A–Z OF POPULAR GARDEN PLANTS

A-Z OF POPULAR GARDEN PLANTS

Consultant Editor
Alan Titchmarsh

OCTOPUS BOOKS

Contributors

Kenneth A. Beckett · Ann Bonar · Graham Clarke
John Clayton · Allen J. Coombes · Jane Courtier
Michael Gibson · Gill Page · Philip Swindells
Alan Titchmarsh · Michael Upward · Dennis Woodland
Text Editor · Kenneth A. Beckett

First published in 1985 by
Octopus Books Limited
59 Grosvenor Street, London W1.

© 1985 Hennerwood Publications Limited

ISBN 0 7064 2195 7

Produced by Mandarin Publishers Limited
22a Westlands Road, Quarry Bay, Hong Kong.

Printed in Hong Kong

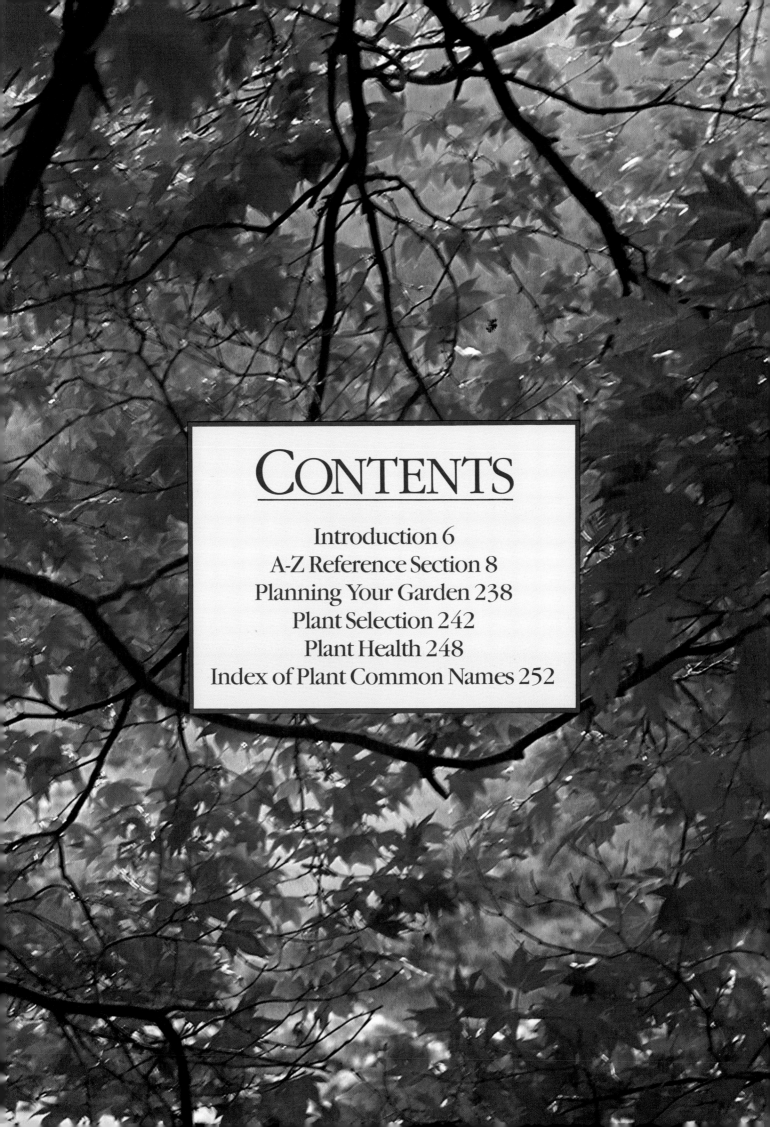

CONTENTS

Introduction

Choosing which plants to grow in a garden has never been such a challenge as it is today. It's not that there is a shortage of plants: on the contrary, there's an embarrassment of riches. At the last count there were about 250,000 different species of flowering plants in the world: and while by no means all of these will grow in British gardens, there are countless variants on the thousands of species that do thrive in Britain.

The choice, then, is bewildering. This book aims to make the job of choosing easier, for the beginner as well as for the experienced gardener, by concentrating on the most popular garden plants and, in particular, on some of the latest reliable forms that are generally available from nurseries, seedsmen, and garden centres.

Plant Names

All over the world a plant is identified by its Latin botanical name. It is only by using this name, rather than the plant's common name (which may vary from one country to another, or even from one region to another within a single country), that gardeners in different parts of the world can be sure that they are talking about the same plant.

In the A–Z section that forms the major part of this book it is the botanical names, rather than the common ones, that are placed alphabetically. But the common names are listed in their own index at the back of the book. If the common name of a plant is the only one you know, look it up in the index and you will be directed to the appropriate place in the A–Z section.

Botanical names are not as confusing as they may at first appear. The plant kingdom (like the animal kingdom) is divided into groups, subgroups, and so on in descending order of magnitude. The largest groups mentioned in this book are plant families, whose names, for ease of identification, we print in small-capital letters; they appear immediately below the main alphabetical headings in the A–Z section.

A typical example is LABIATAE. This is the botanical name for the dead-nettle family. In turn, a family is made up of subgroups known as genera (singular: genus). The genus is the basic unit of the A–Z section, which consists of information on almost 400 genera placed in alphabetical order.

The LABIATAE family includes a number of genera of garden value, including *Salvia*, commonly known as sage. The generic name can be regarded as a plant's surname. On the same basis, a plant's specific epithet can be looked upon as its Christian or given name. A familiar sage species, for instance, is *Salvia officinalis*, the botanical name of the plant used as a culinary herb. The name *officinalis* is the specific epithet which, when combined with the generic name, identifies the plant species. The name of a species is normally written in *italics*, with the generic name beginning with a capital letter. Just as related genera make up a plant family, so a genus is made up of related species. Within the genus *Salvia*, for example, there are more than 700 species, each identified by its specific epithet.

Sometimes the natural offspring of a species differs in certain ways from its parent – but not sufficiently to justify its being classed as a separate species. If these differences are repeated in subsequent generations, the offspring is classified as a natural variety. To take an example, *Lathyrus vernus*, a member of the sweet-pea genus, has purple and blue flowers. But one of its offspring, which has rose-pink flowers, is classified as *Lathyrus vernus roseus*. It is a natural variety, and it can be recognised as such because its varietal epithet (*roseus*) is written, like the rest of its name, in italics.

When reading a nurseryman's catalogue one often comes across a species name (in italics) followed by another name in roman (upright) letters within quotation marks – thus: *Salvia splendens* 'Blaze of Fire'. This denotes the name of a variety that has been produced, from parents of the same species, by a plant breeder or seedsman. Such plants, strictly speaking, are cultivated varieties, or cultivars for short; though many gardeners refer to them simply as varieties.

A cultivar is one example of the plant breeder's work. Another is a hybrid – the result of a deliberate cross between two species, usually of the same genus. *Caryopteris × clandonensis*, the blue spiraea, is a typical hybrid; its parents were *Caryopteris incana* and *Caryopteris mongolica*. The multiplication symbol (×) indicates that the plant is of hybrid origin. Not all plant hybrids are deliberately created: many more occur naturally in the wild.

The name of a cultivar of a hybrid is expressed thus: *Achillea ×* 'King Edward'. If the identities of a cultivar's

parents (whether species or hybrids) are in doubt, the multiplication symbol is omitted; thus: *Cistus* 'Silver Pink'.

Crosses between species of two different genera are called bigeneric hybrids. They are rare; but one that is familiar to many gardeners is × *Cupressocyparis leylandii*, the Leyland cypress. Its parents were *Cupressus macrocarpa* and *Chamaecyparis nootkatensis*. The offspring's first name consists of parts of each of its parents' generic names. Placing the '×' before the name indicates that this hybrid is of the bigeneric type.

Botanists frequently change plant names. The ones in this book are those most regularly used today. In quite a few cases we have listed alternative botanical names, or synonyms – thus: *Fothergilla major* (syn. *F. monticola*) – that still appear in some books or catalogues.

Below Trees, shrubs, perennials, and annuals – all in evidence in this garden – offer infinitely varied ways to furnish your plot.
Right An example of a natural variety: *Lathyrus vernus roseus* has pinker flowers than *Lathyrus vernus*, its sweet pea parent.

Using the A–Z Section

This section presents basic facts about a very wide selection of first-rate garden plants. Care has been taken to recommend only the best and most popular species and hybrids within each genus, along with their most up-to-date and reliable cultivars. The information includes the name of the plant family to which the genus belongs, the distribution of the genus throughout the world, and the nature of the plants within it – be they trees, shrubs, annuals, perennials, or whatever. The country or region of origin of each species is also given, along with such details as typical height and spread at maturity, foliage colour, flowering time, and so on. General information includes notes on site and soil, propagation and cultivation. Where appropriate, there is information about pruning and about any pests and diseases that commonly attack the plants. Information on how to recognise and deal with particular pests and diseases is given in tabular form beginning on page 248.

Planning and Plant Selection

The big A–Z section of this book present basic facts about a selection of first-rate garden plants. It is followed on pages 238–47 by short sections designed to help you to use the plants to best effect. The section on garden planning, for instance, has suggestions on layout, how it affects maintenance, and how it can be altered as your needs change.

The section on plant selection features lists of plants that enjoy the same growing conditions – chalky or clay soil, dry soil, shade, maritime conditions, and so on; and plants which, though they may differ in form, share certain attributes of garden value – evergreen foliage, say, or vivid autumn colour, or attractive fruits. If you wish to know more about a particular plant in any of the lists, just turn to the appropriate place in the A–Z section.

Abelia

CAPRIFOLIACEAE

Deciduous and evergreen flowering shrubs of mainly Asiatic or hybrid origin, particularly suitable as wall shrubs. Most have an extended season of trumpet-shaped flowers.

A. chinensis (China). Height and spread 1–1.5m (3–5ft). Mound-forming, with ovate leaves about 25mm (1in) long. Fragrant white or pale pink flowers freely produced in July–August.

A. floribunda (Mexico). Will reach up to 3m (10ft) and more in milder areas. Glossy green ovate leaves. Bright magenta-red, tubular flowers, up to 50mm (2in) long, crowd branches in June. Most spectacular abelia in flower – but the least hardy.

A. × grandiflora. Vigorous evergreen or semi-evergreen. Height and spread up to 2m (6½ft). Glossy dark green leaves up to 50mm (2in) long. Pink and white trumpet-like flowers with persistent, purplish sepals freely produced in July–October. Hardy and reliable in gardens in southern England when correctly sited.

Site All abelias are best sited in full sun in a sheltered position near a south-facing, wall.
Soil Well-drained, fertile.
Propagation Semi-ripe stem cuttings (with heel if possible) rooted in propagator or cold frame in late summer or early autumn.
Cultivation Plant container-grown shrubs in spring, summer, or early autumn; protect autumn-planted specimens through first winter with bracken fronds or similar material. Plant out cuttings in spring.
Pruning On maturing specimens, cut out older branches after flowering to encourage new basal growths. On established shrubs, cut back frost-damaged stems to sound wood in May.

Above *Abelia × grandiflora*

Abutilon

MALVACEAE   Indian mallow

A large genus of herbs, shrubs, and a few trees from temperate and warm-temperate parts of the world, excluding Europe. In Britain they are grown as deciduous shrubs, most of which have large, saucer-like or dangling bell-shaped flowers on plants of upright, fairly open habit.

A. × 'Ashford Red' (Britain). Hybrid 2m (6½ft) or more high and 1m (3¼ft) or more wide. Large bell-shaped flowers about 50mm (2in) long, coloured deep rose-red in profu-sion throughout summer. Upright plant with large, light-green leaves (evergreen in really warm situations in south and south-west England).

A. vitifolium (Chile). Erect shrub. Height 2–3m (6½–10ft) or more; spread 1.2m (4ft) or more in favourable positions. Leaves maple-like, grey-green, softly hairy, 100–150mm (4–6in) long and nearly as wide. Five-petalled, saucer-shaped, pale purplish-blue flowers, about 75mm (3in) wide, in May–July. Short-lived, but flowers and sets seed freely. 'Alba' is a form with white flowers.

Site Abutilons need warmth, and survive winter best with wall protection and a south-facing position.
Soil Must be fertile and well-drained.
Propagation Sow seed in warmth in March; pot up when large enough to handle; and grow in pots until planting outdoors in May a year later. Semi-hardwood cuttings can be rooted in late summer under cover and planted similarly.

Cultivation Plant outdoors in late April–May. Tie new shoots to supports on wall as they lengthen, and thin out a few if crowding occurs.
Pruning In early spring cut back ends of shoots killed by frost to healthy growth tissue.
Pests and Diseases Yellow variegation on leaves of certain abutilons is due to a virus disease, but does little harm and is acceptable for its ornamental effect.

Above *Abutilon vitifolium*

Acaena

ROSACEAE   New Zealand burr

A large family of evergreen perennials, mostly native to New Zealand, useful as ground-cover plants. They are invasive and have insignificant flowers, but from July they produce attractive burrs, whence their common name. Their foliage colour is varied enough to create all-the-year round interest.

A. adscendens (New Zealand and Falklands). Tall species 225mm (9in) high, less tidy than its fellows, but valuable for its blue-grey toothed leaves. Its cultivar 'Blue Haze' is slightly less tall at 150–200mm (6–8in).

A. buchananii (New Zealand). Its grey-green leaves form a dense mat about 100mm (4in) high. Amber-coloured burrs.

A. caesiiglauca (syn. *A. glauca*; New Zealand). Forms prostrate mats of blue-grey foliage about 75mm (3in) high.

Site Any situation will do, although dense shade may make them grow too tall.
Soil Any tolerated, but plants usually attain better colours in poor soil.
Propagation By division: rooting stems can be potted up or planted out at any time; or tips of stems can be inserted as cuttings in June–July.

Cultivation Plant on rock garden, where they can spread, or in an alpine lawn with dwarf bulbs planted underneath. If planted along edges of paths they recover quickly from trampling.
Pruning Cut mats back if they become too invasive.

Right *Acaena caesiiglauca*

Acanthus

ACANTHACEAE Bear's breeches

Herbaceous perennials native to Europe and North Africa. Striking plants with large, glossy leaves and tall flower-spikes, popular for flower arranging.

A. longifolius (W. Yugoslavia). Height 600–900mm (2–3ft); spread 600mm (2ft). Compact plant with dark green leaves, deeply incised. Lilac flowers on 300mm (1ft) spikes in June–July.

A. mollis (Italy). Height 1.2m (4ft); spread 600mm (2ft). Glossy, mid-green leaves with wavy edging. White and purple flowers on 450mm (1½ft) spikes in July–August. 'Latifolius' is a more vigorous form.

A. spinosus (S.E. Europe). Height 1.2m (4ft); spread 900mm (3ft). Dark green, spiny leaves. White and purple flowers on 450mm (1½ft) spikes in July–August.

Site Sun or light shade.

Soil Deep, well-drained.

Propagation Sow seeds in March in a cold frame; prick out, 150mm (6in) apart, in beds when large enough to handle; grow on for two years before planting out in final positions. Root cuttings can be taken in December–February. Choose thick roots and cut them into 75mm (3in) long sections; push into boxes of sandy soil and leave in a cold frame; move to nursery beds when cuttings are rooted, and plant out when well established. Plants can be divided October-April.

Cultivation Plant in autumn or spring. Plants do not like being disturbed, so leave until overcrowded and then divide.

Pruning Cut back nearly to ground level in late autumn.

Right *Acanthus spinosus*

Acer

ACERACEAE   Maple

A large family of mainly deciduous and hardy trees and shrubs of varied size and wide natural distribution in the northern hemisphere. Notable for their shape and form and for beautiful autumn leaf colour; some have attractive striated or peeling bark, others strikingly variegated leaves.

A. *campestre* (Europe, Near East, North Africa), field maple. Picturesque, hardy, round-headed tree usually reaching 6–11m (20–36ft). Five-lobed leaves are pink-tinted in spring, turning bright yellow in autumn. Often used in hedges.

A. *capillipes* (Japan). One of the best snake-bark maples, with coral-red young shoots and long white striations on trunk and branches. Small tree with rounded crown up to 10m (33ft) high; three-lobed bright green leaves turning orange and crimson before falling.

A. *griseum* (China), paper-bark maple. Delightful small tree of upright, spreading habit, usually 6–11m (20–36ft) high. Effective in all seasons, with dark, cinnamon-brown bark peeling to reveal orange new bark beneath on trunk and branches. The trifoliate leaves, glaucous beneath, colour magnificently in various red hues in autumn.

A. *japonicum* (Japan), full-moon maple. Elegant small tree or large shrub 6m (20ft) high or more. Delicate, soft-green, rounded and lobed leaves colour well in autumn. Best represented by cultivars 'Aconitifolium' (deeply lobed, bright-green leaves turning to rich hues of scarlet, carmine, and purple) and 'Aureum' (very slow-growing and compact; soft yellow leaves all summer and autumn).

A. *negundo* (North America), box elder. Very hardy, wide-spreading tree, fast growing to 12m (40ft). Leaves bright green with usually three to five pinnate leaflets. Best garden varieties include 'Auratum' (golden yellow leaflets conspicuous throughout the growing season); 'Elegans' (syn. 'Ele-

gantissimum', with leaflets broadly margined with yellow); and 'Variegatum' (syn. 'Argenteomarginatum', similarly bordered creamy-white). Cultivars make superb garden trees, often less massive than type species.

A. *palmatum* (Japan, China, Korea), Japanese maple. Upright-growing, round-headed tree up to 10m (33ft) high. Leaves palmate, five- or seven-lobed, with red, orange or yellow autumn colour. Many cultivars, giving wide diversity of size, habit and leaf form. Among the best: 'Atropurpureum' (upright-growing to 5–6m (16½–20ft), usually bronze-crimson foliage throughout the growing season); 'Bloodgood' (new, superior deep-red-leaved selection of 'Atropurpureum'); 'Dissectum' (with low hummocks of cascading branches up to 2m (6½ft) ultimately, leaves finely divided, green in summer, scarlet in autumn, sometimes available grafted as a short standard); 'Dissectum Atropurpureum' (leaves purple in summer, turning crimson in autumn); 'Heptalobum Osakazuki' (upright habit, attaining 6–8m (20–26ft), with seven-lobed leaves, green in summer turning fiery red); 'Senkaki' (syn. 'Sangokaku', coral-bark maple, erect habit to 6–8m (20–26ft), bright-green leaves turning soft-yellow to pale-orange in autumn, invaluable for coral-coloured winter bark). Note that cultivars of A. *palmatum* usually attain a third to a half their ultimate heights in 10 years from planting.

A. *platanoides* (Europe), Norway maple. Handsome, fast-growing, very hardy medium or large tree ultimately 20m (66ft) or more. Large five-lobed, bright green leaves turning brilliant yellow in autumn. Conspicuous corymbs of yellow flowers appear before the leaves in April. Garden cultivars

Left *Acer griseum*   **Right** A. *pseudoplatanus* 'Brilliantissimum'

Left *Acer palmatum* 'Atropurpureum'   **Above** *A. platanoides* 'Crimson King'

include 'Columnare' (erect-growing form); 'Drummondii' (6m (20ft), with leaves margined white); 'Globosum' (mop-headed small tree to about 5m (16½ft) high); 'Crimson King' (syn. 'Goldsworth Purple', about 18m (59ft), leaves crimson-purple all growing season).

A. pseudoplatanus (Europe), sycamore. Familiar large, round-headed tree up to 30m (100ft), with large five-lobed leaves. Vigorous, dominating and self-seeding, only its dwarfer slow-growing varieties are suitable for small gardens. These include 'Brilliantissimum' (young leaves shrimp-pink in early spring, changing to pale green, ultimately about 5m (16½ft) high); 'Prinz Handjery' (young leaves suffused yellow above and purple-tinted beneath, forming a small shrubby tree to 6m (20ft) high).

A. rubrum (E. North America), red or Canadian maple. Ultimately a tall, round-headed tree. Three- or five-lobed leaves with blue-white undersides, giving striking orange and scarlet autumn colours on moist acid soils. Garden cultivars include 'Scanlon' (up to 12m (40ft), of narrow upright habit); 'Schlesingeri' (up to 10m (33ft), a form selected and deservedly popular for its exceptionally rich scarlet autumn colour).

Site Open situations for larger-growing trees; less-exposed sites suit *A. capillipes, griseum,* and *negundo* cultivars; *A. japonicum* and *palmatum* varieties require light shade and shelter from cold winds.

Soil Moist, well-drained loams preferred; chalk soils tolerated but reduce autumn colour and may cause chlorosis (yellowing or bleaching of leaves).

Propagation Species by seed sown after winter stratification; cultivars by budding or grafting in early spring (*A. palmatum* and *japonicum* under glass) and summer for others outside.

Cultivation Plant container-grown shrubs or trees in autumn or spring, and field-grown trees November–March. Water copiously. Mulch, particularly if spring-planting.

Pruning Little needed for larger trees, apart from careful removal of crossing branches to give a well-balanced tree with good leading shoots. Prune out reverted green-leaved branches on variegated forms of *A. negundo* and *platanoides*. With varieties of low shrubby growth (*A. palmatum* and *japonicum*) ensure unrestricted development by pruning back competing nearby trees and shrubs where necessary.

Pests and Diseases Verticillium wilt may attack Japanese maples, causing die-back of twigs.

Achillea

COMPOSITAE   Yarrow

Hardy herbaceous perennials native to Europe, northern Asia, and Middle East. They bear flattened clusters of small, round flower-heads, and are popular subjects for mixed borders or rockeries.

A. filipendulina (Caucasus). Height 900mm–1.5m (3–5ft); spread 900mm (3ft). Mid-green, fern-like, toothed leaves. Flat heads of long-lasting yellow flowers in June–September. Two popular varieties are 'Coronation Gold' and 'Gold Plate'. The flowers can be used for drying.

A. × 'King Edward' (hybrid). Height 100mm (4in); spread 200mm (8in). Forms hump of grey-green foliage with primrose-yellow flowers, 40–65mm ($1\frac{1}{2}$–$2\frac{1}{2}$in) across, in May–September.

A. millefolium (Europe, W. Asia), common yarrow. Height 750–900mm ($2\frac{1}{2}$–3ft); spread 375mm ($1\frac{1}{4}$ft). Dark green, pointed, deeply cut leaves. Small white flower-heads in June–September. 'Cerise Queen' has cherry-red flowers in June–July. Species can become a nuisance as a lawn weed.

A. × 'Moonshine'. Height 600mm (2ft); spread 450mm ($1\frac{1}{2}$ft). Feathery grey-green leaves topped by rich sulphur-yellow, flattened flower-heads in summer.

A. ptarmica (Europe to Siberia), sneezewort. Height 600–750mm (2–$2\frac{1}{2}$ft); spread 375mm ($1\frac{1}{4}$ft). Narrow mid-green, toothed leaves. Clusters of white, button-like flowers in June–August. Cultivar 'The Pearl' has white double flowers which last into September.

A. × *taygetea* (Middle East). Height 450mm ($1\frac{1}{2}$ft); spread 125mm (5in). Silver-grey, toothed leaves. Pale yellow, long-lasting flowers in June–September; the flat heads, 50–100mm (2–4in) across, are good for cutting. 'Flowers of Sulphur' is a vigorous variety with light-yellow blooms.

A. tomentosa (Europe, N. Asia). Height 150–225mm (6–9in); spread 300mm (1ft). Rock-garden plant with downy grey leaves. Makes mat of bright yellow flowers 75mm (3in) across in July–September.

Site Sunny position.
Soil Must be well-drained.
Propagation Sow seeds in unheated greenhouse in March; prick off into boxes, and plant out in rows when large enough; plant out in final site in autumn or spring. Plants can be divided in spring.
Cultivation Tall varieties should be cut back to the ground in November.

Aconitum

RANUNCULACEAE   Monkshood

Hardy herbaceous perennials native to Europe and Asia. Distinctively hooded flowers. NOTE *All parts of these plants are poisonous.*

A. carmichaelii (syn. *A. fischeri*; China). Height 900mm (3ft); spread 375mm ($1\frac{1}{4}$ft). Dark green, glossy, lobed leaves. Spikes of violet-blue, hooded flowers in September–October. *A. c. wilsonii*, a somewhat larger variety, has dark green, three-lobed leaves, and spikes of bright-blue hooded flowers in September-October; 'Kelmscott Variety' has lavender-violet flowers.

A. napellus (Europe, Asia), common monkshood. Height 1.1m ($3\frac{1}{2}$ft); spread 450mm ($1\frac{1}{2}$ft). Dark green, deeply cut leaves in fine segments. Spikes of deep-blue, hooded

Below *Achillea* × 'Moonshine'

flowers in July–August. Usually available in cultivar forms: 'Bicolor' (blue and white flowers); 'Bressingham Spire' (violet-blue); 'Carneum' (shell-pink); 'Grandiflorum Album' (white); 'Spark's Variety' (violet-blue).

A. septentrionale (Norway, Sweden). Height 900mm (3ft); spread 450mm (1½ft). Dark green, rounded, toothed leaves form a neat bush. Purple, hooded flowers with fine hairs. Variety 'Ivorine' has ivory-white blooms in May–July.

A. vulparia (syn. *A. lycoctonum*; Europe, N. Asia), wolfsbane. Height 1–1.2m (3¼–4ft); spread 450mm (1½ft). Dark green, finely divided leaves. Spikes of pale-yellow flowers freely produced in June–August.

Site Light shade.
Soil Moist, fertile.
Propagation Plants divided in October–March. Sow seeds indoors in March–April and transplant to nursery beds when large enough; plant out in permanent positions in October.
Cultivation Plant in October–March. Make sure they do not dry out. Cut off dead flower-heads in October. *A. napellus* should be cut back to ground-level after flowering.

Right *Aconitum napellus* hybrid

Above *Actinidia kolomikta*

Actinidia

ACTINIDIACEAE

Vigorous, mainly hardy deciduous climbing shrubs of Asiatic origin grown for their handsome leaves, flowers, and edible fruit.

A. chinensis (China), Chinese gooseberry. Very vigorous climber reaching 9m (30ft) or more. One-year-old stems covered with crimson hairs carry heart-shaped leaves up to 200mm (8in) long and wide. Unisexual flowers, 40mm (1½in) across, in pendulous clusters, white in bud, opening pale apricot-yellow, produced on short spurs in July. On female plants these are followed by cylindrical, brown, hairy, palatable fruits 50–75mm (2–3in) long and up to

40mm (1½in) wide. Plants of both sexes are required to produce these fruits. Selected clones are grown and fruits widely exported from New Zealand as Kiwi fruit.

A. kolomikta (China, Japan). Elegant, less-vigorous species than above, 3m (10ft) or more in height. Grown mainly for its white, pink-flushed leaf-tips. The fragrant white flowers, 13mm (½in) across, in June are rather hidden.

Site Sheltered south- or west-facing wall, pergola or rustic tripod.
Soil Fertile, well-drained.
Propagation Semi-ripe cuttings in July rooted in propagator or shaded frame.
Cultivation Plant from containers in early autumn or spring. Provide supporting wires on walls and train them to cover their allotted space.
Pruning Winter pruning of well developed specimens of *A. chinensis* essential to maintain a tidy condition and to produce fruit. Shorten lateral growths to one or two buds to encourage production of flower/fruit spurs. Cut out older growths and tie in replacement shoots during summer.

Aethionema

CRUCIFERAE

A sun-loving genus of dwarf evergreen perennials from the Mediterranean and Middle East, suitable for a warm corner of the rock garden with good drainage, or on a dry wall.

A. grandiflorum. Height and spread up to 450mm (18in). In early summer flower heads 75mm (3in) long adorn plant; flowers are deep pink at the tips, but paler below.

A. pulchellum. About 180–200mm (7–8in) tall, with shell-pink flowers produced above the blue foliage.

A. 'Warley Rose'. Most popular hybrid, it reaches about 150mm (6in) in height, with small glaucous leaves and neat habit; produces heads of bright rose-pink flowers from spring to early summer.

Site Sunny. The plants will thrive on a dry wall, where they may self-seed.
Soil Must be well-drained, preferably light.
Propagation Sowing seed produces variable plants (and sometimes the plants seed themselves). Cuttings ensure true plants. Take non-flowering soft-wood cuttings in June–July, inserting them in peat and sand in a propagating frame. Pot up into John Innes No. 2 potting compost when they have rooted, and keep in frame until following spring. Pinch out leading growths to ensure a bushy plant.
Cultivation Plant out in spring in a not too rich soil.
Pruning Remove dead flower heads to produce growth suitable for cuttings and the chance of a second crop of flowers.

Below *Aethionema* 'Warley Rose'

African lilies. Good for cutting; the dried seedheads are also decorative. Hardy except in very cold districts, and excellent plants for late-summer effect. Cultivars include 'Loch Hope' (tall, china-blue flowers); 'Cherry Holley' (dark blue); 'Lilliput' (dwarf, rich blue).

Site All prefer full sun and a warm, sheltered position, but tolerate part shade.
Soil Must be well-drained but not too dry; all plants grow well on chalky soils.
Propagation Divide clumps carefully in April, just as young leaves start to show; take care not to damage the brittle fleshy roots. Sow seed of the hybrids, which is very freely produced, in March–April under glass. Seedlings flower within 2–3 years; good-coloured plants can then be retained, the remainder discarded.
Cultivation Plant in the open, April–May, just as growth is beginning. Water well in dry weather. In cold districts and on heavy wet soils, apply a protective mulch in autumn and ensure good drainage.
Pests and Diseases Purpling of base of leaf is followed next year by die-back—probably a physical condition caused by excessive moisture or root disturbance.

Above *Agapanthus* 'Headbourne Hybrid'

Agapanthus

LILIACEAE   African lily

Deciduous and evergreen perennials, native to southern Africa, producing showy, round clusters of funnel-shaped flowers on erect, fleshy stems above bold clumps of strap-shaped leaves. Apart from the Headbourne Hybrids, most are somewhat tender.

A. campanulatus (Natal). Height 600mm–1.2m (2–4ft); spread 450mm (1½ft). Dense globular heads of pale-blue flowers, 65mm (2½in) long, in August-early September. Narrow greyish-green leaves are deciduous. One of the hardier species; needs winter protection only in colder districts.

A. inapertus (S. Africa). Height 900mm–1.2m (3–4ft); spread 600mm (2ft). Stiffly erect stems above green leaves. Open, rounded heads of dark violet-blue tubular flowers, 50–65mm (2–2½in) long, in July–September, the opened flowers hanging down beneath erect buds.

A. praecox (syn. *A. umbellatus*; Cape Province, Natal). Evergreen. Height 900mm–1.2m (3–4ft); spread 600mm (2ft). Broad greyish-green leaves form a large clump. Tall stems and large round heads of rich-blue flowers, 50–65mm (2–2½in) long, opening wide at the end in July–September. Widely grown, but tender.

Headbourne Hybrids (garden origin). Deciduous. Height 450mm–1.2m (1½–4ft); spread 450mm (1½ft). Bold clumps of narrow green or greyish leaves. Erect, slightly curving stems and round heads of lily-like, tubular flowers, 50–75mm (2½–3in) long, ranging from deep violet-blue to pure white, in late July–September. The most widely grown

Ageratum

COMPOSITAE

Half-hardy annuals and biennials native to Central and South America. Those cultivars listed are popular plants for summer bedding at the front of borders.

A. houstonianum (syn. *A. mexicanum*; Mexico). Annual. Height 125–150mm (5–10in); spread 150–300mm (6–12in). Mid-green, heart-shaped leaves are covered in hairs. Mounds of fluffy blue, white or pink flowers in June–October. F_1 hybrid forms, giving best blooms, include 'Adriatic' (mid-blue flowers); 'Bengali' (rose-carmine); 'Blue Danube'; 'Blue Surf'; 'Ocean' (light blue); 'Sprindrift' (white); 'Summer Snow' (white). The tetraploid varieties such as 'Blue Mink' also give good results.

Site Sunny and sheltered.
Soil Well-drained, fertile.
Propagation Sow seeds in gentle heat in February–March; prick off seedlings into boxes; harden off before planting out in late May–June after the chance of frost has passed.
Cultivation Plants that are dead-headed regularly will flower into October. Water well in dry weather.
Pests and Diseases Foot- and root-rot may occur.

Below *Ageratum houstonianum*

Agrostemma

CARYOPHYLLACEAE Corn-cockle
The common corn-cockle is familiar as an annual weed of cornfields. The form described here is a popular hardy annual.
A. githago 'Milas'. Height 750–900mm (2½–3ft). Large pink or purple flowers on slender stems in June–August. The blooms make excellent cut flowers.

Site Sun or a little shade.
Soil Any, preferably well-drained.
Propagation Sow seed outdoors in prepared seed-bed in March, April or May.

Cultivation Keep soil free of weeds. Thin seedlings twice to a final spacing of not less than 225mm (9in).
Pests and Diseases Greenfly, froghoppers.

Above *Agrostemma githago* 'Milas'

Ajuga

LABIATAE
Annuals or herbaceous perennials native to all continents except America. All have short spikes of tubular, lipped flowers and green or variegated leaves. Those listed have a prostrate mat-forming habit of growth and make good ground-cover plants.
A. pyramidalis (Europe). Perennial. Height 150–300mm (6–12in); spread 300mm (12in) or more. Clump-forming plant with bluntly oblong leaves, slightly toothed. Intense gentian-blue flowers in 100–150mm (4in–6in) spikes, in June–July. Cultivars include 'Crispa' (syn. 'Metallica'), with bronzed leaves. Spreads less rapidly than *A. reptans* (q.v.).
A. reptans (Europe, including Britain), bugle. Perennial. Height 50–150mm (2–6in); spread 300–500mm (12–20in) or more. Vigorous prostrate carpeter that roots at the leaf joints. Oblong, slightly waved, green leaves. Whorls of rich-blue, tubular, lipped flowers on erect, 75–100mm (3–4in) spikes in May–June. Cultivars include handsome cream, green, and rose-pink variegated-leaved forms 'Burgundy Glow' and 'Rainbow'. Largest is green-leaved hybrid 'Jungle Beauty', with 300mm (1ft) spikes of intense blue.

Site All grow well in shade, but variegated-leaved forms need full sun to develop their best colour.
Soil Must be reasonably moist and fertile; plants are lime-tolerant.
Propagation Divide clumps into individual rooted runners

at any season except when plant is in flower.
Cultivation Maintain fertile growing conditions, and divide clumps when they become bare in centre.
Pests and Diseases
Occasionally attacked by mildew.

Above *Ajuga reptans*

Alchemilla

ROSACEAE Lady's mantle
Hardy, herbaceous perennials native to Europe, Greenland, and Asia. The foliage is widely used in flower arranging.
A. alpina (Europe, Greenland, N. Asia), alpine lady's mantle. Height 150mm (6in); spread 225mm (9in). Light green, divided leaves, silky beneath. Star-shaped green flowers 6mm (¼in) across in June–August. The almost identical *A. conjuncta* is more widely available.
A. mollis (Carpathians, Asia Minor), lady's mantle. Height 300–450mm (1–1½ft); spread 600mm (2ft). Light green, hairy leaves with serrated edges, particularly attractive after rain when droplets settle on the leaves. Star-shaped, lime-green flowers, 3mm (⅛in) across, in June–August.

Site Sun or partial shade.
Soil Moist, well-drained.
Propagation Self-sown seedlings usually produced in abundance. Divide in autumn, or spring.

Cultivation Plant in October–March when weather is favourable. Cut back stems after flowering.

Below *Alchemilla mollis*

Allium

ALLIACEAE   Onion

Bulbous and clump-forming herbaceous perennials native to the northern hemisphere. Most have narrow, flattened, keeled or tubular basal leaves and dense umbels of small, six-petalled, starry or bell-shaped flowers on erect stems. Onion, leek, chives, and garlic are familiar alliums of the vegetable garden.

A. cernuum (North America). Height 200–450mm (8–18in); spread 150–300mm (6–12in). Sparingly tufted, with flattened leaves like broad grass blades. Flowers pink to red-purple, bell-shaped, in distinctive, stiffly nodding heads in summer.

A. christophii (syn. *A. albopilosum*; W. Iran, C. Asia). Height 300–500mm (12–20in); spread 300mm (12in) or more. Leaves strap-shaped and hairy. Blue-purple starry flowers with metallic hue borne in spherical heads 115–200mm (4½–8in) wide in summer. Good for cutting and drying.

A. cyaneum (W. China). Height and spread about 150mm (6in). Densely tufted, grass-like plant with deep-blue flowers in summer. Good for rock gardens.

A. giganteum (Iran, C. Asia). Height 900mm–1.2m (3–4ft); spread 450–600mm (1½–2ft). Strap-shaped, blue-green leaves fade at flowering time. Starry, metallic-lilac flowers carried in dense spheres, 100–150mm (4–6in) wide, in early to mid-summer.

A. karataviense (Turkmenistan). Height 150–200mm (6–8in); spread to 300mm (12in). Grey-green, purple-backed elliptical leaves unlike those of any other onion. Whitish to purplish starry flowers borne in heads 150mm (6in) or more wide in late spring. Handsome foliage plant.

A. moly (S.W. Europe). Height about 250mm (10in); spread about 150mm (6in) or more. Leaves lance-shaped, grey-green. Bright yellow, starry flowers open in loose clusters in summer. Soon forms clumps; good for naturalising.

A. narcissiflorum insubricum (France, N. Italy). Height and spread 200–300mm (8–12in). Leaves greyish-green, like those of broad grass blades. Rose-purple, bell-shaped flowers 15mm (⅝in) long carried in small pendant clusters in early summer. Good rock-garden plant.

Site All are best in a mainly sunny place; *A. cernuum* and *A. moly* tolerate part shade.
Soil Must be reasonably well-drained; light, chalky, and sandy ground should be enriched with organic matter.
Propagation Divide established plants of clump-forming species in autumn or spring. Separate offsets from others when dormant. All may be raised from seed under glass in spring.
Cultivation Plant clump-formers in autumn to spring; bulbous types when dormant in autumn.

Below Allium cernuum

Above *Alstroemeria aurantiaca*

Alstroemeria

ALSTROEMERIACEAE   Peruvian lily

Hardy and tender herbaceous perennials native to South America. All have fleshy rootstocks and brightly coloured blossoms which are excellent for cutting.

A. aurantiaca (Chile). Height 900mm (3ft); spread 600mm (2ft). Bright-orange, tubular flowers, up to 40mm (1½in) long, borne in long branching spikes in June–July among small lance-shaped, grey-green leaves.

A. ligtu (Chile). Height 600mm (2ft); spread 450mm (1½ft). Small narrow grey-green leaves on stout stems. Tubular blossoms, up to 40mm (1½in) long, varying in colour from white through pink to red produced in June–July. Selected hybrid strains with much wider colour range available from seedsmen.

Site Open, sunny, not too exposed; a little shade tolerated.
Soil Moderately fertile medium loam preferred.
Propagation Division of the crown in September–October or February–March best for *A. aurantiaca*. Seed sown in spring in trays of seed compost best for increasing *A. ligtu*; young seedlings should be potted individually immediately they are large enough to handle; pot-grown plants should be ready to plant in their permanent positions the following spring. Do not disturb root-ball when planting or plant may die.
Cultivation Planting is best in February–March. Ensure roots are well covered with soil, but avoid too-deep planting. Provide stakes in early spring so foliage can develop naturally around them. Cut down old foliage in autumn. Sprinkle bonemeal around roots in spring when fresh growth is evident.
Pests and Diseases Slugs and snails frequently attack emerging shoots in spring.

Althaea

MALVACEAE   Hollyhock

Hardy annuals, biennials, and perennials native to Europe, Asia, and North Africa. All have showy trumpet-shaped flowers.

A. ficifolia (Siberia), Antwerp hollyhock. Perennial. Height 1.8m (6ft); spread 600mm (2ft). Enormous terminal spikes of single or double orange or yellow blossoms, each some 75mm (3in) across, in July. Coarse fig-shaped green leaves.

A. officinalis (Europe, including Britain), marsh mallow. Perennial. Height 900mm–1.2m (3–4ft); spread 600mm (2ft). Spires of blush-pink, open, trumpet-shaped flowers up to 40mm (1½in) across in July. Bushy, oval, softly hairy foliage. Requires moist growing conditions, preferably beside a pool or stream.

A. rosea (Asia), hollyhock. Perennial. Height up to 2.4m (8ft); spread 900mm (3ft). Handsome spikes of brightly coloured trumpet-shaped flowers, up to 100mm (4in) across, in June–July. Coarse heart-shaped leaves clothe lower stems. A large selection of double, dwarf, and rust-resistant strains available.

Site Sheltered from wind: all plants are fairly tall and can suffer wind damage.

Soil All types; on light soils provide a mulch in warm summer months.

Propagation Treat all as biennials to ensure best results. Seed sown either in trays and placed in a frame in July, or in well-prepared bed in open ground at same time, produce plants that can be moved to flowering positions in October.

Cultivation When treated as biennials they are planted during October, flower the following summer, and should then be discarded. Stakes required from early spring and should be strong enough to support the weight of the flower spikes. Some gardeners grow plants in lee of a wall and do not need to stake as the wall provides protection.

Pests and Diseases Flea beetles sometimes attack seedlings. Rust often affects older plants.

Below *Althaea rosea*

Above *Alyssum saxatile*

Alyssum

CRUCIFERAE

Hardy and half-hardy annuals and perennials native to Europe, Asia, and North Africa, many of which have very showy flowers and make good rock-garden plants. Few annual alyssums are cultivated in Britain. Those that are have now been classified under genus *Lobularia*.

A. argenteum (S. Europe). Perennial. Height 300–450mm (12–18in); spread 450mm (18in). Shrubby plant forming a dense hummock of narrow silvery-grey leaves smothered in July–August with tiny bright-yellow flowers.

A. montanum (Europe). Perennial. Height 75mm (3in); spread 250mm (10in) or more. Creeping, tufted plant with tiny, dense, grey-green foliage and fragrant, bright-yellow flowers in June–July.

A. saxatile (E. Europe), gold dust. Perennial. Height up to 300mm (12in); spread 450mm (18in). Shrubby-forming plant with long grey-green leaves and dense corymbs of yellow flowers in April–June. Varieties include 'Citrinum' (lemon); 'Compactum' (neat habit); 'Plenum' (double flowered); 'Variegatum' (foliage variegated with yellow).

A. serpyllifolium (Spain). Perennial. Height 75mm (3in); spread 250mm (10in). Tiny grey-green leaves smothered in pale-yellow flowers in June.

Site Open, sunny situation essential.

Soil Light, free-draining. Do not over-feed plants or they will rapidly grow out of character.

Propagation Increase annuals from seed sown under glass in March; prick out seedlings, harden them off in a frame, and plant out in late May or early June. Increase perennials from seed sown in trays of seed compost in early spring; grow seedlings on in pots until ready

for planting out. Alternatively grow perennials from short soft cuttings taken in June–July and rooted in a propagator.

Cultivation Perennials for the rock garden can be transferred from pots into prepared pockets of free-draining compost on the rock garden at any time.

Pests and Diseases Flea beetles attack seedlings. Downy mildew and club root affect both young and mature plants.

Amaranthus

AMARANTHACEAE

Half-hardy annuals valued for their brilliantly coloured foliage and plumes of catkin-like flowers, the latter being popular with flower arrangers.

A. caudatus (tropics), love-lies-bleeding. Height 1–1.2m (3–4ft); spread 450–600mm (1½–2ft). Long, showy tassels of plum-red flowers carried among coarse, mid-green, ovate leaves in late summer and early autumn. Flowers last well when dried; the variety 'Viridis', with green tassels, is especially striking.

A. hypochondriacus (tropical America), prince's feather. Height 600mm–1.5m (2–5ft); spread 450mm (1½ft). Similar to *A. caudatus*, but flowers in upright spikes. 'Pygmy Torch', a dwarf variety 300–600mm (1–2ft) tall, suitable for pots or front of a border; 'Green Thumb' has green-tinged white flower-spikes.

A. tricolor (Indonesia), Joseph's coat. Height 600–900mm (2–3ft), spread 300–450mm (1–1½ft). Pointed, ovate leaves are mottled, striped and splashed with green, crimson, yellow, cream, and bronze. Flower spikes usually pinched out as the species is grown for its foliage. Variety 'Molten Fire' has deep-crimson leaves strongly variegated with purple and bronze.

Site Sunny and warm.
Soil Well-drained, preferably good loam, though plants will grow reasonably well in thin, poor soil.
Propagation Sow in a propagator in March at 15°C (60°F); prick off seedlings into boxes; harden off before planting out in May. Alternatively, sow outdoors where they are to flower in mid- to late April, thinning seedlings to about 300–450mm (1–1½ft) apart.
Cultivation Keep plants well watered, particularly while they are getting established. Pinch out flowering shoots on *A. tricolor* (they detract from the brilliant foliage). Pull up and discard plants in autumn.
Pests and Diseases Aphids may attack growing tips.

Below *Amaranthus caudatus*

Above *Amelanchier lamarckii*

Amelanchier

ROSACEAE   Snowy mespilus

Beautiful, very hardy small trees or large shrubs, most native to North America, producing abundant white spring flowers, black fruits, and notable autumn leaf-colour.

A. canadensis (E. North America). Tall suckering shrub or shrubby tree up to 6m (20ft) high; thicket-forming. Elliptical to oblong leaves, about 50mm (2in) long, green- and white-felted when young. Erect racemes of star-like white flowers in April, followed by black juicy fruits. Often confused with *A. lamarckii* (q.v.).

A. lamarckii (syn. *A. × grandiflora*; North America; naturalised in N. Europe and Britain). Bushy, spreading large shrub or small tree up to 10m (33ft) high. Coppery young leaves and lax flower racemes spectacular in spring; crimson, finally black fruits produced in June. The best species, especially for larger gardens.

Site Open, sunny position needed for good autumn colour. Avoid dry, exposed sites.
Soil Well-drained, moist, lime-free or neutral.
Propagation Suckering species by layering or division during winter or early spring. Seed sown in spring outdoors following stratification.
Cultivation Plant open-ground shrubs or trees in November–March; container-grown specimens can be planted at any time.
Pruning Suckering species may need removal of thin superflous growth; single- or multi-stemmed trees require little pruning once a branch system is formed.

Anaphalis

COMPOSITAE   Pearl everlasting

Hardy herbaceous perennials from Asia and North America, with attractive grey leaves and flat heads of creamy white 'everlasting' flowers which are good for cutting and drying.

A. cinnamomea (*A. yedoensis* of gardens; India). Height and spread 600mm (2ft) or more, depending on situation. Bushy, erect plant, with narrow, pointed, greyish leaves, white beneath. Flat heads of papery white flowers with deep creamy-yellow centre in August–October. More open in habit than other species, with spreading growth. Best anaphalis for garden effect and for cutting.

A. triplinervis (Himalaya). Height 400mm (16in); spread 600mm (2ft). Bushy, compact plant with a domed habit of growth. Erect stems covered in white hairs, and narrow leaves, grey-green above and white beneath. Flat heads of white flowers with yellow centres, 75–100mm (3–4in) across, in August. (*A. margaritacea* is similar in effect, but the plant is somewhat less compact).

Site All thrive in full sun but tolerate a little light shade.
Soil Any well-drained, fertile soil is suitable (including chalk), provided that it does not dry out in hot weather.
Propagation Divide clumps in September–October or February–March.

Cultivation *A. cinnamomea* should be staked in April–May, when plants are no more than 100–150mm (4–6in) high. Leave dead stems on plants (until spoilt by weather) to enjoy their winter effect.

Below *Anaphalis triplinervis*

Above *Anchusa azurea* 'Loddon Royalist'

Anchusa

BORAGINACEAE   Alkanet

Hardy biennials and herbaceous perennials from Europe, Asia, and Africa. Most cultivated species provide large sprays of true blue flowers, without a hint of purple, on vigorous, bushy plants.

A. azurea (syn. *A. italica*; Caucasus). Perennial, best treated as a biennial. Height 900mm–1.5m (3–5ft); spread 600–900mm (2–3ft). Vigorous plant with rather coarse, hairy, pointed leaves, and tall branching habit. Large loose sprays of rich blue flowers, 13mm (½in) across, in June–August. Cultivars include 'Loddon Royalist', royal blue, compact.

A. caespitosa (Crete). Perennial. Height 50–75mm (2–3in); spread 150–225mm (6–9in). Forms a prostrate rosette of narrow, bristly, grey-green leaves, in the centre of which clusters of small vivid blue flowers with a white eye appear in May–June. Best grown in pots of gritty compost in the alpine house, or in scree beds outdoors.

A. capensis (Africa). Biennial, usually grown as an annual. Height and spread 225–300mm (9–12in). Neat, erect, bushy plant with dark green leaves. Bears a profusion of ultra-marine-blue flowers 13mm (½in) across in July–September. 'Blue Bird' is a popular cultivar.

Site All need full sun; taller species and cultivars need shelter from strong winds.
Soil Well-drained and fertile, but too much manure produces tall, weak plants which need to be well staked. On heavy soils dig in weathered ashes or strawy compost to improve drainage.
Propagation Propagate perennials from root cuttings taken in February and placed in a cold frame or propagator. Sow seed in the open in May–June, transplanting to flowering position in September. Sow seed of *A. capensis* as a hardy annual outdoors, where plants are to flower, in March–April; or in October in pots for early flowering under glass the following spring.
Cultivation Stake tall perennials securely when 100–150mm (4–6in) high, using twiggy brushwood or other firm supports.
Pruning Pinch out growing tips of young shoots of tall perennial types to produce compact dome-shaped plants which need much less staking.
Pests and Diseases Mildew may appear on leaves in wet weather.

Above *Androsace sempervivoides*

Androsace

PRIMULACEAE   Rock jasmine

A group of attractive cushion- and mat-forming plants from the higher mountains of Europe and Himalaya. (The cushion-forming species are subjects for the alpine house, and are not considered here.)

A. jacquemontii (syn. *A. villosa*; Himalaya). Distinctive grey-leaved species. Unusual lavender-pink or white flowers, on 50–75mm (2–3in) stems, in May–June.

A. primuloides (syn. *A. sarmentosa*; E. Himalaya). 'Chumbyi', the best form of this species, makes a mat of silvery leaved rosettes from which emerge 100mm (4in) stalks of small, rose-pink primrose-like flowers in April–June. Several other varieties available.

A. sempervivoides (Himalaya). A smaller plant, producing flower stems, 50–65mm (2–2½in) tall, of bright-pink flowers in early summer. It has small, neat, emerald-green leaf rosettes and does well in scree.

Site All thrive in sunny, well-drained situation, producing tight rosettes in rock-garden scree or in a trough, where they look attractive hanging over the sides.
Soil Need not be rich but should include some moisture-retentive material such as peat or leaf-mould.

Propagation Remove non-flowering rosettes and insert in cutting frame in summer, potting rooted cuttings when they are ready.
Cultivation Hairy rosettes tend to hold moisture in winter, which rots them off; protect them against rain-showers with a sheet of glass.

Anemone

RANUNCULACEAE   Windflower

Showy herbaceous, tuberous or rhizomatous perennials from North America, Asia, Europe, and South Africa.

A. blanda (E. Europe). Height and spread 150mm (6in). Deeply cut, bright-green foliage studded with bright-blue daisy-like flowers in February–March. Varieties include 'Atrocoerulea' (deep blue flowers); 'Radar' (cerise pink).

A. coronaria (S. Europe, C. Asia). Height 150–225mm (9in); spread 225mm (9in). Large poppy-like blossoms in many bright colours, flowering about three months after planting the small brown tubers. Foliage is bright green, lacy, and much divided. Florists' anemones are derived indirectly from this species and include mixed strains like 'St Brigid'

(double) and 'De Caen' (single). All make excellent cut flowers.

A. hupehensis (Asia). Height 600–900mm (2–3ft); spread 600mm (2ft). Coarse-leaved, fibrous-rooted border plant with attractive pink, saucer-shaped blossoms, 50mm (2in) across, in July–October. The plant known in gardens (and in many catalogues) as *A. japonica* is in fact *A. hupehensis japonica*, a natural variety.

A. × hybrida. Height 1.2m (4ft); spread 600mm (2ft). The well-known *A. japonica* of gardens, with fine cultivars such as 'Bressingham Glow' (rose-red flowers); 'Margarete' (pink); 'Queen Charlotte' (rose-pink).

A. × lesseri (hybrid origin). Height 300–450mm (1–1½ft); spread 450mm (1½ft). Long-stalked, round leaves. Saucer-shaped, deep-red flowers, 50mm (2in) across, in May–June.

A. nemorosa (Europe, including Britain), wood anemone. Height 150mm (6in); spread 225mm (9in). Shade-loving plants of great variability. Flowers about 25mm (1in) across in March–May in white or with a pinkish flush. Leaves deeply cut and dull green. Varieties include 'Allenii' (blue).

A. pavonina (S. Europe). Height 225–300mm (9–12in); spread 225mm (9in). Handsome palmate leaves support solitary red or purple flowers, 50mm (2in) or more across, in March–April. Improved garden anemone 'St Bavo' is derived from this species.

A. vitifolia (Nepal). Height 600mm (2ft); spread 450mm (1½ft). Hummocks of large vine-like leaves with downy undersides support pure-white saucer-shaped blossoms 50mm (2in) or more across in July.

Site Few except *A. coronaria* enjoy a position in the full sun; dappled shade is ideal. Protect taller kinds from winds.
Soil Free-draining moist loam.
Propagation Sow seeds of tuberous kinds, soon after gathering, in pans of seed compost and place in a frame or greenhouse; prick out seedlings immediately the first rough leaves appear, and grow on in boxes or pots until they are large enough to plant out. Divide fibrous-rooted species in spring or autumn; alternatively take short-root cuttings about 50mm (2in) long in September–October and plant in a sandy compost in a cold frame. The tiny plants thus produced can be lifted and potted the following spring. Rhizomatous species can be divided in the spring.
Cultivation Plant tuberous-rooted kinds in their permanent positions at any time March–October. Late-planted ones will flower the following spring; others will flower about three months after planting. Plant fibrous-rooted and rhizomatous kinds in September–March. Stake tall-growing kinds in early spring. Remove foliage in the autumn.
Pests and Diseases Plum rust and smut often a problem.

Below *Anemone blanda*

Above *Anthemis tinctoria* 'Wargrave Variety'

Anthemis

COMPOSITAE

Herbaceous perennials native to Europe. Those of garden value have daisy-like flowers; some also have leaves that emit scent when bruised.

A. cupaniana (Italy). Height 150–300mm (6–12in); spread 300–450mm (12–18in). Spreading plant with scented, grey, finely divided leaves forming a mound on which white daisy flowers 50mm (2in) across with yellow centres appear in May–August.

A. nobilis (syn. *Chamaemelum nobile*; Europe, including Britain), common chamomile. Height 150–225mm (6–9in); spread 300–375mm (1–1¼ft). Finely divided, green leaves form a dense mat. White flowers, 450mm (1½in) across, with yellow centres in June–August. Common chamomile can be used to form a lawn instead of grass, but it is not so hard wearing; leaves give off a pleasant scent when walked on. 'Treneague', a non-flowering variety, is best for lawn cultivation and is now widely available.

A. sancti-johannis (Bulgaria). Height 450mm (1½ft); spread 375mm (1¼ft). Compact plant with grey-green, downy deeply lobed leaves. Bright yellow flowers 50–65mm (2–2½in) across in June–August.

A. tinctoria (Europe), ox-eye chamomile. Height 750mm (2½ft); spread 375–450mm (1¼–1½ft). Mid-green lobed leaves. Yellow flowers, 50–65mm (2–2½in) across, in June–August. Popular varieties include 'Mrs E.C. Buxton' (primrose-yellow); 'Grallagh Gold' (golden yellow); 'Wargrave Variety' (sulphur-yellow).

Site Sunny.
Soil Well-drained.
Propagation Take 50–75mm (2–3in) cuttings of young shoots in spring; root them in pots or in a cold frame; plant out in nursery beds until autumn, when they can be moved to their permanent positions. Plants can be divided in September–April.
Cultivation Plant September–April, when weather is suitable; taller plants need to be supported. Cut back to within a few inches of the ground after flowering. To make a lawn, plant *A. nobilis* (or its cultivar 'Treneague') in spring 150mm (6in) apart each way. Established lawns may need mowing once a year; older lawns become patchy, and the gaps should be replanted.

Antirrhinum

SCROPHULARIACEAE Snapdragon

Annuals and perennials native to Europe. Only the one perennial species is widely grown, but it is short-lived and so is treated as an annual.

A. majus (Mediterranean). Height 225mm–1.2m (9in–4ft); spread 225–450mm (9in–1½ft). Smooth, mid-green, ovate leaves. Pink tubular flowers carried on spikes 150–900mm (6in–3ft) long in June–September.

There are three major groups of garden varieties derived from this species, as follows:

A. majus 'Maximum'. Height 600–900mm (2–3ft); spread 460mm (1½ft). Many varieties, including 'Madame Butterfly' (double azalea-like flowers); 'Wedding Bells' (rust-resistant); 'Bright Butterflies Improved'; 'Spring Giant'. All F1 forms come in a wide range of colours – yellows, reds, pinks, orange, white.

A. majus 'Nanum'. Height 450mm (1½ft); spread 250mm (10in). Semi-dwarf varieties include 'Cheerio' (F2 hybrid, mixed colours); 'Coronette' (F1, rust-resistant); 'Little Darling' (F1, mixed); 'Black Prince' (crimson with bronze leaves); 'Monarch' (various colours, rust-resistant); 'Purple King'; 'Rembrandt' (orange with gold tips); 'Hyacinth Flowered Mixed'.

A. majus 'Pumilum'. Height 100–150mm (4–6in); spread 225mm (9in). Good quality selections include 'Delice' (pale apricot); 'Floral Carpet' (F1, mixed); 'Magic Carpet' (mixed); 'Pixie' (F1, mixed); 'Tom Thumb' (mixed); 'Trumpet Serenade' (mixed).

Site Bright sun essential.
Soil Well-drained, preferably with compost added.
Propagation Sow seeds in January–March indoors in gentle heat; prick out seedlings into boxes when large enough to handle; harden off before planting out in March–June. Can also be sown in July–September in cold frame; will flower the following year.
Cultivation Pinch out growing tips after planting out to promote bushy growth. Tall varieties need staking. Deadhead flowers regularly. In areas prone to rust disease, grow rust-resistant varieties only.
Pests and Diseases Aphids may be a problem on young plants. Damping off, foot- and root-rot, grey mould, mildew, and rust may occur.

Below *Antirrhinum majus* 'Pumilum'

Aquilegia

RANUNCULACEAE   Columbine

Hardy herbaceous perennials native to Europe, North America, and Japan. Erect, bushy plants with attractive fern-like leaves and graceful funnel-shaped flowers carried on thin, wiry stems, usually with a characteristic spur behind each petal. Aquilegias make very effective border plants, and are particularly good for naturalising in less formal parts of the garden; the smaller species are more suited to the rock or peat garden.

A. alpina (Switzerland). Height 600mm (2ft); spread 300mm (1ft). Dainty, erect small plant with much-divided green leaves. Large, rich blue or white flowers, 50mm (2in) across, with long incurving spurs, in May–June. Variety 'Hensol Harebell' is taller.

A. canadensis (Canada, United States). Height 450–600mm (1½–2ft); spread 300mm (1ft). Graceful, erect plant with fern-like greyish green leaves. Strong, straight stems and nodding flowers, 50mm (2in) across, with red sepals, yellow petals, and straight red spurs, knobbed at the end, in June–early July.

Garden Hybrids. Interbreeding of several species has produced a race of very ornamental strains, usually 600–900mm (2–3ft) in height, with 300–450mm (1–1½ft) spread. Large, long, spurred flowers in a variety of colours carried on graceful wiry stems above finely divided fern-like leaves in May–July. 'McKana Hybrids' are one of several such strains; 'Nora Barlow', 700mm (2ft) high and 300mm (1ft) across, is a beautiful double form with red, pink, and green flowers, which comes true from seed.

Site Preferably open and sunny, although all will tolerate light shade. Hardy but not long-lived plants, producing seed freely in right conditions.
Soil Fertile, well-drained, but not too dry.
Propagation Sow seed in cold frame or in open in April–May; transplanting to permanent site in October. Divide established clumps into single rooted pieces in October–March.

Cultivation Mulch in early spring to conserve moisture; water regularly in dry weather. Unless seed is required, dead-head and cut stems to ground after flowering, leaving foliage intact.

Pests and Diseases Aphids may be troublesome in spring. Leaf-spot fungus and rust may occur.

Right Aquilegia vulgaris

Above Arabis ferdinandi-coburgii

Arabis

CRUCIFERAE

Evergreen perennials, popular in the rock garden but over-dominant if planted unwisely. They are traditionally grouped with *Alyssum* and *Aubrieta* (q.v.) – commonly known as the three As.

A. caucasica (syn. *A. albida*; S.E. Europe and Iran). Height up to 150mm (6in). The common white arabis with grey foliage and masses of white flowers in spring. Of several named forms double-flowered 'Plena' is perhaps the best; there is also a pink form, 'Rosabella'.

A. ferdinandi-coburgii 'Variegata' (N. Greece). Forms a prostrate mat of attractive cream and green variegated foliage of interest throughout the year. The white flowers in spring are insignificant and best removed.

Site Anywhere for *A. caucasica*, but best where it can cascade down a wall or over a rock; the more starved and/or sunny the situation the less rampant it becomes. *A. ferdinandi-coburgii* anywhere on rock garden with good drainage.
Propagation By division, taking rooted stems in the autumn or spring and potting them up. If quantities are required, take cuttings in July with a heel or a bit of the old stem at the base.

Cultivation Plant out in autumn or spring. If plants are allowed to flower, remove flower stems when flowering has finished.
Pruning Cut back *A. caucasica* in early spring after flowering. If winter has been severe, dead shoots may need to be removed before flowering.
Pests and Diseases Mosaic virus may infect plants, causing pale yellowish leaves and ring patterns; plants should be removed and burnt.

Site Young plants require a sheltered position. Good as lawn specimens. *A. unedo* is tolerant of coastal exposure.
Soil European species and hybrids thrive on all fertile soils and are excellent on lime (chalk) soils.
Propagation Species from seed sown under glass in spring. Cultivars and hybrids by cuttings in propagator in autumn or spring, or by grafting on to *A. unedo* stock under glass in spring.
Cultivation Plant container-grown plants in early autumn or spring.
Pruning Straggly old specimens will regenerate if severely cut back in late winter.
Pests and Diseases Leaf spot diseases may occur.

Right *Arbutus unedo*

Armeria

PLUMBAGINACEAE   Thrift

A group of sun-loving, clump-forming evergreen rock-garden perennials with grass-like foliage; the flower-heads develop on relatively tall stems.

A. caespitosa (Spain). Compact domes form 100mm (4in) tall clumps with almost stemless pink flowers in April–May. The form 'Bevan's Variety' is smaller and more compact with deeper pink flowers.

A. maritima (Europe), sea-pink. Height 150–225mm (6–9in); spread 250–300mm (10–12in). Forms dark green clumps of linear leaves, above which are carried 150mm (6in) tall flower stems with large heads of pink flowers. It has given rise to several forms, notably the cultivars 'Alba' (pure white); 'Bloodstone' (deep blood-red); 'Vindictive' (taller, with rich rose-pink flowers).

Site Sunny.
Soil Free-draining, not too rich. Plants are lime-tolerant.
Propagation Take small cuttings in July–August with 5mm (¼in) of old wood attached to base, and insert in cutting frame or around rim of a clay pot; pot on into gritty, limy compost; plant out the following spring. Seed is not a reliable form of increase for named forms.
Cultivation Plant out in spring or September. Remove flower-heads when blooming is over.
Pruning If plants spread too far, cut back to size with spade.
Pests and Diseases Armeria rust is fairly common.

Below *Armeria maritima* 'Vindictive'

Arbutus

ERICACEAE   Strawberry tree

Very ornamental, slow-growing evergreen tree and shrubs native to the Mediterranean countries, south-west Ireland, and north-west North America. They display attractive shredding bark, heather-like flower clusters, and strawberry-like fruits from autumn to spring.

A. × andrachnoides (Greece; also of gardens), Grecian strawberry tree. Hardy. A noble hybrid up to 10m (33ft) high and of spreading habit, with magnificent cinnamon-red trunk and branches. The toothed, leathery leaves have glaucous undersides and set off the white pitcher-shaped flowers, 6mm (¼in) long, produced in terminal panicles in autumn or spring.

A. unedo (Mediterranean, S. W. Ireland), Killarney strawberry tree. Usually a small spreading tree or large shrub 5–10m (16½–33ft) high, with fibrous brown bark. Leaves dark green, narrowly oval. Parchment-coloured or pinkish flowers appear in autumn with ripening, orange-red, hanging fruits 20mm (¾in) across from the previous season's flowers. 'Rubra', with deep-pink flowers and more compact habit, is a desirable form.

of silver-white flowers develop in September–October.

A. maritima nutans (*A. nutans* of gardens; Sicily). Perennial. Height 600mm (2ft); spread 450mm–600mm (1½–2ft). Silver, narrowly divided leaves. Pale yellow, insignificant flowers in August–September can be cut off before they develop to encourage better leaf growth.

A. stellerana (North America, Asia), dusty miller, old woman. Herbaceous perennial. Height 450–600mm (1½–2ft); spread 300mm (1ft). Silver, deeply lobed leaves. Clusters, 150mm (6in) long, of yellow flowers appear in August–September.

Site Full sun.
Soil Light, well-drained, reasonably fertile.
Propagation Herbaceous perennials divided in October–April. Propagate shrubs by taking 75–100mm (3–4in) long heel cuttings in August; root in a cold frame; pot up the following spring; plunge pots outside; plant out into final positions in May.
Cultivation Plant herbaceous perennials in October–March in reasonable weather; plant shrubs in spring. Remove faded flowers from shrubs.
Pruning Cut back herbaceous perennials to ground in October. Remove leggy stems from shrubs and cut *A. absinthium* back to 150mm (6in) high in April.
Pests and Diseases Aphids attack leaves. Rust diseases can occur.

Left *Artemisia absinthium* 'Lambrook Silver'

Artemisia

COMPOSITAE

Half-hardy and hardy herbaceous perennials and shrubs native to Asia, Canada, South America, and Europe. They are grown mainly for their scented grey foliage; the flowers are insignificant.

A. abrotanum (S. Europe), lad's love, old man, southernwood. Shrub. Height 600mm–1.2m (2–4ft); spread 1.2m (4ft). Upright, bushy plant with semi-evergreen, grey-green, finely divided leaves. Small yellow flowers in July–September.

A. absinthium (Europe, including Britain), common wormwood. Sub-shrub. Height and spread 900mm (3ft). Deciduous plant with silver, feathery foliage. Yellow flowers in July–August. 'Lambrook Silver' is a good variety.

A. dracunculus (S. Europe), French tarragon. Perennial. Height 450–600mm (1½–2ft); spread 300mm (1ft). Dark-green, shiny leaves, strongly scented. Small clusters of globular white flowers which open fully only in warm climates in July. Leaves can be dried or used fresh to flavour sauces, salads, chicken, and in a *fines-herbes* mixture; also used for making tarragon vinegar.

A. lactiflora (China, India), white mugwort. Herbaceous perennial. Height 1.2–1.5mm (4–5ft); spread 450mm (1½ft). Lobed, green leaves. Plumes of creamy-white flowers 150–200mm (6–8in) long in August–October.

A. ludoviciana (syn. *A. purshiana*; North America), white sage. Herbaceous perennial. Height 600mm–1.2m (2–4ft); spread 450mm (1½ft). Silvery, willow-like leaves. Clusters

Aruncus

ROSACEAE   Goat's-beard

Imposing herbaceous perennials from northern Asia. They form bold clumps of foliage, above which rise handsome plumes of tiny starry flowers.

A. dioicus (*A. sylvester* of gardens; Siberia). Height 1.2–2m (4–6½ft). Vigorous, stately plant with compound, fern-like leaves up to 1.2m (4ft) long forming a large clump. Erect stems and loose spikes or plumes of tiny, 6mm (¼in), creamy white flowers in July. Suited to larger border, or as specimen plant in lawns. Variety 'Kneiffii', growing to 750mm (2½ft) high and 450mm (1½ft) across, is dwarfer, with similar graceful plumes of flowers but more-finely divided leaves: a better choice if space is limited.

Site Sun or shade, but not very hot or dry.
Soil Fertile; must be kept adequately moist at all times of the year.
Propagation Divide roots in early autumn or spring. Established plants usually produce self-sown seedlings which can be transplanted; or seed can be sown in a cold frame in April.
Cultivation Plant October–March. Water in dry weather. Cut plant down to ground level in November.

Below *Aruncus dioicus*

Arundinaria

GRAMINEAE   Bamboo

Hardy and half-hardy, woody-stemmed perennial grasses from Asia and North America; some yield bamboo canes.

A. anceps (Himalayas). Height 3m (10ft); spread 1.8m (6ft). Graceful arching, purplish-green stems with bright-green leaves. Can be invasive if not isolated from other plantings.

A. fastuosa (syn. *Semiarundinaria fastuosa*; Japan). Height up to 6m (20ft), usually less; spread 1.8m (6ft). Dark green, shiny leaves carried on purplish stems. The tallest hardy bamboo.

A. japonica (syn. *Pseudosasa japonica*, *Bambusa metake*; Japan), metake. Height 3m (10ft); spread 1.8m (6ft). Slim, tapered canes with long, wide glossy leaves of rich green.

A. murielae (syn. *Sinarundinaria murielae*; China). Height 2.4m (8ft); spread 1.2m (4ft). Slender, bright, green-gold canes with small, rich-green, lance-shaped leaves.

A. nitida (syn. *Sinarundinaria nitida*; China). Height 2.4–3m (8–10ft); spread 1.2m (4ft). Slender dark-purple canes with small, rich-green, lance-shaped leaves.

A. viridistriata (syn. *A. auricoma*; Japan). Height up to 1.5m (5ft), often less; spread about 2m (6½ft). Evergreen leaves striped bright yellow and green. Good for small gardens.

Site Open preferred, but all species must be sheltered from cold winds.
Soil Heavy or loamy preferred; free-draining but moisture-retentive even in dry summer periods.
Propagation Divide rootstock or separate emerging shoots or culms in May, planting in permanent sites at once.
Cultivation Freshly planted material needs careful watering throughout summer. Give mature plants a mulch of well-rotted manure or leaf-mould in spring. Remove dead canes and untidy foliage in autumn.

Below *Arundinaria viridistriata*

Asperula

RUBIACEAE

Annuals and herbaceous perennials native to Europe and Asia Minor. Most are low-growing, neat plants with clusters of small tubular flowers, often sweetly scented.

A. odorata (syn. *Galium odoratum*; Europe, including Britain), woodruff. Perennial. Height 150–225mm (6–9in); spread 300–600mm (1–2ft). Small, erect plant with whorls of lance-shaped, shining green leaves. Slender stems and clusters of small, tubular, white flowers appear in May–June. When dried the plant smells of new-mown hay.

A. orientalis (syn. *A. azurea setosa*; Syria). Annual. Height and spread 150–225mm (6–9in). A neat plant with rings of green, pointed leaves and erect, slender stems. In July–August plant is covered in pale blue, starry, sweet-scented flowers, 19mm ($\frac{3}{4}$in) across. An attractive hardy annual.

A. suberosa (Greece). Perennial. Height 50–75mm (2–3in); spread 100–150mm (4–6in). Choice alpine plant for dry wall or scree bed, forming dense carpets of tiny, hairy, greyish leaves, covered in June–July with 13mm ($\frac{1}{2}$in) long tubular, rich-pink flowers.

Site *A. odorata* prefers cool shade; others require open sun.
Soil Must be really well-drained for annual and alpine species (latter probably better grown in an alpine house); *A. odorata* prefers moist, well-drained, leafy soil.
Propagation Sow annuals outdoors in April where they are to flower, or under glass in September to flower as pot plants. Root short basal cuttings of alpine species in cold frame in May–June. Divide roots of herbaceous species in October–March.
Cultivation Stake annuals with twiggy branches when 100mm (4in) high, having thinned seedlings in two stages to 100–150mm (4–6in) apart. Pull up and discard annuals after flowering.

Below *Asperula orientalis*

Aster

COMPOSITAE

Hardy herbaceous perennials native to Europe, North America, and Asia. All are bushy plants with showy, daisy-like flowers, and range in height from tall, erect plants to compact low domes. Indispensable for the autumn flower border and for cutting, Michaelmas daisies can be supplemented by other species which extend the start of the flowering season back to July.

A. acris (syn. *A. sedifolius*; S. Europe). Height 900mm (3ft); spread 500mm (1½ft). Best represented in the garden by form 'Nanus', a bushy plant, making round dome of erect stems with narrow, pointed, roughly hairy green leaves. Clouds of star-shaped, rosy mauve flowers, up to 25mm (1in) across, with yellow centres cover the plant in August–September.

A. amellus (S. Europe), Italian aster. Height and spread 300–450mm (1–1½ft). Low, open, branching plant with bluntly oblong, rough, grey-green, faintly aromatic leaves. Flowers appear in loose clusters on the end of the stems, 50mm (2in) across, pink, blue, or mauve, with yellow centres, in August–September. Cultivars include 'King George' (large, violet-blue); 'Pink Zenith' (rich pink).

A. × frikartii (garden origin). Height 900mm (3ft); spread 450mm (1½ft). A fine garden plant, bushy and erectly branching, with dark-green pointed leaves. Well-formed clusters of lavender-blue flowers, 75mm (3in) across, with a deep-gold centre, in July–September. 'Mönch' is best of several cultivars.

A. novae-angliae (E. North America), Michaelmas daisy. Height 1.2–1.5m (4–5ft); spread 600mm (2ft). Tall, erect plant with light-green pointed leaves mainly on upper parts of woody stems. Flowers in clusters on the ends of the stems, 50–65mm (2–2½in) across, pink or rose-red, in September–October. Cultivars include 'Harrington's Pink', 'Alma Potschke' (deep rose). Good for cutting. Place it at back of a border, with other plants in front, in order to hide its bare lower stems.

A. novi-belgii (E. North America), Michaelmas daisy. Height ranges from 150mm (6in) hummocks to erect plants 900–1.2m (3-4ft) tall, with spread up to 600 mm (2ft). All have dense, bushy habit, stiffly erect, rather woody stems, and smooth lance-shaped leaves. Flowers 25–40mm (1–1½in) across in broad, domed clusters. Many forms – single, semi-double or completely double, white, pink, red, and many shades of blue (the prevalent colour) – flowering in September–October; typical are 'Crimson Brocade'; 'Fellowship' (semi-double, deep pink); 'Marie Ballard' (double, blue); 'White Ladies' (semi-double). All are good for cutting.

Site All prefer full sun and an open situation, with a free flow of air to reduce incidence of mildew.
Soil Well-drained, fertile and moist; lime tolerated.
Propagation Root tip cuttings of young shoots under glass in February–March; transplant to flowering position in May. Divide established plants in February–March or in autumn, retaining only single shooted pieces from outside of clump and discarding rest. Divide plants every two or three years as older plants become susceptible to mildew.
Cultivation Stake taller cultivars securely when plants are 100–150mm (4–6in) high. Spray regularly with fungicide from late June onwards to reduce attacks of mildew.
Pests and Diseases Tarsonemid mites can cause dwarfing of plants and malformed flowers. Slugs and caterpillars may attack stems and leaves. Mildew is most serious of several diseases. Verticillium wilt may also be troublesome.

Left Aster novi-belgii 'Marie Ballard'
Below A. acris

Above *Astilbe × arendsii*

Astilbe

SAXIFRAGACEAE

Hardy herbaceous perennials native to China and Japan. Bushy plants with attractive, finely divided leaves and graceful, feathery spires of blooms, they are ideal for cool, moist parts of the garden.

A. × arendsii (garden origin). Group of fine hybrids of complex parentage that has superseded most species for general garden use. Height 450mm–1.2m (1½–4ft); spread 600–900mm (2–3ft) or more. Bushy erect plants, forming handsome clumps of finely divided, fern-like leaves, often tinged with bronze or purple. Graceful wiry stems and more-or-less branching feathery plumes or sprays of tiny white, pink, red, or lilac flowers in June–August. Leaves of the taller types make effective ground cover. Cultivars include 'Fanal' (low-growing, flowers deep crimson), 'Irrlicht' (medium height, white), 'Ostrich Plume' (tall, rich-pink). There are now many dwarf hybrids, 300–450mm (1–1½ft) high and wide; one of the best is 'Sprite', with feathery, pale-pink plumes.

A. chinensis (China) 'Pumila'. Height 225–300mm (9–12in); spread 600mm (2ft). Low, spreading, bushy plant forming creeping mat of fern-like green leaves, above which rise stiff erect spikes of pinkish mauve flowers in July–September.

A. simplicifolia (Japan). Height and spread up to 200mm (8in) or more. Low-growing plant with attractive bronzed leaves. Cultivar 'Bronze Elegance' has graceful arching sprays of soft, rose-pink flowers in August.

Site All prefer a cool, moist position and tolerate quite deep shade, but will grow in the open if never allowed to get dry at the roots. Excellent plants near pools or streams or in damp woodland.
Soil Must be moist at all times; avoid shallow chalky soils.
Propagation Divide woody clumps in March–April, ensuring each new piece retains two or three developing growth-buds.
Cultivation Water well in dry weather. A surface mulch of compost, leaf-mould or completely rotted manure in early spring will promote growth and help to conserve moisture. Cut down to ground level only in February, as dead foliage and flower heads can have an attractive winter effect.

Astrantia

UMBELLIFERAE   Masterwort

Hardy herbaceous perennials native to Europe and western Asia. Most are bushy plants with divided leaves and clusters of small round flower-heads with a collar of papery bracts beneath. All are good for cutting.

A. major (Europe). Height 600mm (2ft); spread 450mm (1½ft). Erect plant with a basal group of much-divided, fresh-green leaves. Wiry branching stems carry clusters of small, round, pinkish green flowers, surrounded by a ring of papery textured silvery white bracts in June–August. Variety *A. m. involucrata* (also known as 'Margery Fish' or 'Shaggy') has looser, longer, more prominent collar of bracts; 'Rubra', has deep-crimson bracts; 'Sunningdale Variegated' has young leaves splashed and striped with yellow in spring.

A. maxima (Europe). Height 600mm (2ft); spread 450mm (1½ft) or more. Growth and effect are similar to *A. major*, but much bolder, with rich-pink bracts and bright-green, three-lobed leaves.

Site All do best in partial shade, but will grow well in full sun.
Soil Well-drained and fertile; must not be dry.
Propagation Divide roots of cultivars, which will not come true from seed, in autumn or spring. Sow seed of species in the open or in unheated frame when ripe or in spring.
Germination may be delayed if seeds stored dry over winter.
Cultivation Apply a mulch of compost or manure in April–May to encourage strong growth and conserve moisture. Water in dry spell. Cut plants to ground level in November.

Below *Astrantia major*

Above *Aubrieta deltoidea* varieties

Aucuba

CORNACEAE

Useful hardy and shade-tolerant evergreen shrubs of Asiatic origin, having a bushy habit and large, handsome, often variegated leaves. The sexes are on different plants, female varieties having large, bright-red berries.

A. japonica (Japan), spotted laurel. Dense rounded shrub 2–3m (6½–10ft) high and wide with fleshy green branchlets and leathery, glossy green leaves 75–200mm (3–8in) long and 40–75mm (1½–3in) wide. Male plants have erect terminal panicles of purplish flowers and females compact clusters of shining scarlet berries about 13mm (½in) long. Notable cultivars includes 'Crotonifolia' (leaves speckled golden-yellow, male); 'Nana Rotundifolia' (compact female with smaller green leaves, upper half toothed); 'Picturata' (strikingly variegated with elongated central golden splashes, male); 'Salicifolia' (Longifolia group, a narrow-leaved, free-fruiting form); 'Variegata' (syn. 'Maculata', a female with large, yellow-blotched leaves).

Site Almost any situation: will thrive even in considerable shade under trees, but variegation and berrying are better in more open sites.
Soil Any reasonably fertile soil.

Below *Aucuba japonica*

Propagation Cuttings 100–200mm (4–8in) long root readily in shaded frame in late summer.
Cultivation Plant container-grown specimens in open weather at any time. Plant both sexes if berries are required.

Aubrieta

CRUCIFERAE

A valuable plant for the early spring, when its colourful mats can cascade over walls and rocks. It is tolerant of sun and favours limy soils.

A. deltoidea (E. Mediterranean). All the garden aubrietas derive from this species. Some of the best are: 'Argenteo-variegata' (tight, white-variegated foliage and 50mm (2in) tall, light-purple flowers); 'Bob Saunders' (new cultivar, with double, reddish purple flowers, slightly more vigorous at 200mm (8in) tall); 'Dr Mules' (well-established cultivar about 150mm (6in) tall, unsurpassed for the deep violet-purple of its flowers); 'Bressingham Pink' (double, rich pink); 'Gurgedyke' (long-established favourite with deep-purple flowers).

Site All need full sun and well-drained position, preferably with lime or chalk added.
Soil Not too rich; plants enjoy a little starvation.
Propagation If seed-sown (in March), plants will not come true to type. Better to divide rooted stems in August–September; alternatively take cuttings at same time and insert in a cold frame in a mixture of

equal parts of peat and sand.
Cultivation Aubrietas need to be planted carefully or they are likely to quarrel with their neighbours.
Pruning Most gardeners are too gentle with aubrietas. Take shears to them immediately after flowering to remove the dead flower heads and encourage tight rather than straggly growth.

Ballota

LABIATAE

Herbaceous perennials and sub-shrubs native to the Mediterranean region and North Africa. The species listed, the main one in general cultivation, is valued for the silvery-white effect of its leaves and stems.

B. pseudodictamnus (Mediterranean). Height 300–600mm (1–2ft); spread 600–900mm (2–3ft). Low, loosely branching sub-shrub with soft woody stems and almost round leaves entirely covered with yellowish white woolly hairs. Whorls of dull lilac-pink, lipped flowers up to 25mm (1in) long in July. Hardy except in severe winters; grows well by the sea. Excellent for foliage effect. *B. acetabulosa* is very similar but with white woolly hairs on leaves.

Site Must have full sun and shelter from cold winds and severe frost.

Soil Good drainage essential; prefers light soils, the drier the better; tolerates chalk.

Propagation Cuttings of short, non-flowering side-growths taken in July–August and rooted in sunny frame or propagator. Sow seeds in pots under glass in April.

Cultivation In cold districts, treat as a tender plant, lifting old plants in September to overwinter under glass.

Pruning Cut back branches by a third in late April to keep the plant bushy.

Below *Ballota pseudictamnus* (with pelargonium)

Begonia

BEGONIACEAE

A very large genus of half-hardy perennials, found throughout the tropics and sub-tropics of both hemispheres, with brightly coloured flowers and attractive foliage. Most of those grown in Britain are houseplants, but the following are suitable for summer bedding.

B. semperflorens (Brazil), fibrous-rooted begonia. Usually grown as annual. Height and spread 150–225mm (6–9in). Bright green or bronze, glossy, rounded leaves. Clusters of small pink, red or white flowers 25mm (1in) across in June–October. Many F1 hybrids available including 'Cocktail' (mixed flowers, bronze leaves); 'Coco Ducolor' (white with scarlet edge, leaves bronze); 'Electra' (cerise-red, flushed with orange); 'Frilly Pink'; 'Lucia' (mixed); 'New Generation' (mixed); 'Organdy' (mixed); 'Pink Avalanche'; 'Rosanova' (cerise-pink); 'Rosita' (rose-pink); 'Scarletta' (orange-scar-

Left *Begonia × tuberhybrida*

let); 'Thousand Wonder' (mixed); 'Volcano' (orange-scarlet, leaves bronze).

B. × tuberhybrida, tuberous begonia hybrids. Height 200–600mm (8–24in); spread 300mm (12in). Midgreen, smooth, rounded leaves. Large, rose-like flowers 25–150mm (1–6in) across in June–September. Many varieties, including 'Bertini Fascination' (large blooms in wide colour range from pink to gold); 'Cameo' (double, camellia-like flowers); 'Chanson Mixed' (hanging variety, semi-double); 'Lloydii' (hanging, mixed); 'Multiflora Double Fiesta Mixed'; 'Nonstop' (F1 hybrid, very free-flowering, double).

Site Sun or light shade.
Soil Well-drained; enriched with peat or leaf-mould.
Propagation Sow seeds of *B. semperflorens* and tuberous begonias indoors in gentle heat, December–March; prick off into boxes and harden off before transplanting to flowering site from late May onwards. Stem cuttings of *B. semperflorens* are taken in May–August. Stem cuttings of tuberous begonias are taken in April; use 75–100mm (3–4in) long basal shoots, root in propagator. Divide tubers in March–April when repotting; cut into pieces, each with a shoot attached.
Cultivation Start tuberous begonias into growth in March–April in boxes of peat; pot up when leaves appear. Harden off before planting out in early June; lift before frosts in autumn. Leaves die down in winter; keep in cool, frost-free place, watering occasionally. *B. semperflorens* are usually discarded after flowering.
Pests and Diseases Weevils and eelworms attack roots; tarsonemid mites feed on leaves and buds. Grey mould, powdery mildew and viruses may occur; damping off can affect seedlings.

Bellis

COMPOSITAE Daisy

Hardy and half-hardy perennials native to Europe, North Africa, North America and Asia. The main garden strains of the common daisy are excellent for borders or for use as ground-cover.

B. perennis (Europe, including Britain, Asia Minor), common daisy. Height 75–100mm (3–4in); spread 250mm (10in). Used in Monstrosa or miniature forms as a dwarf carpeting plant with double-daisy flowers 25–50mm (1–2in) across in white, pink or red in April–May. Glossy, almost evergreen foliage. Many unnamed strains of mixed colours are available from seedsmen; named varieties include 'Alice' (pink); 'Dresden China' (pink); 'Victoria' (red and white).

Site Plants prefer full sun but do tolerably well in shade.
Soil Almost any; bigger plants prefer heavy soil.
Propagation Mixed selections raised from seed sown either in boxes or in the open in May; grow on in a nursery bed and plant out in October. Named varieties increased by division immediately after flowering.
Cultivation Seed-raised plants are usually treated like wallflowers and other spring bedding plants. Plant in October and discard after they flower the following spring.
Pests and Diseases Aphids sometimes attack plants in summer.

Right *Bellis perennis*

Berberis

BERBERIDACEAE   Barberry

Large genus of spiny deciduous and evergreen shrubs from the Americas, Europe, and Asia. Many make first-class hardy garden plants notable for abundant yellow or orange spring flowers, summer leaf colour, and attractive autumn fruits and foliage.

B. × 'Buccaneer' (garden origin). Spreading habit, 1.5m (5ft) high and wide. Small soft-green leaves turn brilliantly flame coloured in autumn. Fruits pink, turning scarlet and persisting into winter.

B. darwinii (Chile), Darwin's barberry. Handsome evergreen, 2m (6½ft) high by 1.5m (5ft) in moist areas. Small, glossy, dark-green leaves. Spectacular displays of golden flowers in April, then bloomy blue-purple berries.

B. gagnepainii (China). Hardy, compact, erect-growing evergreen, up to 2m (6½ft) or more high with 1.5m (5ft) spread. Up to 100mm (4in) long crinkled, dark-green leaves and abundant yellow flower-clusters; bloomy black berries. Makes an impenetrable hedge.

B. × *ottawensis* 'Purpurea' (syn. 'Superba'). Vigorous hybrid. Height and spread 2m (6½ft). Upright and arching branches. Nearly oval leaves, larger and of richer purple than those of *B. thunbergii* 'Atropurpurea'. Yellow spring flowers and red autumn berries.

B. × 'Parkjuweel' (garden origin). Excellent ground-covering, semi-evergreen, very spiny hybrid, up to 1m (3¼ft) high and wide. Dark glossy green leaves turning various shades of crimson in autumn and often persisting until spring. Golden flowers in spring.

B. × *stenophylla*. Arching stems of small, narrow, evergreen leaves forming dense thickets. Height up to 3m (10ft); spread 2m (6½ft). Spectacular in April–May when wreathed with golden-yellow flowers. Makes a fine informal hedge. 'Corallina Compacta' at 600mm (2ft) is an excellent, neat dwarf form, with coral-red buds opening to golden flowers.

B. thunbergii (Japan, China). Compact, deciduous, hardy species, usually 1.5m (ft) high and 1.2m (4ft) wide. Leaves fresh green in summer, turning brilliant scarlet in autumn. Excellent hedge plant. Several cultivars notable for habit and leaf colour include 'Atropurpurea Nana' (syn. 'Little Favourite'), 600mm (2ft) high and wide, a dwarf edition of 'Atropurpurea', with rich bronze-red foliage; 'Aurea') 1–

Above *Berberis darwinii*   **Below** *B. thunbergii* 'Rose Glow'

1.5m (3¼–5ft) high, slow-growing with golden-yellow leaves turning pale green by September; 'Rose Glow', 1.5m (5ft) high by 1.2m (4ft) wide, with purple leaves attractively variegated pink and white.

B. verruculosa (China). Dense, compact evergreen ultimately 1.2–1.8m (4–6ft) high. Glossy, dark green, often red-tinted, leathery leaves, glaucous beneath. Solitary golden flowers and bloomy blue-black bottle-like berries. Makes a superb hedge.

Site Foliage, flower, and fruit at their best in open, sunny site.
Soil Ordinary, well-drained.
Propagation Species by seed sown in spring following stratification; hybrids and cultivars by cuttings with heel in shaded frame – deciduous varieties June–July, evergreen August–September.
Cultivation Plant field-grown deciduous species and varieties November–March. Most evergreens are now container-grown for planting at any season.
Pruning Unless plants are used for hedging, pruning should aim to retain natural growth habits; remove dead wood from deciduous species in summer. With *B. × stenophylla* cut back arching growths to suitable replacement shoots after flowering.

Above *Betula nigra*

Bergenia

SAXIFRAGACEAE

Evergreen perennials native to Asia. Low, spreading plants with rounded, glossy leaves which contrast well with other foliage and make excellent ground cover. The nodding clusters of bell-shaped flowers are also attractive. Both foliage and flowers are good for cutting.

B. cordifolia (Siberia). Height 300–450mm (1–1½ft); spread 600mm (2ft) or more. Bold, orbicular leaves, with wavy or undulating margins. Erect fleshy stems carry large clusters of pink to rose flowers, 8mm (⅓in) across, in March–April. The form 'Purpurea' has large, rounded leaves, which turn purple in winter, and dense heads of magenta-pink flowers.

B. crassifolia (Siberia, N. Asia). Height 300mm (1ft); spread 600mm (2ft). Spoon-shaped leaves which often turn red in winter. Loose sprays of pink flowers, up to 20mm (¾in) across, on tall stems in March-April.

Garden Hybrids. Generally more handsome than the species in both foliage and flower effect. Especially good cultivars include 'Abendglut' (syn. 'Evening Glow', deep magenta-red); 'Ballawley' (large, shining leaves and ruby-red flowers); 'Morgenrot' (syn. 'Morning Blush', rich pink, often flowers a second time in June).

Site Most grow almost anywhere, in full sun or shade. Grow in the open for best winter leaf-colour, and sheltered from spring frosts for the best show of flowers.
Soil Must be reasonably moist and fertile.
Propagation Divide and replant single-rooted pieces in autumn just before or after flowering.
Cultivation Remove dead and damaged leaves, and cut down old stems after flowering. Apply general fertiliser in March.
Pests and Diseases Leaf spot and mildew may occur seasonally.

Right *Bergenia cordifolia* hybrid

Betula

BETULACEAE   Birch

Elegant medium-sized or large, hardy trees and shrubs found widely in North America, Asia, and Europe (including Britain). Much admired for their beauty of bark, graceful habit, spring catkins, and golden autumn leaves.

B. ermanii (E. Asia). Magnificent tall tree forming a broad cone up to 20m (65ft) or more; trunk peeling, creamy-white when young, is later pink-tinted; branches orange-brown. Leaves are very variable in size and shape, usually 50–75mm (2–3in) long.

B. jacquemontii (W. Himalaya). Of spreading habit to about 10m (33ft), perhaps the most beautiful white-barked birch. Leaves, usually toothed, are golden in autumn.

B. papyrifera (N. America), paper birch. Grows up to 20m (65ft) or more with light, open crown; white bark, shredded in layers. Leaves large, ovate, 40–90mm (1½–3½in) long, up to 50mm (2in) broad, with superb golden autumn colour.

B. pendula (N. Asia, Europe, including Britain), silver birch. Graceful, much-loved tree attaining 12–18m (40–60ft) with rounded crown, silvery-white trunk, and branches pendulous at the ends. Notable cultivars include 'Dalecarlica' (Swedish birch, an elegant and distinct form with pendulous branchlets, leaves very deeply lobed); 'Tristis' (graceful, narrow-headed, tall tree with upright leading shoot and slender, drooping branches); 'Youngii' (syn. 'Young's Weeping Birch', 6m (20ft) high by 5m (16ft) wide, forming a mound-like specimen weeping to the ground).

B. utilis (Himalaya, China). Handsome tree up to 15m (50ft) or more with spreading habit and variable flaking bark, cream-white or cinnamon-brown.

Site All succeed in sun or semi-shade. Weeping forms of *B. pendula* make ideal lawn specimens singly (especially 'Youngii') or in groups.
Soil Best on well-drained loam, but plants are tolerant of chalk; *B. pendula* succeeds on poor sandy soils.
Propagation Sow seed of species outdoors in early spring; bud or graft cultivars on to seedling stocks in early spring or summer.
Cultivation Plant field-grown trees November–March, water well in first spring or summer. container-grown trees available for out-of-season planting. Roots spread over a wide area: plant birches away from walls, fences, hedges.
Pruning Little pruning required, but ensure a central leader is maintained until desired height is reached.
Pests and Diseases Leaf spot may occur.

Above *Borago officinalis*

Borago

BORAGINACEAE   Borage

Hardy annual native to Europe. Used as a culinary herb, it gives a slightly salty taste similar to that of cucumber.

B. officinalis (Mediterranean). Height 450–900mm (1½–3ft); spread 300mm (1ft). A sturdy plant with large, grey-green leaves covered in coarse grey hairs. Bright blue star-shaped flowers, 13mm (½in) across, in June–September. The white and pink forms are less common.

Site Sunny.
Soil Any, well-drained.
Propagation Sow seed in April–September outdoors. Self-sown seedlings may become a nuisance.

Cultivation Thin out seedlings to 300mm (1ft) apart. Plants will reach maturity in six to eight weeks.

Briza

GRAMINEAE

Hardy annual and perennial grasses native to the northern temperate zone and South America. The flower spikes are useful for dried-flower arrangements.

B. maxima (Mediterranean), great quaking or pearl grass. Annual. Height 450–600mm (1½–2ft); spread 200–250mm (8–10in). Graceful, heart-shaped seed-heads hang from tall, wiry stems. The long, narrow leaves are bright green.

B. media (Europe, Siberia), quaking grass. Perennial. Height 300–450mm (1–1½ft); spread 150–250mm (6–10in). Leaves are pale green; seed-heads are small, heart-shaped and purplish-brown.

B. minor (Europe). Annual. Height 300mm (1ft); spread 150–200mm (6–8in). A much smaller version of *B. maxima*, with dainty spikelets.

Site Sunny and reasonably sheltered.
Soil Free draining; plants will tolerate poor, dry soils.
Propagation Sow *B. maxima* and *B. minor* in flowering positions in March–April, thinning seedlings to 150–230mm (6–9in) apart. Divide creeping rootstocks of *B. media* in March.
Cultivation Cut flower-heads for drying on a dry day as soon as they are fully expanded. Discard annuals after flowering. Trim old flower heads from *B. media* in autumn; lift and divide plants every two or three years.

Right *Briza maxima*

Brunnera

BORAGINACEAE

Hardy herbaceous perennials native to the Caucasus. Easy, quick-growing plants, providing good ground-cover and foliage effect, with sprays of vivid blue flowers resembling forget-me-nots.

B. macrophylla (syn. *Anchusa myosotidiflora*). Height 450mm (1½ft); spread 600mm (2ft) or more depending on situation. Vigorous, spreading plant with large, dull-green, roughly hairy, heart-shaped leaves, soon producing large clumps of foliage. Bright blue flowers borne on dainty 450mm (1½ft) sprays in April–May. 'Variegata', a beautiful form, has leaves boldly splashed with creamy white; 'Langtrees' is splashed with silvery grey.

Site Prefers part or full shade, but will grow in the open. Variegated forms must have a cool sheltered position that is not too dry.
Soil Any fertile soil; grows well on chalk.
Propagation Divide the plants in autumn or early spring.
Cultivation Remove old stems after flowering, and cut plant down to ground level in November.
Pruning Carefully remove any reverted green-leaved shoots which may appear on the variegated forms, taking care not to damage roots.
Pests and Diseases Mildew may occur on the leaves.

Below *Brunnera macrophylla*

Above *Buddleia davidii* 'White Profusion'

Buddleia

LOGANIACEAE

Popular deciduous and evergreen, summer-flowering shrubs native to tropical and temperate regions, especially eastern Asia. Showy, fragrant flowers in many colours; particularly attractive to butterflies.

B. alternifolia (China). Vigorous deciduous, weeping-willow-like shrub or small tree 3m (10ft) or more high with alternate lanceolate leaves. Densely covered with lilac-purple flowers in June.

B. davidii (China), butterfly bush. Widely planted and naturalised in many countries. Usually a wide-spreading shrub up to 4m (13ft) high. Lanceolate leaves 100–300mm (4–12in) long; flower panicles up to 450mm (18in) long in July–October. Best cultivars include 'Black Knight' (deep-purple flowers); 'Empire Blue' (upright habit, violet-blue flowers with orange eyes); 'Harlequin' (attractively varie-gated creamy-white foliage, and purple-red panicles of flowers); 'White Profusion' (pure white flowers).

B. globosa (Chile, Peru), orange-ball tree. Handsome semi-evergreen bush of large, open habit. Height and spread 3–5m (10–16½ft). Leaves lanceolate, 125–200mm (5–8in) long, felted beneath. Round, tangerine-coloured flower clusters 20mm (¾in) in diameter in June.

B. × 'Lochinch'. Handsome, hardy hybrid. Height and spread 2.5m (8¼ft). Leaves grey-green, white beneath, up to 200mm (8in) long and 50mm (2in) wide. Flower spikes, mauve with orange eye, in July–September.

Site Sunny site essential for best results. Shelter necessary in cold districts. Excellent plants in seaside areas and town gardens.
Soil Must be well-drained.
Propagation Short, soft cuttings in late June in propagator or sun frame; *B. davidii* also by hard-wood cuttings outside in October.

Cultivation Plant from containers in autumn or spring.
Pruning *B. alternifolia* and *globosa* require occasional thinning of old wood after flowering or in early spring. Hard-prune *B. davidii* cultivars annually in early spring to lowest buds to maintain compact habit and encourage long flower spikes.

Buxus

BUXACEAE Box

Evergreen shrubs or small trees native to Europe, North Africa, Asia, and America. Their leaves are small, leathery, and either toothed or lobed; their wood is hard and close-textured. The plants are often clipped to make formal hedges and topiary.

B. sempervirens (Europe, including Britain, North Africa, W. Asia), common box. Long-lived hardy shrub or small tree. Height 6m (20ft) or more; spread up to 1.5m (5ft). Slow-growing, of dense habit, with small, dark-green leaves. Many forms, some with variegated leaves; few are readily available apart from the following: 'Elegantissima' (small, domed shrub 1–1.5m (3–5ft) high, with creamy-white-margined leaves: the best 'silver' box); 'Handsworthensis' (vigorous, erect shrub with thick, leathery, round or oblong leaves, making an excellent tall screen); 'Suffruticosa' (edging box, with ovate, small, glossy leaves, much used to make low hedge in formal gardens or parterres).

Site Successful in sun or considerable shade, even under trees.
Soil Any fertile; excellent on chalk.
Propagation Take cuttings 75–150mm (3–6in) long in early autumn in propagator or cold frame. divide 'Suffruticosa' in early spring.
Cultivation Plant container-grown specimens at any time. Water and mulch in spring and summer.
Pruning Old 'leggy' specimens may be heavily stooled down in early spring to encourage compact regeneration. Clipping formal specimens and hedges is best done in July–August.

Below *Buxus sempervirens*

Calamintha

LABIATAE   Calamint

Hardy perennials native to Europe. Can be used as a herb.
C. alpina (S. Europe). Height 100mm (4in); spread 200mm (8in). Rounded, slightly toothed, light-green leaves. Small mauve flowers on trailing stems in June–August.
C. grandiflora (syn. *Satureja grandiflora*; S. Europe). Height 225mm (9in); spread 450mm (18in). Low-growing, bushy plant with rounded, coarsely toothed leaves. Small, deep-pink flowers in June–September.
C. nepeta (syn. *C. nepetoides*; Europe). Height 300mm (1ft) or more; spread 450mm (18in). Rounded bush with light-green leaves on erect woody stems. Small, palest lilac flowers in August-October.

Site Full sun or half shade.
Soil Moisture-retentive.
Propagation Divide in spring. Basal cuttings can also be taken in spring; root in a cold frame or open ground.
Cultivation Suitable for growing on rock gardens.

Calceolaria

SCROPHULARIACEAE   Slipper-flower

Annuals, biennials, and herbaceous and shrubby perennials with inflated, pouch-shaped flowers. Suitable for alpine gardens, as bedding plants, or for pots and tubs.
C. darwinii (Magellan Strait). Slightly tender perennial. Height 200–300mm (8–12in); spread 300–400mm (12–16in). Orchid-like flowers, yellow, spotted and blotched with brown, with broad white band along the lip of the pouch. Mid-green leaves form a neat rosette.

C. integrifolia (syn. *C. rugosa*; Chile). Slightly tender shrub. Height 450–600mm (1½–2ft); spread 300–450mm (1–1½ft). Mid-green, oblong, deeply veined leaves and small, yellow, pouch-shaped flowers from midsummer to autumn. 'Sunshine' is a vigorous, free-flowering variety.

Site Full sun or part shade in warm, sheltered position.
Soil Rich, well-drained; preferably lime-free.
Propagation Sow February–April in greenhouse or propagator; do not let the temperature rise above 15°C (60°F); mix tiny seeds with silver sand and sow on the surface of the compost; keep seedlings cool and lightly shaded; harden off and plant out in May. *C. integrifolia* can be raised from late-summer cuttings.
Cultivation Protect plants with cloches during winter; take care to give good protection in first year. Always keep soil moist. *C. integrifolia* often best if grown as annual after rooted cuttings have been overwintered under glass.
Pests and Diseases Aphids may attack growing points and young foliage. Excessive winter damp leads to root rot.

Above *Calceolaria integrifolia*   **Below** *Calamintha nepeta*

Calendula

COMPOSITAE   Pot marigold

Hardy annuals, perennials and sub-shrubs found from the Mediterranean region to Iran. The orange and yellow blooms of the species listed make a cheerful contribution to borders or as cut flowers.

C. officinalis (S. Europe). Height 300–600mm (1–2ft); spread 300–375mm (1–1¼ft). Bushy plant with long, narrow leaves. The bright pom-pom flowers, 100mm (4in) across, appear in May–September. Varieties include 'Art Shades' (mixture); 'Apricot Beauty'; 'Baby Orange'; 'Geisha Girl' (red-orange); 'Fiesta Gitana' (mixed); 'Mandarin' (orange); 'Lemon Gem'; 'Orange King'; 'Pacific Beauty' (mixed).

Site Bright sun.
Soil Any, including poor ones, preferably well-drained.
Propagation Sow seeds outdoors in March–May. Thin to 375mm (1¼ft) apart. Can also be sown in September to flower in spring.

Cultivation Dead-head regularly to encourage more flowers. Self-sown seedlings can become a problem.
Pests and Diseases Caterpillars may eat leaves. Mosaic virus, powdery mildew, and rust may occur.

Callistephus

COMPOSITAE   China aster

A genus of one half-hardy annual native to China and Japan. The many garden varieties derived from it are valued for their chrysanthemum-like blooms.

C. chinensis. Height 600–800mm (2–2½ft); spread 300mm (1ft). Flowers purple and daisy like. Numerous garden forms have been raised in a wide range of colours. Flower types include double, semi-double, single, pompone, ostrich-feather, duchess, and quilled. Good dwarf-bedding strains: 'Milady', 'Thousand Wonders', and 'Roundabout'.

Site Open, sunny, and not too exposed to wind.
Soil Any good garden soil; light, free-draining preferred.
Propagation Sow outdoors where plants are to flower in April, thinning seedlings to 300mm (1ft); or sow in greenhouse or propagator in March, pricking seedlings off into boxes and hardening off before planting out in May.
Cultivation Stake tall-growing varieties before the flowers open. Remove dead flower-heads to encourage succession of blooms.
Pests and Diseases Aphids may attack young shoots. Wilt disease causes collapse of plants; some varieties are listed as resistant to this disease.

Below *Calendula officinalis*   **Right** *Callistephus chinensis*

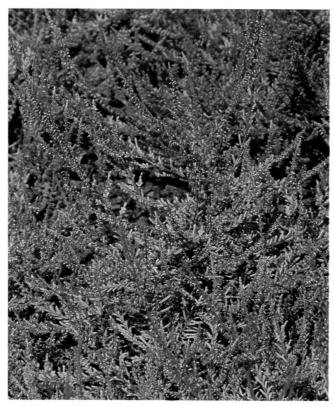

Above *Calluna vulgaris* 'Blazeaway'

Calluna

ERICACEAE   Heather, ling

A monotypic genus of evergreen, bushy shrublets, native to moorlands of Europe, including Britain, and North Africa. The plants are covered in a mass of tiny purple or white flowers in late summer and autumn and are much worked by bees. Careful selection from wild and nursery-grown varieties has produced a great number of forms, varying in flower and foliage colour, which make a striking patchwork of colour if planted *en masse*.

C. vulgaris. Height and spread 225–600mm (9–24in). Scale-like leaves, closely packed, cover the twiggy shoots. Tiny purple flowers form slender, spike-like clusters 150–300mm (6–12in) long; there may be several clusters on a stem. Some cultivars from a vast selection: 'Alba Plena' (free-flowering, double white, flower spikes up to 450mm (18in) high); 'Beoley Gold' (white flowers August–September, golden foliage); 'Blazeaway' (lilac-mauve flowers, deep-red winter foliage); 'County Wicklow' (double shell-pink flowers, spreading, low growth habit); 'Gold Haze' (white flowers, bright-yellow foliage all year, 600mm (24in) high); 'H.E. Beale' (double, pink flowers in 225mm (9in) long clusters September–November); 'J. H. Hamilton' (fuchsia-pink double flowers, semi-prostrate habit 225–300mm (9–12in) high); 'Silver Queen' (woolly silvery-grey foliage, pale mauve flowers); 'Sunset' (orange, yellow, and gold foliage, pink flowers).

Site All callunas need an open situation; they should on no account be coddled, otherwise they become soft, leafy, and prone to disease; an exposed, light site is best.
Soil Must be acid (callunas are lime-haters), containing peat; poor, with good drainage.
Propagation Divide or layer in autumn; take cuttings of new growth about 25mm (1in) long in August and root in peaty compost under cover.
Cultivation Little regular care needed beyond shearing in early spring to remove dead flower-heads and straggly growth; an occasional mulch with peat in spring is beneficial.
Pests and Diseases Heather wilt is an occasional problem.

Caltha

RANUNCULACEAE

Herbaceous perennials native to Europe, North America, Asia, and Australia. Most are bog-garden plants grown for their showy flowers in spring.

C. leptosepala (N.W. North America). Height and spread 300mm (1ft). Makes neat clumps of dark-green, shiny, heart-shaped leaves. Silvery white flowers, 25mm (1in) across, in May–June. Enjoys damp conditions at pool-side.

C. palustris (Europe including Britain, North America, Asia), marsh marigold or king-cup. Height 300–450mm (1–1½ft); spread 300mm (1ft). Very adaptable, growing on wet ground and in up to 225mm (9in) of water. Glossy, green, kidney-shaped leaves in neat hummocks, smothered in large, shiny, golden-yellow flowers up to 50mm (2in) wide in March–April. Varieties include 'Alba' (white) and 'Flora Plena' (double yellow); latter is best garden form.

C. polypetala (Asia). Height 600 (2ft); spread 600–900mm (2–3ft). Like a larger version of *C. palustris*. Large, glossy leaves up to 300mm (1ft) in diameter. Dense clusters of bright golden-yellow flowers, each 75mm (3in) across. For bog garden or marginal shelf of pool.

Site Full sun or part shade.
Soil Preferably heavy, moisture-retentive neutral or slightly acid loam.
Propagation All except double forms raised from fresh seed sown on trays of wet seed compost in July and planted out the following spring. Alternatively divide in early spring as their young shoots are appearing.
Cultivation Spring planting preferable in wet positions. Pool-margin varieties should be accommodated in aquatic planting baskets in March–August. Use a heavy soil free from too much organic matter. Apply a layer of pea-shingle to top of each basket to prevent soil fouling the water. Remove old leaves and stems in autumn as they may harbour aquatic insect pests.
Pests and Diseases Some kinds are prone to mildew; all are attacked by water-lily aphis.

Below *Caltha palustris* 'Alba'

Above *Camassia leichtlinii*

Camassia

LILIACEAE   Quamash

Bulbous hardy perennials from western North America. They have basal tufts of tapered, narrow leaves and long, erect spikes of starry flowers.

C. cusickii (N.W. United states). Height 900mm (3ft); spread 450mm (1½ft). Leaves greyish-green, arching. Flowers pale blue, about 40mm (1½in) wide, in early summer. Needs staking in windy sites.

C. leichtlinii (California to British Columbia). Height 900mm–1.2m (3–4ft); spread about 450mm (1½ft). Leaves rich green, usually erect. Flowers violet, blue, or white, 40–75mm (1½–3in) wide, in early summer. Varieties: 'Atro-violacea', 'Eve Price', and 'Orion' have purple-blue flowers; 'Plena' is a double form and creamy-white.

C. quamash (California to British Columbia). Height 600mm (2ft) or more; spread about 300mm (1ft). Leaves very slender, almost grassy, pale to mid-green. Flowers 40mm (1½in) wide, blue or white, in early summer. Tends to be floppy in shaded positions.

Site Moderately sunny.
Soil Most types, provided they do not dry out rapidly in spring.
Propagation Separate congested clumps of bulbs.

Seeds can be sown when ripe in spring or early summer, but take several years to flower.
Cultivation Plant bulbs in autumn, the earlier the better.

Camellia

THEACEAE

Beautiful, mostly hardy, large or medium-sized evergreen shrubs of Asiatic origin flowering, often spectacularly, in winter or spring.

C. × 'Inspiration' (hybrid between *C. reticulata* and *C. saluenensis*). Of upright habit, up to 3m (10ft) high in sheltered areas. Dark green ovate and pointed leaves. Deep pink semi-double flowers in profusion. Fine wall shrub.

C. japonica (Japan, Korea), common camellia. Large shrub or small tree up to 5m (16ft) or more. Glossy green leaves 75–100mm (3–4in) long, oval tapering to short point. Flowers are 65–100mm (2½–4in) diameter. Parent of many cultivars, most 1.5–3m (5–10ft) high. Of good garden value are: 'Adolphe Audusson' (vigorous, with large semi-double, blood-red flowers); 'Apollo' (vigorous growth, flowers semi-double, rose-red with white blotches); 'Elegans' (spreading habit, deep peach-pink anemone-form flowers); 'Gloire de Nantes' (erect habit, deep rose-pink, semi-double flowers); 'Preston Rose' (vigorous growth, salmon-pink peony-form flowers with darker veins); 'Snowflake' (single, white flowers).

C. × williamsii (hybrid group between *C. japonica* and *C. saluensis*). One of the best, most free-flowering camellias for British gardens; grows to 1.5–3m (5–10ft) high. Leaves usually ovate and tapering, up to 65mm (2½in) long; flowers 65–100mm (2½–4in) in diameter. Recommended cultivars: 'Anticipation' (upright habit, rose-pink peony-form flowers); 'Debbie' (clear pink, semi-double); 'Donation' (vigorous, upright habit, large mid-pink with paler veining); 'J. C. Williams' (first named variety of this hybrid group, with single flowers a unique shade of pink).

Site Avoid south- or east-facing sites; excellent for light woodland, for north- or west-facing walls, or for tubs on a shaded patio or in a conservatory; good in town gardens.
Soil Acid (lime-free) or neutral essential. Add peat if soil is heavy.
Propagation Leaf-bud or semi-ripe stem cuttings 100–150mm (4–6in) long in propagator or under mist in late summer.
Cultivation Plant container-grown camellias in autumn or spring. Ensure roots are adequately moist at all times or bud drop will occur. Mulch in summer. Feed camellias in tubs in summer.
Pruning Correct any tendency to legginess by spring pruning young growths before new buds break to induce a thick, bushy habit.
Pests and Diseases Scale may attack camellias under glass. Virus-infected plants should be destroyed.

Below *Camellia × 'Inspiration'*

flowers in dense clusters on ends of stems in June–August. Cultivars include 'Superba' (violet-blue); 'Crown of Snow'. For herbaceous borders.

C. isophylla (Italy), star of Bethlehem. Perennial. Height 150mm (6in); spread 300mm (1ft) or more. Spreading bushy plant with greyish green heart-shaped leaves, toothed at ends. Loose heads of wide, starry blue or white flowers 25mm (1in) across over long period in spring to autumn. Half-hardy in all but mildest districts; popular as a pot plant or for hanging baskets.

C. lactiflora (Caucasus). Perennial. Height 1–1.2m (3–4ft); spread 600mm (2ft). Vigorous bushy plant, with pale-green, pointed leaves on stiff, erect stems. Large branching heads of many pale-lilac bell-shaped flowers 25mm (1in) across in July–August. Cultivars include 'Loddon Anna' (lilac-pink); 'Pouffe', 300mm (1ft) tall. For border or naturalising.

C. medium (S. Europe), Canterbury bell. Biennial. Height 450–750mm (1½–2½ft). Bushy erect plant with soft green pointed leaves. Large loose heads of inflated bell-shaped blue, pink or white flowers, 40–50mm (1½–2in) across in May–June. *C. m. calycanthema* is the popular cup-and-saucer variety. Dwarf strains of both types are now available, making dense, dome-shaped plants smothered in flowers requiring no staking.

C. persicifolia (Europe, N. Asia), peach-leaved bellflower. Herbaceous perennial. Height 450–900mm (1½–3ft); spread 450mm (1½ft). Upright plant, with slender stems rising from rosettes of narrow, toothed evergreen leaves. Clusters of large, open, bell-shaped flowers, 40mm (1½in) across, in June–July, blue or white, single or double. A favourite border plant. Cultivars include 'Telham Beauty' (rich blue); 'Hampstead White' (cup-and-saucer flowers).

Above *Campanula cochlearifolia*   **Right** *C. lactifolia*

Campanula

CAMPANULACEAE   Bellflower

Annual, biennials and herbaceous perennials native to Europe, Asia, and North Africa. Most have showy bell-shaped flowers, and range in height from prostrate alpines to tall, erect plants for the perennial border.

C. carpatica (Carpathian Mts). Perennial. Height 300mm (1ft); spread 375mm (1¼ft) or more. Forms neat bushy tufts of green heart-shaped leaves. Cup-shaped flowers, 25–40mm (1–1½in) across, blue, pink, or white, borne in great profusion of erect wiry stems in June–August. *C. carpatica turbinata* (*C. turbinata* of gardens) has larger, more richly coloured flowers. For front of border or rock garden.

C. cochlearifolia (syn. *C. pusilla*; Alps). Perennial. Height 100–150mm (4–6in); spread 300mm (1ft). Vigorous, quickly forming low mats of tiny, round, green leaves. Dainty bell-shaped flowers on thin wiry stems, blue or white, up to 13mm (½in) across in July–August. For rock gardens.

C. garganica (Italian Alps). Perennial. Height 100–150mm (4–6in); spread 225–300mm (9–12in). Creeping plant, forming carpets of green heart-shaped, toothed leaves. Profusion of flat, star-shaped blue or white flowers up to 20mm (¾in) across in May–August. For dry walls or rock gardens.

C. glomerata (Europe, including Britain), clustered bell-flower. Herbaceous perennial. Height 300–600mm (1–2ft); spread 450mm (1½ft). Erect plant with coarse, dark green, oval leaves. Purple or (rarely) white, pointed, bell-shaped

Site All prefer full sun, but perennials tolerate some shade.
Soil Must be well-drained, especially for rock-garden plants, and fertile; all grow well on chalky soils.
Propagation Sow seed of all species in pots under glass in March–April; grow on until large enough to plant in the open. Sow seed of biennials and herbaceous species in the open in May–June, transplanting in July and planting out in flowering positions in October. Cultivars and double-flowered forms do not come true from seed. Take cuttings of short basal shoots under glass in March–May, or in August after flowering. Divide established clumps of herbaceous cultivars in autumn or February–March.
Cultivation Tall-growing perennials need secure staking when the plants are 150mm (6in) high.
Pests and Diseases Slugs and snails may be a problem; froghoppers often attack young shoots. Leaf-spot fungus and rust may occur on larger-leaved perennials.

Above *Campsis × tagliabuana*

Campsis

BIGNONIACEAE   Trumpet vine
Deciduous, climbing, woody perennials of which there are two species only. Their large trumpet flowers are most decorative, appearing late in the season.
C. radicans (S.E. United States). Hardy. Climbing by aerial roots like ivy, its height in the wild is 9–12m (30–40ft), but in Britain is 2.1–3m (7–10ft) or more in favourable positions. Pinnate leaves 225mm (9in) or more; long, trumpet-shaped red and orange flower clusters in August–September, each 75mm (3in) long and half as much wide.
C. × tagliabuana 'Mme Galen' (hybrid between *C. grandiflora* and *C. radicans*). Hardy. Similar in habit to *C. radicans*; flowers are salmon-red. Needs support for its long stems.

Site Sheltered and sunny wall is essential.
Soil Fertile and well-drained, with well-rotted garden compost mixed in.
Propagation Layer in late summer. Semi-hardwood cuttings about 150mm (6in) long in August under cover, with bottom heat if possible.
Cultivation Plant in autumn or spring. Mulch in spring with rotted garden compost. Tie stems to supports. Water well in dry weather.
Pruning If space is needed, prune in late winter to leave about two buds on shoots produced the previous year; occasionally cut one of the oldest main stems down by one-third to provide replacement growth.
Pests and Diseases Aphids may attack young growth. Powdery mildew may occur.

Canna

CANNACEAE   Indian shot
Perennials from tropical and subtropical America grown as summer bedding plants. They have large, handsome, lance-shaped leaves and spikes of showy flowers on erect stems above the foliage.
C. × generalis (*C. × hybrida* of gardens). Name covers a number of cultivated varieties derived from hybridising *C. indica* with other species. Height 600mm–1.2m (2–4ft); spread 450–750mm (1½–2½ft). Leaves bright-green or purple-flushed, depending on cultivar, carried on erect stems. Flowers 50–75mm (2–3in) wide in shades of yellow, red and orange, opening mid to late summer. Several named cultivars are available.
C. indica (C. and South America). Resembles *C. × generalis* but has green leaves and flowers about 40mm (1½in) wide, usually in shades of red or pink.

Site Must be sunny, preferably sheltered from strong winds.
Soil Moisture-retentive and humus-rich, but well drained.
Propagation Divide tuber-like rhizomes into single-shooted pieces when they start into growth. Seeds may be sown in early spring at not less than 21°C (70°F). The hard seeds are best soaked in warm water for 24 hours; germination is erratic.
Cultivation Barely cover rhizomes with moist peat in early spring and keep at 15–18°C (60–65°F). When shoots are about 60mm (2½in) tall, divide into single-shooted pieces and pot into 100mm (4in) containers. Plant out when fear of frost has passed. Lift in autumn and store in frost-free conditions in slightly moist peat or leaf-mould.
Pests and Diseases Slugs may damage young leaves.

Below *Canna × generalis* 'Lucifer'

Carpenteria

PHILADELPHACEAE
A genus, allied to *Philadelphus*, comprising one handsome evergreen shrub from California.

C. californica Height and spread 2m (6½ft) or more. Leaves lanceolate, 50–100mm (2–4in) long, bright-green above and white-felted beneath. Terminal clusters of three to seven fragrant white flowers, each 50–75mm (2–3in) in diameter, produced in June–July.

Site Plant in sunny position near south- or west-facing wall.
Soil Any well-drained fertile soil.
Propagation Best by soft to semi-ripe cuttings, 75–100mm (3–4in) long, in a propagator in early summer; over-winter under glass in pots.

Cultivation Plant from containers in spring.
Pruning With mature specimens, remove old, exhausted, or winter-damaged branches to encourage new basal growths.

Below *Carpentaria californica*

Carpinus

CARPINACEAE   Hornbeam
Picturesque medium-sized to large, deciduous, hardy trees native to North America, Asia, and Europe. Their foliage is rather like that of the beech tree; they bear attractive hop-like seed clusters.

C. betulus (Asia Minor, Europe, including Britain), common hornbeam. Graceful tree ultimately 15–25m (50–82ft) high with grey, fluted trunk. Ovate, ribbed and toothed, dark-green leaves, 40–75mm (1½–3in) long and 25–50mm (1–2in) wide, turning yellow in autumn. Often grown clipped as a hedge. There are several cultivars, notably 'Columnaris' (slow-growing, small, spire-like, of dense, compact growth ultimately about 5m (16ft) high); 'Fastigiata' (syn. 'Pyramidalis', conical when young, becoming onion-shaped with age, ultimately about 14m (46ft) high by 3m (10ft) wide).

Site Suitable for waterside or parkland. 'Columnaris' makes a striking specimen in a formal garden setting; 'Fastigiata', which is higher at maturity, is better in larger gardens.
Soil Excellent in moist clay; tolerant of chalk.
Propagation Species by seed sown in spring after stratification; cultivars by grafting in early spring.
Cultivation Plant field-grown trees November–March.

Right *Carpinus betulus* 'Fastigiata'

Caryopteris

VERBENACEAE   Blue spiraea
A small genus of mainly deciduous shrubs from eastern Asia which have the double merit of being late-blooming and blue-flowered, both unusual attributes in shrubs. Commonly represented in gardens by forms of the hybrid listed.

C. × clandonensis 'Arthur Simmonds' (*C. incana* × *C. mongolica*). Deciduous shrub. Height and spread about 600mm (24in). Forms a rounded mound which looks attractive tumbling over a low wall. Pointed-toothed, aromatic leaves, silvery-green on under-surface. Bright blue flowers form rounded clusters in September. Hardy except in severely cold winters, but stems may be killed back to some degree by frost. Variety 'Kew Blue' is similar, but with deeper-blue flowers.

Site Sunny, sheltered from wind.
Soil Any, particularly chalk.
Propagation By soft cuttings 70mm (3in) long in July–August under cover; divide in late March–early April.
Cultivation Plant in spring; protect the crown in winter with a deep mulch.

Pruning Prune hard in early spring to remove previous year's new growth to within 25–50mm (1–2in) of stem.
Pests and Diseases Occasionally attacked by capsid bugs – usually a sign of water or sun shortage.

Below *Caryopteris* × *clandonensis*

Catalpa

BIGNONIACEAE   Indian bean-tree

A genus of small or medium-sized deciduous trees from North America and Asia with magnificent foliage and summer flowers. Excellent in city gardens, especially in southern parts of the country.

C. bignonioides (E. United States). Forms a wide-spreading, vigorous, dome-like, hardy tree, 8–12m (26–40ft) high and wide. Large, broadly ovate leaves 100–250mm (4–10in) long and 75–200mm (3–8in) wide, unfurling in June. Horse-chestnut-like flower panicles 200–250mm (8–10in) long and wide, white, spotted yellow and purple, in July–August. Slender, bean-like seed-pods, 300mm (1ft) long, hang down in autumn. 'Aurea', a striking golden-leaved cultivar, is somewhat slower-growing and makes an attractive specimen tree.

Site Sunny, protected against harsh winds, but with room to spread.
Soil Must be well-drained.
Propagation Species by seed sown in prepared seed-bed outside in spring. Cultivars by root cuttings in a propagator in spring or by grafting under glass in early spring.
Cultivation Plant field-grown trees November–March; container-grown specimens at any time.
Pruning Older specimens need regular dead-wooding.

Catananche

COMPOSITAE   Cupid's dart

Hardy herbaceous perennials and annuals, native to Europe. The species listed makes a good border plant.

C. caerulea (W. Mediterranean). Height 450–750mm ($1\frac{1}{2}$–$2\frac{1}{2}$ft). A short-lived perennial with narrow, grey-green leaves. Lavender-blue flowers, resembling cornflowers, in July–September; suitable for cutting and drying. Usually sold under species name, but several good varieties include 'Bicolor' (white with blue centres); 'Major' (large, lavender-blue flowers); 'Perry's White'.

Site Sunny.
Soil Light, well-drained.
Propagation Sow seeds in February–March, under glass with some heat, or in April–June in cold frame. Seeds sown in heat will flower same year if planted out in May. Named varieties can be propagated by root cuttings taken in March; this method ensures they grow true to type.
Cultivation Plant out in September–May.
Pruning Cut off dead flowers at base.

Below *Catananche caerulea* 'Major'

Below *Catalpa bignonioides*

Ceanothus

RHAMNACEAE   Californian lilac

A large genus of attractive evergreen and deciduous shrubs or small trees from North America, producing clusters of flowers in various shades of blue (a few are pink or white).

C. × 'Autumnal Blue' (hybrid). Evergreen. Height and spread 1.8–2.7m (6–9ft). Large, oval, glossy leaves, about 40mm (1½in) long. Blue flowers in rounded clusters in July–October. Best grown close to a south- or west-facing wall or fence; otherwise free-standing but sheltered from wind and in a sunny place. One of the hardier sorts.

C. × 'Burkwoodii' (hybrid). Evergreen, with a wide-spreading habit. Height 3m (10ft); spread 2.1m (7ft) against a wall. Shiny leaves, grey beneath, 30mm (1¼in) long. Lightly scented, deeper blue flowers than 'Autumnal Blue', in smaller clusters but larger numbers in July–October.

C. × 'Gloire de Versailles' (hybrid). Deciduous with vigorous arching growth. Height and spread 2.1m (7ft) or more in favourable position. Large leaves up to 65mm (2½in) long, powder-blue flowers in profusion carried in rounded clusters June–October. One of the most attractive species.

C. impressus (California). Half-hardy evergreen wall shrub, up to 3m (10ft) high and wide. Small dark green leaves. Small deep blue flowers in clusters in April–May.

C. thyrsiflorus repens (California). Evergreen prostrate shrub forming mounds about 1m (3¼ft) high and spreading twice as much or more. Glossy green leaves, average 25mm (1in) in length; light-blue flowers in roundish clusters late April–May. Reasonably hardy.

C. × 'Topaz' (hybrid). Deciduous shrub. Height 1.8m (6ft); spread 1.2m (4ft). Belongs to same group of hybrids as 'Gloire de Versailles' but is less vigorous. Indigo-blue flowers in July–early September.

Site Most do best grown with the protection of a sunny wall, especially evergreens, but will grow in open if there is shelter from wind and plenty of sun. Severe winters can kill them, although well-established plants may survive.

Soil Well-drained, light rather than heavy; if chalky add peat or leaf-mould.

Propagation Take soft cuttings 50–75mm (2–3in) long in July–August, and root in sandy compost under cover, with a little warmth if the summer is cool; pot on when they have rooted; plant out late the following spring.

Cultivation Some ceanothus do not like being transplanted, so they are all better planted from pots in late spring. Remove faded flowerheads. Tie shoots and branches of evergreen kinds to wall supports to ensure maximum exposure to light.

Pruning Prune deciduous late-summer- and autumn-flowering kinds in early spring by cutting preceding year's growth back to within 75mm (3in) of stem. Evergreen kinds may be cut back a little to tidy after flowering and to maintain a bushy habit. Remove shoots that are crowded, unproductive, or straggling.

Pests and Diseases Scale insect and sooty mould pose occasional problems.

Right *Ceanothus impressus*

Centaurea

COMPOSITAE   Cornflower, knapweed

Annuals, biennials, perennials, and shrubs from the northern temperate zone and South America. Only a few of the annuals and perennials are widely grown; some are hardy, others tender. Those listed have showy flower-heads resembling double or semi-double daisies.

C. cineraria (Italy, Sicily), dusty miller. Half-hardy, woody-based evergreen perennial often listed as *C. gymnocarpa*. Height (as a bedding plant) up to 600mm (2ft); spread about 450mm (1½ft). Fern-like, grey-white hairy leaves up to 300mm (1ft) long. Flowers, rose-purple, seldom produced on young plants.

C. cyanus (S. E. Europe), cornflower. Hardy annual. Height up to 900mm (3ft); spread about 300mm (1ft). Erect plant usually well-branched, with lance-shaped leaves. Flowers 40–50mm (1½–2in) wide in shades of blue, purple, red, pink, and white in summer. Several seed strains available, including the 300mm (1ft) tall 'Polka Dot'.

C. dealbata (Caucasus). Hardy perennial. Height 450–750mm (1½–2½ft); spread 600mm (2ft). Clump-forming habit. Pinnately dissected leaves, green above and grey-white, hairy beneath. Pink flower heads 50–65mm (2–2½in) wide from summer to autumn. A good variety, 'Steenbergii', has rose-crimson flowers.

C. hypoleuca (Turkey, Iran, Caucasus). Resembles *C. dealbata* but leaves are whiter beneath and flowers are slightly smaller. Variety 'John Coutts' has deep rose-pink flowers.

C. macrocephala (Caucasus). Hardy perennial. Height 900mm (3ft) or more; spread 450–600mm (1½–2ft). Erect clump-former with narrowly oblong to lance-shaped leaves. Flower-heads are deep yellow, about 75mm (3in) wide, opening in summer.

C. montana (European mountains). Hardy perennial. Height 450mm (1½ft) or more; spread to 600mm (2ft), sometimes more. Erect, winged stems bear ovate to lance-

shaped deep-green leaves which are woolly beneath. Flower heads, 50–65mm (2–2½in) wide, deep purple-blue in late spring and summer. Good varieties: 'Alba' (white); 'Rubra' (rose-red); 'Rosea' (syn. 'Carnea', pink).
C. moschata (S.W. Asia), sweet sultan. Hardy annual or biennial. Height about 600mm (2ft); spread 225–300mm (9–12in). Grey-green, lance-shaped leaves, sometimes pinnately lobed. Flower heads red-purple to pink, yellow, and white; fragrant. *C. m. imperialis* is commonest form in gardens, with larger flowers up to 75mm (3in) wide in summer.
C. rutifolia (syn. *C. candidissima*; S.E. Europe). Half-hardy evergreen perennial. Height and spread (as bedding plant) about 300mm (1ft),. Deeply lobed, velvety, silvery-white leaves. Flowers pink but rarely produced on plants in first two years or so.

Site Sunny; hardy perennials stand up to half-day shade.
Soil Fertile, well-drained.
Propagation Sow annuals where they are to grow in April or September. Divide hardy perennials in spring or autumn; or sow seed under glass in spring. Take cuttings of tender perennials in late summer, and overwinter young plants under glass; or sow seed in warmth in early spring.
Cultivation Plant hardy perennials in autumn–spring. Plant half-hardy perennials in spring only when fear of frost has passed.

Right *Centaurea montana* 'Rosea'

Cerastium

CARYOPHYLLACEAE
A group of easily grown spring- and summer-flowering rock-garden perennials. *Cerastium tomentosum* (snow-in-summer) has attractive grey foliage with myriads of white flowers produced in summer, but it is an ineradicable weed that should be avoided, as it will eliminate almost any other plant in the rock garden.
C. alpinum lanatum (Europe). Useful carpeting plant with comparatively large white flowers on short 75mm (3in) stems. Leaves attractively covered with grey hairs.
C. tomentosum columnae. Neater, less-invasive form of *C. tomentosum*. Makes a carpet of silvery white foliage. White flowers on 75mm (3in) stems in June–July.

Site Sunny, well-drained; a south-facing bank is ideal.
Soil Preferably poor; too rich a diet will throw plants out of character.
Propagation By division in July; pot or plant directly.
Cultivation After division and planting out the plants look after themselves; covering them with a pane of glass in winter will protect the woolly foliage against excess water.

Below *Cerastium tomentosum columnae*

Ceratostigma

PLUMBAGINACEAE

Showy tender and half-hardy shrubs and herbaceous perennials from Asia and tropical Africa bearing attractive tube-shaped flowers in summer to autumn.

C. plumbaginoides (syn. *Plumbago larpentae*; China). Perennial. Height 300–450mm (1–1½ft); spread 900mm (3ft). Bristly, much-branched reddish stems support hairy green leaves; brilliant, purplish-blue blooms 20mm (¾in) in diameter in August–October. May be invasive.

C. willmottianum (W. China). Deciduous shrub. Height 600mm–1.2m (2–4ft); spread 1.2m (4ft). Bristly, purplish stems with small, coarse green leaves. Dense clusters of brilliant blue blossoms in July–October. Can be cut back to ground in a hard winter.

Site Sheltered position facing south or west, preferably at base of a wall and getting plenty of sun.
Soil Free-draining sandy loam.
Propagation Perennials can be increased by division in the spring just as young shoots are emerging. Both can be propagated from softwood cuttings taken in June–July and rooted in a propagator.
Cultivation Plant in the spring. Allow existing stems to remain over winter to act as protection. All old growth can be cleared away in the spring when new shoots have emerged.

which has deep purple-red foliage throughout the growing season.

C. siliquastrum (E. Mediterranean), Judas tree. Low, branching, bushy tree usually not more than 8m (26ft) high; often a large, multi-stemmed shrub. Leaves rounded 65–100mm (2½–4in) across, grey-green. Flowers variable from pink to purple, 13–20mm (½–¾in) long in clusters in May. Purple seed-pods, 75–125mm (3–5in) long, hang from July onwards.

Site Sunny, sheltered.
Soil Well-drained and fertile; sandy loam preferred. Plants are lime-tolerant.
Propagation By seed sown in seed-bed outside in spring. Cultivars by layering or by grafting in spring.
Cultivation Plant from containers at most seasons.
Pruning Remove promptly any died-back or dead branches.
Pests and Diseases Coral-spot fungus may be troublesome in wet seasons.

Right *Cercis siliquastrum*

Above *Ceratostigma plumbaginoides*

Cercis

LEGUMINOSAE

Small trees and shrubs native to North America, eastern Mediterranean, and China, much prized for their distinctive foliage and colourful pea-flowers in spring.

C. canadensis (North America), redbud. Small, hardy, spreading, shrubby tree up to 5m (16½ft) high with heart-shaped leaves 75mm (3in) or more across. Clusters of pale pink flowers occasionally produced in Britain in late spring. Best represented by excellent new variety 'Forest Pansy',

Chaenomeles

ROSACEAE   Japonica, flowering quince

Deciduous shrubs, native to northern Asia, grown for their mostly light-reddish flowers which appear in spring before the leaves; in hot summers they set aromatic, yellow-green fruits which can be used for making jelly. Growth habit is rather stiff and untidy, but plants can be trained by pruning, and do well as wall shrubs.

C. speciosa (syn. *C. lagenaria, Cydonia japonica*; (Japan). Dense, spreading, tangled habit, slowly growing to about 3m (10ft) high and wide, with a greater spread if against a wall. Spiny branches clothed with glossy leaves. Light-red, open flowers in clusters in March–May (January–February in very mild conditions). Good forms, 1.2–1.8m (4–6ft) tall, are: 'Moerloosii' (apple-blossom pink and white); 'Nivalis' (white); 'Simonii' (semi-horizontal habit, velvety deep red, double).

C. × superba (*C. japonica × C. speciosa*). Low and spreading, height about 1.2m (4ft), suitable for herbaceous borders or rock gardens. Range of flower colour is considerable; some good selections: 'Crimson and Gold' (large, deep-red flowers with prominant golden stamens, suckers on some soils); 'Knap Hill Scarlet' (brilliant salmon-scarlet, free-flowering); 'Rowallane' (large, deep, brilliant crimson, free-flowering, does well against wall).

Site Best against a wall, where plants can be grown and trained much taller than in the open; they flower best in sun.
Soil Well-drained, rich.
Propagation Layer in autumn; remove suckers in November or March. Seeds sown outdoors in autumn. Cultivars will not be true to type.
Cultivation Plant autumn-spring. No special cultivation needed beyond annual mulching with completely rotted organic matter.

Pruning Remove straggling shoots in July and thin crowded or weak shoots. Spur-prune wall-grown plants by cutting back sideshoots to five leaves above basal cluster in July and two-three buds in winter; prune sub-sideshoots in July to two-three leaves. Train wall-grown plants fan-wise when young and tie in, removing shoots growing at right-angles to the wall.
Pests and Diseases Iron chlorosis may occur in very chalky soils.

Above *Chaenomeles* × *superba*

Chamaecyparis

CUPRESSACEAE   False cypress

Conifers, evergreen shrubs, and trees from North America, Japan, and Taiwan. A small genus with a vast number of cultivars, from miniatures only a few inches tall and growing slowly over many years, through moderate-sized shrubs to large, stately specimen trees. Grown for their shape and evergreen foliage, which consists of minute scale leaves clasping the stems in groups of four, with the branchlets produced as flat sprays.

C. lawsoniana (Oregon, California), Lawson's cypress. Pyramidal shape when young, ultimately a forest tree up to 60m (200ft) tall, with soft, thick, red-brown bark. Most varieties of the genus grown in cultivation derive from this species. Good examples: 'Chilworth Silver' (slow-growing, somewhat columnar, to 1.2m (4ft), silvery blue foliage); 'Columnaris' (narrowly columnar, to 3m (10ft) tall, 1.2m (4ft) wide in 10 years, ultimately 7.5m (25ft) after many years, blue-grey); 'Ellwoodii' (upright, somewhat pyramidal, quickly reaching 1.8m (6ft) tall, 1m (3¼ft) wide, then grows about 150mm (6in) a year to 3.5mm (12ft) and more, grey-green becoming blue in winter); 'Ellwood's Gold' (a slower-growing sport of the above, yellow shoot-tips); 'Fletcheri' (broadly conical, slow-growing to 1.8m (6ft) tall, 600mm (2ft) wide after 10 years, eventually 10m (33ft) and more); 'Kilmacurrugh' (narrow columnar habit with dense growth resembling Italian cypress, 3m (10ft) tall after 10 years, ultimately 15m (50ft) or more tall, deep-green foliage); 'Minima Aurea' (dwarf, slow-growing pyramid to 300mm (12in) and nearly as wide after 10 years, ultimately about 1m (3¼ft), bright yellow, tight-packed sprays of foliage); 'Pembury Blue' (broadly conical, moderately slow-growing to about 10m (33ft), silver-blue foliage, colour most marked when young); 'Winston Churchill' (broadly columnar, slow-growing to about 2.1m (7ft) tall, 1m (3ft) wide after 10 years, ultimately 7.5m (25ft), densely-packed, bright yellow foliage all year).

C. obtusa (Japan), Hinoki cypress. Tree growing to about 21m (70ft) in Britain, 30m (100ft) and more in the wild; graceful in outline and with feathery foliage. Attractive specimen in its own right, but also has good small forms: 'Crippsii' (slow-growing to 1.8m (6ft) after 10 years, ultimately about 12m (40ft), dense habit, frond-like sprays of deep yellow foliage); 'Nana Gracilis' (conical, compact, slow-growing to 600mm (24in) after 10 years, eventually about 3m (10ft), deep green, shell-like sprays of foliage); 'Pygmaea' (bushy, wide-spreading, 300mm (12in) tall, 600mm (24in) wide, brown-green foliage, red-brown in winter).

C. pisifera (Japan), Sawara cypress. Species seldom grown and is less attractive than *C. obtusa*, but has some fine varieties, such as: 'Boulevard' (more-or-less conical, silvery blue, feathery foliage becoming purplish in winter, best in neutral-acid soil and some shade); 'Plumosa Aurea Compacta' (syn. 'Plumosa Aurea Nana', dense conical habit, slow-growing to 1m (3¼ft) after 10 years, feathery golden foliage, brightest in spring).

Site Open or slightly shaded; none object to cold.
Soil Any except heavy clay; ideally, well-drained but moist; shallow chalk soils result in slow, less good growth, and *C. obtusa* and *C. pisifera* should have lime-free soil.
Propagation Take heel cuttings – 25–50mm (1–2in) long for dwarf and miniature forms, 100–150mm (4–6in) long for others – using young side-shoots in July–September, and put in sandy compost under cover.
Cultivation Plant mid- to late spring; do not remove soil from root-ball or spread out the roots. Keep well-watered if no rain after planting, and spray foliage with water daily; protect from wind until established.
Pruning Tidy up straggling shoots in September.

Below *Chamaecyparis lawsoniana* 'Pembury Blue'

Cheiranthus

CRUCIFERAE   Wallflower

Shrubby perennials often treated as biennials, grown for their (usually) scented, brightly coloured spring flowers. Very popular as spring bedding plants.

C. × allionii (syn. *Erysimum allionii*; garden origin), Siberian wallflower. Perennial grown as biennial. Height 300–400mm (12–16in); spread 200–250mm (8–10in). Four-petalled orange or yellow blooms carried in late spring and early summer. Growth compact, the mid-green leaves forming a dense mound. 'Orange Queen' and 'Golden Queen' are commonest cultivars.

C. alpinus (syn. *Erysimum alpinum*; Scandinavia). Perennial. Height 150–250mm (6–10in); spread 100–150mm (4–6in). Small, delicate wallflower for rock gardens. Leaves deep green and lanceolate. Flowers yellow in May. 'Moonlight' has pale, creamy yellow flowers.

C. cheiri (Europe), common wallflower. Perennial grown as a biennial. Height 300–600mm (1–2ft); spread 250–450mm (10–18in). Spring bedding plant available in a wide range of forms and colours. Erect plant with tough, wiry stems and mid-green, lanceolate leaves. Flowers are red, orange, or yellow, usually carried in May–June. Cultivars include 'Tom Thumb' (150–225mm (6–9in), for front of border or container); 'Fair Lady' (300mm (1ft), in a wide colour range); 'Vulcan' (300 (1ft) rich, deep crimson); 'Cloth of Gold' (400mm (16in), large, scented, yellow); 'Persian Carpet' (300mm (1ft), mixed, muted shades). 'Harpur Crewe' is yellow, fully double, grown as a perennial.

C. semperflorens (syn. *C. mutabilis*; Morocco). Perennial. Height 300–450mm (1–1½ft); spread 250mm (10in). Bushy, compact plant with grey-green leaves. Small flowers start off cream, become striped pink, and turn purple as they age.

Site Full sun, reasonably sheltered.
Soil Well-drained, preferably alkaline.
Propagation Sow seeds in a seedbed outside in May–June; prick out seedlings into nursery rows 150mm (6in) apart; plant in their flowering positions in October, after summer bedding has been cleared. Increase perennials from cuttings, using 50–75mm (2–3in) long sideshoots taken in June–July; keep in sheltered position over first winter. The double 'Harpur Crewe' is sterile, setting no seed, so must be increased by cuttings taken in June–July.

Cultivation Plant firmly, pinching out tips of tall-growing types to encourage bushy, branching habit. Apply lime to the soil before planting to deter clubroot. Pull up biennials after main flowering period, to make room for summer bedding.
Pests and Diseases Flea beetles may attack seedlings, biting small holes in the leaves. Cabbage-root fly larvae cause wilting and collapse of plants by damaging the roots. Clubroot disease stunts growth and causes large swellings on roots.

Right *Cheiranthus alpinus* 'Moonlight'

Chimonanthus

CALYCANTHACEAE

Genus of three species of shrubs from China, of which only one has become established as a garden species.

C. praecox (syn. *C. fragrans*), winter sweet. Deciduous spreading plant, slow-growing to about 2.4m (8ft) tall and 1.8m (6ft) wide, but much larger if given wall protection. Pale yellow, bell-shaped, strongly fragrant flowers with wine-coloured centres in November–February. Cultivar 'Grandiflorus' has larger flowers with conspicuous purple centres, but is less fragrant; 'Luteus' is completely yellow, but may be slow to flower.

Site Sheltered with sun, or against a south or west wall.
Soil Well-drained, preferably deep and moist; plant is lime-tolerant.
Propagation Layer in autumn; sow ripe seeds under cover.

Below *Chimonanthus praecox*

Cultivation Plant in autumn or spring; mulch annually with a layer of peat.
Pruning None required when grown in open; on walls prune in February to remove weak and crowded shoots and to shorten the strongest growths, tying in at the same time.

Chionodoxa

LILIACEAE   Glory-of-the-snow

Bulbous perennials from the eastern Mediterranean and Asia Minor. Each bulb has two to four almost grassy leaves and a short raceme of starry, blue to lilac and white flowers in early spring.

C. gigantea (Turkey). Height 150mm (6in) or more; spread about 100mm (4in). Flowers are 30mm (1¼in) wide, lilac-blue with small white eye. The form 'Alba' is pure white.

C. luciliae (Turkey). Height 100–150mm (4–6in); spread about 75mm (3in). Flowers 20–25mm (¾–1in) wide, deep blue with large white eye. Varieties include 'Rosea' (pink); 'Zwanenburg' (bright blue); 'Pink Giant' (extra-large flowers).

C. sardensis (Turkey). Height 100mm (4in) or more; spread about 75mm (3in). Flowers 20mm (¾in) wide, clear, deep blue March–May.

Site Moderately sunny, in open position.
Soil Moisture-retentive, but not wet in growing season.

Propagation Separate offsets when plant is dormant. Sow seeds when ripe or as soon afterwards as possible.
Cultivation Plant in autumn, the earlier the better.

Left *Chionodoxa luciliae*

Above *Choisya ternata*

Choisya

RUTACEAE

A small genus of evergreen flowering shrubs from Mexico and south-west United States, of which only one is commonly cultivated.

C. ternata (Mexico), Mexican orange blossom. Evergreen spreading shrub. Height and spread about 1.5m (5ft); in favourable situations to 2.4m (8ft). Attractively rounded bush with shiny, aromatic, light green leaflets usually in threes. Many clusters of strongly fragrant white flowers, 30mm (1¼in) wide, with orange stamens in May, and usually again in late summer and autumn. Severe winters are likely to kill plant back to ground level.

Site Sunny, but will take a little shade; shelter from wind. Preferably south- or south-west-facing.
Soil Well-drained; plant does well in chalky soil.
Propagation Insert half-ripe, 75mm (3in) long, cuttings in summer under cover.
Cultivation Plant autumn, or spring. Mulch occasionally with rotted organic matter; protect in cold weather.
Pruning Remove dead shoot-tips and leaves damaged by cold in March.
Pests and Diseases Occasionally capsid bug on leaves; white discoloration on top leaves due to cold.

carinatum but flowers have yellow discs and yellow to white ray florets; some are double.

C. frutescens (Canary Is), marguerite, Paris daisy. Half-hardy shrub. Height 600mm (2ft) or more; spread 450mm (1½ft). Deeply lobed leaves greyish or bright green. Flowers 65mm (2½in) wide with yellow disc and white ray florets opening from spring to autumn.

C. maximum (Pyrenees), Shasta daisy. Hardy perennial. Height 600–900mm (2–3ft); spread 450–600mm (1½–2ft). Robust clump-former with erect stems and lance-shaped, toothed leaves. Flower-heads 75mm (3in) or more wide, with yellow disc and white rays, opening in summer. Most cultivated varieties are double or anemone centred; typical are 'Everest', 'Mayfield Giant', 'Wirral Supreme'.

C. parthenium (S.E. Europe to Caucasus), feverfew. Short-lived hardy perennial, often grown as annual. Height 300–900mm (1–3ft); spread 300mm (1ft) or more. Deeply cut leaves. Large terminal clusters of small, white, single or double daisies in July–September. Variety 'Aurea' has green-gold foliage. Dwarf cultivars under 300mm (1ft), such as 'White Gem', 'Golden Ball', used as annual bedding plants, are listed in seed catalogues under *Matricaria eximia*.

C. rubellum (Japan). Hardy perennial. Height 600mm (2ft); spread 300–450mm (1–1½ft). Wide-spreading clump-former with lobed leaves and pink daisy flowers. Most cultivars are of hybrid origin, some in shades of red, yellow, and apricot.

C. segetum (S.W. Asia), corn marigold. Hardy annual similar to *C. coronarium* but with more coarsely cut grey leaves and all-yellow flowers.

C. uliginosum (E. Europe), moon daisy. Hardy perennial. Height 2m (6½ft), spread 600mm (2ft). Clump-forming and erect, an elegant plant with narrow, lobed leaves. White

Above *Chrysanthemum carinatum* **Right** *C. maximum*

Chrysanthemum

COMPOSITAE

Annuals, perennials, and shrubs from the northern temperate zone. They are mostly bushy plants with lobed or toothed leaves and showy daisy flowers.

C. carinatum (syn. *C. tricolor*; N. Africa). Hardy annual. Height up to 600mm (2ft); spread about 250mm (10in). Leaves coarsely dissected, bright green. Flowers 50mm (2in) or more wide, purple discs surrounded by white, yellow-based ray florets. Modern cultivars have rays variously banded red, maroon, or purple or wholly red. Double-flowered selections available. All flower in summer and early autumn.

C. coccineum (syn. *Pyrethrum roseum*; Caucasus), pyrethrum. Height 600–900mm (2–3ft); spread 450mm (1½ft). Bushy plant with divided leaves and erect stems. Rayed, daisy-like flowers, 50–75mm (2–3in) across, single or double, pink, crimson, or white in May–June. Easy to grow border plants. Varieties include 'Brenda' (cerise pink); 'Scarlet Glow'.

C. coronarium (Mediterranean, Portugal). Similar to *C.*

daisies in October–November. Useful as late-flowering perennial; thrives in wet soils.

Florists' Chrysanthemums. The familiar, mainly double-flowered plants grown as pot plants and cut flowers are derived from *C. vestitum* (syn. *C. morifolium*), *C. indicum*, and probably other Chinese and Japanese species. A group of early-flowering cultivars can be grown outside for late-summer to early-autumn flowering, but are not fully winter hardy. A wide selection is available from specialist nurserymen in almost every colour except blue.

Site Sunny positions are best, but hardy perennials will stand some shade.

Soil Fertile, well-drained.

Propagation Sow annuals on site in April; divide hardy perennials in autumn or spring or take cuttings in spring. Take cuttings of the *C. frutescens* hybrids in late summer or spring, in warmth. For florists' chrysanthemums, take cuttings from overwintered plants in early spring. Both *C. frutescens* and the florists' cultivars (notably 'Charm', 'Korean', and 'Cascade' types) can be raised from seed sown in warmth in late winter.

Cultivation Plant hardy perennials from autumn to spring; half-hardy ones only in spring after fear of frost has passed. Stake florists' cultivars; also annuals in windy sites. Lift florists' cultivars in autumn, cut back spent stems, and heel-in in a frame; or plant in boxes of soil in a cold greenhouse. *C. frutescens* must be overwintered in a frost-free greenhouse.

Pruning Cut back overwintered *C. frutescens* in late winter to induce bushy growth and young shoots for cuttings. Pinch out tips of young plants of florists' cultivars when about 150mm (6in) tall to initiate plenty of flowering stems.

Pests and Diseases Leaf miner, aphids, earwigs, capsid bugs may attack; grey mould disease is sometimes troublesome.

Above *Cimicifuga foetida*

Cimicifuga

RANUNCULACEAE Bugbane, black cohosh

Perennials native to the northern temperate zone. Those cultivated are clump-forming, erect, stately plants with long spikes or bottle-brush-like clusters of small white flowers. Suitable for mixed borders.

C. americana (E. United States). Height about 2m (6½ft); spread 600mm (2ft) or more. Large basal leaves formed of several separate leaflets. Flowers creamy white in long spikes in late summer.

C. foetida (N. E. Asia). Height 1.5m (5ft); spread 450–600mm (1½–2ft). Leaves cut into several leaflets and branched spikes of white and pale yellow flowers in late summer. *C. f. simplex*: see *C. simplex*.

C. racemosa cordifolia (E. United States). Sometimes listed as *C. cordifolia*, this is almost identical to *C. americana* and is confused with it in gardens. (Each flower of this species has one—rarely two or three—stigmas, that of *C. americana* three to eight.) Creamy-white flowers on long, erect spikes in August–September.

C. simplex (Russia, Asia, Japan). Height 1.2m (4ft); spread 450mm (1½ft) or more. Divided leaves and branched stems. Flowers pure white in arching, bottle-brush spikes in autumn. The most decorative species, useful for its late flowering. Varieties include 'Elstead' (purple buds); 'White Pearl' (coppery leaves); *C. s. ramosa* (*C. ramosa* in many catalogues), 2m (6½ft) tall).

Site Part shade best; full sun tolerated in moist sites.

Soil Moisture-retentive, fertile.

Propagation Divide established clumps in autumn or spring; sow seeds when ripe or in spring.

Cultivation Plant in autumn to spring. Staking is seldom required.

Above *Cistus × corbariensis*

Cistus

CISTACEAE   Rock rose, sun rose

Evergreen shrubs from the Mediterranean area, with abundant but short-lived flowers in late May–July. The rounded bushes are covered by large saucer-like blooms in white or in various shades of pink, purple and maroon, which flower in the mornings and then fall, with fresh ones taking their place on successive days. Some have aromatic leaves, whose odour is released in hot sunny conditions. None is completely hardy.

C. × corbariensis (hybrid). Height 1m (3¼ft); spread 1.2m (4ft). Dark-green leaves. White and yellow flowers in June.

C. × cyprius (hybrid). Height and spread 2.1m (7ft) in favourable situations. Grey-green leaves. Large white flowers with maroon blotch in June–July.

C. ladanifer (S.W. Europe, North Africa), gum cistus. Height 1.5m (5ft); spread 750mm (2½ft). Dark-green leaves. Large white, red-blotched flowers, 100mm (4in) wide, in June.

C. laurifolius (Mediterranean). Height 1.8m (6ft); spread 1m (3¼ft). Dull-green, wavy leaves, very aromatic in hot, sunny weather. White flowers in June. Hardiest cistus.

C. palhinhae (Portugal). Height 600mm (24in); spread 900mm (3ft). Dark green leaves with conspicuous white under-surface. Solitary large, white flowers, 100mm (4in) wide, in May–June. One of the hardiest.

C. × purpureus (hybrid). Height 1.2m (4ft); spread 1.5m (5ft), more in favourable conditions. Grey-green aromatic foliage. Red-purple flowers with dark brown blotches in May–June. Not very hardy.

C. 'Silver Pink' (hybrid). Height and spread 900mm (3ft). Dark green foliage. Flowers silvery pink with prominent golden stamens in June–July. Not good on poor soil; otherwise reasonably hardy.

C. × skanbergii (Greece). Height 900mm (3ft); spread 900mm (3ft); spread 1.2m (4ft). Grey-green leaves. Small, beautiful clear-pink flowers, six in a cluster, in June–July.

Site Full sun, away from wind.
Soil Well-drained, poor, even rocky (except for C. 'Silver Pink'); plants do well in chalk.
Propagation Sow seed when ripe or in spring in gentle warmth. Take semi-hardwood cuttings about 75mm (3in) long in July–August under cover; atmospheric humidity particularly important; grow on in pots and plant from these, as cistus do not like to be transplanted.
Cultivation Plant mid-late spring; no cultivation required.
Pruning Remove dead growth after hard winters, and occasionally the oldest flowered stems.

Clarkia

ONAGRACEAE

Hardy annuals native to North America. With their showy flowers, they are ideal for cutting or as container-grown or border plants.

C. elegans (syn. *C. unguiculata*; California). Height 600mm (2ft); spread 300mm (1ft). Graceful border plant with lanceolate, mid-green leaves. Long flower-spikes bearing deep-pink double flowers in July–September. Cultivars include 'Mixed' (pink, mauve, purple, and red blooms); 'Brilliant' (carmine-pink); 'Orange King'.

C. pulchella (N. America). Height 300–450mm (1–1½ft); spread 300mm (1ft). Erect plant with shorter flower spikes than *C. elegans*. Double or semi-double flowers in July–September in mixtures of white, lavender, pink, salmon, and purple.

Site Bright sun.
Soil Fairly light, preferably slightly acid.
Propagation Sow March–May where they are to flower; thin out to 225–300mm (9–12in). Can also be sown in September in mild southern areas or if cloches are used.
Cultivation For best results do not over-feed as this encourages leaf growth at expense of flowers.
Pests and Diseases Grey mould and foot- and root-rot may occur.

Below *Clarkia pulchella* mixture

Clematis

RANUNCULACEAE

Climbing, woody, deciduous and evergreen perennials native to temperate regions, including Britain, in the northern hemisphere. Old man's beard or traveller's joy (*C. vitalba*) is the native British species, whose greenish white, late-summer flowers and feathery seed-heads ('beards') are a familiar sight in British woods and hedgerows. The cultivated hybrids mostly have large showy flowers from spring to autumn, depending on variety; all climb by twining their leaf petioles around their host or other support. Most of the popular cultivated species and their cultivars bloom in spring or early summer and have rather smaller flowers than the hybrids.

Hybrids. This large-flowered group can be divided into two: those that flower early, in late May-end June, and those that flower from late summer into autumn. Good earlies, each growing to about 3m (10ft) include: 'Lasurstern' (purplish-blue flowers with prominent yellow stamens); 'Nellie Moser' (very pale mauve-pink with carmine stripe, best on north-facing wall); 'The President' (purple-red with lighter central stripe, silver reverse); 'Vyvyan Pennell' (double, deep violet-blue with crimson shading, also makes single flowers in autumn). Good late-flowering kinds include: 'Jackmanii Superba' (6m (20ft), rich, dark purple, free-flowering); 'Perle d'Azur' (3.5m (12ft) tall, sky-blue, free-flowering); 'Etoile Violette'(4.5m (15ft), deep violet, yellow stamens, very free-flowering); 'W.E. Gladstone' (3.5m (12ft), lavender, large flowers, lighter stripe and white stamens).

Above *Clematis C.* × 'Jackmanii Superba'   **Below** *C.* × 'Nellie Moser'

C. alpina (C. Europe) 'Frances Rivis'. Height 2.1m (7ft). Bright blue outer sepals, 50mm (2in) long, with inner white 'petals' in April–May; soft, silky white seed-heads are longlasting and decorative.

C. armandii (China). Evergreen. Height 6m (20ft). Creamy white flowers. Not completely hardy. Variety 'Apple Blossom' has pink and white flowers.

C. montana (Himalaya). Height 9m (30ft). Produces masses of small white flowers in May. Variety *C. m. rubens*, with bronze-green foliage, has rose-pink flowers in June.

Following are a few unusual but garden-worthy species.

C. florida 'Sieboldii' (Japan). Semi-evergreen. Height 3m (10ft). Flowers (in June and July) are white and green, with prominent central cluster of purple petaloids.

C. orientalis (Himalaya), orange-peel clematis. Height 4.5m (15ft), narrow grey-green leaflets. Thick, fleshy yellow, slightly fragrant flowers in August–September.

C. tangutica (C. Asia). Height 3–4.5m (10–15ft). Yellow, lantern-shaped flowers in July–October; decorative, silky seed-heads.

Right *Clematis tangutica*   **Below** *C. armandii*

Site Sun or some shade for top growth, but roots must be shaded; choose site carefully as clematis dislike transplanting.

Soil Deep, moist, well-drained and fertile, preferably with some chalk.

Propagation Layer 18-month-old shoots in autumn–spring. Take inter-nodal cuttings in summer, and keep in warmth under cover. Pot on both types as necessary.

Cultivation Plant from pots in autumn or spring the year after rooting; ensure cool, shaded root run by laying stones over the roots or surrounding with other plants. Mulch generously in spring with rotted manure. Water well in dry weather. Tie in shoots as they grow.

Pruning Early summer, large-flowered kinds: prune lightly in early spring, to cut back the tips of last year's shoots and remove weak or straggling growth. Late-flowering species and large-flowered kinds: either cut down hard in February to leave 600–900m (2–3ft) of main stem, or cut back last year's growth to leave one pair of buds – this will result in longer and longer bare main stems. Spring-flowering kinds: remove oldest flowered growth, and tips of remainder to keep in bounds, immediately after flowering.

Pests and Diseases Earwigs eat petals; slugs and snails like new young shoots; greenfly, scale insect, adult weevils eat leaves. Mildew may affect leaves. Clematis wilt attacks young plants, causing leaves to wither and shoots to wilt completely within days.

Above *Cleome spinosa* mixture

Cleome

CAPPARIDACEAE   Spider-flower

Annuals and shrubs native to South America. The cultivated species listed has fragrant flower heads. Useful on its own or in a mixed border.

C. spinosa (syn. *C. pungens*; tropical America). Annual. Height 900mm–1.2m (3–4ft); spread 450mm (1½ft). Half-hardy plant with bushy, upright growth and thorns at the base of each leaf; mid-green leaves divided into five to seven leaflets. White flower-heads flushed with pink, 100mm (4in) across, with narrow petals and long stamens, in July to late autumn. Cultivars include 'Golden Sparkler' (bright yellow); 'Helen Campbell' (white); 'Pink Queen'; 'Cherry Queen'; 'Violet Queen'; 'Colour Fountain Mixed'.

Site Full sun.
Soil Rich, well-drained.
Propagation Sow seeds in March in heated greenhouse; prick out into 75mm (3in) pots;

harden off before planting out in May; pinch out shoot tips to encourage bushiness.
Cultivation Dig in organic matter before planting out.

Above *Cobaea scandens*

Cobaea

COBAEACEAE

Half-hardy perennials native to Central and South America.
C. scandens (Mexico), cathedral bells, cup-and-saucer vine. Treated as half-hardy annual when grown outdoors. Quick-growing climber, using tendrils to reach 6m (20ft). Mid-

green leaves with three pairs of leaflets. Purple bell-shaped flowers, 65–75mm (2½–3in) long, with prominent stamens in May–October. Variety 'Alba' has white flowers.

Site Sunny, sheltered spot with wall or trellis for support.
Soil Well-drained, not too rich.
Propagation Sow seeds in February–April in gentle heat; pot on when large enough;

harden off before planting outside in June.
Cultivation Water well and often in dry weather.
Pests and Diseases Aphids sometimes a problem.

Above *Colchicum speciosum*

Colchicum

LILIACEAE   Autumn crocus, naked ladies.

Cormous perennials, most of which flower in autumn. They are unrelated to *Crocus*, the corms of the two genera being quite different in shape, although the flowers are somewhat similar. The leaves, which are relatively large, are carried in clusters of three to eight and mature in spring. Good for borders or in rough grass.

C. autumnale (Europe, including Britain). Height and spread about 300mm (1ft), with lance-shaped leaves. Flowers 150–250mm (6–10in) tall, lilac pink (sometimes faintly chequered) in early autumn. Varieties include 'Album' (pure white); 'Plenum' (syns. 'Pleniflorum', 'Roseum-Plenum', 'Flora-Pleno', double pink flowers).

C. speciosum (Caucasus, Iran, and Turkey). Height and spread about 400mm (16in). Leaves oblong-eliptic, lustrous; flowers about 250mm (10in) tall, lilac-rose to red-purple in mid-autumn. Variety 'Album' is pure white and of excellent substance. Several hybrid cultivars are available, including 'Lilac Wonder' (rosy-violet); 'The Giant' (rose-lilac); 'Violet Queen' (red-purple); 'Water Lily' (rosy-lilac, fully double).

Site Sunny.
Soil Well-drained.
Propagation Separate offsets or divide congested clumps while plants are dormant. Sow seed when ripe; these germinate erratically and take

several years to flower.
Cultivation Plant corms in late summer or early autumn – the earlier the better.
Pests and Diseases Corms and flowering shoots sometimes attacked by slugs.

Convallaria

LILIACEAE   Lily-of-the-valley

A showy, creeping, hardy perennial native to Europe, North America, and Asia.

C. majalis. Height 150–230mm (6–9in); spread 1m (3¼ft) or more, by creeping rootstock. Sprays of tiny, waxy, fragrant white flowers in graceful arching sprays in April–May; they make good cut flowers and are ideal for buttonholes. Lance-shaped, deep-green leaves arise directly from rootstock. Cultivars include 'Fortin's Giant' (white); 'Rosea' (pink); 'Variegata' (gold-striped foliage).

Site Shade preferred; will tolerate full sun if sufficient moisture in soil.
Soil Heavy, richly organic is ideal. Mulch with leaf-mould in autumn.
Propagation Separate small pieces of root with bud attached at any time during dormant season, and plant in their permanent position.
Cultivation Plant 'pips' (root pieces with buds) up to 50mm (2in) deep.

Below Convallaria majalis

Right Convolvulus tricolor

Convolvulus

CONVOLVULACEAE

Annual or perennial, twining, prostrate, or erect herbaceous plants and sub-shrubs from temperate and tropical regions. One or two are all-too-familiar natives in our gardens, such as field bindweed (*C. arvensis*), with its small pink and white flowers. Those listed here are much less rampant and make desirable plants.

C. cneorum (S. Europe). Shrub. Height and spread 600–900mm (2–3ft). Evergreen silvery grey, narrow leaves. Small, pale-pink and white trumpet-flowers in June–September. Not completely hardy, it thrives best near a south-facing wall.

C. mauritanicus (syn. *C. sabatius*; Italy, Sicily). Low-growing, trailing perennial suitable for rock garden, with greyish foliage. Bright-blue, funnel-shaped flowers in succession in July–October. Not fully hardy.

C. tricolor (Mediterranean region, Portugal). Annual. Height 300mm (1ft), dark-green foliage. Flowers blue, with white or yellow throats, in July–September. Many garden varieties in various colours derived from hybridising. 'Blue Flash' is a particularly good bushy plant whose blooms are deep blue with yellow and white centre; it is a little shorter than the type species.

Site Sunny, sheltered; perennials do well on rock gardens or on banks.
Soil Well-drained, even dry.
Propagation Annuals from seed sown outdoors in spring. Perennials by tip cuttings taken in summer and kept covered in gentle heat; or by division in spring.
Cultivation Plant or sow in mid-late spring; protect from cold while establishing; thin annuals to 120mm (5in) apart when 50mm (2in) tall; keep free of weeds.
Pests and Diseases Slugs and snails may eat seedlings.

Cordyline

AGAVACEAE   Cabbage palm

Evergreen trees and shrubs from South America, India, Australasia and the Far East. Most are tender or half-hardy plants that need to be grown under glass in Britain, but the species below is quite common in mild areas in south-west England.

C. australis (New Zealand). Slow-growing bushy tree, eventually reaching 9m (30ft) height and up to 3m (10ft) spread. Sword-shaped leaves up to 900mm (3ft) long borne in large clusters at end of erect branches. Creamy white, fragrant flowers in loose panicles in June–July. Form 'Atropurpurea' has purple leaves and is less tall. A good 'accent' plant in summer bedding.

Site Sheltered, sunny; must be frost-free.
Soil Well-drained, with peat or leaf-mould mixed in before planting.
Propagation By seed sown 13mm (½in) deep in warmth in March.
Cultivation Plant indoors in moist soil in May; be careful to avoid injury to the roots. Do not over-water while plants are establishing, as the fleshy roots may rot if they have not taken hold. Lift the plants in autumn and over-winter under glass.

Below *Cordyline australis*

Above *Coreopsis verticillata*

Coreopsis

COMPOSITAE   Tickseed

Hardy annuals or herbaceous perennials native to North America. The garden species are easy-to-grow border plants with an erect bushy habit, producing a mass of yellow daisy flowers throughout the summer. All are good for cutting.

C. drummondii (S. United States). Hardy annual. Height and spread 300–450mm (1–1½ft) or more. Bushy erect plant with slender branching stems and divided, dull-green leaves. Bright yellow 'daisies', 40–50mm (1½–2in) across, produced in profusion in July–September. Double-flowered strains are available, and others with flowers blotched or ringed with brown and red.

C. grandiflora (United States). Perennial, often short-lived. Height 600–900mm (2–3ft). Vigorous, bushy plant with narrow, toothed leaves. Strong, erect stems with clear-yellow daisies 50–75mm (2–3in) across continuously in June–September; excellent as cut flowers. A prolific border plant. Cultivars include 'Mayfield Giant' (deep yellow); 'Goldfink' (bright yellow, only 230mm (9in) high); 'Sunray' (double or semi-double yellow flowers).

C. verticillata (E. United States). Perennial. Height 450–600mm (1½–2ft); spread 450mm (1½ft). Neat, erect, bushy plant with finely divided, almost threadlike leaves. Covered continuously with small, star-shaped, shining golden-yellow flowers with pointed petals, 25mm (1in) across, in July–September. Cheerful front of border plant.

Site All prefer full sun in an open border.
Soil Must be well-drained and fertile; all species listed tolerate chalky soils.
Propagation Sow seed of annuals where the plants are to flower in March–April. Sow seed of perennials in May–June, transplanting to nursery beds in late summer; or sow under glass in early spring. Divide perennials in early autumn or in February–March. Take cuttings of short basal growths of *C. grandiflora* in July–August, rooting them in frame or greenhouse.
Cultivation Cut back stems of one or two plants of *C. grandiflora* in August to prevent them setting seed and to encourage production of perennial growth. Stake annuals with twiggy branches when they are 100mm (4in) high. Pull up and discard plants after flowering.
Pests and Diseases Froghoppers ('cuckoo-spit') sometimes appear on young shoots.

Above *Cornus alba*

Cornus

CORNACEAE   Cornel, dogwood

A genus mainly of shrubs and trees, with a few herbaceous species, mostly deciduous but with one or two evergreens; from northern temperate zones. The species native to Britain is the common dogwood, *C. sanguinea*, with purple-red stems, dull white but heavily scented flowers in June, and black fruits in autumn. The cultivated species and varieties are grown either for their coloured bark and foliage or for their flowers.

C. alba (Siberia, China). Deciduous shrub. Height 3m (10ft), spreading considerably to form a thicket of bright red stems, attractive in winter but rather rampant. Recommended forms: 'Elegantissima' (grey-green leaves margined in creamy white, and much less rampant); 'Sibirica' (syn. 'Westonbirt', with vivid red stems in winter, less rampant than parent, but with plain leaves); 'Spaethii' (bright yellow leaves having deep, irregular margins all summer, and bright red bark in winter).

C. canadensis (syn. *Chamaepericlymenum canadense*; North America), creeping dogwood. Creeping herb with wiry stems, 250mm (10in) tall, topped with horizontal leaves to form a flat carpet. Tiny flowers surrounded by prominent white bracts in June, followed by red berries.

C. kousa chinensis (China). Deciduous tree. Height and spread 3m (10ft) or more. White bracts stand up along horizontal branches, producing tiers of blooms in May–June; edible red, strawberry-like fruit in good summer; bright red autumn leaf colour.

C. mas (Europe), cornelian cherry. Deciduous shrub, 1.8m (6ft) high by 1.5m (5ft) wide; or small tree, 4.5m (15ft) high.

Tiny bright-yellow flower clusters in February; edible red fruit in late summer. Cultivar 'Aurea Elegantissima' has leaves with yellow border, sometimes also tinged pink.

C. stolonifera (North America) 'Flaviramea'. Deciduous shrub. Height 2.4m (8ft). Suckers freely; bark of young shoots is greenish yellow.

Site Sun or light shade, protected against persistent wind; *C. canadensis*, in particular, needs shade.
Soil *C. canadensis* must have acid soil, with some peat added; *C. kousa chinensis* flowers best in deep, moist, neutral-to-acid soil, with peat; *C. mas* does not object to dry and limy soil.
Propagation By layering in autumn; by rooted suckers in late autumn; by half-ripe hardwood cuttings, 75mm (3in) long, in July–August in warm conditions; *C. mas* should be propagated by cuttings from a fruiting tree.
Cultivation Plant autumn to spring; mulch flowering and herbaceous kinds annually in spring with peat.
Pruning If *C. alba* and other species and varieties are grown for bark effects, cut half the shoots down close to ground level if height required; otherwise, prune all the shoots of *C. alba* and varieties to ground level in February.

Above *Cortaderia selloana* 'Sunningdale Silver'

Cortaderia

GRAMINEAE   Pampas grass

Perennial grasses from South America and New Zealand. Those cultivated are decorative, evergreen and clump-forming, with tall, showy, plume-like flower panicles.

C. richardii (New Zealand), toetoe or New Zealand pampas. Height 2–3m (6½–10ft); spread 1.5–2m (5–6½ft). Forms dense clumps with slender, pointed leaves. Tiny, silvery to creamy white flowering spikelets form arching floral plumes and expand in late summer. Sometimes listed as *Arundo conspicua*.

C. selloana (syn. *C. argentea*; temperate S. America). Height 2–3m (6½–10ft) or more; spread 2m (6½ft). Similar to *C. richardii*, but leaves more greyish-green and floral plumes erect, appearing in September. Varieties include 'Pumila' (dwarf and compact); 'Rendatleri' (tall with pink-tinted plumes); 'Sunningdale Silver' (feathery white plumes). New cultivars 'Gold Band' and 'Silver Comet' have respectively yellow and white variegated leaves.

Site Full sun essential for free flowering; give shelter from north winds.
Soil Must be well-drained and moderately fertile.
Propagation Divide established clumps; or sow seeds under glass in spring.
Cultivation Plant where they are to grow in spring.
Pruning Dead leaves may be cut off or burnt off for the sake of tidiness; beware of cuts from the sharp-edged leaves.

Corydalis

FUMARIACEAE   Fumitory

A diverse group of hardy perennials that are both valuable and a challenge to the rock gardener.

C. cashmeriana (Himalaya). Height up to 150mm (6in). Has lovely sky-blue flowers in June and does well out of doors in a cool, peaty situation. Has a reputation for being difficult, but worth persevering with as its deeply cut, fern-like leaves as well as flowers on 75mm (3½in) stems are attractive.

C. cheilanthifolia (China). A less-demanding plant that will self-seed. Likes part shade. Bronzed ferny foliage in tufts from which arise dense racemes of yellow flowers on 200mm (8in) stems from spring through summer.

C. solida (N. E. Europe, Balkans, and Asia Minor). Ideal plant for a dry, shady position. Delicate foliage appears briefly in early spring. Purple-pink flowers grow on sturdy 100–150mm (4–6in) stems. Often confused with similar but more robust *C. bulbosa*.

Site Varies between species: see above.
Soil *C. cashmeriana* requires cool, peaty, lime-free soil; *C. cheilanthifolia* tolerates most soils; *C. solida* prefers dry soil.
Propagation By division (take care, as tubers are brittle). *C. cheilanthifolia* also increases well from self-sown seed; otherwise sow in autumn or winter.
Cultivation See individual species.

Below *Corydalis cheilanthifolia*

Above *Corylus avellana* 'Contorta'

Corylus

CORYLACEAE   Hazel

Deciduous trees and shrubs native to North America, Europe, North Africa, and Asia. In gardens and woodland they are grown for their edible nuts and attractive male catkins and foliage.

C. avellana (Europe, including Britain, W. Asia and North Africa), cobnut. Much-loved native forming a dense thicket of erect stems up to 5m (16ft) or more high with downy, roundish leaves 50–100mm (2–4in) long and wide, turning yellow in autumn; male catkins 40–75mm (1½–3in) long, soft-yellow in February; tasty nuts 20mm (¾in) across ripen in September–October. Varieties include 'Aurea' (soft-yellow leaves – a weaker grower); 'Contorta' (corkscrew hazel); Harry Lauder's Walking Stick (3m (10ft) tall, makes a winter feature of contorted branches hung with lamb's-tail catkins, but is slow-growing).

C. maxima (S. Europe), filbert. Similar to but more robust than *C. avellana*, attaining 6m (20ft), with larger leaves, longer catkins, and larger nuts concealed by long husks. The variety 'Purpurea', with leaves and catkins of dark purple, is a reliable and effective coloured shrub.

Site Species ideal in woodland conditions. Associate different-coloured leaf forms to provide a contrast. *C. avellana* 'Contorta' makes a good lawn or courtyard specimen.
Soil Any, fertile; hazels tolerate chalk.
Propagation Species by seed sown in seed-bed in spring following stratification. Varieties by division, layering, or (*C. avellana* 'Contorta') grafting in early spring.
Cultivation Plant field-grown shrubs in November–March; container-grown cultivars often available and may be planted at any season.
Pruning Remove unwanted suckers in winter. Coppice old wood periodically to encourage new growth. Remove basal suckers from grafted specimens. Laterals from previous year carry crop.

Cosmos

COMPOSITAE   Cosmea

Annuals and perennials native to South America. The two most widely grown species are half-hardy annuals that make a colourful contribution to borders or containers well into the autumn.

C. bipinnatus (Mexico). Height 450mm–1.2m (1½–4ft); spread 600mm (2ft). Fern-like, mid-green leaves. Brightly coloured flowers up to 125mm (5in) across in August–September. Many good cultivars, including 'Candy Stripe' (white flowers splashed with crimson); 'Gloria' (very large, rose-pink blooms); 'Sensation Mixed' (flowers ranging from white to deep pink).

C. sulphureus (Mexico). Height 600–900mm (2–3ft); spread 450mm (1½ft). Darker, coarser foliage than *C. bipinnatus*. Among varieties are 'Bright Lights' (small, double flowers in yellow, orange, and scarlet); 'Klondyke' (best-known cultivar, with double orange, red, and yellow flowers); 'Sunset' (early cultivar producing masses of flame-coloured flowers); 'Sunny Gold' (dwarf strain 300–375mm (1–1¼ft) high, with small, golden flowers).

Site Bright sun.
Soil Light, not too rich.
Propagation Sow seeds in March–April in gentle heat; prick out into boxes; harden off before planting out in late May. Seeds can also be sown outside in April–May.

Cultivation Plants do best when weather is warm and dry. Will need staking. Dead-head the flowers regularly.
Pests and Diseases Aphids may cause problems.

Right *Cosmos sulphureus* 'Bright Lights'

Above *Cotinus coggygria* 'Notcutt's Variety'

Cotinus

ANACARDIACEAE   Smoke-tree

A genus of two small deciduous trees providing brilliant autumn foliage colours. Only one species is widely cultivated in Britain.

C. coggygria (syn. *Rhus cotinus*; S. Europe, Himalaya, China). Height and spread 1.8m (6ft) after 10 years, but can grow much larger. Light-green oval leaves turn bright yellow to red in October. Small purple flowers in July. Good cultivars include 'Flame' (orange and red leaves in autumn); 'Notcutt's Variety' and 'Royal Purple' (both with deep wine-purple leaves all season). Species and cultivars have a filmy, pinkish grey inflorescence partly covered in silky hairs in June-August.

Site Best colour achieved in sun; shelter from cold wind essential.
Soil Well-drained; best colours on poor sandy soils.
Propagation By layering and rooted suckers in autumn; by rooted cuttings (taken in autumn) in early spring.

Cultivation Plant in autumn-early spring.
Pruning Remove dead growth and straggling shoots in spring.
Pests and Diseases Occasionally capsid bugs on leaves. Shoots on young plants may wilt owing to soil-borne fungus disease.

Cotoneaster

ROSACEAE

A large genus of attractive evergreen and deciduous shrubs and a few small trees native to Europe, North Africa, and northern Asia except Japan. Many are suitable for the garden, with growth habits from prostrate to tree-form; they are easily grown, with coloured berries and pretty, small flowers. Some deciduous species colour well in autumn.

C. × 'Cornubia' (hybrid). Tall deciduous shrub, semi-evergreen in mild areas. Height and spread 6m (20ft) and more, growing about 300mm (12in) a year, with arching branches. Creamy white flowers in June; heavy clusters of brilliant red berries from autumn into winter.

C. dammeri (syn. *C. humifusus*; China). Evergreen prostrate shrub with shoots that root as they go. Spreads about 600mm (24in) a year, with dark-green, glossy foliage. White flowers in June, followed by red berries.

C. horizontalis (China), fishbone cotoneaster. Deciduous shrub. Height 600–900mm (2–3ft) if grown prostrate; trained against wall will reach 3m (10ft). Tiny, inconspicuous pink flowers in May, followed by profuse bright-red

Above *Crataegus monogyna*

Crataegus

ROSACEAE Thorn, may

Tough, hardy, dense, and spiny small deciduous trees or large shrubs native to North America, Europe, North Africa, and Asia. The flowers, usually white, come out in May or June; the fruits develop from August onwards. Excellent both in towns and in exposed areas.

C. × lavallei (syn. *C. carrierei*). Handsome and garden-worthy hybrid making a sparsely thorned small tree attaining 6m (20ft) or more, of upright habit, spreading with age. Leaves are leathery, glossy, oval, and dark-green, often colouring red in autumn and persisting into winter. Flowers 25mm (1in) wide in erect clusters abundant in June, and succeeded by large, pear-shaped, orange fruits retained almost to spring.

C. monogyna (Europe, including Britain, North Africa, Asia), common hawthorn, quickthorn. Familiar native tree of rugged outline up to 10m (33ft) tall. Leaves are deeply lobed. Abundant spring flowers are strongly scented; red 'haws' (berries with a single stone) make an autumn feature. A vigorous hedging plant. The upright-growing cultivar 'Stricta' makes a useful specimen in exposed areas.

C. oxyacantha (syn. *C. laevigata*; Europe, including Britain), hawthorn, may. Dense, small, round-headed tree up to 5–6m (16–20ft), less spiny than *C. monogyna*. Leaves with fewer rounded or pointed lobes; flowers larger; fruits with two or three seeds. Several cultivars make good garden trees: 'Paul's Scarlet' (syn. 'Coccinea Plena', with double rose-red flowers); 'Plena' (syn. 'Alba Plena', with double-white flowers); 'Rosea Flore Pleno' (double-pink flowers).

C. × prunifolia (garden origin). Excellent small tree up to 6m (20ft) high, often broader than tall, with compact rounded head. Glossy oval leaves colour orange and scarlet in autumn. Clusters of white flowers in June; crimson haws persist into winter.

Site Open; most species tolerate considerable exposure, drought or waterlogging.
Soil Any, fertile; plants are lime-tolerant.
Propagation Species by seed sown outdoors in spring, following 18 months' stratification. Cultivars by budding or grafting in summer.
Cultivation Plant field-grown trees in November–March. Container-grown cultivars often available for out-of-season planting.
Pruning Dense heads of matted branches may require thinning as trees mature.

globular berries; leaves turn bright orange and red in autumn.

C. × hybridus pendulus (hybrid). Semi-evergreen shrub, usually available as grafted weeping tree. Height 2.1m (7ft); spread 1.5m (5ft), with weeping shoots to ground level clothed in glossy leaves. White flower clusters in June, red berries in autumn.

C. × rothschildianus (hybrid). Evergreen shrub. Height 3m (10ft); spread 2.1m (7ft), leaves green above, grey beneath. White flowers in June; deep-yellow berries in clusters in autumn–early winter.

C. salicifolius (China) 'Autumn Fire'. Evergreen or semi-evergreen, low-growing and spreading. Height 450mm (1½ft); spread 3.5m (12ft), leaves glossy green above, light grey and hairy beneath. Bright orange-red berries after small June flowers.

Site Any is suitable, as all are hardy; sun with some shade is preferred.
Soil Any.
Propagation Sow seed 25mm (1in) deep outdoors in March. For cultivars and hybrids, take semi-hardwood cuttings under cover in July or August, or layer in autumn.
Cultivation Plant autumn–spring; no special needs.
Pruning Remove dead and damaged growth in spring.
Pests and Diseases Birds often eat the berries during the winter.

Right *Cotoneaster horizontalis*

Above *Crocosmia masonorum* 'Firebird'

Crocosmia

IRIDACEAE

Perennial bulbs from central and southern Africa with sword-shaped leaves and branched spikes of showy six-petalled flowers in mid- to late summer or early autumn.

C. × crocosmiiflora (garden origin), montbretia. Height 450–600mm (1½–2ft); spread 200–300mm (8–12in) or more. This is the common orange-red montbretia of gardens which also occurs naturalised on roadside verges in rural areas of western Britain. It is apt to be invasive. Among choicer cultivars are: 'Citronella' (soft lemon-yellow flowers); 'Emily McKenzie' (red and deep orange); 'Jack-anapes' (dark red and yellow); 'Solfatare' (apricot yellow, leaves bronze-tinted, not fully hardy in severe winters).

C. masonorum. Height 1m (3¼ft) or more; spread 450–600mm (1½–2ft). Leaves distinctively pleated; flowering stems arch over at the top. Flowers about 30–40mm (1¼–1½in) wide, vermilion-orange. Hybrids between this and the related *Curtonus paniculatus* include 'Vulcan' (burnt-orange flowers); 'Lucifer' (brilliant flame red); 'Firebird' (flame orange).

Site Sunny; sheltered from cold winds.
Soil Well-drained and fertile; water well in summer.
Propagation Divide clumps of corms in early spring just as growth commences.

Cultivation Plant in spring or in autumn after flowering is over, setting corms about 100mm (4in) deep.
Pests and Diseases Occasionally corms attacked by gladiolus dry rot.

Crocus

IRIDACEAE   Crocus

Cormous perennials from Europe and the Mediterranean to central Asia, with grassy leaves and showy, six-petalled, chalice-shaped flowers in spring, autumn, and winter.

C. ancyrensis (C. Turkey). Height and spread 70mm (2¾in). Rich orange-yellow flowers, opening in late winter. Variety 'Golden Bunch' has more flowers per corm.

C. angustifolius (syn. *C. susianus*; Crimea). Height and spread about 70mm (2¾in). Orange-yellow flowers, the buds feathered brownish bronze, in late winter.

C. biflorus (Italy to Caucasus and Iran), Scotch crocus. Height and spread about 100mm (4in). Flowers white or blue with purple veining, often with yellow throat, opening early spring. Varieties include 'Alexandrei' (undersides of petals a lustrous purple); *C.b. weldenii* (white, freckled or suffused with purple-blue); *C.b.w.* 'Albus' (pure white).

C. chrysanthus (Yugoslavia to Turkey). Height and spread about 70mm (2¾in). Flowers with broad orange petals with darker feathering, opening late winter. Typical cultivars (some of hybrid origin): 'Advance' (yellow-bronze and lilac-mauve flowers); 'Blue Bird' (blue and white); 'Cream Beauty' (cream and coppery-lilac); 'E. P. Bowles' (butter yellow); 'Ladykiller' (rich purple-blue and white); 'Princess Beatrix' (clear blue); 'Zwanenburg Bronze' (yellow and bronze).

C. flavus (syn. *C. aureus*; Yugoslavia to Turkey). Height and spread 70–100mm (2¾–4in). Flowers usually orange-yellow, sometimes paler, in winter to early spring. Cultivar 'Dutch Yellow' is bright orange-yellow.

C. goulimyi (S. Greece). Height and spread 100mm (4in). Flowers lavender-blue, before or with short young leaves in October–November.

C. imperati (Italy). Height and spread up to 100mm (4in). Flowers satiny lilac-purple, light buff in bud, variably lined or feathered purple, opening mid- to late winter.

C. kotschyanus (syn. *C. zonatus*; Turkey to Syria). Height and spread about 65mm (1½in). Flowers lilac with deep yellow throat, before the leaves in early autumn. Variety *C. k. leucopharynx* (syn. *C. karduchorum*) has white-throated blooms.

C. laevigatus (Greece). Height and spread 50mm (2in). Flowers strongly scented, usually lilac, sometimes white, the backs of the outer petals variably violet-striped, opening in winter. *C. l. fontenayi* is a nurseryman's name for a clone with well-striped petals.

C. sativus (Italy to Iran), saffron crocus. Height and spread 100mm (4in). Flowers violet-purple with darker veining and prominent red styles (the source of saffron), opening late autumn. Shy flowering unless deep-planted in rich soil. *C. s. cashmirianus* is freer flowering.

C. sieberi (Greece, Crete). Height and spread 65–100mm (2½–4in). Flowers white to purple with yellow throat,

Left *Crocus chrysanthus* varieties   **Above** *C. vernus* 'Pickwick'

opening late winter to spring. Varieties include *C. s. atticus* (lavender-purple, the largest and finest form in cultivation); *C.s.* 'Hubert Edelsten' (petals zoned in purple and white); 'Violet Queen' (entirely purple).

C. speciosus (W. Turkey to Caspian Sea). Height and spread 100–125mm (4–5in). Flowers bright lilac to purple-blue with darker veining, opening before the leaves in autumn. Cultivars include 'Albus' (white); 'Aitchinsonii' (one of the largest); 'Oxonian' (darkest form).

C. tomasinianus (Yugoslavia). Height and spread to 75mm (3in). Flowers lilac to purple, silvery buff in bud, in later winter with young leaves. Variety 'Whitewell Purple' has petals tipped red-purple; 'Ruby Giant' is larger and darker.

C. vernus (France to Yugoslavia). Represented in gardens by large-flowered Dutch crocus, the small wild mountain species being rarely seen. Height and spread 100–150mm (4–6in). Flowers white to purple in spring. Cultivars include 'Jeanne d'Arc' (pure white flowers); 'Little Dorrit' (silvery-amythyst blue); 'Pickwick' (silvery-lilac with dark lilac stripes); 'Queen of the Blues' (soft blue); 'Remembrance' (violet-purple, large).

Site All need sun if flowers are to open properly.
Soil Well-drained, moderately fertile.
Propagation Separate clumps or remove offsets when dormant. Sow seeds when ripe or as soon as possible.

Cultivation Plant corms of autumn-blooming sorts in summer, those of winter and spring sorts in early autumn.
Pests and Diseases Flowers pecked by birds; corms and shoots eaten by mice and squirrels.

Cryptomeria

TAXODIACEAE   Japanese cedar

Genus of single species of evergreen conifer from China and Japan related to redwoods (*Sequoia*).

C. japonica. Tall pyramidal tree growing to 30m (100ft) or more, with red-brown, shredding bark. Dark-green leaves densely crowded on slender branchlets. Best represented in small garden by variety 'Elegans', with soft, billowy, longer, permanently juvenile leaves, glaucous green in summer, turning bronze-red in autumn and winter. Makes an excellent bushy specimen up to 6m (20ft) tall, or may be grown as an informal hedge about 2m (6½ft) high.

Site Ideally sheltered but open in sun or semi-shade.
Soil Moist, deep loam best; plants will tolerate chalk.
Propagation Autumn or winter cuttings in propagator or cold frame.
Cultivation Plant container-grown shrubs whenever soil conditions allow.
Pruning *C.j.* 'Elegans' often improved by cutting out branched tips of 'leggy' specimens, which can be damaged by snowfall. Trim hedges in August.

Above *Cryptomeria japonica* 'Elegans'

× Cupressocyparis

CUPRESSACEAE

Hybrid genus represented by a large, evergreen, coniferous tree, originating at Leighton Hall, Welshpool (Wales), which can also be used for hedging.

× *C. leylandii*, Leyland cypress. Large, columnar, fast-growing tree, extending by 900mm (3ft) a year and reaching 18m (60ft) and more. Foliage is grey-green. Two good cultivars are 'Leighton Green' and 'Haggerston Grey'; a recently distributed form is 'Castlewellan', from Ireland, a beautiful yellow-green tree not as fast growing; useful for shelterbelts, and can be grown as a 1.2m (4ft) hedge.

Site Any; widely planted in seaside gardens.
Soil Any, deep.
Propagation Take semi-hardwood cuttings 75mm (3in) long in late summer, place in sand with bottom heat.
Cultivation Plant in September–November using plants lifted from open ground (pot-grown kinds, unless planted in spring, are likely to be blown out of the ground). Keep watered if weather is dry after planting, and spray foliage overhead daily until rain falls.

Right × *Cupressocyparis leylandii* 'Castlewellan'

Cyclamen

PRIMULACEAE   Sowbread

A genus of excellent tuberous plants that collectively provide almost year-round colour in the rock and peat garden. Some are hardy; others are tender and need winter warmth.

C. coum (syn. *C. orbiculatum*; S.E. Europe). Height 75–100mm (3–4in). Winter- and spring-flowering species with flowers varying from near white to deep crimson, all with a red or purple blotch at base of petals. Leaves rounded or kidney shaped, plain or silver marbled.

C. hederifolium (syn. *C. neapolitanum*; Europe). Most widespread and popular dwarf cyclamen. Mauve, pale pink, or white flowers appear in August and last well into October. Ivy-shaped leaves with attractive marbling on upper surface

Above *Cyclamen hederifolium* mixture

makes them a centre of interest at other times of the year. *C. purpurascens* (syn. *C. europaeum*; Alps). Height 100mm (4in). Lime-loving and one of the hardiest cyclamens. Has circular or heart-shaped leaves; short-petalled rose-carmine or pink, highly scented flowers in mid- to late summer. *C. repandum* (Mediterranean). Height 100–150mm (4–6in). Spring-flowering woodland plant with heart-shaped silver-mottled leaves. Carmine-red flowers have twisted petals.

Site *C. repandum* requires peaty woodland with some shade; *C. hederifolium* thrives anywhere, but looks well around the base of a tree; *C. coum* is hardy, but the flowers may benefit from the protection of a nearby shrub; *C. purpurascens* can be planted more in the open. All need shade from intense sun and must have some protection against strong winds.
Soil Well-drained but moisture-retentive; *C. purpurascens* benefits from addition of limestone chippings.

Propagation By seed, sown fresh. Collect them immediately from pods that have burst and sow thinly in a peat-based seed compost in a pot. (Cyclamen corms do not produce offsets.)
Cultivation Plant when dormant, 150–250mm (6–10in) apart and about 25–50mm (1–2in) deep. Mulch with peat or leaf-mould annually.
Pests and Diseases Vine weevils may attack corms, causing plants to wilt and die. Aphids may also be a problem. Cyclamen grown outdoors are seldom infected by disease.

Cytisus

LEGUMINOSAE Broom

Deciduous and evergreen shrubs and a few small trees native to Europe, particularly the Mediterranean area, and North Africa. All flower profusely in spring and early summer; short-lived, though they are easily propagated.
C. battandieri (north-west Africa), pineapple broom, Moroccan broom. Deciduous shrub. Height 3.5–4.5m (12–15ft), large trifoliate silvery leaves. Smoothly hairy, bright-yellow flowers in fat cylindrical spikes, 75–152mm (3–5in) long and strongly pineapple-scented, in May–June. Not completely hardy in severest winters; best against a south-, east- or west-facing wall. Sets seed only in hot summers.
C. × kewensis (hybrid, originated at Kew). Prostrate, deciduous shrub. Height 30mm (1ft); spread 1.2–1.8m (4–6ft). Pale yellow to creamy white flowers cover plant completely in May. Excellent for rock gardens.
C. × praecox (hybrid), Warminster broom. Height 1.2–1.5m (4–5ft); spread slightly greater. Pale yellow flowers in early May. Variety 'Allgold' is slightly larger selected seedling with deep-yellow flowers covering arching branches.
C. scoparius (Europe, including Britain), common broom. Height and spread 1.5m (5ft). Yellow flowers in May–June. Many named hybrids, including 'Andreanus' (deep brown-red wings and yellow standards); 'Cornish Cream' (ivory-cream standards, pale yellow wings); 'Goldfinch' (crimson and yellow standards, pink and yellow wings); 'Killiney Red' (red, with darker red wings, smaller with compact habit); 'Killiney Salmon'; 'Zeelandia' (lilac and cream standards, pink and cream wings, long arching shoots).

Site Open, sunny; sheltered location best for somewhat tender *C. battandieri*.
Soil Very well-drained to dry; poor, not too limy.
Propagation Sow seed outdoors in spring. Take 40–75mm (1½–3in) long heel cuttings of ripe growth in August, place in sandy compost under cover; when roots appear in spring, pot them into small pots, and plant out in the same summer (or immediately) if plenty of root growth).
Cultivation Plant while small in autumn and firm the soil round them well.

Pruning Immediately after flowering has finished cut back to just above any strong new growth; avoid cutting into old growth, as it is likely to cause die back. Encourage *C. battandieri* to produce new growth from near the base.
Pests and Diseases Gall mite attacks buds in late spring. Dieback, due to fungus disease, causes tiny black spots on leaves followed by withering, blackened shoots with cankers, and early leaf-fall; lift and destroy infected plants.

Below *Cytisus × praecox*

Daboecia

ERICACEAE   St Dabeoc's heath

A genus of two species from Europe and the Azores. Both are dwarf evergreen shrubs whose flowers resemble those of the bell-heathers.

D. cantabrica (syn. *Menziesia polifolia*; S.W. Europe, western Ireland, Azores). Height and spread 600mm (24in). Rosy purple, bell-shaped flowers 6mm (¼in) long on spikes 75–150mm (3–6in) long in June–September. Good cultivars include 'Alba' (white flowers); 'Atropurpurea' (deep red-purple); 'Bicolor' (white, rosy purple, and striped).

Site Exposed and sunny; do not coddle plants.

Soil Should be lime-free, acid, ideally containing leaf-mould or peat.

Propagation Layer in September. Take tip cuttings, 25–40mm (1–1½in) long, of sideshoots in August under cover. Sow seed in early spring under cover.

Cultivation Plant in spring or mid-autumn, adding peat if soil is short of organic matter. Mulch lightly with peat annually.

Pruning Clip over in early spring with shears to remove dead flower-heads and maintain compact habit.

Pests and Diseases Heather wilt may occur.

Below Daboecia cantabrica

Right Dahlia: ball (yellow), decorative (pink), cactus (red)

Dahlia

COMPOSITAE

Half-hardy perennials native to Mexico. The garden hybrids, with their large, brightly coloured flower in a variety of forms, fall into two groups: bedding dahlias and border dahlias.

Bedding Dahlias

Height 300–500mm (12–20in); flower width 50–75mm (2–3in). Single or semi-double flowers from July onwards. Cultivars include 'Coltness Hybrids', 'Figaro', 'Rigoletto', 'Unwins Dwarf Hybrids', and 'Unwins Ideal Bedding', all of mixed colours.

Border Dahlias

Mid-green leaves divided into ovate leaflets. Wide range of flower shapes and colours in single and double forms, grouped as follows:

Single-flowered Height and spread 450–600mm (1½–2ft); flower width 65–100mm (2½–4in). Single flowers from early August onwards. Cultivars include 'Orangeade'; 'Sion' (bronze).

Anemone-flowered Height 600mm–1.1m (2–3½ft); flower width 65–100mm (2½–4in). Outer circle of petals with densely packed inner petals from August onwards. Cultivars include 'Bridesmaid' (white with yellow centre); 'Comet' (maroon).

Collerette Height 760mm–1.2m (2½–4ft); flower width up to 100mm (4in). Outer circle of petals with inner ring of smaller ones from early August onwards. Cultivars include 'Can Can' (pink with yellow inner ring); 'Ruwenzori' (scarlet and yellow). Even better are the miniature forms, 375–500mm (15–20in) high: 'Esther' (yellow with orange centre); 'Alsterguss' (red with yellow centre); 'King of Hearts' (pink with yellow centre).

Decorative Height 900mm–1.5m (3–5ft); flower width 100–250mm (4–10in). Double flowers, various shades, from August onwards. Cultivars include 'Allemagne' (red); 'Gerrie Hoek' (pink); 'Harlequin' (lemon-splashed red); 'House of Orange'; ('Kelvin Floodlight' (yellow); 'Thomas Edison' (purple). Dwarf forms, 375–600mm (1¼–2ft) high, include 'Garden Wonder' (red); 'Little Erna' (yellow); 'Little Tiger' (red and cream).

Ball Height 900mm–1.2m (3–4ft); flower width 100–150mm (4–6in). Spherical double flowers similar to Decorative, but with floret edges more inward-curving. A good form is 'Trendy' (yellow tipped with orange).

Pompon Height 900mm–1.2m (3–4ft); flower width 40–50mm (1½–2in). Smaller flowers than ball dahlias, the blooms forming a slightly flattened sphere; from August onwards. Cultivars include 'Kochelsee' (dark red); 'Little William' (red tipped with white); 'Nero' (maroon); 'Yellow Jewel'; 'White Aster'.

Cactus Height 900mm–1.5m (3–5ft); flower width 100–250mm (4–10in). Double flowers with narrow, quilled petals from early August onwards. Cultivars include 'Apple Blossom' (pink with paler centre); 'Bach' (yellow); 'Highness' (white); 'Herbert Smith' (cerise pink); 'Mallorca' (deep orange); 'Queen Fabiola' (rich red).

Site Full sun; open site protected against frosts and strong winds.

Soil Well-drained, with added compost, manure, or peat (avoid excessive manure, which promotes leaf growth at expense of flowers). Rake in bonemeal before planting.

Propagation *Bedding dahlias* Sow seeds in February–March in gentle heat; prick off into pots; harden off in cold frame; plant out late May–early June, after last frosts. *Border dahlias* Plant over-wintered tubers in boxes of peat and sand in March; keep in frost-proof place; divide when 'eyes' begin to swell; cut into pieces, each with an 'eye'; pot up or plant 100mm (4in) deep in cold frame; plant out when danger of frost has passed. Take cuttings from tubers started into growth in February; place in boxes of peat; must be kept warm; cut off shoots 75mm (3in) long and root in pots in propagator; move to cold frame when well rooted; plant out after last frosts.

Cultivation *Border dahlias* Plant tubers mid-February to mid-April in greenhouse or cold frame; harden off before planting out late May. Can also be planted outdoors in early May, but will need frost protection. Pinch out growing tip four weeks after planting. Support with canes. Cut off dead flowers. Lift tubers in autumn after first frosts; cut back to 150mm (6in) from ground; hang upside down to drain water from stems; put in boxes with shallow covering of peat; keep in frost-proof place. *Bedding dahlias* Keep well watered. Cut off dead flower heads. Over-winter as for border dahlias or discard.

Pests and Diseases Aphids, caterpillars and earwigs may be a problem. Damping off, grey mould, petal blight, sclerotinia, verticillium wilt may occur.

Daphne

THYMELAEACEAE

Evergreen and deciduous shrubs mostly from Europe, a few from Asia. Notable, for their strongly fragrant flowers, which are often also decorative. The small kinds look good and do well in rock gardens. NOTE *All the species listed are poisonous in all their parts.*

D. cneorum (Europe). Evergreen trailing shrub. Height 300mm (12in); spread 900mm (3ft). Profusion of deep rose-pink, fragrant flowers in clusters at the tip of shoots in April–May.

D. laureola (S. and W. Europe, including England, North Africa, Azores), spurge laurel. Evergreen shrub. Height and spread 600mm–1.2m (2–4ft). Greenish-yellow flowers, occasionally fragrant in February–March; black berries. Not particularly gardenworthy, but will grow in woodland and fairly deep shade.

D. mezereum (Europe, including Britain, Siberia), mezereon. Deciduous shrub. Height and spread 900–1.5m (3–5ft). Very fragrant purplish-red flowers in clusters all along the leafless branches in February–March; red berries.

D. odora (China) 'Aureo-marginata'. Evergreen shrub. Height 1.2m (4ft); spread 1.5m (5ft). Light green leaves with pale yellow marginal variegation. Reddish purple to pale purple, fragrant flowers in February–March.

Site Daphnes have a largely undeserved reputation for being difficult to suit and prone to die suddenly, for no apparent reason (drought is often the cause). All like sunny position, though *D. laureola* will accept some shade.

Soil Well-drained, acid or alkaline; must be moist and cool, with shaded root run. Organic matter is important, preferably as peat.

Propagation Layering in autumn. Semi-hardwood cuttings, 50–75mm (2–3in) long, in June–July. Seed sown as soon as berries begin to acquire colour.

Cultivation Plant in autumn or spring from pots (daphne dislike transplanting); mix in organic matter at time of planting. Cover root-run with stones if likely to be exposed to hot sun and drying-out.

Pests and Diseases Greenfly in dry conditions. Daphne are prone to various virus diseases producing yellow mosaics, mottling and crumpling of leaves, and become vulnerable to frost. Those growing poorly for no apparent reason may also be infected. Do not use such plants for propagation.

Below *Daphne mezereum*

Delphinium

RANUNCULACEAE

Annuals and herbaceous perennials native to the northern temperate zone and mountains farther south. Most have large, showy flower-spikes in shades of blue and purple.

D. ajacis (syn. *D. ambiguum*; Mediterranean), rocket larkspur. Annual. Height 300–900mm (1–3ft); spread 300mm (1ft). Upright plant with mid-green, fern-like leaves. Slender flower spikes 600mm (2ft) long in various shades of blue, pink, and white in June–August. The Hyacinth-flowered varieties are best. Typical are 'Tall Rocket'; 'Dwarf Rocket'.

D. consolida (syn. *D. regale*; Europe, including Britain), larkspur. Annual. Height 900mm–1.2m (3–4ft); spread 300–375mm (1–1¼ft). Upright plant with mid-green, fern-like leaves. Dense flower spikes, 225–375mm (9–15in) long, in range of colours in June–August. Giant Imperial varieties, with very long spikes ideal for cutting, include 'Blue Spire'; 'White Spire'; 'Giant Imperial Mixed'. Earlier-flowering Stock-flowered varieties also good for cutting.

D. elatum (Pyrenees, Siberia). Perennial. Height 900mm–1.8m (3–6ft); spread 450–600mm (1½–2ft). Erect plant with mid-green, hand-shaped leaves. Large spikes 300–600mm (1–2ft) long of blue, purple, and white flowers with brown 'eye' in June–July. Many hybrid cultivars now available, notably 'Blackmore and Langdon' (mixed, very large blooms); 'Blue Fountains' (dwarf, double flowers, no need to stake); 'Blue Heaven' (dwarf, sky blue with white 'eye'); 'Connecticut Yankees' (Mixed, single flowers); 'Mount Everest' (white). Among the Belladonna group are 'Blue Bees'

(pale blue); 'Lamartine' (deep blue); 'Peace' (bright blue); 'Pink Sensation' (rose pink); 'Rich Blue'; 'Wendy' (gentian blue). The Pacific hybrids – taller versions of the Belladonnas – include 'Astolat' (lilac and pink, semi-double); 'Black Knight' (deep violet, black eye); 'Blue Jay' (mid-blue, white eye); 'Cameliard' (lavender blue, white eye); 'Galahad' (white); 'Pacific Giants Mixed'.

D. grandiflorum (syn. *D. chinense*; China, Siberia). Perennial. Height 300–600mm (1–2ft); spread 300mm (1ft). Mid-green, hand-shaped leaves. Deep blue, funnel shaped flower spikes, 300mm (1ft) long, in July–August. 'Blue Butterfly' and 'Blue Mirror' (dwarf and bushy) are good varieties.

D. nudicaule (California). Perennial. Height 300–375mm (1–1¼ft); spread 150–230mm (6–9in). Short-lived plant with three- to five-lobed fleshy leaves. Deep red flowers, 40mm (1½in) long, in loose clusters in April–July.

Site Sunny, sheltered.
Soil Well-cultivated, fertile.
Propagation Sow annuals and perennials outdoors where they are to grow in March–May or September. Divide perennials in March–April. Take basal cuttings of *D. elatum* hybrids in April; root in rows, transplanting to final site in September.

Cultivation Plant perennials in October–March. Stake tall varieties with canes; dwarf varieties and annuals with pea sticks if needed. Pull up and discard annuals after flowering.
Pruning Cut back perennials to ground level after flowering.
Pests and Diseases Slugs and snails may damage young shoots. Crown, root and stem rot, cucumber mosaic virus and powdery mildew may occur.

Above *Deutzia × hybrida* 'Mont Rose'

Below *Delphinium elatum* Belladonna

Deutzia

PHILADELPHACEAE

Reliable and rewarding summer-flowering small or medium-sized deciduous shrubs. The species, all of Asiatic origin, have given rise to many garden hybrids. Most are hardy, easy to cultivate, and produce conspicuous clusters of pink or white flowers.

D. × elegantissima. Elegant hybrid attaining 1.5m (5ft). Leaves broadly ovate. The variety 'Rosealind', with deep-pink midsummer flowers, is the best form.

D. × hybrida. This group of hybrids provides the most striking pink-flowered deutzias – strong-growing shrubs of upright habit 2m (6½ft) high and wide, often with orange-brown, peeling bark on mature stems. Leaves 75–100mm (3–4in) long, lance-shaped, and deeply veined. Typical examples are 'Magician' (large, pink-tinted blooms with prominent purple markings on petal reverses); 'Mont Rose' (large, open, lilac-pink flowers). Both are June-flowering.

D. monbeigii (China). Arching, branched shrub about 1.5m (5ft) high by 1.2m (4ft) wide. Shredding bark on older branches reveals orange-brown stems beneath. Small, lanceolate, grey-green leaves have whitish undersides. Many clusters of shining white 'starry' flowers weigh down branches in July.

D. × rosea. Compact, graceful hybrid about 1m (3¼ft) high and of smaller spread. Bell-shaped pink flowers appear in May. The form 'Carminea', with deep carmine-pink flowers, is the best.

Site Sun or semi-shade; avoid exposed north- and east-facing positions.
Soil Any, fertile; deutzias are lime tolerant.
Propagation By semi-ripe cuttings 75–100mm (3–4in) long in late summer in propagator or cold frame; robust growers by hard-wood cuttings of pencil thickness in autumn.
Pruning Keep small specimens neat by removing flowering stems almost to the base when last flowers fade.

D. chinensis (E. Asia), Indian or Chinese pink. Annual or biennial. Height 300–450mm (1–1½ft); spread 300mm (1ft). Erect, stiff, grass-green foliage with bold heads of bright pink or red flowers, up to 25mm (1in) across, in July–August. Many strikingly coloured dwarf strains available, listed under Heddewigii in seedsmen's catalogues.

D. deltoides (Europe, including Britain), maiden pink. Perennial. Height 150–225mm (6–9in); spread 225mm (9in). Short green leaves on prostrate stems, forming dense carpet. Tiny, bright pink flowers, 10mm (⅜in) across, in abundance on short, wiry stems in late May–June. Varieties include 'Albus' (white); 'Brilliant' (pinkish red).

D. plumarius (S. E. Europe), pink. Perennial. Height 225–300mm (9–12in); spread 300mm (12in). Narrow, grey-green leaves form tight mounds. Flowers up to 25mm (1in) across, fragrant, bright pink, in June–July. Ancestor of many hybrid garden pinks, including 'Inchmery' (pink); 'Mrs Sinkins' (white).

Site Open, sunny essential.
Soil Good, free-draining, alkaline; acid soils can be treated with liberal dressings of ground limestone.
Propagation Annuals, biennials, and rock-garden types raised from seed in trays in cold frame in spring. Alpine species increased by small cuttings of young shoots in propagator in July–August. Pinks grown from cuttings removed by snapping off healthy non-flowering shoot tips 75–100mm (3–4in) long. Border carnations increased this way or by stem layering. Grow all young plants except annuals in pots until ready for planting out.
Cultivation Plant young stock from pots in spring. Remove old flower-heads and trim unruly plants in late summer. Foliage improved by applying a handful of coarse bonemeal to each plant every spring.
Pests and Diseases Aphids may cause problems. Anther smut and rust may occur.

Left *Dianthus barbatus*
Below *D. deltoides* 'Brilliant'

Dianthus

CARYOPHYLLACEAE   Carnation, pink, sweet william
Hardy and half-hardy annual, biennial and evergreen perennial plants native to Europe, Asia and Africa. All have showy flowers (most of them are fragrant) which are widely used for cutting.

D. × allwoodii (hybrid). Perennial. Height 150–450mm (6–18in); spread 300mm (1ft). Attractive grey-green foliage in tight mounds. Fragrant, brightly coloured flowers (white through pink to deep port-wine) in May–July. Ideal for the rock garden. This hybrid is parent of the fast-growing, many-flowered modern pinks, including dwarf forms.

D. alpinus (Europe). Perennial. Height and spread 150mm (6in). Forms mats of short, rich-green foliage. Studded with scentless pink or purplish red blooms, 25mm (1in) across, in June–August. Good rock-garden plant.

D. barbatus (S. and E. Europe), sweet william. Perennial usually grown as biennial. Height 300–600mm (1–2ft); spread 450mm (1½ft). Erect stems clothed in bright green, lance-shaped leaves. Fragrant flowers in dense, flat heads, up to 150mm (6in) across, in June–July; colours from white to deep red, some striped. Excellent for cutting and in a border.

D. caryophyllus (France), carnation, gilliflower. Perennial. Height 300–900mm (1–3ft); spread 300mm (1ft). Handsome grey-green leaves on stout, upright stems. Fragrant flowers with sweet, clove-like scent; 25mm (1in) across, varying from white to pink and rose, in July–August. Parent of present-day border carnations. Varieties include 'Beauty of Cambridge' (yellow); 'Bookham Lad' (white, striped scarlet); 'Clarinda' (salmon-pink); 'Polar Clove' (white).

Dicentra

FUMARIACEAE

Hardy perennials from Asia and North America. The garden species have ferny foliage and racemes of decorative, locket-shaped, pendant flowers.

D. eximia (E. United States). Height about 300mm (1ft); spread 600mm (2ft) or more. Spreads by creeping rhizomes and has finely cut leaves. Narrow heart-shaped, rose-red flowers 20mm ($\frac{3}{4}$in) long, from late spring to autumn. Variety 'Alba' has white blooms.

D. formosa (W. United States). Resembles *D. eximia*, but flower clusters (in May–June) somewhat larger and petal tips reflexed. Good cultivars include 'Spring Morning' (grey-green leaves and pale-pink flowers); 'Pearl Drops' (similar foliage but pearly-white blooms); 'Luxuriant' (fresh green leaves and bright red flowers).

D. spectabilis (China, Korea, Japan), bleeding heart. Height 450–600mm ($1\frac{1}{2}$–2ft); spread about 450mm ($1\frac{1}{2}$ft). Elegant clump-former with greyish tinted, coarsely dissected leaves. Arching wands of 30mm ($1\frac{1}{4}$in) long rose-crimson, heart-shaped flowers in late spring and summer. 'Alba' has pure white blooms.

Site Partial or dappled shade gives best results.
Soil Moisture-retentive but well-drained, preferably rich in humus.
Propagation Divide plants in autumn or spring. Take root cuttings of *D. spectabilis* in late winter. Sow seeds when ripe.

Cultivation Plant autumn–early spring. Mulch with organic matter, preferably every spring.
Pests and Diseases Slugs and snails may eat young shoots and leaves.

Below Dicentra spectabilis 'Alba'

Dictamnus

RUTACEAE

Hardy perennials of eastern Europe and Asia, whose aromatic foliage and flowers exude a volatile oil. The garden species listed makes an attractive and durable border plant.

D. albus (syn. *D. fraxinella*: E. Europe, Asia), burning bush. Height 600mm (2ft); spread 450mm ($1\frac{1}{2}$ft). Bushy habit with fragrant, dark-green leaves. Spires of small white or purple flowers in May–June. Natural variety *D. a. purpureus* has rose-purple flowers.

Site Sunny.
Soil Generally happy in any well-drained soil.
Propagation Raise from seed sown in a frame when ripe or in spring; grow seedlings singly in pots until plants are large enough to be planted in their permanent positions. Root cuttings 50mm (2in) long taken during September–October inserted in sandy compost in frame; these make sizeable plants by late summer the following year.
Cultivation Remove decaying foliage in autumn. Occasionally put handful of coarse bonemeal around crown of plant in early spring.
Pests and Diseases Slugs often attack seedlings.

Below Dictamnus albus

Dierama

IRIDACEAE   Wand-flower, angel's fishing-rod

Bulbous, clump-forming perennials, native to South Africa, with long, grassy leaves and clusters of bell-shaped flowers on tall gracefully arching stems. The species listed is hardy except in the coldest parts of Britain, and is useful for giving a contrast of texture and lightness among other perennials in a border.

D. pulcherrimum. Evergreen. Height 1.2–1.5m (4–5ft); spread 1m ($3\frac{1}{4}$ft) or more when fully established. Vigorous, forming a large clump of narrow grass-like leaves. Clusters of silvery pink or purple, bell-shaped flowers, 40mm ($1\frac{1}{2}$in) long, on top of elegant arching, wiry stems in August–September. 'Album' is a good white form.

Site Prefers a sunny, sheltered situation, but tolerates some shade. Good as a single specimen or among other plants.
Soil Must be moisture-retentive in dry weather. Lighter soils preferred; chalk soils tolerated.
Propagation Divide congested mass of corms in early autumn; replant singly or in groups of three to five. Sow seed in pots under glass in early spring.
Cultivation Cut old stems to the ground in autumn; and remove dead or damaged leaves in the spring. Plant resents disturbance and may take a year or two to flower if transplanted. In cold districts plant only in the spring and give winter protection.

Right Dierama pulcherrimum

Digitalis

SCROPHULARIACEAE Foxglove

Biennials and perennials native to Europe, North Africa, and western Asia. Familiar as a wild-flower in woodlands. There are also several cultivars.

D. ferruginea (S. Europe). Biennial. Height 1.2m (4ft); spread 450mm (1½ft). Smooth, mid-green leaves fringed with hairs. Tubulat hairy-tongued flowers of golden brown tinged with red, on 600–900mm (1–3ft) spikes in July–August.

D. grandiflora (syn. *D. ambigua*; Europe, Caucasus). Perennial. Height 900mm (3ft); spread 300mm (1ft). Green, hairy leaves with serrated edges. Soft-yellow flowers spotted with chocolate inside on 600mm (2ft) spikes in July–August.

D. lutea (S.W. Europe, N. Africa). Perennial. Height 300–900mm (1–3ft); spread 300mm (1ft). Glossy, green leaves with serrated edges. Small yellow flowers on narrow spikes in May–July.

D. × mertonensis (hybrid). Perennial. Height 600–900mm (2–3ft); spread 300mm (1ft). Broad, somewhat lustrous leaves. Large flowers, 25mm (1in) across, in crushed-strawberry colour in June–September.

D. purpurea (Europe, including Britain), common foxglove. Biennial. Height 900mm–1.5m (3–5ft); spread 300mm (1ft). Mid-green, downy leaves that form a rosette. Large spikes, up to 900mm (3ft) high, of mottled pink flowers in June–July. Will grow as a perennial in suitable conditions. Cultivars include 'Alba' (pure white); 'Excelsior Hybrids' (from cream to purple); 'Dwarf Sensation Mixed' (compact form); 'Foxy' (mixed; can be grown as annual).

Site Light shade.
Soil Any, reasonably moist.
Propagation Sow seeds outdoors in April–mid-June; plant out in final positions in September.
Cultivation Plant in September–April. Leave flower spikes on plants if self-sown seedlings required.
Pests and Diseases Root rot may occur in waterlogged soil.

Right *Digitalis* 'Excelsior Hybrids'

Above *Dimorphotheca barberiae*

Dimorphotheca

COMPOSITAE African daisy, Cape marigold

Annuals and perennials from South Africa bearing attractive daisy flowers. Although half-hardy, the species listed will thrive in sunny, sheltered borders in southern Britain.

D. barberiae (syn. *Osteospermum barberiae*). Perennial. Height 300–450mm (1–1½ft); spread to 600mm (2ft). A spreading plant with aromatic, lance-shaped leaves. Rose-purple flowers 50–70mm (2–2¾in) wide in June–September.

D. calendulacea (syn. *D. sinuata*). Annual. Height 300mm (1ft); spread 150–300mm (6–12in). Erect, usually well-branched with narrow leaves. Yellow to white flowers, 65mm (2½in) wide, in July–September. Summer-blooming seed strains, mostly of hybrid origin, have white to orange flowers sometimes marked blue to violet in the disc or at the base of the ray florets.

D. ecklonis (syn. *Osteospermum ecklonis*). Perennial. Height and spread 600m (2ft). Bushy plant with lance-shaped leaves. Pink and dark blue flowers, 75mm (3in) wide, in July–August. Variety 'Prostrata' is mat-forming, with flowers on 225mm (9in) stems.

Site All need full sun and sheltered position.
Soil Must be well drained and fertile (but over-manuring leads to too much leaf growth).
Propagation Take cuttings in late summer. Sow seeds under glass in spring.
Cultivation Plant in spring as weather warms up. In cold areas protect perennials with a cloche in winter. Keep rooted cuttings in a frame in winter. Old plants of perennials can be cut back by half each spring for a few years, but it is better to replace them regularly with young stock.
Pests and Diseases Slugs may attack leaves.

Above *Dodecatheon pulchellum* 'Red Wings'

Dodecatheon

PRIMULACEAE   Shooting star, American cowslip

Hardy perennials from North America which enjoy a very moist situation, similar to that for primulas. There is considerable confusion over naming. *D. meadia* is only species widely grown in Britain, although the other listed is available if sought after.

D. meadia. Height 250mm (10in) or more. Attractive yellow-centred pink to lilac flowers with swept-back petals. Flowers appear in May. Plants die down in late summer and need to be marked or they may be lost.

D. pulchellum. Height about 225–300mm (9–12in). Flowers are lilac to magenta, in loose clusters. 'Red Wings', a selection with crimson flowers, is perhaps most handsome of all dodecatheons.

Site Damp pond edge or moist woodland ideal.

Soil Must be moisture-retentive in spring, so should contain a lot of humus or leaf-mould.

Propagation Seed is acceptable, but variable; sow immediately it is harvested or in January. Or propagate by division in April or August.

Cultivation No problem provided plants are given moist conditions.

Pests and Diseases Attack by greenfly may distort stem and leaves.

Doronicum

COMPOSITAE   Leopard's bane

Hardy herbaceous perennials, native to Europe, producing bright yellow or gold daisy-like flowers in late spring above clumps of fresh green leaves. The species listed makes a good cut flower.

D. plantagineum (W. Europe, including Britain). Height 750mm (2½ft); spread 450mm (1½ft). Vigorous bushy plant with rich green, slightly hairy, heart-shaped leaves. Erect stems, each bearing several large rich yellow daisies 65mm (2½in) across, in April–June.

Site Sun or dappled shade.

Soil Fertile, moist.

Propagation Divide roots in September–October, retaining only healthy outer pieces. Sow seed in the open in May–June, transplanting seedlings to nursery rows in July.

Cultivation Plant in autumn rather than spring.

Pests and Diseases Powdery mildew may appear on leaves.

Left *Doronicum plantagineum*

Eccremocarpus

BIGNONIACEAE

Vigorous, evergreen, perennial climbers with showy, tubular flowers. They are hardy only in the milder areas and for this reason the species listed is often treated as a half-hardy annual.

E. scaber (Chile), Chilean glory flower. Climber reaching 3–3.5m (10–12ft). Evergreen pinnate leaves culminate in branched twining tendrils. Flowers are orange, carried in racemes through summer and into autumn. 'Aureus' has yellow flowers; 'Carmineus' has red ones.

Site Full sun in sheltered position at base of south- or west-facing wall.

Soil Well-drained but moisture-retentive; good loam preferred.

Propagation Sow seeds (produced freely) in a greenhouse or propagator in early March at 12–15°C (55–60°F); prick off seedlings into individual 90mm (3½in) pots; harden off before planting them out in May.

Cultivation Provide a trellis or similar support for plant to climb. In colder areas protect roots in winter by covering them with bracken, straw, or similar material. Water plants well in dry spells. Dead-heading will prolong the flower display, but if plant is to be treated as an annual, allow some flower-heads to remain to provide seeds for next year.

Pruning Cut away dead growths in early spring. In all but coldest areas, new shoots will be produced from below soil level.

Pests and Diseases Aphids may attack tips of shoots.

Below *Eccremocarpus scaber*

Echinacea

COMPOSITAE   Purple cone-flower

Hardy herbaceous perennials, native to North America, bearing handsome rayed, daisy-like flowers with prominent central cones. Closely related to the other cone-flower genus, *Rudbeckia* (q.v.), they make good cut flowers.

E. purpurea (E. United States). Height 900mm–1.2m (3–4ft); spread 450mm (1½ft). Vigorous, erect plant with stout stems covered in rough, dark-green, lance-shaped leaves. Broad-petalled flowers, 90–100mm (3½–4in) across, purple with raised central cone of brownish orange in July–September. Cultivars include 'Robert Bloom' (intense rosy purple); 'White Lustre' (creamy white with orange centre).

Site All prefer full sun.

Soil Must be well-drained and moderately fertile.

Propagation Divide roots in October–March. Sow seed in the open or under glass; seedlings will vary, but the best can be selected; plants may not flower for two or three years.

Cultivation Mulch with compost or manure in spring. Water in dry weather. Staking may be needed in exposed gardens. Dead-heading prolongs flowering. Cut down remaining stems in autumn.

Right *Echinacea purpurea*

Above *Echinops ritro* hybrid

Echinops

COMPOSITAE   Globe thistle

Hardy herbaceous biennials and perennials, native to Europe and Asia, making stately plants with soft, thistle-like leaves and round 'drumstick' flower-heads.

E. ritro (of gardens; Balkans, Caucasus). Perennial. Height 1.2m (4ft); spread 600mm (2ft). Upright plant with ragged, thistle-like, dark green leaves, grey beneath. Round heads up to 40mm (1½in) across of steel-blue flowers on ends of silvery brown stems in July–August. Cultivar 'Veitch's Blue' is more compact, with rich blue flowers that make attractive winter decoration if dried. (The true *E. ritro* is a plant about 600mm (2ft) in height, but it is rarely available.)

Site Prefers full sun and some shelter from strong wind.

Soil Well-drained; a deep-rooter, thrives on poor soils.

Propagation Divide roots in October–March. Root cuttings, taken under glass in February, transplanted to nursery beds outdoors in May.

Cultivation Stake plants securely before they are 150mm (6in) high.

Echium

BORAGINACEAE   Viper's bugloss

Annuals and biennials with spikes of flowers in shades of blue and pink. Colourful border plants.

E. pininiana (Canary Isles). Height up to 3.5m (12ft); spread 1m (3ft) or more. A monocarpic species: it takes two or three years to flower, and dies when flowering is over. Foliage is rough, hairy and silvery green, forming an elongated rosette. Flower-spike tall and very showy, with many blue, funnel-shaped flowers in summer. Cultivar 'Tresco Blue' is very vigorous, with flower spike reaching 6m (20ft) or more.

E. plantagineum (syn. *E. lycopsis*; S. and W. Europe). Hardy biennial or annual. Height to 600mm (2ft); spread 300–450mm (1–1½ft). Bushy plant with hairy, mid-green leaves. Violet-blue flowers on 300mm (12in) branching spikes. Forms include 'Dwarf Hybrids' (compact strain with flowers in blue, rose, purple, and white) and 'Blue Bedder' (bright blue flowers), both about 300mm (1ft) tall.

Site Open, sunny beds or border. *E. pininiana* needs a sheltered spot in mild south or south-west areas of England for successful over-wintering.
Soil Ordinary, well-drained. Plants tolerate poor, dry soils.
Propagation Sow seeds of hardy species in flowering positions in March or mid- to late September; thin out to required distance in April. Sow *E. pininiana* under glass in April; grow plants singly in pots and plant out in summer.
Cultivation Clip off dead and dying flowerheads. Stake tall flower-spikes in exposed positions. Pull up and discard when flowering finishes.

Right *Echium plantagineum* (dwarf)

Above *Elaeagnus pungens* 'Variegata'

Elaeagnus

ELAEAGNACEAE

Deciduous and evergreen, mainly fast-growing shrubs or small trees from Asia, southern Europe, and North America. They are especially valuable for their garden-foliage display, particularly the variegated forms. They bear small, fragrant, white or silvery, bell-shaped flowers in clusters. Excellent for windbreaks and maritime exposure.

E. angustifolia (W. Asia, naturalised in S. Europe), oleaster. Superb wide-spreading large shrub or small deciduous tree up to 10m (33ft) high and wide, making a striking specimen. Lanceolate leaves up to 90mm (3½in) long have silvery-white undersides. Fragrant flowers in June, followed by oval silvery amber fruits.

E. commutata (syn. *E. argentea*; N. America), silver-berry. Deciduous shrub of suckering habit and upright growth attaining 2–3m (6½–10ft). Leaves narrow-ovate, up to 75mm (3in) long, and silvery-white. Flowers show in profusion in May, followed by small, silvery, egg-shaped fruits.

E. × ebbingei. Vigorous, fast-growing, evergreen. Height 3m (10ft) or more; spread 2m (6½ft). Large, leathery leaves up to 100mm (4in) long, silvery beneath. Fragrant flowers form on old wood in autumn. Excellent screening shrub in exposed areas. Cultivars: 'Gilt Edge' (leaves boldly margined with gold; slower growing to 1.5m (5ft)); 'Limelight' (leaves with large central, yellow blotch, quickly attains 3m (10ft) height with 2m (6½ft) spread).

E. macrophylla (Korea, Japan). Impressive evergreen up to 3m (10ft) high and often greater spread. Leaves 50–100mm (2–4in) long, silvery on both surfaces but becoming green above. Fragrant silvery white flowers in autumn.

E. pungens (Japan). Dense, spreading evergreen 4m (13ft) or more high with brown, scaly shoots. Leathery oval or oblong leaves, about 50mm (2in) long, glossy dark-green above and dull white beneath. Silvery flowers in October–November. 'Maculata' (syn. 'Aureo-variegata'), with central golden splash to leaves, is one of the most striking hardy variegated evergreens; it slowly reaches about 2m (6½ft) in height and width, makes an attractive hedge plant, and is readily available.

Site Open, sunny or semi-shaded.
Soil Well-drained, fertile.
Propagation Deciduous species by seed sown in spring. Evergreen species and cultivars by summer cuttings 100mm (4in) long in propagator or cold frame.

Cultivation Plant container-grown shrubs in most seasons; field-grown deciduous species are planted in November–March.
Pruning Cut out branches of reverting foliage on variegated forms and suckers from grafted plants.

Embothrium

PROTEACEAE

Evergreen shrubs or trees, native to South America and Western Australia, noted for their brilliantly coloured flowers. The plant listed, the only garden species, is tender and will thrive outdoors only in south-west England and the west of England.

E. coccineum (Chile), Chilean fire-bush. Shrub or small tree. Height up to 9m (30ft); spread 3m (10ft). Upright-growing, with small, glossy, dark green oval or lance-shaped leaves. Brilliant red flowers in dense terminal and axillary clusters, 100mm (4in) across, produced in May–June. Varieties include *E. c. lanceolatum* (red) and cultivar 'Norquinco Valley' (red); both are hardier and may survive winters elsewhere than the south and west.

Site Warm, sheltered spot essential.
Soil Good neutral to acid loam, well-drained but moisture-retentive.
Propagation Seed sown in frame in spring produces young plants for planting out

two seasons later. Suckers can be detached from roots of main plant in April–May, potted, and grown on for planting the following year.
Cultivation Best planted from pots into permanent positions.
Pruning Remove dead or winter-damaged shoots in early spring.

Left *Embothrium coccineum*

Endymion

LILIACEAE   Bluebell

Bulbous hardy perennials from western Europe and North Africa, with strap-shaped leaves and spikes of bell-shaped flowers in spring.

E. hispanicus (syn. *Hyacinthoides hispanica*, *Scilla campanulata*, *S. hispanica*; W. and S. Europe, North Africa). Height 200–300mm (8–12in) or more; spread 150–200mm (6–8in). Leaves up to 40mm (1½in) wide. Flower-spikes erect, with the blue, wide bells facing outwards and inclined downwards in April–June. Cultivars listed under this name are mainly hybrids with the species below. They include 'Blue Queen' (light blue); 'Excelsior' (deep blue); 'Rose Queen' (lilac pink); 'Alba Maxima' (white); all have large, nodding blooms.

E. nonscriptus (syn. *Hyacinthoides nonscripta*, *Scilla nutans*, *S. nonscripta*; W. Europe, including Britain), common bluebell or wild hyacinth. Similar in general form to *E. hispanicus*, but leaves rarely more than 13mm (½in) wide; flower spikes arch at tip, and bells are narrow and fully pendant.

Site Part shade preferred but full sun tolerated.
Soil Moisture-retentive but adequately drained and, ideally, humus-rich.
Propagation Separate congested clumps when dormant. Sow seeds in shallow drills when ripe or in spring; or allow them to grow where they fall. Seedlings take several years to develop flowering-size bulbs.
Cultivation Plant in autumn, the earlier the better.
Pests and Diseases Rust may infect leaves.

Right *Endymion hispanicus* hybrid

Above *Enkianthus campanulatus*

Enkianthus

ERICACEAE

Choice deciduous shrubs from north-eastern Asia, notable for their brilliant autumn leaf colour and unusual drooping bell-shaped flowers in spring. The example below is the best species for British gardens.

E. campanulatus (Japan). Erect-growing hardy species attaining about 3m (10ft). Reddish young twigs. Obovate or oval leaves, up to 60mm (2½in) long in clusters, colour magnificently golden and scarlet in autumn. Flowers freely produced in May, yellow-bronze and subtly-veined, about 8mm (⅓in) long, in pendulous clusters beneath the leaves.

Site Ideally associated with rhododendrons and azaleas in dappled shade.
Soil Lime-free essential; preferably peaty or leafy.
Propagation By seed sown under glass in February; or by semi-ripe cuttings of current season's growth in late summer in peat-sand mixture in propagator or shaded frame.
Cultivation Plant container-grown shrubs in autumn or spring. Mulch and water liberally in dry weather.
Pruning Leggy, overgrown specimens will regenerate if heavily cut back in late winter.

Epimedium

BERBERIDACEAE   Barrenwort, bishop's hat

Perennials native to North Africa, northern Italy, and the Middle and Far East. The garden species listed here have attractive foliage and small but pretty flowers and, since they are evergreen or semi-evergreen, make good ground-cover plants.

E. alpinum (Italy, Albania). Height about 300mm (1ft); spread to 600mm (2ft). Clump- or colony-forming, with each leaf divided into heart-shaped leaflets, reddish flushed when young. Flowers dark red and yellow on slender racemes in spring.

E. grandiflorum (syn. *E. macranthum*; Japan). Height 250mm (10in) or more; spread 300mm (1ft). Neat clump-forming habit, leaves divided into triangular to oval leaflets. Flowers white to purple, with four long spurs, in spring. Cultivars: 'Rose Queen' (crimson-pink); 'White Queen'; 'Violaceum' (deep lilac).

E. pinnatum (Iran). Height about 300mm (1ft); spread 600mm (2ft) or more. Leaves evergreen, with three to nine oval leaflets. Yellow flowers in late spring-summer. *E. p. colchicum* is taller, with fewer but larger leaflets and flowers.

E. × rubrum (hybrid). Much like *E. alpinum* but more robust, with strongly red-tinted leaves, and red flowers with white spurs in May.

E. × versicolor (hybrid). Height 300mm (1ft). Leaves similar to those of *E. pinnatum* (q.v.). Flowers yellow and pink with red-tinted spurs in May. Variety 'Sulphureum' has pale yellow blooms.

E. × warleyense (hybrid). Height 250mm (10in); spread 600mm (2ft). Young leaves have red blotches. Orange flowers in April–May.

E. × youngianum (hybrid). Clump-forming, deciduous.

Height up to 230mm (9in); spread 300mm (1ft). Leaves divided into triangular leaflets and are red-marked when young. Pink flowers with short spurs in April–May. Variety 'Niveum' has pure white flowers.

Site Best in partial shade.
Soil Moisture-retentive but not wet, with plenty of humus.
Propagation Divide after

flowering finishes, in autumn or in early spring.
Cultivation Plant in autumn or early spring.

Above *Epimedium × rubrum*

Eranthis

RANUNCULACEAE   Winter aconite
Useful bulbous plants that flower in the depths of winter. They prefer alkaline soil, but will grow on other soils if left undisturbed.
E. 'Guinea Gold'. Cultivar of the hybrid *E. × tubergenii*, with much larger flowers in March–April, and bronzy leaves.
E. hyemalis (Europe). Easiest eranthis to grow. Bright yellow flowers, about 100mm (4in) high, from February, with leaflike bracts beneath petals. Pale-green leaves deeply dissected.

Site Plant beneath shrubs where they can naturalise and associate with other winter-flowering bulbs.
Soil Woodland soil with plenty of peat or leaf-mould.
Propagation Sow seed in late spring and place in a frame; pot on or plant out the following spring, feeding in meantime to help build up corms. Separate

offsets from mature corms or cut into two when dormant.
Cultivation Little needed once corms are planted (they resent disturbance). Keep soil weed-free at all times.
Pests and Diseases Aphids may cause whole plant to become sticky and sooty. Birds may peck out flowers and flower-buds.

Above *Eranthis hyemalis*

Eremurus

LILIACEAE   Foxtail lily
Perennials from western and central Asia. They have rosettes of strap-shaped leaves and tall, tapered, dense racemes of six-petalled flowers. Statuesque plants, they deserve to be featured in prominent positions.
E. himalaicus (N. W. Himalaya). Height 1–1.5m (3¼–5ft); spread 600mm (2ft) or more. Leaves 300mm (1ft) or more long by 40mm (1½in) wide. White flowers, 30mm (1¼in) wide, in May–June.
E. olgae (Iran, N. Afghanistan). Similar to above, but leaves narrower and flowers white or pink in June–July.
E. robustus (Turkestan). Height 2–3m (6½–10ft); spread 900mm (3ft) or more. Leaves 1m (3¼ft) or more long, bluish-green. Flowers about 40mm (1½in) wide, peach pink, opening in summer. *E. r. elwesii* has pure pink flowers which open a little earlier.
E. × 'Shelford Hybrids'. Range of cultivars whose flowers open in June–July in colours from yellow to orange-buff, pink, and white.
E. stenophyllus (Iran, Turkestan). Height 900mm–1.2m (3–4ft); spread about 600mm (2ft). Grey-green leaves 300mm (1ft) or more long, 13mm (½in) wide (narrowest of all cultivated eremurus). Flowers bright yellow, about 20mm (¾in) wide, in summer.

Site All need full light, but preferably shaded from early morning sun (young leaves are frost prone).
Soil Must be well-drained and fertile.
Propagation Divide carefully at planting time. Sow seeds when ripe or in spring (seedlings take about five years to flower).
Cultivation Plant when dormant in late summer- or early autumn.
Pests and Diseases Young shoots may be eaten by slugs or snails.

Right *Eremurus robustus*

Erica

ERICACEAE   Heath

A large genus of evergreen shrubs and small trees, similar in all respects to *Calluna* except that it is the corolla of the flower which is coloured, not the calyx. The plants are natives of Africa and Europe, including Britain; about three-quarters of the species come from South Africa. The European species are hardy and a selection will provide plants in flower for most of the year, although the main flowering period is autumn and winter.

E. carnea (syn. *E. herbacea*; central and southern European Alps). Height 250mm (10in); spread 450mm (18in). Rosy red or white flower spikes 25–75mm (1–3in) long in December–March. Many forms, of which the following are outstanding: 'Ruby Glow' (bronze foliage, large dark red flowers in January–February); 'Springwood White' (semi-prostrate, spreading to 600mm (24in), flowers in January–March; 'Vivellii' (bronze-red foliage in winter, deep carmine flowers in January–March); 'Winter Beauty' (syn. 'King George', rose-pink flowers in November–February).

E. cinerea (W. Europe, including Britain), bell heather. Height 225–600mm (9–24in); spread 150–450mm (6–18in). Rosy purple flowers in June–September. Good cultivars (from a large selection): 'C.D. Eason' (225mm (9in) tall, bright-red flowers in June–July); 'Eden Valley' (150mm (6in) tall, lilac-pink flowers in June–July); 'Golden Drop' (100mm (4in) tall, 200mm (8in) wide, deep gold- to copper-coloured foliage, turning rust-red in winter, pink flowers due in June–July but seldom appear); 'P.S. Patrick' (300mm (12in) tall, long spikes of large, deep-purple flowers in June–July); 'Velvet Knight' (225mm (9in) tall, black-purple flowers in June–August).

E. × darleyensis (hybrid). Height and spread 450–600mm (1½–2ft). Rosy lilac flowers in January–April. Two good forms: 'George Rendall' (deep-pink flowers); 'Silber-schmelze' (syn. 'Molten Silver', scented white flowers in February-May).

E. mediterranea (syn. *E. erigena*; S.W. Europe, including Galway), Irish or Mediterranean heath. Upright shrub, height in favourable conditions 1.2–3m (4–10ft); spread 600–900mm (2–3ft). Rosy red flowers in March–May. The white form 'Alba' reaches 1.2m (4ft) or less.

Site Open situation; do not coddle the plants. *E. mediterranea*, however, is less hardy than others and suffers damage in cold winds and freezing temperatures.

Soil Acid, peaty, well-drained preferred, except for *E. carnea*, *E. mediterranea*, and *E. × darleyensis* forms, which will grow in alkaline soils (but not shallow chalky kinds).

Propagation Divide or layer in autumn. Take cuttings of new growth about 25mm (1in) long in August and root in peaty compost under cover.

Cultivation Little regular care needed; give a spring mulch.

Pruning Clip over with shears after flowering annually or every second or third year.

Pests and Diseases Heather wilt may occur.

Below *Erica carnea* (at front)

Erigeron

COMPOSITAE   Fleabane

Annuals, biennials, and herbaceous perennials of worldwide distribution but especially North America. The perennial species and garden hybrids are useful border plants, with rayed daisy-like flowers borne over a long period in summer. Many are good for cutting.

E. aurantiacus (Turkestan). Perennial. Height and spread 250–300mm (10–12in). Low mat-forming plant with oblong, soft, grey-green leaves. Flowers deep orange-yellow on erect leafy stems in June–August.

E. glaucus (W. United states). Perennial. Height 300mm (1ft); spread 600mm (2ft) or more. Vigorous low plant quickly forming broad mats of greyish green leaves. Flowers on short erect stems, 50mm (2in) across, lilac, pink or mauve, with yellow centre, blooming continuously in April–October. Grows well in coastal gardens; too tender for colder inland districts.

E. mucronatus (Europe). Perennial. Height 150mm (6in); spread 75–100mm (3–4in). Dainty little plant of erect habit with tiny dark green leaves. Small pale pink or white flowers, up to 13mm (½in) across, resembling the lawn daisy, in May–October. Sometimes invasive.

E. speciosus (W. North America). Perennial. Height and spread 600mm (2ft). Attractive bushy plant with loosely erect leafy stems. Bears profusion of rayed daisy-like flowers, up to 75mm (3in) across, pale lilac with yellow centres, in July–September. One of the parents of many fine garden hybrids, including 'Darkest of All' (deep violet); 'Dimity' (pinkish mauve); 'Foerster's Liebling' (pink); 'Prosperity' (violet blue).

Site All need full sun and some shelter in cold districts.
Soil Must be well drained; cold heavy soils may kill plants.
Propagation Divide roots in late winter or early spring rather than autumn. Root tip

Left *Erigeron speciosus* 'Dimity'

cuttings of non-flowering shoots under glass in July.
Cultivation If growing against grass, plants will need staking to prevent damage to verge. Plant in February–March, and do not cut established plants down until then to give added winter protection.

Erinus

SCROPHULARIACEAE

A small genus of plants mainly from South Africa, but one species comes from Europe and it is this one and its cultivars that are in cultivation, making useful subjects for the rock garden and dry walls.

E. alpinus (European Alps), summer starwort. Neat little plant of mounded habit; will seed readily around the rock garden and in paving. Pink flowers produced on 75mm (3in) upright spikes from May onwards. Good cultivars include 'Albus' (white flowers); 'Dr Hanaele' (crimson); 'Mrs Charles Boyle' (light pink).

Site Well-drained and sunny preferred.
Soil No especial requirement; the poorer the soil the neater the mounds become.
Propagation Scatter the seed where it is to grow; most

named forms come true from seed. Sow in January; prick out seedlings into boxes.
Cultivation Plant out seedlings in April.

Below *Erinus alpinus*

Above *Erodium chamaedryoides* 'Roseum'

Erodium

GERANIACEAE   Heron's-bill, stork's-bill

Native to the Mediterranean area and Asia Minor, the erodiums are closely related to crane's-bills (*Geranium*) and are easily cultivated sun-lovers, several of which are suitable perennials for the rock garden.

E. chamaedryoides (syn. *E. reichardii*; Balearic Is). Introduced to Britain in 18th century, forms low mat of small, dark-green leaves. Pink-veined white flowers, 25mm (1in) tall, throughout summer. Most readily available are varieties 'Roseum' (pink), and 'Roseum Plenum' (double pink).

E. guttatum (Spain). Slow-growing species. Height 75–100mm (3–4in). Finely cut leaves. White flowers with crimson-brown veining.

E. macradenum (syn. *E. petraeum glandulosum*; Pyrenees). Height 75–125mm (3–5in). Aromatic fern-like foliage. Flowers, whitish pink with delicate purple veining, in late spring to mid-summer. There is a pink form, 'Roseum'.

Site Plants flower best in full sun, preferably sheltered.
Soil Well-drained, open, on poor side (too rich a soil will cause plants to grow out of character); alkaline or neutral rather than acid.

Propagation Take cuttings with old wood at base late in season and keep in heated frame for winter, or take in April onwards in an unheated sand-peat frame; plant out in September–October.

Eryngium

UMBELLIFERAE   Sea holly

Biennials and herbaceous perennials native mainly to Europe, North Africa, and North and South America. Most have handsome leaves and flowers. Good for cutting and for dried-flower arrangements.

E. alpinum (Europe). Perennial. Height 750mm (2½ft); spread 450mm (1½ft). Erect plant with rounded leaves and blue branching stems. Large cone-shaped blue flower-heads, 65mm (2½in) long, above broad metallic-blue ruff of divided bracts in July–August.

E. giganteum (Caucasus), Miss Willmott's ghost. Biennial. Height 750mm (2½ft); spread 600mm (2ft). Upright, branching plant with pale grey stems and rounded, spiny leaves. Large ivory-blue flower-heads and bracts, 65–75mm (2½–3in), across in July–August. Seeds itself freely.

E. × oliverianum (hybrid). Perennial. Height 1.2m (4ft); spread 600mm (2ft). Deep-cut blue-green leaves. Deep blue flower-cones, 25mm (1in) long, in July–September.

E. tripartitum (of gardens). Perennial. Height and spread 600–750mm (2–2½ft). Upright, spreading plant with many branching stems above rosette of grey-blue leaves. Rich blue heads of flowers, 25mm (1in) long, surrounded by deeper violet-blue bracts in July–September.

E. variifolium (Morocco). Perennial. Height 450mm (1½ft); spread 225–250mm (9–10in). Stiffly erect, compact plant with rounded, green leaves marked with pronounced white veins. Pale blue cones of flowers, 20mm (¾in) long, surrounded by silvery spiny bracts in July–August.

Site All like full sun and an open situation. Deep-rooting, they like dry conditions.
Soil Light, well-drained, not too rich in organic material.
Propagation Take root

cuttings in February–March under glass. Sow seed under glass when ripe or in early spring; or the stronger-growing species outside at same time.
Cultivation Plant October–March. Taller plants may need staking in exposed situations.

Left *Eryngium × oliverianum*

Above *Erythronium revolutum* 'White Beauty'

Erythronium

LILIACEAE

A genus of hardy plants bearing attractive flowers with reflexed petals somewhat resembling small lilies. They thrive in a cool, damp situation that does not dry out entirely.

E. dens-canis (Europe, Asia), dog's-tooth violet. An easy-to-grow plant with heavily blotched leaves. The solitary flowers vary from white through rose to deep cyclamen, with brownish and purplish markings in the centre. The 125mm (5in) tall flower stems appear in April.

E. revolutum (W. North America), American trout-lily. 'White Beauty', of American origin, is a very good white selection, with reddish brown markings near the base and brownish green mottled leaves. It is 250mm (10in) tall. (The plant is probably a form or hybrid of *E. oregonum*.)

E. tuolumnense (N. America). Easy, free-flowering, with up to six pure yellow flowers on a 250–375mm (10–15in) stem. Hybrid 'Pagoda' is outstanding and more easily available than species; produces sulphur-yellow flowers in April on 300mm (12in) stems.

Site Light shade. Plants do best on the peat garden.
Soil Good humus necessary; add peat and leaf-mould to poorer soils.
Propagation For named cultivars division of corms in autumn is best, but on no account allow them to dry out while in storage.
Cultivation Once plants are

established keep area weed-free. Apply top dressing of bonemeal in spring. Foliage dies away fairly quickly, so positions of plants should be marked beforehand.
Pests and Diseases
Erythronium rust may occur, causing yellowish or deep-brown leaf spots; no treatment is necessary.

Above *Escallonia* × 'Edinensis'

Escallonia

ESCALLONIACEAE

Mostly evergreen shrubs and small trees from South America, especially the Andes. Those grown in Britain are evergreen shrubs, with pretty, small tubular flowers in pink, red, or white. They do particularly well in gardens by the seaside.

E. × 'Apple Blossom' (hybrid). Height and spread about 1.2m (4ft) after 10 years. Small, dark green leaves. Pink and white flowers in June.

E. macrantha 'C. F. Ball' (seedling). Height 3m (10ft); spread 1.5m (5ft). Aromatic leaves 75mm (3in) long. Tubular crimson flowers 20mm ($\frac{3}{4}$in) long in June–July.

E. × 'Donard Brilliance' (hybrid). Height and spread 1.5m (5ft). Large leaves. Crimson flowers clothing arching shoots; will repeat-flower if first crop is cut off after flowering; full season is June–September.

E. × 'Edinensis' (hybrid). Height and spread 2m (6½ft) after 10 years. Small leaves. Carmine to pink flowers in profusion in June.

E. × 'Peach Blossom' (hybrid). Height 1.8m (6ft); spread 1.5m (5ft). Small leaves. Peach-pink flowers in June–July.

Site Do well as wall shrubs where they get some sun, or in open in sheltered gardens.
Soil Medium to well-drained; plants may be killed in severe winters if in heavy, badly drained soil.
Propagation Layer in autumn. Plant rooted suckers in spring. Plant semi-hardwood cuttings under cover in July–August.
Cultivation Plant in autumn or mid-spring; keep watered if dry weather follows in spring. Protect plants in a hard winter.

Pruning Remove flowered shoots as soon as they fade, or in spring just as growth is about to start. If in doubt, wait until spring: pruning in autumn followed by even moderate winter may kill the plant. Remove straggling shoots and dead or damaged growths. Low-growing shoots will root if they touch the soil.
Pests and Diseases Virus diseases may cause mottling, streaking, or distorting of leaves and so reduce growth.

Above *Eschscholzia californica* 'Ballerina'

Eschscholzia

PAPAVERACEAE

Annuals and perennials, native to America, bearing brightly coloured flowers resembling poppies.

E. caespitosa (California). Hardy annual. Height 125–150mm (5–6in). Dwarf plant ideal for rock gardens and edging. Blue-green feathery leaves. Bright yellow flowers, 25mm (1in) across, in June–October. Two of the most reliable varieties are 'Sundew' (lemon-yellow) and 'Miniature Primrose' (primrose-yellow).

E. *californica* (W. North America), Californian poppy. Hardy annual. Height 300–600mm (1–2ft). Fern-like, grey-green foliage. Delicate bright-orange flowers, 40–63mm (1½–2½in) across, in June–October. Some good varieties: 'Ballerina' (pink, orange and yellow, with white); 'Cherry Ripe' (cerise); 'Orange King'; 'Milky White'; 'Monarch Mixed' (crimson, cream, orange, yellow, and red).

Site Full sun.
Soil Ordinary, well-drained.
Propagation Sow outside in March–May; thin out to 150mm (6in) apart. If sown outside in

August–September, may need protection with cloches.
Cultivation Sow seeds in succession for continuous flowering.

Eucalyptus

MYRTACEAE   Gum tree
A genus of over 500 species of fast-growing evergreen trees and shrubs, mainly from Australia and Tasmania. Those listed are the best of a dozen or so species that are grown with some success outdoors in Britain. They have attractive bark, handsome and distinct juvenile and adult foliage, and many-stamened white flowers.

E. *dalrympleana* (Tasmania, S. E. Australia), broad-leaved kindling-bark. Elegant, tall tree attaining 15–18m (50–60ft). Trunk and branches display cream, pink and brown patchwork bark. Juvenile leaves glaucous and ovate; adult leaves lanceolate, 100–175mm (4–7in) long. Flowers in October–November. Fairly hardy.

E. *gunnii* (Tasmania), cider gum. Popular, almost hardy tree reaching 30m (100ft) or more, but best grown coppiced or as multi-stemmed bush up to 3m (10ft) high. Juvenile foliage round, stem-clasping, and bright green-blue; adult foliage sage-green, sickle-shaped, up to 75mm (3in) long. Flowers in July–August.

E. *niphophila* (New South Wales, Victoria), alpine snow gum. Small, very hardy tree, slower growing than E. *gunnii*, up to 6m (20ft). Bark grey, cream, and green patchwork on maturing trees; young stems silvery-white. Juvenile leaves roundish, leathery blue-grey, up to 50mm (2in) across; adult leaves up to 150mm (6in) long, lance-shaped, blue-green. Flowers in June.

E. *parvifolia* (New South Wales), small-leaved gum. Dense-crowned, hardy tree up to 10m (30ft) tall, with spreading head and smooth, grey-barked trunk. Adult leaves small, narrow, pointed, blue-green. Flowers in July–August. Notably lime-tolerant.

Site Shelter from north and east winds.
Soil Fertile, moist, preferably lime-free (but E. *parvifolia* and *gunnii* will grow on chalk).
Propagation By seed sown in early spring in frame or under glass; grow on in pots; overwinter under glass.
Cultivation Plant young pot- or container-grown specimens in spring; ensure plant is not pot-bound and prepare site with shallow depression to retain mulch. Stake, water and mulch well; amply feed and mulch coppiced or heavily pruned bushes.
Pruning With species developing *as trees*, cut back leading shoots by one third in March–April on plants established for one year, to strengthen stem and improve anchorage. In *coppicing* treatment, cut down E. *gunnii* to near ground level in mid-March to April annually from the second year onwards; further tipping of vigorous upright shoots may be necessary in July. On plants grown as *taller bushes*, cut back leading shoots in June to suitable lateral shoots, tipping these laterals in July-August;

older 'leggy' specimens will resurrect to more compact bushes if hand pruned to a low framework of branches in late March or April.
Pests and Diseases Leaf spots and rust may infect eucalyptus in wet seasons.

Right *Eucalyptus gunnii* (juvenile)

Above *Eucryphia × nymansensis* 'Nymansay'

Eucryphia

EUCRYPHIACEAE

Mostly evergreen trees and shrubs from Australia and South America grown for their showy flowers.

E. glutinosa (Chile). Deciduous or semi-evergreen shrub. Height 4.5m (15ft); spread 2m (6½ft). Handsome, glossy, green leaves. Pure-white, saucer-shaped flowers 75mm (3in) across in August–September.

E. × nymansensis 'Nymansay'. Evergreen shrub or small tree. Height 6m (20ft); spread 2.5m (8¼ft). Upright, almost columnar shrub with dark green leaves. Abundance of white, saucer-shaped flowers up to 75mm (3in) across in August–September.

Site Sheltered, especially in cold areas.
Soil Neutral to acid, well-drained but moisture-retentive.
Propagation Seed can be sown in the spring in a cold frame, but seedlings will be very variable, most of them inferior. Short soft-wood cuttings from non-flowering laterals taken in July root readily in peat and sharp-sand mixture in a heated propagator. Lower branches can be layered in July–August.
Cultivation Plant in spring. Water young plants diligently for first season.
Pruning Remove badly winter-scorched foliage and any stray shoots or branches that mar plant's symmetry in spring.

Euonymus

CELASTRACEAE

Evergreen and deciduous shrubs or small trees, native to Europe, Asia, North and Central America, and Australia. Evergreen kinds are much used in Britain for formal hedges.

E. europaeus (Europe, including Britain), spindleberry or spindletree. Deciduous hedgerow shrub or small tree. Height 3–7.5m (10–25ft); spread 1.5–2.4m (5–8ft). Oval leaves decorative in autumn. Inconspicuous yellow-green flowers in May–June, followed by bright rose-pink fruits 20mm (¾in) wide with orange-covered seeds. Variety 'Red Cascade' has heavy clusters of larger, red-pink fruits, and is smaller at 1.8m (6ft) tall and 1.5m (5ft) wide.

E. fortunei radicans (Japan). Creeping evergreen shrub, rooting as it spreads; can be grown up walls. Shiny, dark green, oval leaves, about 30mm (1¼in) long. Among other varieties of the type species, 'Silver Queen', a small shrub, will grow to about 2.4m (8ft) trained up a wall, but is smaller if grown in the open, with leaves creamy yellow to green with white irregular margin; 'Variegatus', trailer or climber, has grey-green leaves with white margins tinged pink, especially in cold weather.

E. japonicus (Japan). Evergreen shrub or tree. Height 3–4.5m (10–15ft); spread 2.1–3m (7–10ft). Densely leafy, with shiny obovate leaves up to 75mm (3in) long. Excellent for formal hedges, especially by the sea. Good varieties: 'Aureus' (bright yellow leaves narrowly margined with green, but with tendency to revert to plain green); 'Ovatus Aureus' (wide yellow leaf-edges and green centres, slow to grow and needs sun to maintain variegation).

Site Sun or shade, the former essential for variegated kinds; any position for deciduous kinds; creeping evergreen kinds may not be hardy in severe winter; *E. japonicus* is good in coastal gardens.
Soil Any except waterlogged; do well in chalky kinds.
Propagation By rooted portions of creeping kinds. By heeled hard-wood cuttings taken in autumn, under cover. By layering in early summer. By seed of *E. europaeus*, sown in March under cover.
Cultivation Plant in autumn or spring. No special problems.
Pruning Evergreen kinds may need clipping to tidy them up in spring. Snip out any plain green shoots on variegated cultivars.
Pests and Diseases Blackfly on spindleberry; caterpillars, scale insects, powdery mildew on *E. japonicus* and forms.

Below *Euonymus europaeus* 'Red Cascade'

Euphorbia

Above *Euphorbia robbiae*

EUPHORBIACEAE   Spurge, milkweed

Annuals, biennials, herbaceous perennials, succulents and sub-shrubs of cosmopolitan distribution in the northern hemisphere. Most are handsome plants of distinctive character, with beauty of shape, form, and texture rather than bright colouring; the persistent bracts are usually more showy than the flowers. NOTE *Most species have a milky sap which can irritate sensitive skins.*

E. characias (Mediterranean region). Evergreen perennial. Height 1.2m (4ft); spread 900mm (3ft). Vigorous, bushy sub-shrub with erect stems tinged with red, and short, narrow, grey-green leaves. In May–June cylindrical heads of small yellow flowers, with brown centres, are surrounded by prominent round, yellowish green bracts, 13mm ($\frac{1}{2}$in) across, which persist long after flowers fade. *E. c. wulfenii* is larger and finer, with chrome-yellow flowers.

E. griffithii (Himalaya). Herbaceous perennial. Height 600–900mm (2–3ft); spread 600mm (2ft) or more, depending on situation. Upright, spreading plant with erect stems and narrow, soft-green leaves with paler midrib. Vivid orange-red flowers and bracts in round heads, 100mm (4in) across, on top of stems in June–July. 'Fireglow' is best form.

E. marginata (North America). Annual. Height 600mm (2ft); spread 300mm (1ft). Bushy upright plant with pale green leaves. As plant matures, leaves become edged and splashed with white. Flowers unimportant. Good for cutting.

E. myrsinites (S. Europe). Evergreen perennial. Height 100mm (4in); spread 300mm (1ft) or more. Prostrate plant with trailing stems covered with fleshy, grey-blue, pointed leaves. Heads of lime-green flowers and bracts, 100mm (4in) across, on ends of stems in March–April. For rock garden or front of border.

E. polychroma (syn. *E. epithymoides*; Europe). Hardy perennial. Height and spread 450mm (1$\frac{1}{2}$ft). Forms dense, rounded hummock of stems and mid-green leaves. Domed heads of strident greenish-yellow flowers and bracts, 50–75mm (2–3in) across, in March–June. First flowers open when stems are only a few inches high. Useful for creating an early spring effect.

E. robbiae (Asia Minor). Evergreen perennial. Height 450–600mm (1$\frac{1}{2}$–2ft); spread 900mm (3ft) or more. Spreading plant with upright stems and whorls of dark green, leathery leaves. Loose heads of lime-green flowers and bracts, up to 150mm (6in) long, in March–June, persisting through the summer. Makes excellent ground cover even under trees as it is very shade tolerant.

Site Most prefer full sun, but evergreens tolerate some shade. Sub-shrubs not suited to cold districts.

Soil Must be well-drained, preferably light; will grow on chalky soils.

Propagation Sow seed of *E. marginata* under glass in March for planting out in mid-May; or, if growing conditions are good, in open in April. Sow seeds of other species under glass in spring. Short basal cuttings of herbaceous and sub-shrubby species may be rooted under glass in spring or in autumn. Divide roots of perennials in autumn.

Cultivation Plant shrubby types in spring, not in autumn; provide some shelter from wind until established. Remove flower heads when all colour has faded from the bracts.

Pruning Cut down to ground level old stems of sub-shrubby species when foliage deteriorates, to let young growths develop.

× Fatshedera

ARALIACEAE   Fat-headed lizzie

A hybrid genus between two varieties of *Fatsia japonica* and *Hedera helix*, of which there is only one species, raised in France in 1910.

× *F. lizei*. Evergreen shrub, hardy in sheltered places. Height 1.8–3m (6–10ft); spread 900mm–1.5m (3–5ft). Large, leathery, palmately lobed leaves, 100–250mm (4–10in) wide. Pale green-white flowers in large clusters in October–November. Architecturally handsome plant well-suited to formal surroundings: can also be grown as houseplant. Form 'Variegata' has creamy white leaf edges.

Site Sun or shade, sheltered from wind.
Soil No special requirement.
Propagation Take cuttings of ends of new shoots in summer; grow under cover.
Cultivation Plant in mid- to late spring; provide support, as plant retains some of scrambling quality of its ivy parent. Plant in sun to ensure best chance of flowers, especially if the variegated form is grown.
Pruning Remove dead growth in early spring.

Below × *Fatshedera lizei* 'Variegata'

Fatsia

ARALIACEAE

The only cultivated species is *F. japonica* (syn. *Aralia sieboldii*), the false castor-oil plant, from Japan, an evergreen shrub or, rarely, a small tree. Provides a handsome tropical look, especially suitable at the back of patios. Usually grown as spreading shrub, height and spread 1.8m (6ft), but can be much taller. Glossy, leathery, palmate leaves 300–400mm (12–16in) wide, with nine lobes. Large, branching clusters of small white flowers at end of stems in October–November; then black pea-like berries. Form 'Variegata' has white blotches on tips of leaves.

Site Sheltered, semi-shade; protect plant in severe weather.
Soil Good, well-drained.
Propagation Take semi-hardwood cuttings, 75mm (3in) long, in spring, providing bottom heat. Sow in spring.
Cultivation Plant mid- to late spring. May be killed to soil level in severe winters but usually reappears in spring.
Pruning Remove dead stems in spring.

Right *Fatsia japonica* 'Variegata'

Ficus

MORACEAE   Fig

A very large genus of trees and shrubs, evergreen and deciduous, found in all the warmer regions of the world. It includes the rubber plant (*F. elastica*), weeping fig (*F. benjamina*), and mistletoe fig (*F. diversifolia*), all popular houseplants. There is only one species which is more or less hardy outdoors in Britain.

F. carica (Mediterranean). Deciduous tree or large shrub. Height about 4.5m (15ft), but much more in the wild; spread 3m (10ft). Large leathery, three- to five-lobed leaves 100–200mm (4–8in) or more long. Flowers produced on inside of rounded, hollow, pear-shaped container, nearly closed at top, which develops into sweet edible fruit with or without fertilisation. In Britain, plants crop in August–September – but only on warm, sheltered walls in good summers. Good outdoor fruiters: 'Brown Turkey', 'Brunswick'.

Site Against a south- or west-facing wall, sunny and sheltered.

Soil Light, well-drained, chalky or sandy for best fruiting.

Propagation By layering in summer. By semi-hardwood cuttings in June under cover.

Cultivation Plant in April. Trees will be more fruitful if roots are restricted by planting in hole 1.2m (4ft) square and 600mm (2ft) deep, lined at sides with bricks or concrete and at base with 300mm (1ft) depth of firmly packed drainage material such as broken brick. Avoid regular feeding or mulching with organic matter – this causes too great a growth of stem and leaf and too little fruit. Light mulch helps to conserve water in late winter. Trees must be given protection in hard winters; heavy-duty clear plastic sheet attached to the wall above the plant can be lowered over it at night (and in the day also if necessary); but keep tree ventilated.

Pruning Figs are best grown as fans, tying in suitably placed shoots as they grow, and spacing them so that all receive sun and air. In autumn, after the leaves have fallen, cut some of old, bare, non-fruiting shoots back to a bud or joint to encourage new growth to take its place (the fig fruits on one- and two-year-old shoots). In spring, cut out dead material and any weak or crowding shoots. Fruit carried on tips of young shoots.

Pests and Diseases Scale insect may be a problem. Grey mould on shoot tips and on fruits in cool summers. Coral spot may affect shoots.

Above Festuca glauca

Festuca

GRAMINEAE   Fescue grass

Perennial ornamental grasses native mainly to Europe, including Britain; some are used with other grasses to produce high-quality lawns. Most have a low, tufted habit of growth and fine bluish grey or green foliage, and are useful as ground cover or as a foil for other plants.

F. glauca (S. France), blue fescue. Evergreen. Height and spread 150–200mm (6–8in). Forms dense, bluish-grey tufts of smooth cylindrical leaves. Short spikes of purple flowers, 40–50mm (1½–2in) long, in June–July. Excellent as low edging or among heathers (see *Calluna* and *Erica*) and other foliage plants.

F. rubra pruinosa, salt-marsh red fescue. Height 450mm (1½ft). Bluish green leaves.

Site Full sunshine preferred – and it enhances their colour – though green-leaved types tolerate a certain amount of shade. All stand up well to dry conditions.

Soil Must be well-drained, fertile, but not too rich; all fescues tolerate chalky soils.

Propagation Divide clumps in March–April, just as growth is beginning. Sow seed in open then or in August–September.

Cultivation Good weed-control essential, particularly of other, coarser grasses which may appear amongst clumps. Remove dead stems after flowering to show up the leaves to better effect.

Below Ficus carica

Foeniculum

UMBELLIFERAE   Fennel

Hardy perennial and annual native to Europe. One species is a herb and the other form (a natural variety) is used as a vegetable, but they also earn a place in the garden with their decorative properties.

F. vulgare (Europe), common fennel. Perennial. Height 1.2–1.5m (4–5ft); spread 600mm (2ft). Fine, feathery, blue-green leaves with an aniseed flavour. Flat heads of small, yellow flowers in July–August. The form *F. v. purpureum* has deep maroon young foliage. *F. vulgare dulce* (Italy), finnochio, Florence fennel, is an annual. Height 600mm (2ft); spread 300mm (1ft). Similar to common fennel, but has a swollen leaf base used as a vegetable.

Site Bright sun.
Soil Well-drained.
Propagation Sow seeds of common fennel outdoors in April–May; thin out seedlings to 300mm (1ft) apart. Divide established plants in March. They often seed themselves. Sow seeds of Florence fennel in April or July outdoors; thin out seedlings to 225mm (9in) apart.
Cultivation Leaves of common fennel are used fresh for flavouring fish and soups or for making tea. The flower heads can either be cut off or left on and the seeds harvested to flavour apple pies. Cut back plants to about 100mm (4in) from ground level in autumn. The swollen stems *F. vulgare dulce* can be boiled or braised or eaten raw in salads. Blanch stems by earthing up.

Above *Forsythia × intermedia*

Below *Foeniculum vulgare*

Forsythia

OLEACEAE   Golden bell

A small genus of deciduous shrubs, mostly from Asia. Their brilliant yellow flowers in early to mid-spring are among the first of the flowering shrubs to appear – a welcome herald of finer weather.

F. × intermedia (hybrid appearing in cultivation). Height and spread 1.8–2.4m (6–8ft). Arching stems covered in stalkless, yellow, open-bell-shaped flowers before leaves in late March–April. 'Spectabilis' is the best-known form: height and spread 3m (10ft); vigorous grower, it flowers much more heavily than its parent.

F. ovata (Korea). Height and spread about 1.2–1.5m (4–5ft). Deep-yellow flowers in February–March.

F. suspensa sieboldii (China). Rambling shrub with long slender stems which will cover a wall. Height 6m (20ft) plus; spread greater, but can be retricted as required. shoots take root if they touch the soil, so plant is useful for covering banks or walls. Yellow flowers (in March–April) are less-freely produced than in other species.

Site Any; rambling kind flowers best on a south- or west-facing wall or fence.
Soil Must be free-draining and moderately fertile.
Propagation Take hardwood cuttings in October. Detach rooted stems in spring.
Cultivation Plant October–March. Support *F. suspensa sieboldii* as shoots grow. Mulch all species with rotted organic matter every spring; give a spring dressing of general fertiliser on light sandy soils.
Pruning Every two or three years, immediately flowering finishes, cut out some of the oldest sideshoots, as low down as possible, close to a strong new shoot; this encourages new stems to come from ground level and thus ensure best flowering. Remove straggly shoots, and anything weak, crowded or dying, leaving just enough to clothe the base of the bush.
Pests and Diseases Birds may remove buds and flowers. Fasciation, in which stems are thicker or flattened and flowers unnaturally abundant, is characteristic of *F. × intermedia* and is not harmful. Galls (small swellings on root-producing shoots) are not damaging, but cut them out if unsightly. Capsid bugs may cause damage on leaves.

Fothergilla

HAMAMELIDACEAE

Two species form this genus of choice deciduous, hardy shrubs from the north-eastern United States. That listed is grown in Britain for its spectacular autumn colour of hazel-like leaves and its scented, white, 'bottle-brush' flowers that appear in April.

F. major (syn. *F. monticola*; Allegheny Mts). Rounded shrub with erect stems. Height and spread up to 2m (6½ft). Leaves glossy green, rounded or broadly ovate, 50–100mm (2–4in) long, colouring brilliant gold or scarlet in autumn. Flowers of white stamens in terminal erect spikes (25–50mm (1–2in) long.

Site Sun or light shade, sheltered; associates well with evergreen azaleas.
Soil Must be lime-free; sandy-peaty preferred.
Propagation By layering (a two-year process); or by summer semi-ripe cuttings, 75–100mm (3–4in) long, in propagator with bottom heat.
Cultivation Plant in November–March (container-grown kinds may be planted at any time).

Freesia

IRIDACEAE

Cormous perennials from South Africa grown for their colourful spikes of sweetly scented flowers.

F. × *kewensis* (syn. *F.* × *hybrida*). Height 300–450mm (1–1½ft); spread about 100mm (4in). Leaves sword-shaped in fan-like clusters. Flowers crocus-shaped, in branched spikes. Many named varieties, with flowers in shades of white, cream, red, pink, mauve, purple, yellow. Normally freesias are greenhouse plants which bloom from winter to spring. But it is now possible to buy specially treated corms which flower outside in July–August.

Site Full sun and shelter from cold winds.
Soil Must be well-drained and moderately fertile.
Propagation By offsets or seeds when dormant.
Cultivation Plant in spring when likelihood of severe frost has passed, setting corms no more than 75mm (3in) deep. Lift and dry off in autumn.
Pests and Diseases Shoots, leaves, and flowers may be eaten by slugs. Gladiolus corm rot and dry rot occasionally troublesome.

Above *Freesia* × *kewensis* **Below** *Fothergilla major*

Fremontia

STERCULIACEAE

A genus (syn. *Fremontodendron*) of two species of summer-flowering evergreen shrubs from California and Mexico. Usually represented in British gardens by a hybrid between these species, which is hardier than its parents.

F. × 'California Glory'. Vigorous, free-flowering, upright shrub. Height 4m (13ft); spread 2m (6½ft). Leaves up to 65mm (2½in) long and 50mm (2in) wide, variably-lobed, dark green above and grey beneath; young shoots and leaf-undersides covered with fine brown hairs. Large, single, hollyhock-like golden flowers, up to 65mm (2½in) across, produced all summer.

Site Sheltered, south-facing wall essential except in mild areas.
Soil Well-drained, fertile; plant does well on chalk soil.
Propagation Semi-ripe tip cuttings in late summer will root under mist.

Cultivation Plant container-grown shrubs in early autumn or spring.
Pruning Prune back lateral growths in mid-summer if compact wall shrub is required. Tie main stems securely to wire or trellis.

Above *Fremontia* × 'California Glory'

Fritillaria

LILIACEAE Fritillary

Bulbous perennials from the northern temperate zone. They have erect, unbranched, leafy stems and bear nodding bell-shaped flowers in racemes, small clusters, or singly.

F. imperialis (Iran to W. Himalaya), crown imperial. Height 750mm–1.2m (2½–4ft); spread 200–300mm (8–12in). Largest of the 85 known fritillaries, with robust leafy stem and glossy lance-shaped leaves. Terminal umbel of six or more red bells, 50mm (2in) long, in spring. Variety 'Aurora' is deep reddish-orange; 'Lutea Maxima' is yellow.

F. meleagris (C. Europe to Scandinavia and Britain), snake's-head fritillary. Height about 300mm (1ft); spread to 75mm (3in). Stem slender; leaves sparse, narrowly lance-shaped. Flowers singly or in twos, about 40mm (1½in) long, in shades of red-purple with darker checkering, in spring. *F. m. alba* is a white-flowered form.

F. persica (syn. *F. libanotica*; Cyprus, Turkey, Iran). Height 450–900mm (1½–3ft); spread 150–200mm (6–8in). Robust fritillary rather like a grey-leaved *F. imperialis* but with terminal racemes of much smaller maroon to red or greenish-purple bells in late spring. *F. p.* 'Adiyaman' has deep, plum-purple flowers and grey-green leaves.

Site Full sun is best, but light or dappled shade is tolerated.
Soil Moisture-retentive but well-drained for *F. imperialis* and *F. persica*; *F. meleagris* thrives best in moister ground.
Propagation Remove offsets when dormant. Sow seeds when ripe or in spring, under glass; seedlings take several years to bloom.
Cultivation Plant in autumn (*F. meleagris* early autumn).

Below *Fritillaria imperialis* 'Lutea Maxima'

Fuchsia

Deciduous shrubs or small trees from Central and South America and New Zealand. Usually grown in Britain in cold or cool greenhouse conditions, though they can be used for bedding, and some are hardy. The latter are mostly single-flowered. Beautiful and decoratively flowered shrubs, their natural colours are purple and carmine-red, but hybridisation has produced many variants of white and all shades of pink, lilac, blue, red and crimson; some have orange flowers. All fuchsia flowers consist of an outer round or tubular calyx with four parts, and a corolla of four inner petals, usually in a different colour. In the descriptions below the calyx colours are given first.

The following are some of the hardiest and best fuchsia species and varieties; all flower in August–October – longer in mild autumns.

F. 'Alice Hoffman'. Height and spread 600mm (2ft); pink and white, small, 13–20mm (½–¾in) long, freely produced.

F. 'Corallina'. Height 750–900mm (2½–3ft); scarlet and

purple, large flowers, 40mm (1½in) long, 25mm (1in) wide.
F. 'Lady Thumb'. Height 300mm (12in); spread 450mm (18in); small flowers, carmine and white.
F. 'Mme Cornelissen'. Height and spread 450mm (18in); large, semi-double, white and carmine red.
F. magellanica gracilis 'Versicolor'. Height 1.3m (4½ft), spread 1.2m (4ft); grey-green leaves, tinted pink when young and variegated creamy white, not as hardy as its green-leaved parent; long, slender red and violet flowers.
F. 'Mrs Popple'. Height and spread 900mm (3ft); large scarlet and violet flowers, stamens and style red, profuse flowering.
F. 'Riccartonii'. Height and spread 1.5–1.8m (5–6ft), more in mildest gardens; small red and purple flowers in June–October. An almost hardy form of *F. magellanica*.
F. 'Tom Thumb'. Miniature, height and spread 375mm (15in); purple and carmine red, profusely produced.

Greenhouse fuchsias can be put outdoors for the summer – in beds and borders, also in hanging baskets, urns and other elevated containers which allow their graceful habit and pendulous flowers to be displayed to advantage. Not all of these, however, will survive a winter out of doors. A few from the many hundreds available: 'Angel's Flight' (pink and white); 'Ballet Girl' (red and white); 'Bonita' (light pink, purple); 'Carmel Blue' (white and blue); 'Falling Stars' (pale scarlet, deep red); 'Fascination' (red, pink-rose); 'Gay Fandango' (rosy carmine, magenta); 'Golden Marinka' (red to deep red, golden variegated leaves); 'Marin Glow' (white and deep purple); 'Miss California' (pink); 'Passing Cloud' (rose, violet marbled white); 'Sleigh Bells (white); 'Swingtime' (pink and white, good hanging-basket subject); 'Temptation' (white and orange-rose).

Above *Fuchsia* 'Miss California' **Below** *Fuchsia* 'Mrs Popple'

Site Sheltered, close to protective wall or fence, preferably facing south or west.
Soil Well-drained, fertile.
Propagation Tender kinds: by soft cuttings in spring-early summer, under cover with gentle warmth. Hardy kinds: by tip cuttings in June–July under cover; or by seed sown in spring in warmth.
Cultivation Plant outdoors in April–May, and nip out tips of shoots if extra bushiness required. Mulch crowns heavily in autumn as growth ceases, to protect from cold. Pot tender kinds in March; put outdoors May; remove to a place of protection before first frosts, and keep free of frost through winter. Feed container-grown plants weekly with liquid feed from mid-summer.
Pruning Outdoor kinds should have previous year's growth cut back to ground level if dead, or back to a good pair of new buds low down on the stem in November or early spring. Clip fuchsia hedges in spring. Tender kinds can be trained as standards. Other popular shapes include pyramid, fan, and espalier.
Pests and Diseases Outdoors: capsid bug, greenfly. Indoors: the same, plus whitefly, red-spider mite.

Gaillardia

COMPOSITAE   Blanket flower

Hardy annuals and herbaceous perennials, native to America, with bright, daisy-like flowers; useful for borders and as cut flowers.

G. grandiflora (syn. *G. aristata*; United States). Perennial. Height 300–750mm (1–2½ft); spread 450mm (1½ft). Grey-green alternate leaves. Yellow and red flowers about 75mm (3in) across in June–October. Hybrids include 'Burgundy' (copper red); 'Goblin' (bright red and yellow; a dwarf variety); 'Large Flowered Mixed' (yellows, crimsons, and crimsons edged with yellow).

G. pulchella (United States). Annual. Height 450–600mm (1½–2ft); spread 300mm (1ft). Hairy, grey-green leaves. Single or double flowers up to 75mm (3in) across in July–October. 'Double Mixed' is a selection of cream, yellow, crimson and multi-coloured blooms.

Site Sun or light shade.
Soil Light, well-drained.
Propagation Sow annuals indoors in February–March, and plant out in May after hardening off; or sow outdoors in April–July and thin out to 300mm (1ft) apart. Perennials can be sown either indoors in February–March or outdoors in May–June; latter will need to be grown on in a nursery bed and planted out in March–April of following year.
Cultivation Taller plants need sticks for support. Dead-head flowers to encourage new ones to develop.

Below *Gaillardia grandiflora*

Galanthus

AMARYLLIDACEAE   Snowdrop

Bulbous perennials from Europe and western Asia. Each bulb produces two (sometimes three) narrow leaves and an erect stem bearing one pendent flower composed of three long and three short petals. Good subjects for woodland settings and in grass.

G. elwesii (Turkey). Height 150mm (6in) or more; spread about 100mm (4in). Leaves broad, rolled around each other when young, grey-green. Each flower up to 50mm (2in) wide, white with inner petals bearing a green blotch at base and tip; flowering time variable, from early winter to early spring.

G. nivalis (Europe), common snowdrop. Height 100m (4in) or more; spread about 75mm (3in). leaves narrow and flat, pressed flat together when young, grey-green. Each flower, 20–30mm (¾–1¼in) wide, is white with inner petals bearing a green blotch at the tip; winter to early spring. Cultivar 'Plena' has double blooms; natural variety *G. n. reginae-olgae* flowers in autumn before the leaves.

Site Part shade or full sun equally acceptable, though *G. nivalis reginae-olgae* flowers best in sun.

Below *Galanthus elwesii*

Soil Moisture-retentive but well-drained; must be moist during growing season.
Propagation Plant in autumn, the earlier the better, or immediately flowers fade.

Galega

LEGUMINOSAE   Goat's rue

Hardy perennials from southern Europe and western Asia. They are erect, leafy plants that bear numerous spikes of small pea-flowers.

G. officinalis (Europe to Asia), common goat's rue. Height 1–1.5m (3¼–5ft); spread 600–900mm (2–3ft). Leaves bright green, pinnate, composed of 9 to 17 elliptic leaflets. White to pale purple-blue or lilac-pink flowers in summer. Variety 'Lady Wilson' has rich mauve blooms. (This species now includes the former *G. bicolor* and *G. patula* and hybrid *G. × hartlandii*.)

Site Sunny location is best, though a little shade is tolerated.
Soil Well-drained, preferably not too rich.
Propagation Divide clumps from autumn to spring. Sow seeds in spring.
Cultivation Plant from autumn to spring. Cut down dead stems in early winter. Mulch with organic matter in spring.

Above *Galega officinalis*

Galtonia

LILIACEAE   Summer hyacinth

Bulbous perennials from southern Africa. Cultivated species produce tall racemes of pendent, bell-shaped flowers in shades of white and green, and provide attractive colours in borders late in the season.

G. candicans. Height to 1m (3¼ft) or more; spread about 450mm (1½ft). Leaves strap-shaped, up to 600mm (2ft) long, somewhat greyish-green. Pure white flowers, about 40mm (1½in) long, open in summer–autumn.

G. princeps. Like a smaller version of *G. candicans*, with more widely expanded, very pale green flowers. A useful flower-arranger's plant.

Site Full sun and shelter from strong, cold winds.
Soil Well drained and fertile.
Propagation Separate offsets when dormant. Sow seeds in spring under glass; seedlings take several years to bloom.
Cultivation Plant in autumn in mild areas, in spring in cold ones. In very cold areas, lift the bulbs in autumn and store in slightly moist peat in a cool but frost-free place.
Pests and Diseases Slugs and snails eat leaves and flowers.

Right *Galtonia candicans*

Garrya

GARRYACEAE

Vigorous evergreen shrubs from western North America notable for their leathery leaves and conspicuous catkins early in the year. The species listed has outstanding garden value.

G. elliptica (California, Oregon). Large, bushy evergreen of rapid growth. Height 3m (10ft); spread 2.5m (8¼ft); larger in mild districts and against walls. Leaves oval or rounded, 40–75mm (1½–3in) long, with waved margins, dark green, shiny above and grey-woolly beneath. Male plants have spectacular silky, grey-green catkins, up to 300mm (12in) long in warm districts, produced in January–February. In the female shorter catkins are succeeded by strings of purple-brown berries if fertilised; plant specimens of both sexes for berries.

Site Preferably near a wall, even a north- or east-facing one; in warmer areas it may be grown by itself on a sheltered south- or west-facing slope.
Soil Well-drained. the plant is lime-tolerant. Avoid excessive manuring.
Propagation Selected male or female plants by cuttings 100mm (4in) long in late summer in frame with bottom heat; over-winter in pots under glass. Seed sown in February under glass produces plants of both sexes.
Cultivation Plant from containers in early autumn or spring.
Pruning Size and spread can be restricted by pruning back after flowering before new growth commences in spring. Prune out flowered shoots to maintain an informal bush.

Right *Garrya elliptica*

Above *Gaultheria procumbens*

Gaultheria

ERICACEAE

Evergreen shrubs from Australasia, Himalaya, and North America, belonging to the same family as the heathers and grown mainly for their flowers and berries.

G. procumbens (North America), creeping wintergreen, partridge berry. Low-growing, spreading shrub, forming a dark, glossy carpet. Pink-tinged flowers appear in July–August on stems 75–150mm (3–6in) tall, followed by red berries 8mm (⅓in) in diameter.

G. shallon (North America), salal. Shrub forming dense thickets 1.2m (4ft) and more high and wide. Pinkish white, urn-shaped flowers in June, then purple-black fruit.

Site Sun or shade (listed species do well in woodlands).
Soil Acid, containing peat or leaf-mould; moist but well-drained.
Propagation By division or layering in mid- to late autumn. By seed sown when ripe in February–March under cover.

Cultivation Plant in autumn–spring. Mulch occasionally with organic matter such as peat or leaf-mould.
Pruning Thin out shoots after flowering if crowded or outgrowing the space available.
Pests and Diseases Soil fungi may cause root death.

Gazania

COMPOSITAE

Half-hardy perennials, native to southern Africa, grown in Britain as half-hardy annuals except in very warm areas. Their daisy-like flowers close at night.

G. × hybrida (hybrid). Height 230–375mm (9–15in); spread 300mm (1ft). Dark green leaves with grey undersides. Flowers 50–125mm (2–5in) wide in a range of colours in July–September. Varieties include 'Chansonette' (lemon, gold, apricot, orange, bronze, mauve and carmine); 'Harlequin Hybrids' (yellow, orange, carmine, and orange-and-red); 'Mini-Star' (compact, in wide colour range); 'Sundance' (large blooms, from crimson to cream).

Site Full sun; plants thrive in coastal gardens.
Soil Well-drained.
Propagation Sow seeds in January–March in gentle heat; prick out into pots. Take tip cuttings in July–August; keep in a cool greenhouse over winter.

Cultivation Plant out seed- and cutting-raised plants in June, when they have been hardened off and all danger of frost is past.
Pests and Diseases Grey mould may occur in wet weather.

Above *Gazania × hybrida* 'Chansonette'

Genista

LEGUMINOSAE   Broom

Genistas are distinguishable from *Cytisus* (q.v.) species only by botanists. They can be cultivated in the same way, although they are more tolerant of lime. All bear flowers of various shades of yellow, and are native to the Mediterranean region and western Europe, including Britain.

G. aetnensis (Sicily), Mount Etna broom. Tree-like shrub. Height 3m (10ft) and more; spread 2.4m (8ft) and more. Linear leaves. Yellow pea-flowers cover stems in July. Plant is not completely hardy.

G. hispanica (S.W. Europe), Spanish gorse. Dense, hummocky shrub. Height 300–900mm (1–3ft); spread 2.1m (7ft) and more. Very spiny, with tiny linear leaves forming only on flowering stems. Brilliant golden flowers cover plant in June–July.

G. lydia (S. and E. Europe). Height 600mm (2ft); spread 900mm (3ft). Green pendulous-tipped stems. Bright yellow growth. Golden flowers in May–June.

Site Open, sunny position; plants need protection in hard winters. Small kinds do well on rock gardens.

Soil Well-drained, poor, preferably acid or, if slightly alkaline, with peat mixed in.

Propagation Sow seed under cover in March, outdoors in April. Take heel cuttings in August; put in sandy compost under cover.

Cultivation Plant from pots in spring. Mulch with peat each spring if soil is alkaline.

Pruning G. aetnensis can be cut back several times each season while young to make it bushy; G. hispanica can be lightly sheared after flowering to tidy it up; G. lydia need not be pruned unless it flowers poorly or is straggly, when flowered shoots are cut back to new stems.

Pests and Diseases Gall-mite produces growths on stems; cut these out as soon as seen. Dieback causes black spots on leaves and stems.

Above *Genista lydia*

Gentiana

GENTIANACEAE   Gentian

A large genus of plants, mainly from Europe, Asia and Oceania, that includes perennials of great importance in the rock garden. There is a wide variety of flower and form, and the blooms can continue from spring to autumn.

G. acaulis (syn. *G. excisa, G. kochiana*; Europe), trumpet gentian. Height 65–75mm (2½–3in); spread 450mm (18in) or more. A common sight in the Swiss Alps, in cultivation the species may be shy to flower; if this happens, experiment with different sites until a suitable one is found. The huge blue trumpets, up to 100mm (4in) wide, appear from a prostrate mat of leaves in April. It is lime-tolerant.

G. asclepiadea (Europe), willow gentian. Height 400–600mm (16–24in); spread 300–450mm (12–18in). Too tall for some rock gardens, it will do well in a cool, shady, moist position. Arching stems 600mm (24in) tall produce clusters of gentian-blue flowers in the leaf axils from July to September; a handsome white form is also available.

G. gracilipes (China). Height 150–225mm (6–9in); spread 400mm (16in) or more. Forms a central rosette of narrow leaves from which emerge stems with bell-shaped purple-blue flowers from midsummer onwards. A lime-hater.

G. saxosa (New Zealand). An unusual plant, no taller than 100mm (4in), with rosettes of dark green leaves that offset white cup-like flowers that appear in July and August. Does best in scree conditions.

G. septemfida (Turkey, Caucasus, Iran, and Turkestan). Height 150–250mm (6–10in); spread 250mm (10in) or more. Easiest of all gentians, readily raised from seed, but variable so the best forms should be chosen. Leafy stems bear clusters of bright purplish blue trumpets in July. This species is herbaceous and will tolerate almost any soil and situation.

G. sino-ornata (China). Height 125–150mm (5–6in); spread 300–400mm (12–16in). Finest of the lime-hating autumn gentians, it thrives in a moist but not wet, peaty or leaf-mould soil. Dense mats of fine leaves, 100mm (4in) high, produce dozens of azure-blue trumpets in September and October. Varieties include 'Alba' (white) and 'Brin Form', a free-flowering scrambling form.

G. verna (Europe, Asia), spring gentian. Height 65–75mm (2½–3in); spread 125–150mm (5–6in). Most easily available in the variety *G. v. angulosa*, whose vivid-blue, star-shaped flowers appear in April and May. Needs rich, gritty soil, well-drained yet not drying out. A lime-lover, but will tolerate acid soils.

Site Requirements vary between species. Spring- and summer-flowering species mostly tolerate sunny position, most autumn-flowering species require some shade.

Soil Varies for each species. In particular, check for lime tolerance.

Propagation Straggling clumps of autumn species prised apart in spring as they come into growth and re-planted in peaty soil. G. acaulis divided after flowering in June, or propagated by seed sown in the autumn in seed compost. G. asclepiadea, gracilipes, saxosa and septemfida raised from fresh seed sown in summer (no later than August).

Cultivation See each species.

Below *Gentiana asclepiadea*

Above *Geranium endressii* **Right** *Geranium sanguineum*

Geranium

GERANIACEAE Crane's-bill

Perennials and some annuals of cosmopolitan distribution. Those in cultivation have rounded, lobed leaves and a long season of showy, five-petalled flowers. (Not to be confused with those species of *Pelargonium* commonly known as geraniums).

G. cinereum (Pyrenees). Height 150mm (6in); spread 300mm (1ft). Tufted species with small, downy leaves. Lilac to pink flowers with dark vein pattern 30mm (1¼in) wide in late spring onwards. Variety 'Ballerina' has white flowers with crimson-purple veins.

G. dalmaticum (N. Albania, S. W. Yugoslavia). Height to 125mm (5in); spread 450mm (1½ft) or more. Mat-forming, leaves five-lobed, often red in autumn. Rich clear pink flowers, 25mm (1in) wide, open in summer. Variety 'Album' has white flowers. Excellent rock-garden plant.

G. endressii (S.W. France, S.E. Spain). Height about 400mm (16in); spread 600mm (2ft) or more. leaves to 80mm (3¼in) wide, deeply five-lobed. Flowers 30mm (1¼in) wide, pale pink in summer to autumn. Varieties include 'A.T. Johnson' (silvery pink); 'Rose Clair' (white, purple-feathered); 'War-grave Pink' (bright salmon-pink). The species has also given rise to several excellent hybrids: *G.* × 'Claridge Druce' (like a robust, very vigorous *G. endressii*, with rich, purplish pink blooms, excellent for ground cover); *G.* × 'Russell Prichard' (semi-prostrate, with small greyish leaves and rose-magenta flowers).

G. himalayense (syn. *G. grandiflorum*, *G. meeboldii*; Sikkim). Height 300–450mm (1–1½ft); spread 600mm (2ft) or more. Runs underground and in time can form wide patches. Leaves deeply seven-lobed. Wide bowl-shaped flowers, rich violet-blue with red veins, in summer. Variety 'Alpinum' (syn. 'Gravetye') more compact, rarely above 300mm (1ft) tall.

G. macrorrhizum (S. Europe). Height about 300mm (1ft); spread to 1m (3¼ft) or more. Mat-forming plant, excellent for ground cover. Leaves deeply five- to seven-lobed, aromatic, often red in autumn. Flowers 20mm (¾in) wide, purplish-red, in early summer. Varieties include 'Album' (white); 'Walter Ingwersen' (soft pink); and 'Variegatum' (leaves splashed creamy-white).

G. × *magnificum*. Height 450–600mm (1½–2ft); spread 300–450mm (1–1½ft). Clump-forming plant, often confused with *G. ibericum*, but is more vigorous and never sets seed. White downy leaves are 100mm (4in) or more wide and deeply lobed. Red-veined violet-blue flowers in profusion in summer.

G. pratense (Europe), meadow crane's-bill. Height 600–900mm (2–3ft) or more in shade; spread 450–600mm (1½–2ft) or more. Handsome clump-former, with very deeply lobed leaves to 120mm (4¾in) wide. Violet-blue flowers, 30–40mm (1¼–1½in) wide, open in summer. Varieties 'Plenum Violaceum' (double); 'Striatum' (syn. 'Bicolor', white striped and sectioned petals); 'Johnson's Blue' (large, darker-veined lavender blooms); 'Kashmir White' (new name for the former *G. rectum-album*, bearing white flowers with darker veins, runs at root).

G. psilostemon (syn. *G. armenum*; Armenia). Height to 1.2m (4ft); spread about 900mm (3ft). Clump-forming, like a larger *G. pratense*, with crimson-magenta, black-eyed flowers in summer.

G. sanguineum (Europe, W. Asia), bloody crane's-bill. Height 200–300mm (9–12in); spread to 1m (3¼ft). Rhizomatous and mat-forming, with very deeply cut leaves.

Magenta, 25mm (1in) wide flowers from early summer to early autumn. Varieties include 'Album' (white flowers); *G. s. lancastrense* (smaller and flatter, with pale pink, red-veined flowers).

G. tuberosum (S. Europe). Height and spread 300mm (1ft) or more. Rootstock tuberous and slowly spreading. Leaves cut into slender lobes and distinct from most other species. Flowers 25mm (1in) wide and pale rosy-purple, open in late spring and summer, and plant dies down soon afterwards.

Site All stand partial shade, but *G. cinereum*, *G. dalmaticum*, *G.* × *magnificum*, and *G. sanguineum* prefer full sun.
Soil Well-drained, not too dry.
Propagation Divide in autumn or spring. Sow seeds in spring.
Cultivation Plant autumn–spring. Cut back dead stems of tall species in autumn.

Geum

ROSACEAE

Hardy herbaceous perennials of cosmopolitan distribution, usually grown for their showy flowers, although a number also have decorative seed heads.

G. chiloense (Chile). Perennial. Height 300–600mm (1–2ft); spread 450mm (1½ft). Hairy, green, pinnate leaves form a dense basal clump. Strong, wiry stems support bright red or orange, papery flowers 40mm (1½in) across in June–September. Varieties include 'Coppertone' (coppery pink); 'Lady Stratheden' (yellow); 'Mrs Bradshaw' (red).

G. montanum (S. Europe). Perennial. Height 150–300mm (6–12in); spread 300mm (12in). Useful rock-garden plant with rosette of hairy green leaves. Golden-yellow flowers 40mm (1½in) across carried on short stout stems in May–July.

Site Open, sunny.
Soil Well-drained, but retaining some moisture even in summer; adding leaf-mould helps moisture retention.
Propagation Species increased by seed sown in spring or in July, either directly in nursery rows or in a frame for transplanting later. Named varieties best increased by division in autumn.
Cultivation Old foliage should be tidied up in the autumn. Lift and divide plants every three or four years to maintain their vigour.
Pests and Diseases Sawflies may attack.

Right *Geum chiloense* 'Coppertone'

Gladiolus

IRIDACEAE

Cormous perennials from Africa, Mediterranean, and southern Europe to central Asia. Each corm produces a fan of rigid, sword-shaped leaves and a one-sided spike of colourful and showy funnel-shaped flowers.

G. byzantinus (Mediterranean). Height 600–750mm (2–2½ft); spread about 200mm (8in). Almost hardy; bears 50mm (2in) long, rose-purple flowers in early summer.

Hybrids. Most of the hundreds of popular gladioli are half-hardy cultivars of complex hybrid origin. They vary in flower-size and form and include every colour except true blue. They are classified into several groups, the main ones being as follows. Large-flowered (Exhibition): most popular group, 600–1.2m (2–4ft) high, with massive spikes of wide-open blooms. Miniature: smaller – 450–900mm (1½–3ft) high – and neater, they include the slightly larger Butterfly strain, many of which have blooms startlingly blotched. Primulinus: basically similar in size and form to Miniatures, but each flower has a hooded upper petal. A wide range of very fine cultivars is available in all these groups.

Site Full sun essential; some shelter beneficial.
Soil Must be well drained and preferably humus-rich.
Propagation Remove offsets and cormlets when dormant. Sow seeds under glass in spring.
Cultivation Plant *G. byzantinus* in autumn or spring; half-hardy cultivars in spring only. *G. byzantinus* can be left *in situ* until clumps form; half-hardy sorts should be lifted six to eight weeks after the last flower has faded. Cut off foliage about 50mm (2in) above the corm and dry off as rapidly as possible, ideally at not less than 24°C (75°F) for first three days, at 13–15°C (55–59°F) for following 10 days. Then clean off the previous season's corm and cormlets (spawn) and store at not less than 10°C (50°F) until the next planting season. This method is recommended by the Gladiolus Society and produces good quality corms.
Pests and Diseases Aphids, thrips, slugs, and snails are the main pests. Corm rot, core rot, dry rot, hard rot, and scab can be a nuisance in some areas and seasons.

Below *Gladiolus* 'Peter Pears'

G. triacanthos (E. North America), honey locust. Large tree attaining up to 20m (60ft) height, with branches armed with stout spines. Handsome fern-like, bright-green leaves, 100–200mm (4–8in) long. Flattened, often twisted, dark brown seed pods up to 300mm (12in) long are a feature in warm locations. Several smaller varieties are particularly garden worthy: 'Elegantissima' (forms dense, slow-growing shrub 3m (10ft) high or more, with spineless branches of elegant glossy foliage); 'Sunburst' (usually 5–6m (16–20ft) high, with broad, rounded head, spineless branches, foliage golden in spring and early summer, later becoming a mixture of gold and green).

Above *Gleditsia tricanthos* 'Elegantissima'

Site Open, sunny preferred, but shade is tolerated. 'Sunburst' makes a superb lawn specimen.
Soil Well-drained.
Propagation Species by seed sown in spring, following stratification; varieties by grafting in late winter or early spring.

Cultivation Bare-root trees can be planted in November–March; varieties are usually container-grown for planting at any time.
Pruning Prune and train to encourage good leading shoot; late-summer pruning is preferred. Remove any dead wood in spring.

Gleditsia

LEGUMINOSAE

A small genus of elegant deciduous trees and shrubs, native to North America and western and central Asia, notable for their graceful pinnate foliage and tolerance of drought and town conditions. That listed is the only species grown widely in Britain.

Godetia

ONAGRACEAE

Hardy annuals, native to America, producing brightly coloured flowers for the border or for cutting. They often appear in garden catalogues under *Clarkia* (q.v.).
G. grandiflora (syn. *Clarkia amoena whitneyi*; California). Height 300–600mm (1–2ft); spread 150mm (6in). Compact plant with mid-green, pointed leaves. Flowers, in June–

Below *Godetia grandiflora* 'Crimson Glow'

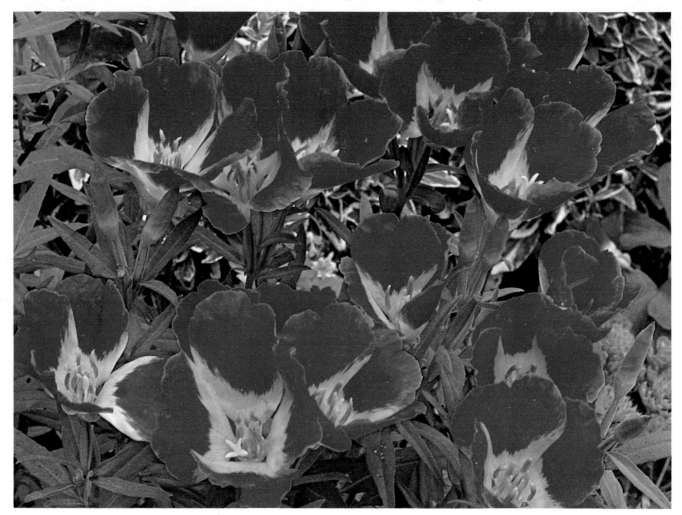

August, are reddish purple and trumpet-shaped. Varieties include 'Azalea-Flowered Mixed' (azalea-like semi-double flowers); 'Crimson Glow' and 'Dwarf Bedding Mixed' (both dwarf plants 300mm (1ft) or less tall); 'Kelvedon Glory' (salmon-orange); 'Sybil Sherwood' (salmon-pink, edged with white); 'Double Crimson'; 'Double White'.

Site Full sun.
Soil Light (if too rich excess foliage will grow).
Propagation Sow seeds outside in March–April to flower same year; in September for the following year. September-sown plants need to be protected with cloches in exposed areas.
Cultivation Thin to 150mm (6in) apart; do not thin autumn-sown plants until spring. Keep well-watered in dry weather.
Pests and Diseases Foot, stem, and root rot may occur.

Above Gunnera manicata

Gunnera

HALORAGIDACEAE
Hardy and half-hardy herbaceous perennials from South America and Australasia, grown in gardens mainly for their decorative foliage.
G. magellanica (South America). Height 75mm (3in); spread varies, the plant creeping and forming a tight mat. Kidney-shaped green leaves, 50mm (2in) wide, interspersed with short reddish-green flower-spikes. Suitable for a damp place on rock garden or by pond.
G. manicata (Brazil). Height 1.8m (6ft) or more; spread 3m (10ft). Enormous, prickly, rhubarb-like leaves with red spiny stems arise from a huge, scaly rhizome. Large reddish-green bottlebrush-like flower-spikes. Imposing by the side of a garden pool.

Site Open, sunny, but not a frost pocket.
Soil Heavy and moist, with plenty of organic matter.
Propagation Divide in early spring. The large scaly buds of *G. manicata* can be removed from rhizome and rooted. Propagation from seed depends on seed being gathered fresh and sown immediately in damp, soil-based compost; resulting plants take up to two years to attain planting size.
Cultivation Plant in the spring. Mulch the larger kinds every spring. Remove large leaves of *G. manicata* as soon as they are blackened by frost, and invert over crowns for winter.

Gypsophila

CARYOPHYLLACEAE   Baby's breath, chalk plant
Annuals and herbaceous perennials native to Europe and western Asia. Most have graceful sprays of tiny flowers, excellent for cutting, and make bushy, erect plants for the herbaceous border, especially in drier gardens.
G. elegans (Caucasus). Hardy annual. Height and spread 300–450mm (1–1½ft). Bushy, upright plant with narrow grey or green leaves. Profusion of 13mm (½in) wide, white or pink flowers cover plants, hiding stems and leaves, in July–September.
G. paniculata (S. Europe, Russia). Hardy herbaceous perennial. Height and spread 600–750mm (2–2½ft). Bushy plant with narrow grey-green leaves and thin, wiry stems which interlace to form a mounded dome. Delicate cloud of small chalk-white flowers, up to 8mm (⅓in) wide, in June–August. Cultivars include 'Bristol Fairy' (completely double, white flowers); 'Rosy Veil' (double, soft pink flowers, effective in front of border or growing over low wall in rock garden).
G. repens (S. Europe). Perennial. Height 100–150mm (4–6in); spread 450–600mm (1½–2ft). Prostrate mat-forming plant with wiry stems and narrow, grey-green leaves. Flowers, 8mm (⅓in) wide, white to soft pink, cover leaves in July–September. Good plants for growing in the rock garden or trailing over dry walls.

Site All need full sun.
Soil Very well drained (especially for alpines), preferably alkaline. Most gypsophila are short-lived on heavy, wet winter soils.
Propagation Sow seeds of annual species where they are to flower in March or September. Basal cuttings of perennials and alpines can be rooted under glass in April, or half-ripe side shoots in July–August. Divide prostrate mat-forming alpines in March.
Cultivation Support taller plants in windy situations with thin brushwood when they are 100–150mm (4–6in) high. Cutting down stems after flowering may induce a second crop of flowers in late autumn.

Below *Gypsophila repens*

Hamamelis

HAMAMELIDACEAE Witch-hazel

Hardy, winter-effective, deciduous shrubs or small trees, from Asia and North America, producing exquisite, sweetly scented, long-lasting, frost-resistant flowers, and rich autumn leaf-colour.

H. × intermedia (hybrid). Height and spread 2.4–3m (8–10ft). Parent of several good varieties, notably 'Jelena' (coppery-orange); 'Diane' (bronze-red). Both of these have good autumn leaf colour.

H. mollis (China), Chinese witch-hazel. Variable wide-spreading shrub. Height and spread 2m (6½ft) or more. Leaves roundish, 75–125mm (3–5in) long, and hazel-like. Stalkless clusters of fragrant golden flowers produced December–February. Variety 'Pallida', of compact habit, 1.8m (6ft) high and 2m (6½ft) wide, with dense clusters of sulphur-yellow, broad-petalled flowers, is best and readily available; its autumn leaves are yellow.

Site Sun or semi-shade; allow room to spread. Effective among spring- or summer-flowering heathers.
Soil Lime-free and loamy preferred.
Propagation Species by seed, spring-sown outside following stratification; hybrids and cultivars by layering or grafting on *H. mollis* or *virginiana* root

stocks under glass in March or early April.
Cultivation Plant from containers at most seasons.
Pruning Little pruning required if shrubs have room to spread. Suckers from root-stocks of grafted plants must be removed as they appear.

Below *Hamamelis mollis*

Above *Hebe* 'Midsummer Beauty'

Hebe

SCROPHULARIACEAE Shrubby veronica

Evergreen shrubs or small trees mostly from New Zealand, also Australia, South America, and Falkland Islands. They are pretty shrubs with oval or pointed leaves and with spikes of flowers all over the bush from spring to autumn; the larger-leaved kinds are not fully hardy.

H. 'Autumn Glory'. Height 450mm (1½ft); spread 750mm (2½ft). Deep purple-blue spikes, 25–50mm (1–2in) long, in June–October.

H. brachysiphon (New Zealand). Height and spread 1.8m (6ft) and more, dense and rounded. Small, oval leaves. Spikes of white flowers, 40mm (1½in) long, in July.

H. 'Carl Teschner'. Height 200mm (8in); spread 600mm (2ft). Violet flowers with white throat in June–July. Useful for ground cover.

H. × franciscana (hybrid). Rounded habit; height and spread 900mm–1.2m (3–4ft). Violet-blue flowers on 75mm (3in) spikes in summer. Of varieties, 'Blue Gem' has brightest colour, 'Variegata' has leaves edged creamy white.

H. 'Great Orme'. Height and spread 750mm (2½ft). Long narrow leaves, bright pink 75–100mm (3–4in) spikes in July–October; less hardy.

H. 'Midsummer Beauty'. Height 1.2m (4ft); spread 900mm (3ft). Long lavender and white spikes in June–July, and again in autumn if seed-heads are removed.

H. pinguifolia (New Zealand) 'Pagei'. Distinctive neat, low-growing hebe providing good ground-cover; somewhat trailing stems covered in grey leaves. Short spikes of tiny white flowers in June–July and in autumn.

H. speciosa. Height 1.2–1.5m (4–5ft); spread 1.2m (4ft). Purple-red or purple-blue flowers on 100mm (4in) spikes in

July–September. Its many beautiful forms thrive only in warm, sheltered places. A few good ones: 'Gauntlettii' (rose-pink and purple, 150mm (6in) spikes); 'La Seduisante' (crimson spikes); 'Midsummer Beauty' (pinkish purple spikes); 'Veitchii' (deep purple-blue). All these are about 1.2m (4ft) high and wide and flower in July–October.

Site Sunny, sheltered.
Soil Medium to well-drained; no objection to chalk; hardiest on poor soils.
Propagation Tip cuttings 50–75mm (2–3in) long in summer under cover.
Cultivation Plant spring; no special care beyond protection in severe winters. Remove the flowerheads as soon as flowering has finished.
Pruning Remove shoots killed by frost in spring.
Pests and Diseases Leaf spot and mildew may occur.

Hedera

ARALIACEAE   Ivy

Hardy evergreen climbers native to Europe and North Africa. They have two different phases of growth: development of juvenile leaves with aerial or stem roots, which attach themselves to any supporting surfaces; and, subsequently, growths that bear flowers, fruits, and adult leaves which are entire, but no aerial roots. Many forms have variegated leaves.

H. canariensis (syn. *H. helix canariensis*; Canary Islands, N. Africa), Canary Island ivy. Height and spread 4.5–6m (15–20ft). Large, leathery, heart-shaped leaves, bright green in summer and bronze in winter; young stems covered with brown felt-like hairs. Variety 'Gloire de Marengo' has creamy-white-edged leaves with silvery-green centres.

H. colchica (Iran), Persian ivy. Height and spread 6–9m (20–30ft). One of the quickest-growing ivies. Leaves heart-shaped and dark green. Form 'Dentata Variegata' has leaves margined creamy yellow with pale green centres.

H. helix (Europe, including Britain), common ivy. Height and spread variable. One of the hardiest of all the evergreen climbers, with glossy leaves. Best forms include 'Buttercup' (rich yellow leaves becoming pale green with age); 'Glacier' (silvery-grey leaves with narrow white margin); 'Goldheart' (leaves with a striking yellow central splash); 'Hibernica' (large, dark-green, lobed leaves, especially good for ground cover).

Above *Hedera helix* 'Goldheart'

Site Any will do, but variegated forms retain their colour longer on south- or west-facing walls.
Soil Any.
Propagation Take 75–125mm (3–5in) cuttings from tips or sections of long shoots in July–August (juvenile growth for climbing ivy, adult growth for bushy ivy); root cuttings in a cold-frame.
Cultivation Plant out between September and March; or grow plants in pots, with extra support and watering in dry weather. Feed potted specimens every month in growing season.
Pruning Prune large, dense specimens hard. Wall-covering ivies should be clipped every other spring to reduce their weight.
Pests and Diseases Scale insects can make plants sticky and sooty; mites may cause leaves to mottle. Leaf spot may occur.

Helenium

COMPOSITAE   Sneezewort

Annuals and herbaceous perennials native to North and South America. Most are easy and colourful summer border plants, with showy heads of daisy-like flowers, and are good for cutting.

H. autumnale (E. North America). Perennial. Height 1.5m (5ft); spread 600mm (2ft). Vigorous, erect plant with woody stems and green, lance-shaped leaves. Broad, rounded heads of many composite yellow flowers, 25–40mm (1–1½in) across, in July–September. A parent of many fine garden hybrids, notably 'Butterpat' (rich yellow), 'Coppelia' (coppery orange, yellow centre) and 'Moerheim Beauty' (bronze, orange centre), all 900mm (3ft) high; 'Riverton Beauty' (yellow) 1.5m (5ft) high; 'Wyndley' (yellow, striped orange, 600mm (2ft) high).

Site Full sun and an open situation.
Soil Fertile; all heleniums are lime-tolerant.
Propagation Divide roots in autumn or spring, retaining only healthy outer growths.
Cultivation Plant in October–March. Stake taller plants securely when they are 100–150mm (4–6in) high. Divide clumps every three years to prevent overcrowding and maintain vigour.
Pests and Diseases Slugs may be troublesome in spring; tortrix caterpillars may bind and eat the leaves.

Below *Helenium autumnale* 'Butterpat'

Above *Helianthemum nummularium* 'Wisley Pink'

Helianthemum

CISTACEAE   Rock rose

Hardy evergreen or semi-evergreen dwarf shrubs native to Europe, North Africa, western Asia and North America. Cultivated mainly for their brightly coloured flowers, especially effective on rock gardens.

H. alpestre (syn. *H. oelandicum alpestre*; C. and S. Europe). Height 75–125mm (3–5in); spread 250mm (10in). Almost evergreen hummocks of small green leaves. Attractive bright-yellow, saucer-shaped, papery blossoms, 20mm ($\frac{3}{4}$in) across, in June–July.

H. apenninum (Europe, including Britain, Asia Minor). Mat-forming evergreen. Height and spread to 450mm (1½ft). Soft, downy, grey-green foliage. Clusters of papery white flowers in June. Varieties include 'Roseum' (rose-red).

H. nummularium (syn. *H. chamaecistus*, *H. vulgare*; Europe, including Britain). Evergreen. Height 300mm (1ft); spread 600mm (2ft). Crowded mounds of small green or grey leaves. Bright yellow, papery blooms in June. Varieties include 'Ben Heckla' (copper); 'Cerise Queen' (rose-red); 'Fire Dragon' (orange-red); 'Wisley Pink'; 'Wisley Primrose' (soft yellow).

Site Open, in full sun.
Soil Light, well-drained. Plants are lime-tolerant.
Propagation Sow seed in trays in a frame in spring; grow on the young plants in pots ready for planting out the following autumn. Propagate named varieties from soft cuttings of non-flowering wood in June–July; they root quickly in an open gritty medium in a propagator, and can be potted and planted out the following spring.
Cultivation Plant in September–October or March–April. Always grow or purchase pot-grown plants. After flowering trim plants with shears to prevent them becoming straggly.
Pests and Diseases Slugs may take succulent young shoots in spring. Powdery mildew may affect leaves.

Above *Helianthus annuus*

Helianthus

COMPOSITAE   Sunflower

Tall annuals and perennials with large, yellow daisy-like flowers.

H. annuus (North America), common sunflower. Annual. Height usually 2–3m (6–10ft), but can exceed 6m (20ft); spread 450–600mm (1½–2ft). Fast-growing plant with thick stem and large, coarse, light-green leaves. Flowers are huge, bright yellow with a brown central disc containing many seeds. Varieties include 'Autumn Beauty' (branching stems with flowers in shades of gold, lemon, bronze and mahogany); 'Sungold' (fully double, golden blooms).

flower-heads, which are very popular with flower-arrangers.

H. angustifolium (syn. *H. italicum, H. serotinum*; Europe), curry plant. Sub-shrub. Height 300–450mm (1–1½ft); spread 300–600mm (1–2ft). Evergreen with silver, needle-like leaves in spikes giving off a strong, spicy, curry smell in hot sun or when brushed. Clusters of tiny, bright yellow button flowers in summer.

H. bracteatum (Australia), strawflower. Half-hardy annual. Height 600mm–1.2m (2–4ft); spread 300–600mm (1–2ft). Grown for its long-lasting flowers with papery bracts in shades of yellow, orange, pink, red and white in mid- to late summer. Leaves are mid-green and lanceolate. Variety 'Bright Bikini' has sturdy stems to support its large flowers in a range of eye-catching colours.

H. splendidum (S. Africa). Shrub. Height 450–900mm (1½–3ft); spread 600–900mm (2–3ft). Slightly tender evergreen with downy, silver-white foliage. Clusters of tiny yellow, rounded flowers in mid-summer.

Site Sheltered, sunny.
Soil Free-draining, preferably not too rich.
Propagation Sow annuals where they are to flower in April, or in a greenhouse or propagator in early March; prick off into boxes and harden off before planting out in flowering positions in May. Shrubs and sub-shrubs can be increased by cuttings of side shoots taken in early summer and rooted in sandy compost in a propagator.

Cultivation Cut flowers for drying before they fully open on a warm, sunny morning. Hang them upside down to dry in an airy shed or room. Species grown for foliage should have flower buds pinched off if they spoil the effect. In wet areas protect woolly, silver-leaved species from winter damp.
Pruning Shrubby species should be cut back moderately hard in April.
Pests and Diseases Mildew may cause white patches to form on the leaves.

Left *Helichrysum angustifolium*

H. debilis (syn. *H. cucumerifolius*; N. United States). Annual. Height 1.2m (4ft); spread 450mm (1½ft). Foliage is shiny, deep green. Bright yellow flowers 75mm (3in) across carried on branching stems. Good for cut flowers.

H. decapetalus (N. America). Clump-forming perennial. Height 1.5–1.8m (5–6ft); spread 600mm (2ft). Flowers freely produced, lemon yellow, 75mm (3in) across, in late summer. Hybrid cultivars include 'Soleil d'Or' (semi-double, with a deeper yellow eye); 'Loddon Gold' (fully double, golden yellow).

Site Sunny, open site protected from strong winds.
Soil Well-drained. Dig in well-rotted manure or compost for extra-large plants.
Propagation Sow annuals where they are to flower, in spring; sow two seeds at each position, removing the weaker seedlings if both germinate. They can also be sown a couple of weeks earlier in a greenhouse, in individual peat or fibre pots. Plant out after last frost. Perennials can be sown in a nursery bed in spring, thinning seedlings to 150–200mm (6–8in) apart; plant in their permanent positions in autumn. Divide roots of perennial species in spring or autumn.
Cultivation Plant perennial species in autumn or spring. Remove dead flowerheads. Divide every two or three years to keep plants vigorous. Keep annuals well-watered while the plants are small. Stake firmly.
Pruning Cut down flowering stems of perennials when flowering has finished.

Helichrysum

COMPOSITAE   Strawflower, everlasting flower
Hardy and half-hardy annuals, herbaceous perennials, and shrubs of Europe, southern Africa, and Australasia, grown for their attractive white, furry foliage and their papery

Heliotropium

BORAGINACEAE   Cherry pie, heliotrope
Tender, evergreen South American shrub, with heads of strongly scented flowers.

H. arborescens (syn. *H. peruvianum*; Peru). Perennial, usually treated as a half-hardy annual. Height and spread to 900mm (3ft) or more, but smaller if grown as annual from seeds or cuttings. Leaves elliptic. Wide heads of mauvish blue, cherry-scented flowers from June until first frosts. Variety 'Marine' has deep-blue flowers and dark foliage.

Site Sunny or lightly shaded; sheltered.
Soil Moisture-retentive but well-drained.
Propagation Sow seeds in February in a greenhouse or propagator at 15°C (65°F); prick out seedlings into individual 85mm (3½in) pots; harden off before planting out in May.
Cultivation Pinch out growing tips to encourage a bushy, branching habit. Water freely while plants are getting established. Support tall plants with twiggy sticks or canes and string. Remove faded flower-heads.
Pests and Diseases Aphids may attack young shoots.

Right *Heliotropium arborescens* 'Marine'

Helipterum

COMPOSITAE

Annuals, perennials and shrubs from Australia (all those listed) and South Africa, with papery 'everlasting' flowers suitable for drying for winter arrangements.

H. humboldtianum. Annual. Height 300–450mm (1–1½ft); spread 250mm (10in). Leaves mid-green and lanceolate, woolly when young. Flower-heads make dense clusters of small, bright yellow blooms in July–September.

H. manglesii (syn. *Rhodanthe manglesii*). Annual. Height 300–600mm (1–2ft); spread 300mm (1ft). Branching stems bear blue-green, ovate leaves. Flowers, in July–September, small and yellow surrounded by papery bracts in shades of rose-pink, red, and purple; double 'flowered' forms are also available.

H. roseum (syn. *Acroclinium roseum*). Annual. Height 300–450mm (1–1½ft); spread 300mm (1ft). Leaves linear, mid-green. Flower-heads yellow with bracts in various shades of pink in July–August. Usually available as a mixture containing pink and white forms.

Site Full sun, sheltered.
Soil Free-draining, light, moderately rich.
Propagation Sow in greenhouse or propagator at 15°C (60°F) in early March, pricking off into boxes, and hardening off before planting out in May. They can also be sown where they are to flower, in late April–early May, thinning the seedlings to 150–230mm (6–9in) apart.
Cultivation Pick flower-heads for drying when they are just fully opened, gathering them on a dry, sunny day. Discard plants after flowering.

Below *Helipterum roseum* mixed

Above *Helleborus orientalis*

Helleborus

RANUNCULACEAE   Hellebore

Perennials from Europe to the Caucasus, including the Mediterranean region. Handsome in foliage and flower, they are among the few perennials to bloom in winter.

H. foetidus (W. Europe), setterwort, stinking hellebore. Height 450–750mm (1½–2½ft); spread 450–600mm (1½–2ft). Clump-forming with erect stems of biennial duration, each bearing several large, hand-shaped, deep green leaves composed of 7 to 11 narrow leaflets. Flowers are 13–30mm (½–1¼in) wide, cup-shaped, pale green edged with brownish purple, borne in large terminal clusters in late winter and spring.

H. lividus corsicus (syn. *H. argutifolius*, *H. corsicus*; Corsica, Sardinia). Height and spread to 600mm (2ft) or more. Similar growth habit to *H. foetidus* but has trifoliate leaves and larger, lime-green flowers in March–April. *H. l. sternii* is variable, its best forms having lightly marbled leaves and purple-tinted flowers.

H. niger (E. Alps, Italian Apennines), Christmas rose. Height 300mm (1ft); spread 450mm (1½ft) or more. True herbaceous perennial with leaves and flower stems arising at ground level, leaves long-stalked, composed of seven to nine oval leaflets. Flowers, shallow bowl-shaped, pure white, 65mm (2½in) wide, in mid-winter to spring. Variety 'Potter's Wheel' has flowers 100mm (4in) wide.

Flowers 100mm (4in) long, clear yellow, brown-tinted in bud, in late spring.

H. Hybrids. Almost all the hundreds of popular day lilies are of hybrid origin. Most have large flowers in shades of yellow, orange, red, pink, ivory and white, some strikingly bi-coloured. Among best: 'Bonanza' (light orange and maroon-brown); 'Burning Daylight' (rich, deep orange); 'Buzz Bomb' (deep velvety red); 'Chartreuse Magic' (canary yellow and green); 'Giant Moon' (moonlight yellow, large); 'Golden Orchid' (deep gold); 'Hornby Castle' (deep brick-red and yellow); 'Marion Vaughan' (canary yellow); 'Morocco Red' (dusky red and yellow); 'Pink Damask' (best pink so far developed).

Site Full sun preferred; a little shade tolerated.
Soil Moist, rich preferred.
Propagation Divide established clumps in early autumn or spring just as young growth starts. Sow seeds of species when ripe or in spring. Seedlings from cultivars do not come true to type.
Cultivation Plant autumn to spring. Remove dead stems and leaves in autumn or winter.
Pests and Diseases Slugs and iris leaf spot may attack the leaves.

Right *Hemerocallis* 'Burning Daylight'

Hepatica

RANUNCULACEAE
A small group of lime-loving plants that enjoy shady conditions. Similar to the smaller species of anemone, they are still sometimes listed as *Anemone hepatica*. They are particularly useful for their early flowers.

H. × *media* 'Ballardii'. Hybrid between *H. nobilis* and *H. transsilvanica*. Exceptionally fine plant that blooms in February–April with intense-blue flowers larger than those of the parent species; also white, pink and double forms.

H. nobilis (syn. *H. triloba*; Europe). The three-lobed leaves are distinctive and form short tufts up to 150mm (6in) tall with starry blue flowers in February–April.

H. transsilvanica (E. Europe). Very similar to *H. nobilis*, but larger in all its parts and with paler flowers.

Site Shady position that does not dry out too much in summer.
Soil Moisture-retaining leaf-mould is ideal; limy soils are best, but plants tolerate acid soils as well.
Propagation Divide in August or September, planting directly into peaty soil; or, if potted, keep in shaded frame over winter. Seed can be sown in March in leafy seed compost; seedlings vary.
Cultivation Plant beneath shrubs or in shady corner where they will not be disturbed. Make sure soil is moist at all times.

Right *Hepatica nobilis*

H. orientalis (of gardens), Lenten rose. Name is used by gardeners for a hybrid group involving several allied species. Height and spread about 450–600mm (1½–2ft). Much like taller, more upstanding versions of *H. niger*, but with more flowers per stem in shades of green, white, pink, red-purple, black-purple, often spotted within, in late winter to spring.

Site Part shade and some shelter from winter winds.
Soil Well-drained but not dry; enriched with organic matter.
Propagation Divide mature plants immediately after flowering. Sow seeds when ripe or as soon afterwards as

possible. Germination may take up to 1½ years and the young plants 2 years to flower.
Cultivation Plant immediately after flowering or in autumn, the earlier the better. Mulch with organic matter at least every other spring.

Hemerocallis

LILIACEAE   Day lily
Perennials from central Europe to eastern Asia. They form clumps of broad, grassy foliage and bear showy, lily-like flowers which last for one day only.

H. fulva (Europe to Siberia). Height 750mm–1m (2½–3¼ft); spread 600mm (2ft). Flowers 100mm (4in) long, buff-orange, in summer. Variety 'Kwanso' has double flowers.

H. lilioasphodelus (syn. *H. flava*; S. E. Europe to Siberia). Height 600mm (2ft) or more; spread about 450mm (1½ft).

Hesperis

CRUCIFERAE   Sweet rocket

Hardy herbaceous biennials and short-lived perennials native to Europe and Asia. The species listed is a cottage-garden plant ideal for herbaceous borders.

H. matronalis (S. Europe, W. Asia), sweet rocket, dame's violet. Height 600–900mm (2–3ft). Dark green, pointed leaves. Tall flower spikes in shades of purple or white in June–July, fragrant in evening.

Site Sun or light shade.
Soil Moist, sandy loam.
Propagation Sow seeds outdoors in April–May. Prick off seedlings into nursery beds in May–June and plant out in permanent positions in autumn, for flowering the following June. Plants can be divided in October–March. Self-sown seedlings will often appear but not necessarily with the same-colour flowers as those of their parent.
Cultivation Remove flowers when they have finished.

Right *Hesperis matronalis*

Above *Heuchera sanguinea*

Heuchera

SAXIFRAGACEAE   Alum root

Hardy herbaceous perennials native to North and Central America. Grown for their delicate spires of flowers.

H. sanguinea (Mexico, S. United States), coral bells. Perennial. Height 300–450mm (12–18in); spread 300mm (12in). Splendid herbaceous border plant with hummocks of heart-shaped, somewhat hairy leaves and wand-like spikes of tiny

bell-shaped red flowers in June–September. Varieties include 'Coral Cloud' (coral-red); 'Pluie de Feu' (crimson); 'Red Spangles' (scarlet); 'Scintillation' (pink).

Site Sun or light shade.
Soil Any garden soil that does not dry out in summer. On light land, mulching will help.
Propagation Mixed colours can be raised from seed sown in nursery rows in the open ground in June or July. Named sorts from division of the rootstock in spring.
Cultivation Planting is best done in the spring, newly planted stock being watered regularly. Drying out causes dwarfed stressed plants. Even established plants suffer in dry spells. Old foliage and flower stalks should be removed in the autumn and the clumps divided up every three or four years in the spring.
Pests and Diseases Mildew sometimes attacks the shoots and foliage.

Above *Hibiscus syriacus* 'Woodbridge'

Hibiscus

MALVACEAE

A large genus of annuals and evergreen and deciduous shrubs. Several of the less-hardy shrubby species are greenhouse favourites. That listed below is the familiar garden species.

H. syriacus (India, China). Hardy shrub. Height and spread about 1.8m (6ft). Rich-green, toothed leaves formed late in spring. Funnel-shaped flowers in white, pink, red, and purple bloom successively in August–October. Some good forms: 'Blue Bird' (large blue flowers); 'Hamabo' (large white flowers, flushed pale pink, with crimson centres); 'Duc de Brabant' (double magenta flowers); 'Woodbridge' (pink flowers with carmine centres).

Site Full sun, sheltered.
Soil Well-drained and reasonably fertile.
Propagation Take semi-hardwood cuttings, 100mm (4in) long, without flower-buds in early-mid July; raise in the greenhouse or cold frame.
Cultivation Plant mid- to late spring; plants are slow to become established.
Pruning If plants become too large, cut back some stems fairly hard in spring.

Hosta

LILIACEAE   Plantain lily

Perennials from eastern Asia, especially Japan. They form clumps of mostly large, handsome, often colourfully variegated leaves and wand-like stems bearing small, lily-like flowers, They make excellent ground-cover plants.

H. crispula (Japan). Height 750mm (2½ft); spread 450–600mm (1½–2ft). Leaves oval to lance-shaped, up to 200mm (8in) long, with broadly white-banded and waved margins. The 40–50mm (1½–2in) long lavender flowers open in late summer–autumn.

H. fortunei (Japan). Height 750–900mm (2½–3ft); spread 600mm (2ft) or more. Leaves greyish to pure green, oval with heart-shaped base, 125–200mm (5–8in) long. Flowers 40mm (1½in) long, lilac to violet, in July. Varieties include 'Albopicta' (yellow leaves with green borders when young); 'Aurea' (leaves totally yellow when young); *H. f. hyacinthina* (grey-green leaves, dark flowers).

H. lancifolia (Japan). Height about 450mm (1½ft); spread to 600mm (2ft). Leaves broadly lance-shaped, to 180mm (7in) long, slender pointed, glossy, and arching. Freely borne, deep-purple flowers, 40mm (1½in) long, expand in July–September.

H. plantaginea (China). Height and spread about 600mm (2ft). Leaves oval, up to 250mm (10in) long, lustrous pale green. Fragrant, pure-white, trumpet-shaped flowers, 100mm (4in) long, expand in autumn. *H. p. grandiflora* has larger flowers and longer leaves; 'Royal Standard' is similar but flowers in August–September.

H. sieboldiana (Japan). Height about 600mm (2ft); spread 900mm (3ft) or more. Leaves oval, 250–375mm (10–15in) long, glaucous and prominently veined. Pale lilac flowers, 40–50mm (1½–2in) long, open in summer but partly obscured by the leaves. *H. s. elegans* has leaves more intensely glaucous and somewhat corrugated.

H. tardiflora (Japan). Effectively a smaller *H. lancifolia* (q.v.), but flowering a little later.

H. undulata (Japan). Height and spread about 600mm (2ft). Leaves to 175mm (7in) long, wavy elliptic, mid-green, with white markings. Lilac-coloured flowers, 50mm (2in) long, expand in August. Varieties include 'Albomarginata' (white-margined leaves); 'Erromena' (rich green leaves, lavender-coloured flowers); 'Univittata' (leaves with central white zone).

H. ventricosa (E. Asia). Height 900mm (3ft); spread about 600mm (2ft). Leaves broadly ovate-cordate to 225mm (9in) or more long, deep glossy green. Deep violet flowers about 50mm (2in) long open in July–August. Varieties include 'Aureomaculata' (leaves with yellow centres); 'Variegata' (leaves boldly yellow-margined).

Site Part or dappled shade.
Soil Moisture-retentive but not saturated; humus-rich.
Propagation Divide established clumps in autumn or spring. Sow seeds under glass in early spring. Seedlings of variegated forms do not come true to type.

Cultivation Plant autumn to spring. Mulch with organic matter every other spring.
Pests and Diseases Slugs and snails attack leaves; rabbits eat shoots.

Below *Hosta undulata* 'Albomarginata' (left), 'Univittata' (right)

Hyacinthus

LILIACEAE   Hyacinth

Bulbous perennials from the central and eastern Mediterranean. Each bulb produces several strap-shaped, channelled leaves and one or more robust stems bearing showy, six-petalled, fragrant bell-flowers.

H. orientalis (E. Europe), common hyacinth. Height about 300mm (1ft); spread 230mm (9in). Flower-spikes usually solitary with dense blooms of mauve-purple to blue, in spring. Parent of the popular Dutch hybrids, including 'Jan Bos' (red); 'Lady Derby' (shell pink); 'Pink Pearl' (deep pink); 'City of Haarlem' (primrose yellow); 'L'Innocence' (pure white); 'Amethyst' (lilac-mauve); 'Delft Blue' (porcelain blue); 'King of the Blues' (deep indigo blue); these flower from mid-December to May. 'Albulus' (S. France) is the so-called Roman hyacinth, with several small flower spikes to each bulb, usually in blue or white.

Site Best in sun, though part shade is tolerated.
Soil Well-drained; the richer the better.
Propagation Separate offsets when dormant.

Cultivation Plant in autumn, the sooner the better. When a small clump forms, lift, separate, and re-plant.
Pests and Diseases Occasionally attacked by the diseases hyacinth yellows, fire, and virus.

Below *Hyacinthus orientalis* 'Pink Pearl'

Right *Hydrangea aspera sargentiana*

Hydrangea

HYDRANGEACEAE

A genus of handsome summer- and autumn-flowering, deciduous and evergreen shrubs or small trees and climbers native to North and South America and southern and eastern Asia.

H. arborescens (E. United States). Vigorous, hardy species of loose bushy habit. Height 1.5–3m (5–10ft). Leaves oval or

roundish 75–175mm (3–7in) long. Plant is usually represented by variety 'Grandiflora', with showy, long-stalked globular heads of creamy-white sterile flowers, 100mm (4in) or more across. Excellent in cold areas.

H. aspera (Himalaya, W. China). Height and spread up to 3.5m (12ft). Variable species with bristly-hairy young shoots; handsome large, green leaves, white-hairy beneath, 100–250mm (4–10in) long and up to 100mm (4in) wide. Flat-topped flower-heads up to 200mm (8in) across, with blue or purple fertile flowers surrounded by pink or white ray florets. *H. a. sargentiana* is a good variety. (*H. villosa* (q.v.) is now united botanically with *H. aspera*.)

H. macrophylla (China, Japan), common hydrangea. This species is usually represented by the two major groups – the Hortensias and the Lacecaps. Hortensia Group (mop-headed hydrangeas). Familiar shrubs of garden origin, usually 1.2–2m (4–6ft) high and wide, more if shaded. Excellent in maritime areas. Large globular heads of sterile florets, white-pink, red, blue or a mixture of these. (Blue shades are not possible in alkaline soils.) Of many cultivars, the following are most reliable. 'Altona' (large, rose-pink, 'blueing' well when treated); 'Ami Pasquier' (dwarf habit, crimson); 'Deutschland' (deep pink, and good autumn leaf colour); 'Générale Vicomtesse de Vibraye' (extremely hardy, vivid pink or clear blue according to soil); 'Mme E. Mouillière' (best white mop-head, perpetual-flowering).

Lacecap Group. Shrubs of similar size to Hortensias but with lace-like flat heads of small, fertile flowers surrounded by marginal ray florets in varying shades depending on soil acidity. Lacecaps are better than mop-heads for natural plantings. Best examples: 'Blue Wave' (bold leaves and large, vivid gentian-blue ray florets in acid soils, but needs some shade); 'Mariesii' (rose-pink or pale-blue ray florets); 'White Wave' (syn. 'Mariesii Alba', pearl-white ray flowers freely produced in open sites).

H. paniculata (China, Japan). Ultimately tree-like shrubs with semi-arching habit to 3.5m (12ft) or more with oval leaves 75–150mm (3–6in) long. Variety 'Grandiflora' is one of the most spectacular hardy garden shrubs, with massive pyramidal panicles of white sterile florets fading to purple-pink (largest blooms produced by spring pruning, feeding, and mulching). Successful in cold localities.

H. petiolaris (Japan, Korea), climbing hydrangea. Popular self-clinging deciduous climber for tree trunks and walls. Height 14m (46ft) and more. Older stems have attractive dark brown, shredding bark. Leaves finely toothed and broadly ovate, 40–100mm (1½–4in) long. Flat flower-heads 150–250mm (6–10in) across with marginal sterile white florets opening in June.

H. quercifolia (S.E. United States), oak-leaved hydrangea. Handsome species, 1.2m (4ft) high and wide. Notable for large scalloped leaves which colour subtle shades of purple, crimson, or orange in autumn. Round-topped, pyramidal white flower-panicles, 100–250mm (4–10in) long, in June–September.

H. serrata (Japan, S. Korea). Hardy, variable small shrub. Height and spread 1m (3¼ft). Leaves lanceolate, 50–150mm (2–6in) long. Flower heads mainly of lacecap type, 75–150mm (3–6in) across, and freely produced. Varieties: 'Blue Bird' (brilliant blue on acid soils, red-purple on chalk); 'Preziosa' (small mop-heads deep-pink shaded crimson by autumn, purple-tinted leaves).

H. villosa (W. China). Beautiful shade-tolerant, spreading shrub; is now classified as a form of *H. aspera*. Height up to 3m (10ft); spread up to 3.5m (12ft). Elegant lanceolate grey-green leaves up to 150mm (6in) long. Flower-heads of lacecap type, lilac-blue in late summer. Excellent on chalk soils.

Above *Hydrangea villosa*

Site Most species need a sheltered north- or west-facing wall and a moist root-run. Some shade from hot sun desirable in dry areas; large-leaved species best in dappled shade or wooded areas.

Soil Any fertile garden type. Very chalky soils produce chlorosis (yellowing of foliage) unless shrubs are generously manured and mulched.

Propagation Semi-ripe cuttings of most species and cultivars root readily in shaded cold frame in summer; pot on; overwinter under glass.

Cultivation Plant from containers in early autumn or spring. Protect autumn-planted shrubs for first and second winter except in favoured maritime areas. Mulch and feed older plants after pruning.

Pruning With *H. macrophylla* (Hortensias and Lacecaps), when spring frosts cease remove dead flower-heads and cut robust stems that have flowered back to strong healthy buds. With older plants remove thin, weak shoots and old woody growths to ground level in spring. With *H. paniculata* and *H. arborescens*, prune back to two pairs of buds in February.

Pests and Diseases Slugs and snails destroy young shoots in moist places in spring. Botrytis and mildew may attack young plants under glass.

Hypericum

GUTTIFERAE   St John's wort

A large genus containing annuals, perennials, shrubs and small trees native to temperate regions and to mountains in the tropics. The garden species listed are characterised by saucer-shaped yellow flowers with central clusters of prominent stamens.

H. calycinum (S.E. Europe, Asia Minor), rose of Sharon. Evergreen. Height 300mm (12in) tall; spreads by tough, wiry stolons. Flowers in June–September. Good ground-cover in sun or shade.

H. × *inodorum* 'Elstead' (*H. elatum* of gardens). Semi-evergreen. Height 900mm–1.2m (3–4ft); spread 900mm (3ft). Rounded flowers with many long stamens in July–August; orange and red egg-shaped fruits.

H. patulum (China) 'Hidcote'. Almost evergreen. Height to 1.8m (6ft); spread 1.2m (4ft). Large flowers, 75mm (3in) wide, in abundance in July–August. Hardy except in severe winters.

Site Sun; *H. calycinum* will also thrive in shade.

Soil Any, including chalky; preferably not too rich.

Propagation By semi-hardwood cuttings 75mm (3in) long in August, under cover. Divide *H. calycinum* in spring.

Cultivation Plant in autumn or spring (*H. calycinum* at any time from autumn to spring, but site it carefully as it is invasive).

Pruning Remove dead and weak growth in spring.

Pests and Diseases *H.* × *inodorum* 'Elstead' may be infected by rust fungus.

Below *Hypericum patulum* 'Hidcote'

Iberis

CRUCIFERAE   Candytuft

A group of easily grown annuals, perennials, and more-or-less evergreen sub-shrubs that flower for long periods in spring and summer. They are useful for the rock garden.

I. amara (Britain). Hardy annual, 300–375mm (12–15in) tall. Fragrant white flowers in mid-summer.

I. gibraltarica (Gibraltar, North Africa). Semi-evergreen sub-shrub, 250mm (10in) tall, of doubtful hardiness. Bears dense-packed heads of pale mauve flowers in April–May.

I. saxatilis (C. and S. Europe). Evergreen sub-shrub. Slow-growing miniature, 75mm (3in) tall. Dark green leaves. White flower-heads in May–July. A slow grower.

I. sempervirens (S. Europe). A comparatively vigorous plant with woody stems, evergreen leaves, and heads of white flowers in May–June. Its smaller cultivars are to be preferred: 'Little Gem' (white, 150mm (6in), of compact habit); 'Snowflake' (white, mat-forming, to 250mm (10in) high).

I. umbellata (S. Europe). Hardy annual. Height 150–400mm (6–16in). Leaves narrow and pointed. Flowers white or pinkish purple in June–July or later. 'Dwarf Fairy Mixed' has white, lavender, pink and red flowers.

Site Sunny, well-drained; best to allow plants to cascade down a wall or over a rock.
Soil Most tolerated provided there is good drainage.
Propagation *I. gibraltarica* and *I. saxatilis* are increased by greenwood cuttings from April to August; soft cuttings of *I. sempervirens* and its named cultivars from June to August and inserted in frame.
Cultivation Dead-head regularly candytufts grown for their blooms; this will extend flowering period.
Pruning Cut the plant back to keep it within bounds; remove dead wood in spring.

Below *Iberis umbellata* 'Dwarf Fairy Mixed'

Above *Ilex aquifolium* 'Pyramidalis'

Ilex

AQUIFOLIACEAE   Holly

A large family of evergreen and deciduous trees and shrubs of world-wide distribution. The hardy evergreen species make small or medium-sized trees or large shrubs, handsome in foliage (often variegated) and berry (on female plants). Many make excellent hedges or screens. Male and female flowers are usually borne on separate plants in spring; plant both sexes to ensure berries.

I. × altaclarensis (garden origin), broad-leaved or Highclere holly. Vigorous hybrid forming large spreading shrub or tree up to 10m (33ft) or more high. Large evergreen leaves with few spines. Excellent for screening; faster-growing than *I. aquifolium*. Notable cultivars: 'Golden King' (superb variegated evergreen with gold-margined, oval leaves and bright-red berries – female in spite of its name); 'Hodginsii' (vigorous male with purple young stems and leaves up to 100mm (4in) long).

I. aquifolium (Europe, including Britain, W. Asia), common holly. Favourite native hardy evergreen, usually makes large, dense, pyramidal shrub or small tree up to 10m (33ft) or more. Dark, glossy, green, wavy, and spiny leaves. Berries usually red, 6mm ($\frac{1}{4}$in) in diameter. Along with yew, makes perhaps the finest of all evergreen hedges. Many handsome cultivars: 'Argenteo-Marginata' (silver, broadly ovate leaves conspicuously wide-margined, female); 'Golden Queen' (leaves with bold, irregular gold margins, male); 'J. C. van Tol' (syn. 'Polycarpa', dark green, oblong-ovate leaves, bright red berries); 'Pyramidalis' (conical habit, green stems, smaller entire, pointed leaves, free-fruiting); 'Pyramidalis Fructuluteo' (bright yellow fruits).

Site Open sun or shady sites under other trees. Hollies tolerate seaside exposure and urban conditions. Variegated cultivars make striking lawn specimens.
Soil Moist, loamy, fertile, well-drained preferred.
Propagation By semi-ripe cuttings with 'heel' in late summer in cold frame or propagator.
Cultivation Root-balled specimens, if well rooted, transplant readily in October–May. Container-grown shrubs planted at any time. Water well in spring and summer. Mulch generously to aid re-establishment. Dryness at the roots may cause leaf-drop.
Pruning Straggly or overgrown specimens may be cut back severely in April or May. Trim hedges in August.
Pests and Diseases Leaf miners may disfigure foliage. Leaf spot may occur.

Impatiens

BALSAMINACEAE

A large genus of annuals, perennials, and soft shrubs native mainly to warmer regions of Africa, Asia and Europe. One showy species has become popular for summer bedding and for hanging basket.

I. wallerana (syn. *I. holstii*, *I. sultanii*; Mozambique, Tanzania), busy lizzie. Height 600mm (2ft); spread 300mm (1ft). Smooth, bright-green leaves and fleshy, translucent stems. Five-petalled flowers, 25–50mm (1–2in) across in April–October. Many dwarf cultivars available in red, orange, pink, salmon, violet, white, and striped. Among best: 'Futura', 'Grand Prix', 'Imp Mixed', 'Novette', 'Rosette', 'Super Elfin' (all mixed varieties); 'Blitz' (vermilion); 'Tangleglow' (tangerine orange); 'Zig-Zag' (striped).

Site Sheltered spot in sun or light shade.
Soil Well-drained.
Propagation Sow seed in gentle heat in March–April; prick out the seedlings into boxes; harden off before planting out at beginning of June (late May in warm areas). Take non-flowering tip cuttings, 75–100mm (3–4in) long, in April–September; root in pots; pinch out growing tips to promote bushy growth.
Cultivation Discard old plants or overwinter at 7°C (45°F).
Pests and Diseases Aphids and slugs may attack plants.

Right *Impatiens wallerana* mixed

Above *Incarvillea delavayi*

Incarvillea

BIGNONIACEAE

Hardy herbaceous perennials, native to China and Tibet, prized for their exotic blooms.

I. delavayi (W. China, Tibet). Height 300–450mm (1–½ft). Clumps of long, divided, dark-green, glossy leaves give rise to short stems which support brilliant rose-red, trumpet-shaped flowers, 75mm (3in) long, in May–June.

I. mairei (syn. *I. grandiflora brevipes*; China). Height and spread 300mm (1ft). Clumps of rounded, glossy, green leaves surmounted by large rose-red, trumpet-shaped flowers, 100mm (4in) long, in May–June.

Site Sheltered and sunny; not a frost pocket.
Soil Light but rich; wet winter soils cause roots to rot.
Propagation Sow seed in trays in a frame in spring; when first rough leaves appear, grow seedlings on individually in pots; plant out following year.
Cultivation Plant in spring, if possible using pot-grown specimens. Remove dead or decaying foliage in autumn. Give a light dressing of dried bracken over the roots in colder districts.
Pests and Diseases Slugs are a menace in early spring.

Ipheion

LILIACEAE

Bulbous perennials from South America. The species listed here has ribbon-like leaves and comparatively large, star-shaped flowers with six petals, and makes an attractive addition to the rock garden.

I. uniflorum (syn. *Brodiaea uniflora*, *Triteleia uniflora*; Argentina, Uruguay). Leaves pale to greyish-green, smelling of onions when bruised. Milky-blue flowers, 40mm (1½in) wide, carried singly on stems, 150mm (6in) long, in late spring (sometimes also in autumn or winter). Varieties 'Violacea' and 'Wisley Blue' have purple-blue blooms.

Site Full sun preferred; part shade tolerated.
Soil Well-drained, moderately fertile.
Propagation Separate offsets or divide clumps when dormant.
Cultivation Plant in early autumn.
Pests and Diseases Occasionally eaten by mice and slugs.

Below *Ipheion uniflorum* 'Violacea'

Above *Iris laevigata*

Ipomoea

CONVOLVULACEAE

Annual and perennial shrubs and climbing plants with large, silky, funnel-shaped flowers.

I. purpurea (syn. *Convolvulus major, C. purpurea, Pharbitis purpurea*; American tropics). Height up to 2.5m (8¼ft); spread up to 1m (3¼ft). Fast-growing twining plant. Leaves light green and lanceolate on thin, strong stems. Flowers trumpet-shaped and carried very freely in shades of red, pink, purple, and blue.

I. tricolor (syn. *I. violacea, Pharbitis tricolor*; American tropics), morning glory. Annual. Height up to 3m (10ft); spread 600mm–1m (2–3¼ft). Strongly twining stems. Large, funnel-shaped flowers, furled in bud, in shades of blue and white. Varieties include 'Heavenly Blue' (large, clear sky-blue); 'Sapphire Cross' and 'Flying Saucers' (blue and white striped).

Site At base of warm, sunny wall or fence.

Soil Ordinary or even poor garden soil.

Propagation Sow in spring in greenhouse or propagator at 15°C (60°F), with two seeds to a 90mm (3½in) pot; plant out after last frost. Alternatively, sow seeds where they are to flower in May.

Cultivation Train plants up twiggy sticks or netting to start them climbing. Pull up and discard plants after flowering.

Pests and Diseases Young plants prone to red-spider mite attack, particularly in greenhouse; aphids may also affect young shoots.

Right *Impomoea tricolor* 'Heavenly Blue'

Iris

IRIDACEAE

Hardy and half-hardy herbaceous plants of world-wide distribution, with creeping tuberous or bulbous rootstocks, distinctive sword-shaped or grassy leaves, and in many cases very showy flowers.

I. chaemaeiris (S. Europe). Perennial, dwarf bearded type. Height up to 225mm (9in); spread 150mm (6in). Short, sword-shaped green leaves. Large blue, purple, white, or yellow flowers. Excellent for the rock garden.

I. danfordiae (Turkey). Perennial, bulbous type. Height and spread 150mm (6in). Narrow, grassy leaves preceded by naked, bright-yellow flowers produced just above ground level in January–February.

I. germanica (S. Europe), German or bearded iris. Perennial, intermediate bearded type. Height 600mm–1m (2–3¼ft); spread 600mm (2ft). Large, green, sword-like leaves arise from thick fleshy rhizome. Large, bright-purple flowers 75mm (3in) across produced on stout stems in May–early June. Hundreds of hybrid cultivars, including 'Blue Rhythm'; 'Cliffs of Dover' (white); 'Dream Castle' (orchid-pink); 'Goldilocks' (yellow); 'Tarn Hows' (brown).

I. histrioides (Turkey). Perennial, bulbous type. Height and spread 150mm (6in). Short, stocky, bright-blue flowers near soil level in January–February. Grassy foliage follows the flowers. Usually represented by form 'Major'.

I. kaempferi (Japan), clematis-flowered iris. Perennial, beardless type. Height 300–600mm (1–2ft); spread 300mm (1ft). Clumps of narrow, grassy foliage. Broad-spreading deep-purple or violet flowers in June–July. Must have moist conditions. Good cultivars include 'Blue Heaven'; 'Man-

darin' (purple-violet); 'Landscape at Dawn' (rose-lavender).
I. laevigata (Japan, Korea). Perennial, beardless type. Height
450–600mm (1½–2ft); spread 300mm (1ft). Upright, narrow,
sword-like foliage similar to that of *I. kaempferi* but lacking
prominent mid-rib. Flowers, usually soft blue, in June. True
aquatic, will grow in up to 225mm (9in) of water on
marginal shelf of a pool. Varieties include 'Colchesteri'
(violet and white); 'Rose Queen' (pink); 'Snowdrift' (white).
I. ochroleuca (Turkey). Perennial, beardless type. Height up
to 1.5m (5ft); spread 600mm (2ft). Upright, sword-like
leaves with bluish bloom. Bold yellow and white flowers in
June–July. Likes moist conditions.
I. reticulata (Turkey to Caucasus). Perennial, bulbous type.
Height and spread 100mm (4in). Deep violet-purple flowers
produced in February–March, just ahead of the long, grassy
green foliage. Varieties include 'Cantab' (light blue); 'J.S.
Dijt' (purple); 'Joyce' (hybrid, sky blue).
I. sibirica (C. Europe to Russia). Perennial, beardless type.
Height 900mm (3ft); spread 300mm (1ft). Slender, grassy
foliage. Small, bright-blue flowers in June–July. Likes a
damp position. Varieties include 'Caesar' (purple); 'Perry's
Blue' (light blue); 'Snow Queen' (white).
I. unguicularis (syn. *I. stylosa*; Algeria, Greece, Syria),
Algerian iris. Perennial, beardless type. Height 450–600mm
(1½–2ft); spread 300mm (1ft). Narrow grassy leaves. Beauti-
ful lilac or blue flowers in November–March. Must have dry
conditions. Useful for cutting.
I. xiphioides (Pyrenees), English iris. Perennial, bulbous
type. Height 300–600mm (1–2ft); spread 150mm (6in).
Upright, narrow green leaves. Showy flowers in July–
August, white, blue, or lavender, useful for cutting. Varieties

include 'Blue Giant' (purplish-blue); 'La Nuit' (reddish
purple); 'Mont Blanc' (white).
I. xiphium (S. Europe, North Africa), Spanish iris. Perennial,
bulbous type. Height 300–600mm (1–2ft); spread 150mm
(6in). Upright habit and narrow green leaves. Very showy
white, yellow, or blue flowers in May–June. Popular for
cutting. Varieties include 'Blue Angel'; 'Cajanus' (yellow);
'L'Innocence' (white). The Dutch irises, derived from *I.
xiphium* and *I. tingitana*, are bulbous, have grassy foliage
and upright habit, and are grown extensively for cutting.
Varieties include 'Jeanne d'Arc' (white); 'Golden Harvest'
(yellow); 'Imperator' (blue).

Site Open, sunny for all except *I. unguicularis*, which must be grown in a sheltered spot alongside a wall.

Soil Varies according to species. All tolerate varying acidity or alkalinity except *I. kaempferi*, a lime-hater, and *I. germanica*, an acid-hater. Except for those requiring moist conditions, soil must be free-draining.

Propagation The species can be propagated from seed sown in friable soil in cold frame when ripe or as soon as possible. Rhizomatous irises increased by pieces of vigorous young rhizome removed from mature plants immediately after flowering. Clump-forming irises can be divided in winter months.

Cultivation Bulbous species planted in autumn together with the clump-forming kinds. Rhizomatous varieties are planted immediately after flowering, the rhizomes resting level with surrounding soil. Regular division of clumps of all kinds is desirable.

Pests and Diseases Iris sawfly can be a nuisance. Bulbous species sometimes attacked by ink diseases; leaf spots and bulb and rhizome rot may also occur.

Below *Iris* Dutch hybrid

Jasminum

OLEACEAE   Jasmine

Mostly evergreen, climbing and trailing shrubby flowering plants native to the temperate and tropical regions. In Britain two species are grown in gardens, though one is not completely hardy. The flowers are tubular, ending in five spreading, petal-like segments.

J. nudiflorum (China), winter jasmine. Hardy, deciduous, rambling plant. Height 3–4.5m (10–15ft) against a wall. Bright-yellow flowers in November–February.

J. officinale (Iran, India, China), common white jasmine. Semi-evergreen climber up to 9m (30ft) high for training against a wall. White flowers 25mm (1in) long, in clusters, heavily fragrant, in June–October. Hardy in sheltered gardens, though young stems killed back in severe winters.

Site Sheltered, sunny for *J. officinale*, any east-facing for *J. nudiflorum* (though it flowers best in sun).

Soil Any, well-drained.

Propagation By semi-hardwood nodal cuttings of *J. officinale* in July–August under cover. By rooted layers of *J. nudiflorum* in autumn.

Cultivation Plant spring, and provide supports; *J. nudiflorum* will need regular tying in as it is not a true climber.

Pruning *J. officinale* can be left unpruned, but remove some of oldest, poorly flowering growth in spring. Cut back flowered sideshoots of *J. nudiflorum* to buds within about 75mm (3in) of base of each shoot in early spring; cut out old, weak stems.

Pests and Diseases
Occasionally greenfly are a nuisance. Yellow mottling is due to virus disease.

Below *Jasminum nudiflorum*

Above *Juniperus sabina* 'Tamariscifolia'

Juniperus

CUPRESSACEAE   Juniper

Coniferous evergreen trees and shrubs from northern temperate regions, the latter including North America, Europe, North Africa, China, and Japan. Their size and habit range from prostrate and creeping to tall, columnar trees 30m (100ft) or more high; the foliage colour can be green, grey, blue or yellow. The plants listed are small versions of various species; they are useful particularly for ground-cover and for the rock garden.

J. chinensis (China) 'Blaauw'. Height and spread 900mm (3ft); cylindrical shape, blue-grey foliage. Good variety: 'Old Gold'. Height 1.2m (4ft); spread 2.1m (7ft). Upright but wide-spreading branches, deep yellow foliage, bronze-gold in winter.

J. communis (Britain) 'Compressa'. Dwarf form of common juniper. Slow-growing to 600–900mm (2–3ft) after 10 years; grey-blue foliage.

J. sabina (S. Europe) 'Tamariscifolia'. Height 900mm (3ft); spread 2m (6½ft). Dense prostrate habit, the stems building up in layers; foliage grey when young.

J. virginiana (North America) 'Grey Owl'. Dwarf form of pencil cedar. Height 900mm–1.2m (3–4ft); spread slightly more. Silver-grey foliage. Pencil-shaped cultivar 'Skyrocket', ultimately reaches 5m (16½ft) high with 300mm (12in) spread; blue-grey foliage.

Site Sun preferred, but will tolerate light shade.

Soil Any reasonably well-drained; junipers like chalk.

Propagation By heel cuttings 50–75mm (2–3in) long in summer or early autumn under cover in mixture of peat and sand; low-growing kinds by layering in autumn.

Cultivation Plant early in autumn or mid-spring; do not spread out root-ball. Water well in dry weather. Spray foliage daily and shelter from strong wind until established.

Kalmia

ERICACEAE

Hardy evergreen (occasionally deciduous) shrubs from North America, thriving in the same conditions as rhododendrons. They are slow-growing with attractive and unusually shaped flowers in spring or summer.

K. angustifolia 'Rubra', sheep laurel. Small evergreen shrub. Height 600–900mm (2–3ft); spread 900–1.2m (3–4ft). Leaves arranged in threes. Deep rosy-red, saucer-shaped flowers in clusters in May–July. Poisonous to grazing animals.

K. latifolia, calico bush, mountain laurel. Evergreen shrub. Height 1.8m (6ft) or more; spread 1.5m (5ft) or more. Leaves 125mm (5in) long. Bright pink, parasol-shaped flowers, 25mm (1in) wide, in clusters cover bush in May–June.

Site sheltered, sunny or a little dappled shade.
Soil Acid, peaty, well-drained but moisture-retentive.
Propagation By layering in October (but plants are slow to root). By seed under cover in early spring.
Cultivation Plant in September–October or April–May; allow plants room to spread without being crowded.

Above Kerria japonica 'Pleniflora'

Kerria

ROSACEAE   Jew's mallow

A one-species genus, native to China. The plant is a deciduous shrub that makes an attractive, early flowering bush.

K. japonica. Height 1.2–1.8m (4–6ft); spread 1.5–2.1m (5–7ft). Stems and leaves bright green. Saucer-shaped flowers, deep yellow, 40mm (1½in) wide, and solitary, freely produced in May. The form 'Pleniflora' (syn. 'Flore Pleno', bachelor's buttons) has fully double flowers, resembling deep yellow rosettes, 40–50mm (1½–2in) wide; it is much taller and less broad than the species and its habit is rather ungainly.

Site Best against walls or fences in sun or shade.
Soil Sandy or otherwise well-drained.
Propagation By division in autumn; remove rooted suckers.
Cultivation Plant in suitable weather in autumn–spring. Mulch in spring.

Pruning Cut out old flowered stems of 'Pleniflora' either to ground level or back to new shoots lower on the stem, when flowering has finished; remove weak shoots and dead growth.
Pests and Diseases Occasionally capsid bugs damage leaves; twig blight causes die-back of shoots.

Above Kalmia angustifolia 'Rubra'

Kniphofia

LILIACEAE   Red-hot poker, torch lily

Perennials from southern and eastern Africa and Madagascar. Those cultivated in Britain are reasonably hardy and are clump-forming, with tufts of narrow, tapering leaves and poker-like spikes of colourful flowers.

K. caulescens (S. Africa). Height 1m (3¼ft); spread about 1.2m (4ft). Massive evergreen perennial forming clumps of thick, trunk-like stems topped by arching, grey-green, strap-shaped leaves up to 900mm (3ft) long. Dense spikes of salmon-red buds open to yellow flowers about 25–30mm (1–1¼in) long in autumn.

K. galpinii (S. Africa). Height about 750mm (2½ft); spread 450mm (1½ft). Grassy green leaves in dense clumps. In autumn, bright reddish-orange, 25mm (1in) long flowers expand in loose spikes.

K. uvaria (syn. *K. alooides*; S. Africa). Height 1.2–1.5m (4–5ft); spread 1–1.2m (3¼–4ft). Most commonly grown and hardiest red-hot poker species. Dense spikes of scarlet buds and yellow, 30–40mm (1¼–1½in) long flowers open in early autumn above robust clumps of strap-shaped leaves. Variety 'Nobilis' (syns. 'Grandiflora', 'Maxima') is taller and earlier-flowering.

Hybrids. Many hybrid cultivars are now available in a variety of heights, leaf-widths, and flower-colours. Among the best are 'Atlanta' (resembling *K. uvaria*, with greyish leaves, flowering early to mid-summer; the similar 'Royal Standard' follows on); 'Buttercup' (yellow); 'Fiery Fred' (900mm (3ft) high, fiery-orange, opening in summer); 'Maid of Orléans' (ivory white); 'Little Maid' (yellow-tipped ivory); 'Timothy' (pink).

Site All need full sun but must be sheltered from cold winds.
Soil Moisture-retentive but preferably well-drained and fertile.
Propagation Divide established clumps in spring. Seedlings of cultivars do not come true to type – but may produce interesting colour combinations.
Cultivation Plant in spring, just as weather warms up, or in early autumn. In very cold areas some protection with straw or bracken is worthwhile.

Right Kniphofia 'Royal Standard'

Kochia

CHENOPODIACEAE   Summer cypress

Annual and perennial herbaceous plants native to Europe; Asia, Australia, and Africa. The most commonly grown species, listed below, is popular as a summer bedding plant. *K. scoparia* (S. Europe, Asia). Half-hardy annual. Height 600–900mm (2–3ft); spread 600mm (2ft). Narrow, pointed leaves and small green, insignificant flowers. Variety 'Tricophylla' (burning bush) has light green foliage which turns to a bronzy scarlet in autumn; 'Childsii' is more compact; 'Acapulco Silver' has light green leaves splashed with silver.

Site Full sun preferred.
Soil Preferably fairly light and free-draining.
Propagation Seeds can be sown indoors in March and hardened off before planting out in May; or they can be sown outside in March–April if the weather is reasonable; thin out to 600mm (2ft) apart, or use as dot plants between other summer bedding.
Cultivation Plants may need staking in windy areas.

Right *Kochia scoparia* 'Tricophylla'

Kolkwitzia

CAPRIFOLIACEAE   Beauty bush

A genus of a single species – a hardy deciduous shrub of upright habit from China, with attractive summer flowers. *K. amabilis*. Height and spread about 2.4m (8ft). Stems have peeling bark, attractive in winter. Pink and yellow foxglove-shaped flowers in May–June cover arching growth. Variety 'Pink Cloud' is improved form, with more flowers.

Site Sunny.
Soil Any except waterlogged; does well on chalk.
Propagation By suckers in autumn; or by semi-hardwood cuttings under cover summer.
Cultivation Plant in autumn or spring. Mulch every spring.
Pruning Occasionally remove from established plants some of the oldest flowered branches after flowering, low on plant.

Below *Kolkwitzia amabilis* 'Pink Cloud'

Laburnum

LEGUMINOSAE   Golden rain

Three species, from central and southern Europe and western Asia, and several hybrids and cultivars make up this genus of small but easily grown, spectacular, deciduous trees. Pods containing poisonous seeds follow the flowers. Removing them as soon as possible will extend the healthy lifespan of members of this relatively short-lived genus.

L. anagyroides (syn. *L. vulgare*; C. and S. Europe), common laburnum. Wide spreading, usually multi-stemmed shrubby tree. Height up to 10m (33ft); spread 4.5m (15ft). Leaves composed of three oval, green, downy leaflets 40–75mm (1½–3in) long beneath. Pendulous racemes, 150–250mm (6–10in), long of golden-yellow pea-flowers in late May–June. Useful in exposed coastal areas. Variety 'Aureum' has golden yellow leaves in summer.

L. × watereri (garden origin). Hybrid with dark, glossy leaves. Most garden-worthy of the genus, particularly its cultivar 'Vossii', of compact erect habit to 6m (20ft) with flower racemes up to 600mm (2ft) long, freely borne in June. Fortunately little seed is produced.

Site Sunny preferred. Several plants may be trained on supports to make a 'laburnum arch' or walk. 'Vossii' makes a superb lawn specimen.
Soil Well-drained, fertile; plants happy on chalk soil.
Propagation Species by seed sown outside as soon as ripe or in spring. Cultivars by budding in summer or grafting in spring on seedling rootstocks.
Cultivation Field-grown trees planted in November–March;

container-grown trees often available for out-of-season planting. Stake all firmly.
Pruning Thin out branches and laterals to keep an open-centre head as specimen develops. On laburnum arches, hard-prune laterals after flowering.
Pests and Diseases Canker may infect trunk and branches of older specimens.

Right, above *Laburnum × watereri*

Lagurus

GRAMINEAE   Hare's-tail grass

An annual grass with fluffy white seed-heads; suitable for drying.

L. ovatus (Europe). Hardy. Height 250–300mm (10–12in); spread 200mm (8in). Slender, silvery green leaves with rough, hairy surface. Rounded, white, fluffy seedheads carried on slender stalks above foliage throughout summer.

Site Open, in full sun.
Soil Any reasonably fertile.
Propagation Sow seed in late March–early April where plants are to grow; alternatively, sow in sheltered nursery row in August–September; thin to 200mm (8in) apart; plant out following April.
Cultivation Gather flower-heads for drying when fully expanded on warm, sunny day. Discard plants after flowering.

Right *Lagurus ovatus*

Above *Lamium maculatum*

Lamium

LABIATAE   Dead-nettle

Annuals and herbaceous perennials, native to Europe and Asia, grown by gardeners mainly as ground cover.

L. galeobdolon (now more correctly *Lamiastrum galeobdolon*; Europe, including Britain), yellow archangel. Perennial. Height 300–450mm (1–1½ft). Spreads by vigorous creeping stems. Usually grown in the form 'Variegata', with nettle-like leaves marbled with silver-grey. Whorled spikes of bright yellow hooded flowers open in early summer. Vigorous, often rampant plant extremely useful in difficult dry and

(pink on cream); 'Red Ensign' and 'Royal Wedding' (white); 'Snoopea' (mixed); 'Winston Churchill' (crimson). ('Snoopea' is a low-growing variety with no tendrils and needs no support.)

L. rotundifolius (E. Europe, W. Asia), Persian everlasting pea. Perennial. Height 1.8m (6ft); spread 450mm (1½ft). Pairs of round, dark green leaflets. Clusters of long-lasting rose-pink flowers, 20–25mm (¾–1in) across, in June–August.

L. vernus (syn. *Orobus vernus*; Europe). Perennial. Height 300mm (1ft); spread 230mm (9in). Bushy species with pale green, ovate leaves in pairs. Rose-purple flowers 13mm (½in) across in April–May. Suitable for border or rock garden.

Site Full sun.
Soil Well-drained, but moisture-retentive and fertile.
Propagation Sow annual forms in January–March in heated greenhouse, or in April–May outdoors, or in September–October in cold frame. Pot indoor seedlings into 75mm (3in) pots when rooted and harden off before planting outside in April or early May. Soak seeds in water before sowing, or nick the seed coat with a sharp knife, to hasten germination. Sow seeds of perennials indoors in March. Pot up seedlings into 75mm (3in) pots and plant out in October after hardening off.
Cultivation Add compost or organic matter to soil before planting out. Pinch out plants when 150mm (6in) high to encourage side shoots. Support annual varieties with pea sticks or posts and wires. Pick flowers regularly for continuous flowering.
Pests and Diseases Slugs attack leaves; thrips and greenfly can also be a problem. Downy mildew, root rot, fusarium wilt, grey mould, powdery mildew and viruses may occur.

Below *Lathyrus odoratus* mixture

shady parts of the garden, but once established is difficult to remove.

L. maculatum (Europe, including Britain, North Africa, W. Asia). Perennial. Height 300–450mm (1–1½ft). Spreads by stolons. Coarse, nettle-like leaves with prominent silvery or white splashes. Broad, leafy spikes of hooded purple flowers throughout summer. Varieties include 'Aureum' (golden foliage); 'Beacon Silver' (silver foliage).

Site Very adaptable – grows in full sun, or part or dense shade.
Soil Ordinary garden soil; coloured-leaf forms will develop a brighter appearance on poorer soils.
Propagation Division and separation of stolons in September–March.
Cultivation Cut back severely each spring to promote colourful, vigorous growth.

Lathyrus

LEGUMINOSAE   Sweet pea, everlasting pea

Hardy annuals and herbaceous perennials native to Europe and Asia. They are mostly climbers with brightly coloured, scented flowers.

L. latifolius (Europe), everlasting pea. Perennial. Height 1.8–3m (6–10ft); spread 450mm (1½ft). Vigorous cottage-garden plant with dull green, ovate leaflets. Small pea flowers, 20mm (¾in) across, in June–September, in mixtures of white, pink, and purple. Suitable for training up a trellis or fence.

L. odoratus (Italy). Annual. Height 3m (10ft); spread 150–300mm (6–12in). Greyish green leaflets with tendrils on ends of leaf stalks. Scented flowers 30mm (1¼in) across in wide range of colours in June–September. Good varieties: 'Antique Fantasy Mixed' (strongly scented); 'Jet Set' and 'Knee High' (dwarf, mixed); 'Leamington' (lavender); 'Mrs R. Bolton' (pink); 'Noel Sutton' (blue); 'Princess Elizabeth'

Laurus

LAURACEAE

Aromatic, hardy, evergreen trees or shrubs from the Mediterranean region, the Azores, and the Canary Islands. The species listed has long been cultivated all over Britain. *L. nobilis*, bay laurel, sweet bay. Forms usually a dense, pyramidal bush up to 6m (20ft) or more high; often tree-like in mild coastal areas. Dark, glossy green leaves, ovate with wavy edges, 40–100mm (1½–4in) long and about 50mm (2in) wide; aromatic when crushed and much used as culinary herb. Small yellowish flowers in April. Subject to browning and die-back in hard winters. 'Aurea' is a golden-leaved form.

Site Sheltered, sunny site is necessary in colder inland areas. Makes an excellent clipped specimen for tub or patio planting. A good hedge in coastal areas.
Soil Well-drained, fertile.
Propagation Late summer cuttings, 100–150mm (4–6in) long, in cold frame or propagator.
Cultivation Plant from containers in spring. Ensure tub specimens have enough root space; pot on frequently; do not allow to dry out in summer.
Pruning Clip formal tub specimens to shape and trim hedges in April and August; with frost-damaged shoots on larger shrubs, cut back to sound wood in spring.

Below Laurus nobilis

Site Bright sun.
Soil Well-drained.
Propagation Take cuttings of non-flowering shoots in August; overwinter in cold frame; transplant to final site in March–April. Cuttings can also be rooted outdoors in September. Sow seed in April–June outdoors in cold frame.
Cultivation Plant in September–March. For growing as a hedge, plant 300mm (1ft) apart. Cut flowers for drying before they fully open; hang upside down to dry, in a cool place; they can be used to make lavender bags or pot-pourris.
Pruning Trim untidy plants in late summer or spring. Cut hedges in spring.
Pests and Diseases Cuckoo-spit-producing froghoppers may infest stems. Grey mould, leaf spot, and scab may occur.

Lavatera

MALVACEAE

Annuals, biennials, herbaceous perennials, and shrubs native to Europe, Asia, Australia, and California. Most have showy trumpet-shaped flowers and an erect, bushy habit. *L. arborea* (Britain), tree mallow. Biennial. Height 2m (6½ft) or more; spread 1m (3¼ft) or more. Erect plant with grey-green, downy, deeply lobed leaves. Pink, purple-veined flowers, 50mm (2in) across, carried on tall spires in July–August. Hardy only in mild seaside localities.
L. olbia (Mediterranean, Portugal). Shrub. Height 1–1.2m

Right Lavandula angustofolia

Lavandula

LABIATAE   Lavender

Hardy evergreen shrubs, native to Europe, well-loved for their fragrant, blue flowers that can be dried.
L. angustifolia (syn. *L. spica*, *L. officinalis*; Mediterranean), old English lavender. Perennial. Height 300–900mm (1–3ft); spread 450mm–1.2m (1½–4ft). Erect plant with silver, narrow, oblong leaves. Purple-blue flowers carried on spikes 65mm (2½in) long in June–September. Varieties include 'Alba' (white); 'Grappenhall' (tall and strong); 'Hidcote' (syn. 'Nana Atropurpurea', compact and free-flowering); 'Munstead' (popular variety readily available from seed); 'Twickel Purple' (long purple spikes).
L. stoechas (Mediterranean), French lavender. Perennial. Height and spread 300–600mm (1–2ft). Erect plant with grey-green, narrow, oblong leaves. Dark-purple flowers topped by purple bracts in 50mm (2in) long spikes in May–July. Less widely grown than other species; not fully hardy.

(3¼–4ft); spread 600mm (2ft). Bushy, upright plant with rich green, rounded or slightly lobed leaves and masses of purplish pink flowers 75mm (3in) wide. Blooms have two-lobed tips and open any time in July–November. Usually seen in its best form, 'Rosea', with bright-pink flowers.
L. trimestris (Mediterranean, Portugal). Annual. Height 1–1.2m (3¼–4ft); spread 600mm (2ft). Bushy, erect plant with rounded or slightly lobed leaves. Large, 100mm (4in) wide, rose-pink, trumpet-shaped flowers carried above and among leaves in July–October. Varieties include 'Silver Cup' (bright pink); 'Mont Blanc' (pure white). Good for cutting.

Site Bright sun; biennials and perennials survive winter more reliably in milder areas.
Soil Well-drained; lighter soils preferred; chalky soils tolerated. Too much manure causes excessive leaf growth.
Propagation Sow annuals outdoors where they are to grow in April or September; sow biennials outdoors in rows in May–June; transplant to final site in September. Take shoot-tip cuttings of perennials and short side-shoots of shrubs in propagator in spring or late summer.
Cultivation Plant container-grown shrubby species in spring. Stake annuals with twiggy branches when they are 100mm (4in) high. Pull up and discard annuals after flowering.
Pruning Cut back all stems on *L. olbia* and its varieties to within 300mm (1ft) of ground when shoots burst into growth in spring.
Pests and Diseases Leaf spot and rust may occur.

Above *Lavatera trimestris* 'Silver Cup'

Layia

COMPOSITAE Tidy-tips
Hardy annuals, native to North America, with daisy-like flowers.
L. elegans (California). Height 300–450mm (1–½ft); spread 250mm (10in). Thin, grey-green leaves with slight scent. Bright yellow flowers tipped with white, with yellow central disk, in June–October.

Site Full sun.
Soil Light, well-drained.
Propagation Sow seeds in flowering position in March–April; thin out to 250mm (10in) apart. Seed can also be sown in September in milder areas.
Cultivation Autumn-sown plants may need to be protected with cloches.

Below *Layia elegans*

Above *Leontopodium alpinum*

Leontopodium

COMPOSITAE   Edelweiss

A hardy herbaceous perennial that grows in alpine meadows throughout Europe. It makes a useful addition to the rock garden.

L. alpinum (Europe). Height up to 200mm (8in). Forms a clump of linear, woolly, grey-green leaves. Yellowish flowers emerge in June–August surrounded by woolly white bracts resembling petals.

L. 'Mignon'. Dwarf version of the above, with a good constitution, making a compact clump with 100mm (4in) flower stalks.

Site Sunny.
Soil Any good soil will suffice, but it must be well-drained.
Propagation By seed in January in seed compost; pot up in April; plant out in September

or following March. Divide the plants in spring as new growth begins.
Cultivation Species is light-demanding: do not let other plants overhang it.

Above *Leptospermum scoparium* 'Nichollsii'

Leptospermum

MYRTACEAE

Small-leaved evergreen shrubs from Australasia which are doubtfully hardy but are most attractive for their white, red, or pink, open flowers. They are not so widely available as other alpine shrubs.

L. humifusum (Tasmania). Small prostrate shrub up to 150mm (6in) high with deep-green leaves on reddish stems, clothed in May–June with many white flowers. Hardiest of the leptospermums.

L. scoparium 'Nanum' (New Zealand), tea-tree. Sub-alpine plant, but hardy outdoors only in favourable conditions. Forms miniature rounded bush, 300–900mm (1–3ft) high, of dark-green leaves, with mass of deep-pink flowers in summer. 'Nichollsii' is a good cultivar. (In cold areas it should be confined to the alpine house).

Site For *L. scoparium* 'Nanum' the warmest and most sheltered site that can be found; for *L. humifusum* a site in full sun.
Soil Well-drained, peaty.
Propagation Cuttings of ripe wood are taken in August and

inserted in cold frame. Seed can be sown in March in a good seed compost.
Cultivation Give annual top-dressing of nutrient-rich peat.
Pruning Remove any straggly branches in mid-spring.

Above *Leucojum aestivum*

Leucojum

AMARYLLIDACEAE   Snowflake

Bulbous perennials from western Europe to the Caucasus, and in Morocco and Algeria. Allied to the snowdrop, they have narrow leaves and bell-like flowers with all six petals of the same length.

L. aestivum (C. and S. Europe to Caucasus), summer snowflake. Height 300–450mm (1–1½ft); spread about 200mm (8in). Rich green, glossy, strap-shaped leaves provide a good foil for the white, green-tipped flowers. Each flower is about 25mm (1in) long and clusters of two to five open on each stem in late spring or early summer. Variety 'Gravetye Giant' is more robust, with somewhat larger flowers.

L. autumnale (Spain, Portugal, Sardinia, Corsica, N.W. Africa), autumn snowflake. Height 200mm (8in); spread about 65mm (2½in). Leaves grassy, developing after flowers. The white flowers, 13mm (½in) long, open in late summer–autumn, one or more at each stem tip.

L. vernum (C. Europe), spring snowflake. Height 150mm (6in) or more; spread about 100mm (4in), more after flowering. Leaves strap-shaped, short at flowering time. Flowers white with green tips, usually solitary but sometimes in pairs, 25mm (1in) long, in early spring.

Site *L. autumnale* needs sunny, sheltered position; others grow in partial shade.
Soil *L. autumnale* must have well-drained soil; the others really thrive only where it is moist; *L. aestivum* does well in the bog garden.
Propagation Separate clumps or remove offsets when dormant. Sow seeds when ripe; seedlings take several years to flower.
Cultivation Plant *L. autumnale* in late summer, earlier if possible. Plant others in autumn, the earlier the better.

Lewisia

PORTULACACEAE

A genus of popular semi-succulents from North America that make an important and colourful contribution to the rock garden. Only the species and hybrids that do well in the garden are listed here (many more, although perfectly hardy, are better in the alpine house).

L. columbiana (British Columbia). Height up to 300mm (12in). Rosette of flat, fleshy leaves gives rise to stems on which pale to bright pink flowers are borne loosely in May and continue through summer. Variety 'Rosea' has deeper pink flowers.

L. cotyledon (North America). Species variable in both leaf and flower; has given rise to many named forms and strains, varying in colour from white through to peach and apricot. Handsome broad, fleshy leaves support 225mm (9in) flower stems that in May carry a mass of flowers in panicles, some of which are distinctively striped with deeper colouring. Natural varieties include *L. c. heckneri* (toothed leaves and pink to deep-rose striped flowers); *L. c. howellii* (narrower, wavy leaves, crinkled at margins, and rich rose-pink flowers). Cultivars include 'Rose Splendour' (attractive rose-pink flowers); 'Sunset Strain' (mixture of pinks, apricots, oranges, yellows, and crimson).

L. leana (California, Oregon). Fleshy rootstock gives rise to many fleshy, grey-green leaves with 225mm (9in) wiry stems producing panicles of pale-pink, deep-veined flowers in June.

L. nevadensis (North America). Height 50–75mm (2–3in). Narrow leaves sprout from thick rootstock and die down early in season. Short-stemmed white flowers, veined green, in June–August.

L. rediviva (North America), bitter-root. Leaves wither as plant produces short-stemmed, large, pink or white flowers; it is no more than 50–75mm (2–3in) tall. One of the beauties of the genus, probably best cared for in the alpine house except in exceptionally warm, sheltered sites.

L. tweedyi (N.W. North America). Perhaps the finest lewisia. Clusters of fleshy leaves, 100–125mm (4–5in) long, emerge from stout rootstock together with flower stalks of the same length. Flower colour varies from yellowy pink mixed with apricot to salmon-pink and red; a white form is also available.

Site Full sun.
Soil Rich but well-drained scree. Lewisias are hungry plants; most are lime-haters.
Propagation Best method is by seed, sown when it is still sticky from the pod. Do not sow after end of August; if seed is still to hand by then, keep it to plant in spring. Seeds require some attention until established. Water when sun is off plants. Take care when watering from September onwards as lewisias resent winter damp. Cuttings can be taken in June–August and inserted in a sand frame, but the percentage take is low.
Cultivation Plant on their sides so that rosettes do not become waterlogged in winter. Lewisias need a rich diet and plenty of water up to flowering time. Thereafter they require less water, but in varying degrees: *L. columbiana cotyledon, leana* and *tweedyi* are evergreen and need water all the year round, but much less between September and February. *L. rediviva* should have water withdrawn immediately after flowering and be given a summer baking; start watering it again about November, when growth resumes.
Pests and Diseases Slugs attack the leaves.

Left *Lewisia cotyledon heckneri*

Leycesteria

CAPRIFOLIACEAE

A small genus of hardy deciduous Asian shrubs of erect habit, of which one is commonly grown in Britain.
L. formosa (Himalaya), pheasant berry, Himalayan honeysuckle. Height 1.5m (5ft) and more; spread about 900mm (3ft). Hollow, green, upright stems. Pendant tassel-like flower-clusters in maroon and white in July–August, followed by red-purple berries much favoured by birds. Not fully hardy, but new shoots grow readily from base.

Site Sun or shade.
Soil Any reasonably fertile.
Propagation Sow seed in spring under cover; germination is excellent.
Cultivation Plant in autumn-spring. Water well in dry weather.

Pruning Remove dead growth killed by frost, and cut out old or weak shoots to ground level in spring. Alternatively cut off all shoots at ground level each spring and manure well.
Pests and Diseases Capsid bugs may be a problem.

Above Leycesteria formosa

Liatris

COMPOSITAE   Button snake-root

Hardy herbaceous perennials from North America grown for their showy spikes of blossom, which attract bees to the garden.
L. pycnostachya (C. North America). Perennial, usually treated as a biennial. Height up to 1m (3¼ft); spread 600mm (2ft). Crowded tufts of green, grassy foliage. Stout, congested spires of fluffy, reddish-purple flowers in July–September. Tolerates quite dry conditions.
L. spicata (syn. *L. callilepis* of gardens; S. and E. North America). Perennial. Height 600mm (2ft); spread 450mm (1½ft). Dense tufts of broad green, grassy foliage. Dense spikes of fluffy purple flowers in August–September. Varieties include 'Alba' (white); 'Kobold' (dwarf, mauve-pink).

Site In the open, in full sun.
Soil Free-draining but moisture-retentive. *L. spicata* happy at poolside.
Propagation Easily raised from seed sown in frame or nursery rows outdoors in July.

Root-stocks can be readily divided in spring.
Cultivation Best planted in spring. Tidy up each autumn.
Pests and Diseases Slugs may attack emerging shoots in early spring.

Above Liatris spicata

Ligularia

COMPOSITAE

Hardy herbaceous perennials, of cosmopolitan distribution, grown for their bold, attractive foliage and heads of daisy-like flowers.
L. dentata (syn. *Senecio clivorum*, *L. clivorum*; China). Perennial. Height 900mm–1.2m (3–4ft); spread 900mm (3ft). Large kidney-shaped leaves up to 450mm (1½ft) across, dark olive-green suffused with purple. Small, bright-orange, daisy-like flowers in large mop-heads up to 300mm (1ft) across in July–September. Varieties include 'Golden Queen' (golden yellow); 'Orange Princess' (bright orange).
L. stenocephala 'The Rocket' (China, Japan). Perennial, clump-forming. Height 1.5–2m (5–6½ft); spread 600mm (2ft). Large, triangular, coarse-toothed leaves; stems dark purple. Yellow flowers in wand-like spikes in July–August. (Sometimes listed as *L. przewalskii*.)
L. veitchiana (syn. *Senecio veitchianus*; China). Perennial. Height 1–2m (3¼–6½ft); spread 600mm (2ft). Coarse, green, almost triangular leaves. Tall spires of golden-yellow flowers up to 75mm (3in) across in abundance in July–September.

Site Open preferred, but most kinds tolerate part shade.
Soil Moist, heavy loam; *L. dentata* and *stenocephala* will grow in bog conditions.
Propagation Divide root-stocks in dormant season.
Cultivation Plant at any time in dormant season. Remove old

foliage in autumn. Remove old flower-heads immediately they fade. Watering important in dry summers.
Pests and Diseases Slugs are a menace, especially with young growth.

Right Ligularia veitchiana

Ligustrum

OLEACEAE   Privet

Deciduous and evergreen shrubs and trees, mostly from temperate and tropical Asia. In Britain privet is usually seen as a formal hedge. The best privet for this purpose is *L. ovalifolium* and its various cultivars, though *L. vulgare* is the native species.

L. japonicum (Japan, Korea). Height 1.8m (6ft); spread 1.2m (4ft). Evergreen leaves resembling those of camellia. White flower clusters, 150mm (6in) long, in August–September.

L. ovalifolium (Japan). Semi-evergreen. Height 3–4.5m (10–15ft); spread 1.5–2.1m (5–7ft). Clusters, 50–75mm (2–3in) long, of tiny white, fragrant flowers in July. Form 'Aureum' is the best golden privet, with yellow and green-centred leaves.

Site Sun or shade, but *L. japonicum* needs shelter.
Soil Any.
Propagation Hardwood cuttings in autumn, outdoors.
Cultivation Plant in autumn or spring. Feed every spring.

Pruning Specimen shrubs need only be tidied up in spring; hedges need clipping two or three times in the growing season.

Right *Ligustrum ovalifolium* 'Aureum'

Lilium

LILIACEAE   Lily

Bulbous perennials of the northern hemisphere. Aptly described as queen of the summer bulbs, they bear large, colourful trumpet-bowl-, star-, or turk's-cap-shaped flowers on strong leafy stems.

L. auratum (Japan), gold-band or golden-rayed lily. Height 1.2–2m (4–6½ft); spread 350–450mm (14–18in). Largest-flowered and most imposing of all lilies. Individual bowl-shaped blooms, 200–300mm (8–12in) wide, pure white with a yellow band down each petal and crimson freckles; strongly fragrant in sunny weather; opening August–September. In forms *L. a. rubrum* and *rubro-vittatum*, yellow bands are replaced by crimson ones.

L. candidum (Balkans), madonna lily. Height 1m (3¼ft) or more; spread about 300mm (1ft). Unusually among lilies, produces leaves in early autumn which may be damaged in severe winters. Flowers pure white, widely bell-shaped (with petal tips recurved), about 100mm (4in) or more wide, in June–July.

L. hansonii (Korea, N. Japan, Sakhalin). Height to 1.5m (5ft); spread about 350mm (14in). Much like a robust *L. martagon* (q.v.), with orange-yellow flowers 65mm (2½in) wide in June–July.

L. henryi (C. China). Height 1.2–2.4m (4–8ft); spread 450mm (1½ft). Long-lived, easy to grow lily, the finest of the turk's-caps. Strong stems, often arching over in the top third, bear up to 20 orange, brown-freckled flowers, each about

Left *Lilium auratum*   **Above** *L. pyrenaicum*

75mm (3in) wide, in August–September. Tolerates lime.

L. martagon (Europe, temperate Asia). Height 1–1.8m (3¼–6ft); spread 350mm (14in). Original turk's-cap or turban lily, and one of a group which bears its leaves in whorls at intervals up the stems. Dark to light reddish-purple flowers, about 40mm (1½in) or more wide, open in July. Variety 'Album' is pure white, free-flowering.

L. pumilum (syn. *L. tenuifolium*; E. Siberia, Korea, China), coral lily. Height 300–450mm (1–1½ft); spread about 125mm (5in). Smallest and brightest species in cultivation. Stems slim and wiry, leaves grassy. Flowers, about 40mm (1½in) wide, of turk's-cap form, bright waxy scarlet, in June.

L. pyrenaicum (Pyrenees, S.W. France), Pyrenean or yellow turk's-cap lily. Height 600mm–1.2m (2–4ft); spread about 225mm (9in). Narrow, bright green leaves all way up the stem. Martagon-like flowers of sulphur-yellow open in June. Natural variety *L. p. rubrum* has orange-red flowers.

L. regale (W. China), regal lily. Height 900mm (3ft) or more; spread about 350mm (14in). Best and easiest of trumpet species. Each fragrant bloom 120–150mm (4¾–6in) long, red-purple in bud opening to pure white with a yellow throat, expanding in summer. *L. r.* 'Album' has white buds.

L. speciosum (syn. *L. lancifolium*; Japan, China, Taiwan). Height 750mm–1.2m (2½–4ft) or more; spread about 350mm (14in). Widely expanded, nodding flowers, 100–150mm (4–6in) wide, with strongly waved petals reflexed at tips; white-suffused crimson, with darker spots, opening in August–September; fragrant. Varieties include 'Album' (pure white); 'Ellabee' (superior form of 'Album'); 'Rubrum' (almost entirely crimson).

L. × *testaceum* (hybrid), nankeen lily. Height 1m (3¼ft) or more. Rather like a more elegant *L. pyrenaicum*; flowers a unique shade of maize or nankeen yellow, often pink-flushed, in summer.

L. tigrinum (syn. *L. lancifolium*; China, Korea, Japan), tiger lily. Height 1–2m (3¼–6½ft); spread about 350mm (14in). Purplish, hairy stems with black-purple bulbils in the leaf axils identify this species. Flowers of turk's-cap form, 50–65mm (2–2½in) wide, bright orange-red with black freckles, in August–September. Varieties include 'Giganteum' (larger in all its parts); 'Splendens' (fiery-orange blooms with dark-crimson spots); 'Flore-pleno' (double flowers); 'Flaviflorum' and 'Golden Souvenir' (yellow tiger lilies).

L. × umbellatum (syn. *L × hollandicum*). Group of cultivars of complex hybrid origin. Height 450–600mm (1½–2ft); spread 200–250mm (8–10in). Erect, cup-shaped flowers in fairly dense clusters. Individual flowers 75–90mm (3–3½in) across, open around mid-summer. Good examples: 'Grandiflorum' (robust, vigorous, apricot-orange flowers); 'Orange Triumph' (orange-yellow flowers with purple freckles).

Lilium Hybrids. In the past 30 years hundreds of lily hybrids have been raised, many of them better garden plants than their parent species. Two groups in particular contain easily grown cultivars of excellent garden value: Mid-Century Group, with wide, upward- or outward-facing blooms in both soft and bright colours, typified by 'Destiny' (lemon-yellow, spotted brown); 'Enchantment' (brilliant nasturtium-red, freckled black); 'Harmony' (orange, with chocolate spots); 'Mont Blanc' (white); 'Paprika' (deep crimson). Trumpet Group lilies have horizontally borne or slightly nodding funnel- to trumpet-shaped blooms, typified by 'Black Dragon' (dark purple buds opening white, similar to *L. regale*); 'Golden Clarion' (rich yellow); 'Green Magic' (white-tinted lime-green); 'Moonlight' (apple-green); 'Pink Perfection' (lilac-pink).

Right *Lilium* × *umbellatum*

Site Part shade is the ideal; full sun acceptable if soil is moist or stems rise through cover of low shrubs which keep soil cool. Shelter from strong winds.

Soil Well-drained but moisture-retentive, with plenty of organic matter. Neutral soil is best – few lilies like extreme alkalinity or acidity; *L. martagon*, *regale*, *pyrenaicum*, *henryi* and *candidum* tolerate chalky soil.

Propagation Divide large clumps, or take scales when dormant. Sow seeds when ripe or in spring. Remove stem bulbils in late summer or early autumn; plant immediately in pots or nursery rows.

Cultivation Plant in autumn or in mild weather in winter or early spring. Remove spent flowers unless seed is required; cut down stems when leaves fade. Mulch with leaf-mould or well-decayed manure every other spring.

Pests and Diseases Aphids, slugs and snails, and lily beetle may damage leaves and flowers. Botrytis (lily disease) and virus can be troublesome.

Left *Lilium regale* (with fuchsia)

'Violetta' (richer-coloured flowers); 'Robert Butler' (dwarfer).

L. sinuatum (syn. *Statice sinuata*; S. Portugal, Mediterranean), statice. Biennial or short-lived perennial, grown as an annual. Height 450–600mm (1½–2ft); spread 300mm (1ft). Leaves about 100mm (4in) long, deeply rounded, lobed, in basal rosette. Wiry, branched stems bear dense clusters of 8mm (⅓in) long, purple everlasting flowers in August–September. Modern seed strains contain a variety of colours including blue, lavender, red, pink, and yellow.

L. suworowii (syn. *Statice suworowii*; Iran, Caucasus, C. Asia). Half-hardy annual. Height about 450mm (1½ft); spread about 300mm (1ft). Leaves in basal tufts about 150–250mm (4–10in) long, lobed and waved. Wiry stems bear fingered spikes of rose-pink flowers, 6mm (¼in) long, in July–September.

Site All need full sun, though *L. latifolium* tolerates some shade.
Soil Well-drained, moderately fertile.
Propagation Divide perennials in spring. Take root cuttings in late winter. Sow seed under glass in spring. Sow annuals where they are to flower in late spring (earlier if under glass).
Cultivation Plant perennials in autumn or spring. Remove dead stems of perennials in late autumn.

Above *Limnanthes douglasii*

Limnanthes

LIMNANTHACEAE   Poached-egg flower
Annuals native to America. The species listed is popular as path-edging or as a front-of-border plant.
L. douglasii (W. North America). Hardy annual. Height 150mm (6in); spread 100mm (4in). Bright green, finely divided leaves. Cheerful, 25mm (1in) wide, yellow flowers edged with white, slightly scented, produced in profusion in June–August. Attractive to bees.

Site Full sun.
Soil Any that allows roots to be kept cool.
Propagation Sow seeds where they are to flower in March; thin out to 100mm (4in). Can also be sown in September outdoors. Produces self-sown seedlings in profusion.
Cultivation Cover autumn-sown plants with cloches in cold, exposed districts.

Above *Limonium latifolium*

Limonium

PLUMBAGINACEAE   Sea lavender
Annuals and perennials of cosmopolitan distribution, especially the Mediterranean region. Variable in habit and foliage, they bear clusters of tiny, often colourful flowers, some useful for drying as everlasting blooms.
L. latifolium (syn. *Statice latifolium*; S.E. Europe, S. Russia). Evergreen perennial. Height and spread 450–600mm (18–24in). Dark green, oblong-elliptic basal leaves up to 250mm (10in) long. Light violet-blue flowers, 6mm (¼in) long, in large cloud-like clusters in late summer. Varieties include

Above *Linaria purpurea* 'Canon Went'

Linaria

SCROPHULARIACEAE   Toadflax
A group of dainty annuals, short-lived perennials, and sub-shrubs found in rocky places in Europe and North Africa. Some of them self-seed about the rock garden in a pleasant and unobtrusive manner.
L. alpina (European Alps). Height 75–150mm (3–6in). Forms trailing stems of blue-grey leaves. Orange and violet flowers are showy all through summer. There is an all-violet form.
L. cymbalaria (syn. *Cymbalaria muralis*; Europe), ivy-

leaved toadflax or Kenilworth ivy. The species is rather rampant, but its variety 'Globosa' makes a neat 50mm (2in) tuft of green, with white and pink flowers all through summer.

L. maroccana (Morocco). Annual. Height to 300mm (1ft). Erect plant with slim, wiry stems. Leaves linear, often in whorls. Wild species has spikes of purple and yellow flowers. Modern seed strains available in shades of purple, blue, red, pink, and yellow, opening in June–September; 'Fairy Bouquet' a good example.

L. purpurea (Italy, Sicily). Height 600mm (2ft) or more; spread 300mm (1ft). Upright plant with wiry stems clothed in narrow grey-green leaves. Spikes of purple flowers (pink in variety 'Canon Went') in July–September. Both come true from seed (variety only if isolated from species, however) and spread by self-sown seedlings.

Site All enjoy sun.
Soil Moderately rich, free-draining.
Propagation Scatter seed where it is to grow in March–April; or sow in February, potting on in March, to plant out in May. Cuttings taken in May are ready by July.
Cultivation In sunny scree plants can be left to seed themselves.

Linum

LINACEAE Flax

Annuals, perennials, and shrubs of cosmopolitan distribution, especially the Mediterranean region. Their main features are slender stems, small narrow leaves, and large five-petalled flowers in a wide colour range. They make attractive plants for rock garden and herbaceous border.

L. flavum (C. and E. Europe), yellow flax. Perennial, woody-based. Height and spread up to 450mm (1½ft), sometimes more. Forms spreading clumps of leaves 20–40mm (¾–1½in) long. Erect stems bear clusters of yellow flowers, each about 25mm (1in) wide, in June–August. Variety 'Compactum' is more compact, only 200mm (8in) tall. *L.* × 'Gemmell's Hybrid' is similar, but with grey foliage and darker flowers.

L. grandiflorum (N. Africa), red flax. Annual. Height 300–450mm (1–1½ft); spread 100–150mm (4–6in). Leaves bright green, about 30mm (1¼in) long. Red flowers, 30mm (1¼in) wide, open in summer. Varieties include 'Album' (white flowers); 'Rubrum' (often listed as *L. rubrum*, bright, satiny red blooms).

L. perenne (C. and E. Europe). Perennial, somewhat woody based. Height to 600mm (2ft); spread to 300mm (1ft). Erect stems bear greyish-green leaves, 25mm (1in) long. Loose clusters of blue flowers, 25mm (1in) wide, in June–September.

Site Sunny.
Soil Well-drained, reasonably fertile.
Propagation Sow seeds of annuals where they are to grow; sow seeds of perennials under glass, in spring. Take cuttings of perennials in summer.
Cultivation Plant perennials in autumn or spring. Remove dead stems in autumn. Replace *L. perenne* about every third year as it is not long-lived; increase it from seed.

Below *Linum flavum*

Lippia

VERBENACEAE

A large genus of shrubs and perennials native to North and South America and Africa. The only species in general cultivation is half-hardy: it will grow outdoors only in the south and west of England; elsewhere it is a greenhouse plant.

L. citriodora (syn. *Aloysia citriodora*; Chile), lemon-scented verbena. Perennial. Height 1.5m (5ft); spread 1.2m (4ft). Narrow, mid-green leaves that smell of lemon when crushed. Small, mauve tubular flowers appear in August.

Site Sunny, sheltered place with protection from a wall.
Soil Well-drained.
Propagation Cuttings can be taken in July using 75mm (3in) long lateral shoots; root in propagator; pot up, and keep frost-free over winter; plant out in May.
Cultivation Plant in spring. May be cut back by frost.
Pruning In April established plants should have main growths cut back fairly hard and laterals to about three buds.

Right *Lippia citriodora*

leaves arching, about 300mm (1ft) long. Rounded flowers, 6–13mm ($\frac{1}{4}$–$\frac{1}{2}$in) wide, lavender-purple, in dense racemes in autumn. Variety 'Majestic', the commonest form grown in Britain, has violet flower-spikes with crested tips.

Site Part shade is best; full sun tolerated if soil is moist.
Soil Well-drained but moisture-retentive; ideally it should be humus-enriched.

Propagation Divide established clumps in spring.
Cultivation Plant in autumn or spring. Do not divide more often than every third year.

Lithodora

BORAGINACEAE

A group of mat-forming perennial and shrubby plants, formerly listed under the genus *Lithospermum*. They are useful in the rock garden and as ground-cover plants.

L. diffusa (S.W. Europe). Height up to 100mm (4in); spread up to 600mm (24in). Type species now largely replaced by selected forms, notably 'Grace Ward', with deep-blue star-like flowers emerging from mat of dark-green foliage in May–August. Another attractive form, 'Heavenly Blue', is nowadays seldom available.

L. oleifolium (Pyrenees). Low, mound-forming, with greyish hairy leaves. Clusters of flowers, pinkish in bud, opening to pale blue, in May–August. Spreads by underground runners; gets straggly with age.

Below *Lithodora diffusa*

Above *Liriope muscari*

Liriope

LILIACEAE   Lily turf

Perennials from eastern Asia, with leathery, rich green, grassy leaves and erect spikes of small, bell-shaped flowers.

L. muscari (syn. *L. platyphylla*; China, Japan, Taiwan). Height and spread 300–450mm (1–1$\frac{1}{2}$ft). Clump-forming, with

Site Bright, sunny, well-drained.
Soil Sandy soils preferred. Must be lime-free for *L. diffusa*, but *L. oleifolium* is lime-tolerant.
Propagation Take soft green cuttings, 38–65mm (1½–2½in) long with no old wood at base, at the end of July, and insert in peat in a shaded frame.
Cultivation *L. diffusa* sometimes makes an untidy mat which requires attention. *L. oleifolium* can also be grown in an alpine house, where it can be planted into an open, limy soil, or it can be pot-grown in compost.
Pruning *L. oleifolium* may need a trim from time to time to remove dead shoots; *L. diffusa* may need to be restrained every year from spreading too far.

Lobelia

CAMPANULACEAE

A large genus of annuals, perennials, and shrubs of cosmopolitan distribution, some of which are widely used as border plants, for summer bedding, and in containers.

L. cardinalis (N. America), cardinal flower. Perennial. Height 300–600mm (1–2ft); spread 300mm (1ft). Very upright habit, with lance-shaped green leaves. Terminal spires of scarlet blossoms in June–September. (Often confused with *L. fulgens* (q.v.) or with hybrids between the two.)

L. erinus (S. Africa). Half-hardy perennial, grown as an annual. Height 150mm (6in); spread 230mm (9in). Popular blue lobelia of bedding schemes. Delicate mounds of bright green foliage. Clusters of blue flowers with conspicuous white throats in May–October. Many varieties, including 'Cambridge Blue' (light blue); 'Crystal Palace' (dark blue); 'Red Cascade' (purple-red); 'White Lady' (white). Pendulous varieties look good in hanging baskets.

L. fulgens (syn. *L. splendens*; Mexico). Half-hardy perennial. Height 300–900mm (1–3ft); spread 300mm (1ft). Upright habit with lance-shaped leaves; entire foliage has a purplish cast or is sometimes almost beetroot coloured. Spires of scarlet flowers about 25mm (1in) long in June–September. Appreciates winter protection in northern districts.

L. siphilitica (E. North America). Hardy perennial. Height 300–600mm (1–2ft); spread 300mm (1ft). Neat, upright growth with rather coarse green, almost oval leaves and spikes of bright blue flowers in August–October.

Site Open, sunny for bedding types; dappled shade for others.
Soil Light and free-draining for bedding types; rich, moisture-retentive for others.
Propagation Sow bedding types in pans in warmth under glass in February; prick out into trays; grow on until all danger of frost has passed (late May or early June), then plant out. Other kinds increased by division of rootstock, by cuttings of young shoots taken in early spring and rooted in a propagator, or from seed sown as for bedding types.
Cultivation Bedding kinds treated as annuals and discarded at end of summer. Perennial herbaceous types planted in spring. In colder districts they are often lifted and boxed for the winter, and kept in a cold frame or covered with cloches.
Pests and Diseases Slugs can be a nuisance.

Below *Lobelia erinus* mixture

Above *Lychnis chalcedonica* (foreground)

Lychnis

CARYOPHYLLACEAE   Campion

Annuals and herbaceous perennials, native to Europe and Asia, they are useful garden plants with vividly coloured flowers and a neat habit of growth.

L. × arkwrightii (hybrid of garden origin). Hardy perennial. Height 300–400mm (12–16in); spread 300mm (1ft). Loosely erect plant with oblong, pointed, brownish-green leaves. Clusters of round, brilliant orange-red flowers, 40mm (1½in) across, on ends of stems in June–July. Often a short-lived plant, but worth growing for its unusual colour.

L. chalcedonica (E. Russia), Maltese cross. Hardy herbaceous perennial. Height 900mm (3ft); spread 450mm (1½ft). Tall, narrowly upright plant with green lance-shaped leaves and stiff erect stems. Closely packed heads of cruciform, vivid scarlet flowers, 8mm (⅓in) across, in July–August. One of the few truly red garden flowers, without a trace of blue in it.

L. coronaria (syn. *Agrostemma coronaria*; S. Europe), dusty miller, rose campion. Hardy perennial. Height 450–600mm (1½–2ft); spread 450mm (1½ft). Erect, open plant with stems and leaves covered in silvery, flannelly hairs. Vivid magenta rose flowers, 25mm (1in) across, in July–September contrast well with the leaves. Softer-coloured pink or white forms are sometimes available. Short-lived, but tends to seed itself freely in lighter soils.

Site Must be open and sunny.
Soil Any fertile garden soil; *L. coronaria* happy in very-well-drained, poor ones.
Propagation Sow seed under glass in early spring or (except for *L. × arkwrightii*) in open in May–June. Divide roots in autumn or spring. Cuttings of short basal growths can be rooted under glass in early summer.

Cultivation Plant in October-March. Stake taller perennials securely when plants are 100mm (4in) high. Dead-head plants regularly unless seed is required. Mulch with peat in March.
Pests and Diseases Aphids may be troublesome in spring. *L. chalcedonica* may be affected by virus, distorting leaves and stunting growth.

Lysichiton

ARACEAE

Herbaceous perennials, native to western North America and eastern Asia, with brightly coloured spathes and large, imposing leaves. They like wet ground and in gardens are used mainly around ponds or pools.

L. americanum (W. North America), skunk cabbage. Hardy perennial. Height 600mm (2ft). Waxy, bright yellow spathes up to 300mm (1ft) high in April, followed by massive, lance-shaped leaves.

L. camtschatcense (E. Asia). Hardy perennial. Pure white arum-like spathes up to 250mm (10in) high in late April–May. Lance-shaped leaves up to 600mm (2ft) high throughout summer. A hybrid between this and *L. americanum* occurs in some gardens.

Site Moist conditions beside a pool or stream, in sun or part shade.
Soil Must be constantly moist and preferably rich in organic matter.
Propagation Fresh seed germinates freely if sown on trays of wet soil in July–August. Divide carefully in early spring.
Cultivation Young plants should be planted in spring, not autumn. Given sufficient moisture they require little attention except for removal of decaying foliage in the autumn.
Pests and Diseases Slugs may attack young leaves and spathes.

Right *Lysichiton camtschatcense*

Lysimachia

PRIMULACEAE

Herbaceous plants and a few shrubs which are widespread natives of North America, Asia, and Europe. Most have a bushy habit and produce attractive spires of showy flowers. Attractive plants for open, damp areas of the garden.

L. clethroides (China, Japan). Perennial. Height 900mm (3ft); spread 600mm (2ft) or more. Numerous small white flowers in dense, arching spikes above dark green foliage in July–August. Make excellent cut flowers.

L. nummularia (Europe, including Britain), creeping jenny, moneywort. Perennial, prostrate and spreading, with shoots rooting at each leaf joint. Bright green glossy leaves studded with yellow flowers in June–September. 'Aurea' a golden-leafed form. Both excellent for ground cover.

L. punctata (Balkans, Turkey). Perennial. Height and spread up to 600mm (2ft). Well-branched, bushy plant with lance-shaped leaves. Long, whorled spikes of yellow blossoms in June–September.

Site Open, sunny; most also flourish in part shade.
Soil Constantly damp or even wet. Most species like the damp conditions at a poolside.
Propagation Divide established clumps in the winter or early spring. Take cuttings of emerging young shoots in late spring.
Cultivation Plant when dormant. Tidy up in autumn.

Below *Lysimachia punctata*

Above *Lythrum salicaria*

Lythrum

LYTHRACEAE

Perennials and shrubs from the temperate regions of both hemispheres. Some have dense spikes of showy flowers and an upright branched habit.

L. salicaria (W. Europe, Asia), purple loosestrife. Hardy perennial. Height up to 1.5m (5ft); spread 1m (3¼ft). Strong-growing with attractive small leaves with purplish cast. Dense terminal spires of reddish-purple flowers in June–August. Varieties include 'Brilliant' (pink); 'Fire Candle' (bright pink); 'Rose Queen' and 'Lady Sackville' (rose-pink).

L. virgatum (Europe). Hardy perennial. Height and spread 600–900mm (2–3ft). Bushy, upright habit with spires of purple flowers in June–August.

Site Open and sunny preferred, but plants tolerate dappled shade.
Soil Damp to wet: plants thrive beside a pool or stream.
Propagation Division at any time in dormant season.
Cultivation Plant open-ground lythrums at any time in dormant season. Plants require tidying up each autumn, and division every third or fourth year.

Macleaya

PAPAVERACEAE

Hardy herbaceous perennials, native to China and Japan, these stately plants of sub-tropical appearance are equally at home in the herbaceous or shrub border.

M. cordata (China, Japan), plume poppy. Height up to 2.5m (8¼ft); spread 2m (6½ft). Towering plumes of delicate, white blooms in July–August above dense mounds of rounded, steel-coloured foliage.

M. microcarpa (China). Height up to 2.5m (8¼ft); spread 2m (6½ft). Of similar appearance to *M. cordata* but with buff-pink flowers.

Site Sun preferred, but plants tolerate a little dappled shade.
Soil Ordinary, well-drained. Wet winter conditions can lead to rotting of root-stocks; dry summer conditions may severely dwarf plants.
Propagation Root-stocks sucker freely. These young shoots, which emerge in early spring, can be detached and planted in permanent positions immediately. In early summer, when plants are in active growth, locate small healthy shoots in axils of leaves; remove these and use as cuttings in a mixture of peat and sharp sand; resulting young plants should be potted ready for autumn planting.
Cultivation Plant in the dormant season. In exposed districts summer growth will require support.
Pests and Diseases Slugs may attack shoots in early spring.

Below *Macleaya cordata* (left), *M. microcarpa* (right)

Above *Magnolia* × *soulangeana*

Magnolia

MAGNOLIACEAE

A genus of deciduous and evergreen flowering trees and shrubs native to east and south-east Asia and North America. They are among the most desirable and splendid of flowering trees that are hardy in the temperate regions. Many have large handsome leaves; flowers, produced in spring or summer, vary in shape and colour and can be up to 250mm (10in) in diameter.

M. grandiflora (S.E. United States). Superb hardy, flowering evergreen. As a south-wall shrub it attains 8–10m (25–33ft) or more; free standing in sun and shelter it eventually achieves about 6m (20ft) height and spread in warm locations. Leaves oval or laurel-like, 150–250mm (6–10in) long and 50–75mm (2–2½in) wide, leathery, dark glossy green above and richly red-brown felted beneath. Flowers globular, thick textured, creamy white, 200–250mm (8–10in) across, exuding rich spicy fragrance in late summer and autumn. Good cultivars include 'Exmouth' (elliptical leaves and erect habit); 'Goliath' (shorter, broader leaves and even larger flowers). Both cultivars bloom at an early age.

M. kobus (Japan). Deciduous hardy tree usually pyramidal when young, round-headed with age. Height 10–13m (33–43ft). Leaves obovate, 75–150mm (3–6in) long. Six-petalled pure white flowers up to 100mm (4in) in diameter very freely produced in April, but only on trees at least 12–15 years old.

M. liliiflora (China). Deciduous shrub of wide spreading habit. Height up to 4m (13ft). Leaves variably oblong or obovate, 75–200mm (3–8in) long. 'Nigra' is a good, com-

pact form with deep purple flowers, creamy white within, in May–June. Fine shrub for small gardens.

M. × *loebneri* (garden origin). Large deciduous shrub or small tree, up to 8m (25ft) high and similar spread. Narrowly obovate leaves. Abundant, many petalled, fragrant, white, strap-shaped flowers in April even on very young plants. Varieties include 'Leonard Messel' (lilac-pink flowers, deeper in bud); 'Merrill' (large, white, fragrant flowers freely produced).

M. sieboldii (syn. *M. parviflora*; Japan, Korea). Wide-spreading, large deciduous shrub. Height up to about 4m (12ft) with ovate or obovate leaves, grey and downy beneath. Fragrant cup-shaped, pendulous, white flowers with prominent crimson stamens, produced intermittently in May–August.

M. × *soulangeana*. Group of cultivars that make the best choice for general planting. Large, deciduous, wide-spreading shrubs up to 4m (13ft) or more high with leaves 75–150mm (3–6in) long. Many large, tulip-shaped, white flowers, often purple-stained, produced before leaves in April–May, even on young plants. Some good examples: 'Alba Superba' (fragrant, early white flowers of exceptional quality); 'Lennei' (leaves larger and broader, flowers broader-petalled, rose-purple outside and white within, for extended season); 'Rustica Rubra' (vigorous, similar to 'Lennei', but with white-flushed rose-red flowers in April–May).

M. stellata (Japan). Distinctive slow-growing, deciduous shrub up to 3m (10ft) high and somewhat greater spread. Leaves 75–100mm (3–4in) long. Flowers white, strap-shaped, produced profusely in March–April before leaves. Cultivars include 'Rosea' (flowers tinted rose-pink); 'Water Lily' (larger white flowers with more petals).

Site All require sheltered sites giving protection from spring frosts and cold north and east winds. Most shrubby species adapt successfully as south- or west-facing wall shrubs in cold districts.
Soil Deep, rich, moist loam, preferably acid and well-drained. Given good soil-depth, *M. grandiflora*, × *soulangeana*, and *stellata* tolerate lime; *M. kobus* and × *loebneri* thrive more readily on chalk soils.
Propagation Species by seed as soon as ripe (in cold frame; may take 18 months to germinate). Deciduous hybrids and cultivars by layering or by summer cuttings of current year's wood in propagator with bottom heat (cuttings of *M. grandiflora* should be taken in late summer, with similar treatment; but they root less easily than others). Layers may not root for two years.
Cultivation Most now available container-grown for planting at most seasons. Transplant root-balled specimens ideally in May; water, mulch, and feed for best results. Support with stakes for first few years.
Pruning Overgrown or wind-damaged specimens regenerate well if cut back in July.

Mahonia

BERBERIDACEAE
Evergreen shrubs with prickly, holly-like leaves, from Asia and North and Central America. Their rather stiff, upright habit is disguised by the whorls of pinnate leaflets that go to make up the large leaves. All have long spikes of small, round flowers (some with a fragrance resembling that of lily-of-the-valley) between autumn and spring, depending on species.

M. aquifolium (North America), Oregon grape. Height 600mm (2ft); spread 1.2m (4ft). Rounded clusters of yellow, slightly fragrant flowers in spring, followed by blue-black berries suitable for jam, jelly, and wine.

M. japonica (China). Most commonly grown mahonia. Height 1.8m (6ft) or more; spread 1.2m (4ft) or more. Lemon-yellow flower spikes, 150mm (6in) long, in January–March.

M. × *media* 'Charity' (hybrid). Height and spread to 3m (10ft). Deep yellow, fragrant flowers on spikes 300mm (12in) long in November–January.

Site Sun or shade; give shelter from north and east winds.
Soil Well-drained, not markedly alkaline.
Propagation For *M. aquifolium*, by rooted suckers in autumn or spring. For others, by semi-hardwood cuttings under cover in July; or by seed sown when ripe.
Cultivation Plant in autumn or spring. Mulch with leaf-mould or peat every other spring. Cut back ground-cover types hard in April.
Pruning Remove old or unwanted growth in spring.
Pests and Diseases Lime-induced chlorosis may occur in chalky soil; also rust fungus.

Below *Mahonia japonica*

Malcolmia

CRUCIFERAE

Annuals and perennials native to Europe, Asia and North Africa. The only species widely cultivated in British gardens is useful as an edging plant.

M. maritima (S. Mediterranean), Virginian stock. Hardy annual. Height 150–230mm (6–9in); spread 150mm (6in). Smooth, grey-green leaves. Flowers are cruciform, scented, in a range from red and lilac to yellow and white, and are abundant in April–August, about four weeks after sowing.

Site Sunny preferred.
Soil Any.
Propagation Make successional sowings outdoors in March–July to ensure long flowering season. Seed can also be sown in September for flowering the following April.
Cultivation Easy to grow; particularly popular with children. Self-sown seedlings may occur. Mix seeds with night-scented stocks (*Matthiola*, q.v.) for improved fragrance.

Right *Malcolmia maritima*

Above *Malope trifida*

Malope

MALVACEAE

A small genus of free-flowering annuals, native to the Mediterrean region, with showy, trumpet-shaped blooms; the species listed makes a good border plant.

M. trifida (syn. *M. grandiflora*; Spain, North Africa). Hardy. Height 600–900mm (2–3ft); spread 300–450mm (1–1½ft). Bushy plant with mid-green leaves and mallow-like purple flowers all summer. Two forms, 'Rosea' (pink) and 'Alba' (white), sometimes available.

Site Open and sunny; useful towards the back of a border.
Soil Any; light preferred.
Propagation Sow seeds in September or early spring where plants are to flower; thin seedlings to 300mm (1ft) apart.

Cultivation Dead heading encourages a succession of blooms. Discard plants after flowering.
Pests and Diseases Aphids may attack growing tips of the young plants.

Above *Malus* 'Golden Hornet'

Malus

ROSACEAE   Crab-apple

Deciduous trees and shrubs widely distributed in northern temperate regions. Useful in small gardens for combinations of showy spring flowers, fruit, and foliage. The fruits can be made into jelly preserve.

M. floribunda (Japan), Japanese crab. Dense, spreading head to 6m (20ft) or more high and often wider. Flowers profusely borne in April, red in bud opening to pale pink, sometimes followed by small yellow fruits.

M. 'Golden Hornet'. One of the better fruiting crabs. Height 6m (20ft); spread 5m (16½ft). White flowers in May followed by abundant yellow fruits, 25mm (1in) wide, retained well into winter (birds permitting).

M. 'John Downie'. Vigorous tree, perhaps the best crab for fruit. Height 8m (26ft); spread 6m (20ft). Flowers pink in bud, opening white in May. Brilliant display of conical, bright orange and red edible fruits.

M. 'Profusion'. Small tree, 5m (16½ft) tall and 6m (20ft) across. Young leaves coppery red, becoming bronze-green. Flowers deep purplish pink, 40mm (1½in) across, freely borne in May. Abundant small, deep-wine-red fruits.

M. 'Red Jade'. Small, weeping tree. Height 5m (16½ft); spread 4m (13ft). White flowers in early May, followed by profuse, persistent, cherry-like, red fruits.

M. 'Red Sentinel'. Height 6m (20ft); spread 5m (16½ft). White flowers in early May followed by glossy, deep-red fruits that persist well into winter.

M. 'Royalty'. Rather upright habit, with very attractive foliage. Height 5m (16½ft); spread 4m (13ft). Leaves shiny, reddish purple. Large crimson flowers in May; fruits deep reddish-purple.

M. tschonoskii (Japan). Strong-growing, erect-branched, conical tree, good for confined spaces. Height 10m (33ft) or more; spread 5m (16½ft). Brilliant autumn foliage colours of yellow, orange, red, and purple. Small, white flowers (May) and green, red-flushed fruits are unremarkable.

Site Almost any position, but full sun is best. Malus generally tolerate more exposure than flowering cherries.
Soil Fertile.
Propagation By budding in July–August; or grafting in March.
Cultivation Plant bare-root trees in November–March; plant container-grown trees at any time.
Pruning Remove crossing branches and suckers.
Pests and Diseases Aphids, scale insects, red-spider mites, apple scab, and fire blight can cause problems.

Above *Malva alcea* 'Fastigiata'

Malva

MALVACEAE   Mallow

Annuals, biennials, and perennials native to Europe, North Africa, and Asia. Those cultivated in Britain are bushy perennials with freely produced funnel-shaped flowers, suitable for borders.

M. alcea (Europe). Hardy. Height 1.2m (4ft); spread 600–900mm (2–3ft). Leaves rounded, often shallowly lobed. Pale rose-purple flowers, 50–70mm (2–2¾in) wide, borne in racemes and opening in July–October. Variety 'Fastigiata' has neater, more erect habit.

M. moschata (Europe, North Africa), musk mallow. Hardy. Height 600–750mm (2–2½ft); spread 450–600mm (1½–2ft). Aromatic leaves, rounded, five-to-seven lobed, the upper one deeply so, with each lobe divided again. Bright rose-purple flowers, 50mm (2in) wide, open soon after midsummer and continue into autumn. Variety 'Alba' has pure white flowers.

Site Full sun best; some shade tolerated.
Soil Well-drained.
Propagation Divide perennials. Sow seeds in early spring. Take cuttings in late spring.
Cultivation Plant in autumn or spring. Cut down dead stems in late autumn or winter.

Matteuccia

POLYPODIACEAE
Hardy perennial ferns from Europe, North America, and the Far East. That listed is the only species commonly cultivated in Britain.

M. struthiopteris (syn. *Onoclea struthiopteris*; Europe, Asia), ostrich-feather fern. Height 900mm (3ft); spread 600mm (2ft). Deciduous fern producing 'shuttlecocks' of foliage which remain bright green until first frosts of autumn turn them yellow to russet.

Site Sun or shade; ample moisture.
Soil Leafy and moisture-retentive preferred. Fern will grow in very wet conditions and will advance towards the edge of a pool or stream.
Propagation Black creeping root-stock gives rise to young plants. These can be detached in early spring, just as they push through soil, and planted in permanent positions immediately.
Cultivation Plant at any time in dormant season. Tidy decaying autumn foliage. Control spread of creeping root-stocks.

Below *Matteuccia struthiopteris*

Above *Matthiola incana* Brompton stocks

Matthiola

CRUCIFERAE   Stock

Annuals, biennials, and perennials, native mainly to Europe, valued in beds and borders for their spikes of fragrant flowers.

M. bicornis (Greece), night-scented stock. Hardy annual. Height 450mm (1½ft); spread 230–300mm (9–12in). Rather straggly plant with long, grey-green leaves. Single four-petalled, lilac-pink flowers in July–August; their strong perfume, released at night, attracts night-flying moths that pollinate the flowers. To improve flower colour, mix seeds with those of Virginian stock (*Malcolmia*, q.v.).

M. incana (Europe). Short-lived perennial, usually grown as an annual or hardy biennial. Height 300–600mm (1–2ft); spread 300–450mm (1–1½ft). Spikes of pale purplish pink flowers carried above the greyish, long, narrow leaves. Many different groups of garden hybrids have been derived from this species, including the following. Brompton stocks: bushy plants up to 450mm (18in) high, grown as biennials to flower in spring, in shades of purple, pink, red, cream, and yellow. Ten Week stocks: summer-flowering annuals in a range of heights from dwarf strains, under 250mm (10in), to giant strains up to 1m (3ft). East Lothian stocks: annuals, about 400mm (16in) high, with white, mauve, or pink flowers in late summer. All these hybrid groups produce mixed double and single flowers.

Site Open, sunny.

Soil Fertile, free-draining loam preferred.

Propagation Sow annuals in greenhouse or cold frame in early March; prick off into boxes; harden off and plant out in May. Annuals can also be sown in April where they are to flower; thin seedlings to 225–450mm (9–18in) according to variety. Sow biennials in June–July in nursery bed; transplant to flowering positions in early autumn.

Cultivation Double-flowered plants are superior to single-flowered. Double strains produce seedlings which can be distinguished at an early stage: at 8–10°C (45–50°F) most seedlings will appear pale green; these are the doubles (darker-green single-flowered seedlings can be discarded). At higher temperatures the difference is difficult to see. Remove dead flower-heads; discard plants after flowering.

Pests and Diseases Flea beetles may bite small holes in the leaves of seedlings. Clubroot may cause swollen roots and stunted growth.

Above *Meconopsis cambrica*

Meconopsis

PAPAVERACEAE

Annual, biennial and short-lived perennial herbaceous plants native to Asia and western Europe, grown for their showy, poppy-like flowers.

M. betonicifolia (syn. *M. baileyi*; W. China, Burma), blue Tibetan poppy, Himalayan blue poppy. Perennial. Height up to 1m (3¼ft); spread 600mm (2ft). Handsome rosettes of hairy green foliage. Stout flower-stems bear nodding heads of blue or lavender flowers, 50mm (2in) across, in May–June.

M. cambrica (western Europe, including Britain), Welsh poppy. Perennial. Height up to 600mm (2ft); spread 300mm (1ft). Delicate hairy, green, deeply divided leaves make neat mounds. Bright yellow or orange flowers in June–September. Seeds freely and can become invasive.

M. grandis (Himalaya). Perennial. Height up to 1.2m (4ft); spread 600mm (2ft). Narrow, bristly green leaves in attractive rosettes. Large, crinkled, blue or purple flowers, up to 100mm (4in) wide, in May–June.

M. napaulensis (Nepal, W. China). Perennial. Height up to 2m (6½ft); spread 600mm (2ft). Outstanding rosettes of bristly green foliage persisting throughout winter. Blue, purple, red, pink, and (rarely) white, papery blossoms, 50mm (2in) wide, on bold branching heads in May–June.

creeping plant. Height 25mm (1in); spread 300mm (1ft). Small, pale green leaves smelling of peppermint. Spikes of small, pale purple flowers in June–August.
M. spicata (syn. *M. viridis*; Europe, including Britain), common mint, spearmint. Hardy. Height 600mm (2ft); spread 900mm (3ft) or more. Lanceolate, mid-green leaves with prominent veins. Spikes of small, pale purple flowers in July–September.
M. suaveolens (syn. *M. rotundifolia*; Europe, including Britain, Asia, North Africa), Bowles' mint, apple mint. Hardy. Height 600–900mm (2–3ft); spread 1.2m (4ft). Ovate, pale green leaves covered in hairs. Spikes of purple flowers in July–September. Probably the best-flavoured mint.

Site Light shade.
Soil Moist; preferably rich.
Propagation Plants can be divided in March. Take 75–100mm (3–4in) long cuttings in April–May, rooting them in cold frame or open ground.
Cultivation Plant in spring on well-prepared ground; to contain roots mint can be planted in a bottomless bucket, otherwise it will become too rampant. Plants die back in winter.
Pests and Diseases Mint rust may occur.

Right *Mentha suaveolens*

Mentzelia

LOASACEAE

A genus of herbaceous annuals, biennials, and perennials. The one species of garden interest – a hardy annual native to California – makes a showy plant for mixed borders.
M. lindleyi (syn. *Bartonia aurea*). Height 450–600mm (1½–2ft); spread 230mm (9in). Narrow, deeply lobed leaves on tough stems. Scented, golden-yellow flowers, 50mm (2in) across, in June–August.

Site Full sun.
Soil Well-drained, fertile.
Propagation Sow seeds outdoors in March–April; thin seedlings to 225mm (9in) apart.

Cultivation Apply compost or general fertiliser to soil before sowing.

Below *Mentzelia lindleyi*

Site Dappled shade best for most species; protect against wind, which spoils flowers.
Soil Free-draining but moisture-retentive; neutral to acid but not alkaline.
Propagation Sow freshly gathered seed in pans of seed compost, placing them in cold frame. Dry, packeted, purchased seed must be sown as soon as possible for best results; pot seedlings individually as soon as they are large enough to handle; plant out in late summer.
Cultivation Old seed-heads and foliage should be removed in late summer.
Pests and Diseases Downy mildew and black-bean aphis may be a nuisance.

Mentha

LABIATAE   Mint

Half-hardy and hardy perennials native to Europe, Africa, and Asia. Some are ornamental plants; others are used to add flavour or fragrance in cooking and other applications.
M. × piperita (Europe, including Britain), peppermint. Hardy. Height 300–600mm (1–2ft); spread 600mm (2ft). Erect red stems and toothed, reddish leaves with fine hairs on undersides. Clusters of purple flowers in September. A natural variety is *M. × p. citrata* (Europe), eau-de-Cologne mint. Hardy. Height 300mm (1ft); spread 450mm (1½ft). Smooth, rounded, dull-green leaves, strongly scented. Short spikes of reddish purple flowers in July–August.
M. requienii (Corsica), crème-de-menthe plant. Half-hardy

Above *Milium effusum* 'Aureum'

Milium

GRAMINEAE

Annual and perennial grasses, native to Europe, Asia, and North America. The species listed is noted for its decorative foliage and feathery flower plumes.

M. effusum (Europe, including Britain, Asia, N. E. North America), wood millet. Perennial. Height up to 300mm (1ft); spread 300mm (1ft) or more. Clumps of soft green, grassy foliage. Handsome pale green (occasionally purplish) flower plumes in June–July. Variety 'Aureum' (syn. 'Bowles' Golden Grass') has bright yellow foliage.

Site Sun or part shade; do not let soil dry out.
Soil Moist, free-draining, with plenty of humus.
Propagation By division in spring. Species also from seed sown in groups in small pots for planting out later; or by direct sowing in open ground.
Cultivation Plant in spring. Untidy growth should be removed in autumn, but plants must not be cut back severely or they may not recover.

Mimulus

SCROPHULARIACEAE   Monkey-flower

Hardy and half-hardy annuals and perennials and a few shrubs, native to North and South America, South Africa, and Australasia, with showy tubular flowers. Garden species are mainly short-lived perennials.

M. aurantiacus (syn. *M. glutinosus*, *Diplacus glutinosus*; California). Shrub. Height up to 1.2m (4ft); spread 900mm (3ft). Almost evergreen, shrubby plant with tangled masses of dark green sticky leaves. Bright orange, peach, or buff-coloured flowers, up to 50mm (2in) long, in axils of leaves in July–September. Plant usually pot-grown and plunged outside for the summer as it is not winter-hardy.

M. cardinalis (S. and W. North America, Mexico). Perennial. Height 300–900mm (1–3ft); spread 300–600mm (1–2ft). Hairy, sticky, grey-green foliage in clumps. Loose spikes of bright red, tubular flowers in July–August. Requires protection in cold districts.

M. cupreus (Chile). Perennial. Height 230–300mm (9–12in); spread 300mm (1ft). Luxuriant, soft green foliage in dense clumps. Bright yellow or orange tubular flowers, some marked or spotted with maroon, throughout summer. Varieties include 'Brilliant' (crimson); 'Fireflame' (scarlet); 'Leopard' (yellow, spotted brown); 'Red Emperor' (crimson); 'Whitecroft Scarlet' (dwarf, vermilion).

M. luteus (Chile), monkey musk. Perennial. Height 150–300mm (6–12in); spread 300mm (1ft). Creeping plant with ascending, congested, bushy, foliage. Bright yellow tubular flowers with conspicuous brownish patches in May–August.

M. ringens (North America), lavender-water musk. Perennial. Height 300–600mm (1–2ft); spread 300mm (1ft). True aquatic for margins of pool. Narrow green leaves arranged up slender, erect stems. Small tubular blue or whitish flowers, 25mm (1in) long, in June–July.

M. variegatus (of gardens; probably of hybrid origin). Perennial. Height 150–300mm (6–12in); spread 300mm (1ft). Creeping habit with ascending, lush green foliage. Yellow tubular flowers sprinkled with dark purplish spots in June–September. Varieties include 'Bonfire' (orange-scarlet); 'Queen's Prize Strain' (mixed colours, boldly spotted).

Site Must be open and sunny.
Soil *M. aurantiacus* needs free-draining soil; the others need moist soil that will not dry out in summer.
Propagation Sow seed in trays in spring and place in cold frame; prick out young plants and grow on as bedding plants; plant out as soon as they are large enough to handle. Soft cuttings can be taken in summer and rooted in a propagator. Those that form winter rosettes can be divided in dormant season.
Cultivation Plant at almost any time, but keep young plants continuously well watered. Remove old and decaying foliage in autumn. Regular lifting and dividing or replacement of plants essential.
Pests and Diseases Aphids and mildew can be nuisance.

Below *Mimulus cupreus* 'Whitecroft Scarlet'

Moluccella

LABIATAE

Annual grown for its unusual flower spikes, very popular with flower arrangers.

M. laevis (W. Asia), bells of Ireland, shell-flower. Half-hardy annual. Height to 600–900mm (2–3ft); spread 300mm (1ft). Tiny white flowers in summer surrounded by bowl-shaped, light green calyx, and carried in tall spike with tuft of leaves at top.

Site Sheltered, full sun.
Soil Ordinary, well-drained, rich loam.
Propagation Sow seeds in greenhouse or propagator at 18°C (65°F) in March; harden seedlings off before planting out in May. In favoured situations seeds may also be sown where they are to grow in April.
Cultivation Cut flower-spikes for drying when fully developed, choosing a dry, sunny day. Pull up and discard plants after flowering.

Monarda

LABIATAE   Bergamot, horsemint

Annual and perennial aromatic herbaceous plants from North America and Mexico. Some are decorative, but bergamots have long been cultivated by herbalists; the flowers are notably attractive to bees and butterflies.

M. didyma (North America), Oswego tea, bee balm, sweet bergamot. Hardy perennial. Height 600–900mm (2–3ft); spread 900mm (3ft) or more. Bushy, downy, fragrant foliage and whorls of bright red flowers in June–September. Varieties include 'Cambridge Scarlet'; 'Croftway Pink' (pale pink); 'Mahogany' (brownish red); 'Snow Queen' (white).

M. fistulosa (North America), wild bergamot. Hardy peren-nial 600–900mm (2–3ft); spread up to 900mm (3ft). Bushy with aromatic foliage, but sparser than the very similar *M. didyma*, with which it is often confused. Lavender-purple flowers in June–September.

Site Sun or part shade.
Soil Preferably heavy and moisture-retentive.
Propagation Sow seed of species indoors in March, planting out in late summer.
Divide named varieties in spring (they will not always come true from seed).
Cultivation Plant in spring.

Below *Monarda didyma*

Below *Moluccella laevis*

Above *Morina longifolia*

grape hyacinths, it has six to eight leaves per bulb. Spikes, 50–75mm (2–3in) long, of bright violet-blue flowers in spring. Varieties include 'Blue Spike' (double flowers); 'Cantab' (single, sky blue); 'Early Giant' (more robust, electric-blue flowers).

M. botryoides (C. and S. Europe to Caucasus). Height 100–150mm (4–6in); spread about 75mm (3in). Two to four leaves per bulb. Deep blue flower-spikes, about 40mm (1½in) long, compact, in early spring. Variety 'Album' (syn. 'Pearls of Spain', pure white).

M. comosum (S. Europe, N. Africa), tassel hyacinth. Height to 300mm (1ft); spread about 125mm (5in). Three to four leaves per bulb, fairly broad. Flower spikes of bluish-olive fertile bells, and a top-knot of purple-blue, smaller, sterile bells, in April–May. Represented in cultivation mainly by variety 'Monstrosum' (syn. 'Plumosum', the feather hyacinth), with flowers reduced to sterile filaments, creating a feathery head 75–125mm (3–5in) long.

M. macrocarpum (syn. *M. moschatum flavum*; E. Mediterranean, S.W. Turkey). Height 200–250mm (8–10in). Five or six leaves per bulb, somewhat fleshy. Flower spikes, about 75mm (3in) long, clear, waxy yellow, from purplish blue buds in spring.

M. tubergenianum (N. W. Iran), Oxford and Cambridge grape hyacinth. Height 150–200mm (6–8in); spread about 125mm (5in). Leaves about three per bulb, fairly broad. Flower spikes 50–70mm (2–2¾in) long in spring; upper flowers much paler than lower rich blue ones.

Site All need full sun to thrive; *M. armeniacum* and *M. tubergenianum* tolerate some shade from time to time.
Soil Well-drained, reasonably fertile.
Propagation Remove offsets or separate clumps when dormant; replant at once. Sow seed when ripe, or in spring.
Cultivation Plant in late summer or autumn, the earlier the better. Divide clumps every few years before they get too congested, after flowering or when dormant.

Below *Muscari armeniacum*

Morina

DIPSACACEAE

Hardy herbaceous perennials, native to south-eastern Europe to central Asia, with a thistle-like mode of growth and crowded whorls of decorative blooms.

M. longifolia (Himalaya). Height and spread 600mm (2ft). Evergreen, tufted, thistle-like leaves. Abundant white flowers, aging to pink, in June–July; bracts persist into autumn. A good border plant.

Site Full sun, but provide shelter from winds.
Soil Free-draining, fertile and of good depth.
Propagation Sow seeds as soon as possible after harvesting; pot-grow young plants to prevent root disturbance; plant out in spring or early summer. Division immediately after flowering also possible, but plants may take a whole season to recover from disturbance.
Cultivation Plant at any time in dormant season, but in colder districts spring planting is preferable. Once established they should be left alone, division taking place only when flower and foliage quality starts to diminish.

Muscari

LILIACEAE   Grape hyacinth

Bulbous perennials from the Mediterranean region and south-western Asia. Most have strap-shaped, channelled leaves and showy spikes of small, urn-shaped flowers.

M. armeniacum (N.E. Turkey). Height 150–200mm (6–8in) or more; spread about 100mm (4in). One of the best known

Myosotis

BORAGINACEAE   Forget-me-not

Annuals and short-lived herbaceous perennials native to Europe. Popular spring-flowering plants with mainly bright-blue flowers.

M. alpestris (Europe, including Britain). Perennial. Height 75–200mm (3–8in); spread 150–200mm (6–8in). Bushy plant with narrow, downy green leaves. Small, bright-blue, star-shaped flowers with yellow centres in April–June.

M. scorpioides (syn. *M. palustris*; Europe, including Britain), water forget-me-not. Aquatic perennial for planting in ponds or bog gardens. Height 230mm (9in); spread 150–230mm (6–9in). Spoon-shaped, hairy leaves. Small, pale blue flowers with yellow centres clustered on tall stems in April–July. 'Semperflorens' is a compact variety.

M. sylvatica (Britain). Biennial. Height 300mm (1ft); spread 150mm (6in). Bushy plant with mid-green, oblong leaves covered in hairs. Sprays of small, bright blue flowers in May–June. Cultivars, including several hybrids with *M. alpestris*, have blue, pink or white flowers. Good examples: 'Blue Ball', 'Bouquet', 'Carmine King', 'Compindi', 'Marine', 'Royal Blue', 'White Ball'; they make ideal plants for border edging.

Site Part shade or sun.
Soil Rich, moisture-retentive.
Propagation Sow seed outdoors in May–July; thin seedlings; plant out in September for flowering the following spring. Plants will naturalise if grown in good soil. Take 50–100mm (2–4in) long basal cuttings of *M. scorpioides* in early spring or late summer; root in boxes, keeping compost well-watered.

Cultivation Apply compost or leaf-mould to soil before planting out. Protect with cloches on heavy soils in winter. Plant *M. scorpioides* in spring or autumn in rich loam. In ponds, cover plants with about 75mm (3in) of water.
Pests and Diseases Grey mould or powdery mildew may occur.

Below *Myosotis sylvatica*

Myrtus

MYRTACEAE   Myrtle

Aromatic and fragrant evergreen shrubs and trees from warm-temperature and tropical regions. The species listed is that most commonly cultivated in Britain.

M. communis (Mediterranean), common myrtle. Height and spread against a warm, sheltered, south-facing wall about 3.5m (12ft); otherwise about 2.4m (8ft). Shiny evergreen leaves, aromatic when bruised. White fragrant flowers in July–August, followed by black berries.

Site Sunny, sheltered, preferably against south-facing wall.
Soil Well-drained.
Propagation Layer in early autumn. Take semi-hardwood heel cuttings in July–August with a little heat.
Cultivation Plant in April–May with peat or leaf-mould mixed into soil.
Pruning If necessary, tidy up plant's shape in May.
Pests and Diseases Occasionally affected by scale insect and leaf-spot.

Below *Myrtus communis*

Narcissus

AMARYLLIDACEAE   Daffodil, narcissus

Bulbous perennials native to western Europe, North Africa, and Asia. All have strap-shaped or rush-like leaves and six-petalled flowers with a central corona shaped like a cup or trumpet. Those with a corona as long as or longer than the petals are known as daffodils, the rest as narcissi.

N. asturiensis (syn. *N. minimus*; Spain, Portugal). Height 50–100mm (2–4in); spread 50–75mm (2–3in). Smallest trumpet daffodil. Grey-green leaves. Yellow flowers, 25mm (1in) long, in February–March. Not always long-lived in the garden.

N. bulbocodium (W. Europe, N.W. Africa), hoop-petticoat daffodil. Height 100–150mm (4–6in); spread about 75mm (3in). Leaves rush-like, dark green. Flowers 20–30mm ($\frac{3}{4}$–1$\frac{1}{4}$in) long, corona large and often flared, pale to deep yellow, and petals small, narrow pointed, in February–March. Varieties include *N. b. conspicuus* (slightly more robust, deep yellow); *N. b. obesus* (orange-yellow with very full corona).

N. cyclamineus (Spain, Portugal), cyclamen-flowered daffodil. Height 150–200mm (6–8in); spread about 100mm (4in). Leaves rich green, usually two or three per bulb. Deep yellow, pendent flowers, with coronas longer than back-swept petals, in February–March; from corona edge to petal tip they may exceed 45mm (1$\frac{3}{4}$in).

N. jonquilla (S. Europe, Algeria), jonquil. Height 300mm (1ft); spread about 125mm (5in). Leaves rush-like, erect. Flowers, 30–40mm (1$\frac{1}{4}$–1$\frac{1}{2}$in) wide, corona 4mm ($\frac{1}{6}$in) long,

Above *Narcissus* 'Edward Buxton'   **Left** *N.* 'Louise de Coligny'

carried in umbels of two to six, rich yellow, sweetly scented, in April.

N. juncifolius (Portugal, Spain, S.W. France). Height 150mm (6in); spread about 75mm (3in). Miniature jonquil, with flowers about 20mm ($\frac{3}{4}$in) wide in May.

N. nanus (Europe). Height about 150mm (6in); spread 100–125mm (4–5in). Smaller version of *N. pseudonarcissus* (q.v.), about 250mm (10in) high. *N. minor* is virtually identical, but about 200mm (8in) high. Both flower in March.

N. × odorus, campernelle jonquil. Height 300mm (1ft) or more; spread 130mm (5in). Much like *N. jonquilla* (one of its parents) but more robust. Flattened leaves and slightly larger flowers, having a fragrant corona, 8–13mm ($\frac{1}{3}$–$\frac{1}{2}$in) long, in April. Of several varieties, 'Rugulosus' has shorter, broader petals which overlap; 'Rugulosus Flore Pleno' has a double corona.

N. poeticus (Spain to Greece), pheasant's eye, poet's narcissus. Height 350–400mm (14–16in); spread 150–200mm (6–8in). Leaves narrowly strap-shaped. Fragrant, pure white flowers, 45–65mm (1$\frac{3}{4}$–2$\frac{1}{2}$in) wide, with very short, crimson-edged yellow-corona, in April–May. Variety 'Actaea' more robust, with larger flowers.

N. pseudonarcissus (Europe), Lent lily, wild daffodil. Height about 300mm (1ft); spread 150mm (6in). Leaves strap-shaped, grey-green. Flowers 50–70mm (2–2$\frac{3}{4}$in) long, with medium to deep yellow, almost straight-sided corona as long as the paler, waved petals, in April.

N. rupicola (Portugal, Spain). Height 100–150mm (4–6in); spread about 75mm (3in). Much like *N. juncifolius*, but with greyish-green leaves and solitary flowers in April–May.

N. tazetta (Portugal to Japan), polyanthus narcissus. Height 300–450mm (1–1½ft); spread 200–250mm (8–10in). Leaves rich to pale green, strap-shaped. Fragrant flowers in umbels of four to eight, each 25–40mm (1–1½in) wide, white with short yellow or white cup, very early – February in mild areas. Not reliably hardy in severe winters. *N. t. canaliculatus* is a later-flowering, hardy, miniature form about 150–200mm (6–8in) tall.

N. triandrus (Portugal, W. Spain), angel's tears. Height about 150mm (6in); spread 75mm (3in). Leaves very narrow, usually greyish-green. White flowers solitary or in nodding umbels of two or three, about 30mm (1¼in) long, in March–April. *N. t. concolor* has yellow flowers and attractive fragrance.

Narcissus Hybrids. The species listed above (and many others) have been extensively hybridised. Hundreds of cultivars are readily available, many of them better garden plants than the wild species. These have been classified in 10 groups according to flower shape and colour. The cultivars listed here are typical of each group and are recommended as garden plants.

Division 1: Daffodils. One flower per stem, corona as long as or longer than perianth (petals). Height 300–450mm (12–18in). 1A (petals and corona same colour, though petals may be paler shade): 'Covent Garden', 'Flower Carpet', 'Rembrandt'. 1B (petals white, corona coloured): 'Queen of

Above *Narcissus* 'Suzy'   **Below** *N.* 'Texas'

the Bicolours', 'Spring Glory'. 1C (petals and corona white, though can be yellow in bud): 'Beersheba', 'Mount Hood'.

Division 2: Large-Cupped Narcissi. One flower per stem, corona more than one third length of petals. Height 300–500mm (12–22in). 2A (petals in shades of yellow, orange and red, corona usually darker): 'Carlton', 'Scarlet Elegance' (red cup). 2B (petals white, corona coloured): 'Flower Record' (orange cup), 'Louise de Coligny' (white petals, pink cup). 2C (petals white, corona white or cream): 'Castella'.

Division 3: Small-Cupped Narcissi. One flower per stem, corona less than one third length of petals. Height 350–450mm (14–18in). 3A (petals and corona coloured): 'Edward Buxton' (yellow and orange). 3B (petals white, cup coloured): 'Verger'. 3C (petals and cup white): 'Verona'.

Division 4: Double-Flowered Narcissi. One flower per stem. Height 300–450mm (12–18in). 'Golden Ducat' (deep yellow); 'Irene Copeland' (white and yellow); 'Texas' (yellow and orange-red).

Division 5: Triandrus Narcissi. Several nodding flowers per stem. Height 200–250mm (8–10in). 'Liberty Bells' (deep yellow); 'Thalia' (pure white).

Division 6: Cyclamineus Narcissi. One nodding flower per stem, with reflexed petals. Height 200–375mm (8–15in). 'Dove Wings' (yellow and white); 'February Gold'; 'Tête-à-tête' (yellow, darker cup).

Division 7: Jonquil Narcissi. Several small flowers per stem. Height 250–450mm (10–18in). 'Suzy' (pale yellow and orange); 'Trevithian' (lemon yellow).

Division 8: Tazetta Narcissi. Several flowers per stem, with resemblance to *N. tazetta*. Height 375–425mm (15–17in). 'Geranium' (white and orange); 'Paper White' (pure white).

Division 9: Poeticus Narcissi. One flower per stem with a very small corona. Height 350–425mm (14–17in). 'Actaea'.

Division 10: All the true wild species.

Division 11: Miscellaneous. All cultivars which do not fit into the previous divisions, e.g. the Collar and Split-corona groups, which have divided, petal-like coronas.

Site Sun or part shade.
Soil Well-drained but moisture-retentive; *N. cyclamineus* will grow in wet soil.
Propagation Separate offsets and divide clumps when dormant. Sow seeds when ripe; seedlings take three to five years to flower.
Cultivation Plant in autumn, the earlier the better. Divide clumps before they get too congested.
Pests and Diseases Narcissus fly, slugs, and stem eelworm are common pests. Among diseases, viruses, basal rot, and white root rot may occur.

Below *Narcissus* Tazetta hybrid

Above *Nemesia strumosa* 'Carnival Mixed'

Nemesia

SCROPHULARIACEAE

Annuals, perennials, and sub-shrubs native to southern Africa. The species listed is an annual with showy, cheerful flowers freely produced that makes an excellent bedding plant.

N. strumosa. Half hardy. Height 300–450mm (1–1½ft); spread 150–200mm (6–8in). Bushy plant with light green, lanceolate leaves. Flowers with open faces and short throats in white, yellow, or purple, carried in clusters in mid-summer. Most strains offered are hybrids in a range of colours including blue, yellow, orange, bronze, scarlet, pink and cream; many have attractively blotched and spotted flowers. Typical are 'Blue Gem' (small, sky blue flowers); 'Carnival Mixed' (compact strain growing to 200–225mm (8–9in) high); 'Sutton's Sparklers' (bicolours and tricolours).

Site Open, in sun or part shade; flowers fade more quickly in very hot situations.
Soil Moisture-retentive but well-drained.
Propagation Sow in March in a greenhouse or propagator at 15°C (60°F), covering the small seed very lightly; prick off into boxes; harden off before planting in flowering positions in May.
Cultivation Keep plants well watered while they get established and in dry spells. Deadheading will encourage more flowers. Pull up and discard after flowering.
Pests and Diseases Aphids may attack growing tips of young plants. Infection due to foot-rot or root-rot may cause plants to collapse at ground level.

Nemophila

HYDROPHYLLACEAE

Hardy annuals from the western United States with freely produced blue flowers. The species listed is suitable for bedding.

N. menziesii (syn. *N. insignis*; California), baby blue-eyes. Height 150mm (6in); spread 150–250mm (6–10in). Spreading or trailing plant with deeply divided, mid-green leaves. Wide, flat, sky-blue flowers with white centres in June–August.

Site Sun or light shade, sheltered; dislikes hot, dry positions.
Soil Free-draining but moisture-retentive; reasonably fertile.
Propagation Sow seeds in flowering positions in March, covering them lightly; thin seedlings to 150mm (6in) in April. Can also be sown in September to overwinter outside; this gives sturdy, early-flowering plants.
Cultivation Water freely in dry weather. In cold spells during winter give cloche protection to plants sown to September. Pull up and discard after they have finished flowering.
Pests and Diseases Aphids may attack young shoots.

Below Nemophila menziesii

Nepeta

LABIATAE   Catmint

Annuals and herbaceous perennials native to Europe and Asia. They are rather invasive plants with small tubular flowers.

N. × *faassenii* (hybrid). Herbaceous perennial; makes an ideal edging plant. Height 300–450mm (1–1½ft); spread 600mm (2ft) or more. Narrow, grey-green leaves. Spikes of lavender-blue flowers, 150mm (6in) high, in May–September. Often confused with one of its parents, *N. mussinii*. Varieties include 'Six Hills Giant' (tougher, taller form, with deeper-coloured flowers); 'Blue Beauty'.

N. nervosa (Kashmir). Herbaceous perennial. Height 300–600mm (1–2ft); spread 300m (1ft) or more. Bushy plant with narrow, mid-green leaves showing prominent veins. Violet-blue flowers on spikes, 150–300mm (6–12in) long, in June–August.

Site Sun or half shade.
Soil Well-drained.
Propagation Plants can be divided in March–April. Take 50–75mm (2–3in) long basal cuttings in April; root in pots and plunge into garden soil when well-rooted; plant out following April.
Cultivation Plant in October–March. Cut back untidy growth in spring.
Pests and Diseases Powdery mildew may occur.

Above Nepeta nervosa

Nerine

AMARYLLIDACEAE

Bulbous perennials from southern Africa. Most species are tender and are best raised in the greenhouse; that listed is hardy in all but the severest winters, and bears umbels of showy flowers in autumn.

N. bowdenii. Height about 450mm (1½ft); spread 200–300mm (8–12in). Leaves strap-shaped, glossy green, about 300mm (1ft) long, arching. Flowers in clusters of 6–12, each with six narrow, waved, pink petals about 70mm (2¾in) long. Flowering usually at its best in October. Variety 'Fenwick's' has intense pink flowers and is more robust. A white form is also available occasionally.

Site Must be sunny and sheltered.
Soil Must be well-drained, of moderate fertility, though quite poor soils are also suitable.
Propagation Separate offsets or divide clumps in spring.
Cultivation Plant in spring, just as growth starts and weather warms up.

Below Nerine bowdenii

Nicandra

SOLANACEAE

A hardy annual with interesting flowers and bladder-like fruits; it makes an attractive and unusual border plant.

N. physalodes (Peru), shoo-fly plant, apple of Peru. Height 600–900mm (2–3ft); spread 600mm (2ft). Strong-growing, branched plant with deeply toothed, wavy edged, mid-green leaves. Short-lived bell-shaped, pale lavender and white flowers in July–September, followed by globose berries enclosed in lantern-shaped green or purple calyces. Plant is reputed to repel flies.

Site Sunny.
Soil Moderately fertile.
Propagation Sow in open in April; thin or transplant to 450mm (18in) apart. Can also be sown in greenhouse or propagator in March; harden off before planting out in May.
Cultivation Best grown as specimen plant in centre of border. Stake in exposed positions. Keep well-watered in dry weather. Cut fully developed fruiting branches for drying on a warm, sunny day.

Right *Nicandra physalodes*

Above *Nicotiana alata* 'Lime Green'

Nicotiana

SOLANACEAE   Tobacco plant

Annuals and perennials, mainly from the warmer parts of North and South America, with attractive flowers, grown mainly for their strong evening fragrance. Most blooms open only at dusk.

N. alata (syn. *N. affinis*; South America), sweet-scented tobacco plant. Half-hardy perennial, usually grown as an annual. Height 600mm–1.2m (2–4ft); spread 450–600mm (1½–2ft). Rather straggly plant with light green, oval leaves. White, tubular flowers, very strongly scented, open in the evening in June–September. Varieties include 'Lime Green' (greenish yellow blooms, popular with flower arrangers); 'Nicki Mixed' (compact, hybrid strain 250mm (10in) high, also available in single colours); 'Sensation Mixed' (red, pink, crimson, yellow, and cream flowers, which remain open during day).

N. × sanderae (hybrid). Half-hardy perennial grown as annual. Height 450–750mm (1½–2½ft); spread 450mm (1½ft). Mid-green, pointed leaves. Yellow flowers with pink tinge in June–September. Varieties include 'Crimson Bedder' (smaller than parent, with glowing red flowers); 'White Bedder' (smaller than parent, with white blooms).

N. suaveolens (Australia). Half-hardy annual. Height 450–600mm (1½–2ft); spread 300–450mm (1–1½ft). Broad, light green leaves form spreading rosettes. Strongly fragrant flowers are white, tinged with purple on the outside.

N. sylvestris (Argentina). Half-hardy perennial, usually grown as an annual or biennial. Height 1.2–1.5m (4–5ft); spread 600mm (2ft). Sturdy, quick-growing plant with large, mid-green leaves. Prefers shaded positions, where large white flowers remain open all day.

Site Sun or semi-shade. *N. sylvestris* prefers shade – a good plant for edge of woodland. Plant fragrant species near house or patio, where scent can be appreciated at night.
Soil Reasonably fertile.
Propagation Sow in greenhouse or propagator in March at 15–18°C (60–65°F); prick out seedlings into boxes; harden off before planting in flowering positions in May.

Cultivation Stake tall-growing varieties in exposed positions. In sheltered gardens in south and south-west England, *N. sylvestris* can be treated as short-lived perennial; but better results are obtained by treating all species as annuals and discarding them after they have finished flowering.
Pests and Diseases Aphids and leaf-spot disease can be a nuisance.

Nierembergia

SOLANACEAE

A group of herbaceous perennials, mainly of South America, of which only one is in general cultivation, where it does well on the rock garden or in paving.

N. repens (syn. *N. rivularis*; Argentina, Uruguay, Chile). Height 65mm (2½in); spread up to 600mm (2ft). Spreads by means of creeping underground stems to produce a thick mat, with large white, bell-shaped flowers in June–September.

Site Full sun, sheltered.
Soil Well-drained but moisture must be available to the roots.
Propagation By division in March or April, replanting

directly or in a container.
Pests and Diseases Aphids sometimes a problem.

Below *Nierembergia repens*

Above *Nigella damascena* 'Persian Jewels Mixed'

Nigella

RANUNCULACEAE

Hardy annuals, native to Europe, with showy flowers followed by attractive seed pods. The species listed, popular in borders, makes excellent cut flowers.

N. damascena (S. Europe), love-in-a-mist. Height 150–450mm (6–18in); spread 225mm (9in). Delicate, dissected foliage on erect stems. Cornflower-like flowers, 40mm (1½in) across, in June–August. Varieties include 'Dwarf Moody Blue' (150–200mm (6–8in) high, violet-blue flowers changing to sky-blue); 'Miss Jekyll' (bright blue semi-double flowers); 'Persian Jewels Mixed' (pink, red, mauve, purple, blue, and white flowers).

Site Full sun.
Soil Well-drained.
Propagation Sow seeds where they are to flower in March–May; thin out to 200mm (8in) apart. Can also be sown in September in sheltered areas. Plants may self-seed.

Nymphaea

NYMPHAEACEAE   Water-lily

Hardy and tender aquatics of cosmopolitan distribution. Most have showy flowers and handsome floating leaves; some are scented.

N. × laydekeri (hybrid). Depth of water required 300–450mm (1–1½ft); spread 600mm (2ft) or more. Excellent plant for the smaller pool. Dark green or purplish-flecked leaves. Brightly coloured flowers in June–September, most heavily scented. Varieties, with flowers 65–75mm (2½–3in) across, include 'Fulgens' (crimson); 'Lilacea' (pink); 'Purpurata' (red).

N. × marliacea (hybrid group). Depth of water required 450mm–1m (1½–3¼ft); spread 1m (3¼ft) or more. Water-lilies for the medium-sized or large pool, with dark green or purplish green floating leaves. Large showy flowers in June–September. Varieties, with flowers up to 150mm (6in) across, include 'Albida' (white); 'Carnea' (flesh-pink); 'Chromatella' (syn. *N. × chromatella*, yellow); 'Flammea' (red) 'Rosea' (deep pink).

N. odorata (North America), sweet-scented water-lily. Depth of water required 450–750mm (1½–2½ft); spread 750mm (2½ft). Rounded, bright-green leaves. Pure white, fragrant flowers, up to 150mm (6in) across, in June–September. Varieties include 'Eugène de Land' (apricot); 'Firecrest' (deep pink); 'Sulphurea' (canary yellow); 'William B. Shaw' (creamy pink).

N. × pygmaea (hybrid group), pygmy water-lilies. Depth of water required up to 300mm (1ft); spread 300–450mm (1–1½ft). Small hybrid cultivars for tub or sink garden, with leaves up to 50mm (2in) across. Miniature blooms 25–50mm (1–2in) in diameter in June–September. Varieties include 'Alba' (white); 'Helvola' (yellow); 'Rubra' (red).

N. tuberosa (North America), magnolia water-lily. Depth of water required 600–900mm (2–3ft); spread 1.2m (4ft). Handsome bright-green, floating leaves. Large, scentless, white blossoms produced in June–September. Varieties, with flowers up to 175mm (7in) across, include 'Paeslingberg' (white); 'Richardsonii' (white); 'Rosea' (pink, scented).

Site Full sun in water of adequate depth for the species.
Soil Good heavy loam devoid of raw organic matter likely to pollute water.
Propagation *N. × pygmaea* 'Alba' from seeds sown onto trays of mud immediately they ripen; once germinating, seed leaves are covered with water; depth of water is increased as leaf growths develop; when large enough to handle, seedlings are potted individually. Other water-lilies propagated from 'eyes' (buds or small growths) on woody root-stocks; these are cut out of root-stock in April–May, potted individually in heavy soil, and covered with 50mm (2in) of water. They quickly root and produce small floating leaves; young plants are grown on until large enough to plant in pool.
Cultivation Plant in plastic planting baskets at any time in April-September, the earlier the better. Remove superfluous foliage likely to give buoyancy to the plant; give plant and basket a good soaking from a watering can to drive out air from soil. Apply generous layer of pea gravel to surface of each basket to prevent soil from escaping into pool and to discourage fish from stirring up soil. Divide plants every three to five years. Feed occasionally with coarse bonemeal.
Pests and Diseases Water-lily aphids, water-lily beetle, and caddis flies may cause problems, as may pointed pond snails. Leaf spots and water-lily root-rot are common diseases.

Below *Nymphaea × marliacea* 'Chromatella'

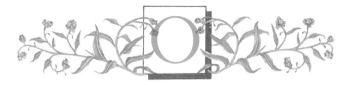

Oenothera

ONAGRACEAE

Annuals, biennials and perennials from the Americas with yellow or white funnel-shaped flowers that remain open in the evening. The garden species listed are hardy and suitable for border or rock garden, depending on size.

O. acaulis (Chile). Perennial. Height 150mm (6in); spread 450mm (1½ft). Rock-garden plant with rosettes of deeply toothed, mid-green leaves. Large flowers, opening white and turning deep rose-pink, carried all summer and autumn.

O. biennis (North America), evening primrose. Biennial. Height 600mm–1.2m (2–4ft); spread 300–450mm (1–1½ft). Vigorous plants with rosettes of lanceolate, mid-green leaves. Tall spikes bearing clusters of large, pale-yellow flowers in June–October. Increases rapidly from self-sown seed. Larger-flowered *O. × erythrosepala* is similar.

O. fruticosa (North America). Perennial. Height 600mm (2ft); spread 300mm (1ft). Mid-green, lanceolate leaves. Golden yellow flowers in June–August. 'Yellow River' is a particularly free-flowering variety.

O. missouriensis (C. United States). Perennial. Height 150mm (6in); spread 300–450mm (1–1½ft). Rock-garden or low-growing border plants. Trailing stems bear lanceolate, mid-green leaves. Large yellow flowers in profusion through the summer.

O. perennis (syn. *O. pumila*; E. North America). Perennial. Height and spread 300mm (12in) or more. Small, yellow flowers are carried above lanceolate, pale green leaves on short spikes in mid-summer.

Below *Oenothera fruticosa*

O. tetragona (syn. *O. riparia*; E. North America). Perennial. Height 600mm–1m (2–3¼ft); spread 300–450mm (1–1½ft). Branching, bushy plant with ovate, mid-green leaves. Spikes of small yellow flowers in June–September. Cultivars include 'Highlight' (free-flowering with wide, yellow blooms); 'Fireworks' (bright yellow flowers, red in bud).

Site Full sun or light shade.
Soil Light, free-draining.
Propagation Sow seeds outdoors in nursery rows in late spring; transplant to permanent positions in autumn. *O. acaulis* best sown under glass in early spring, the young plants grown on in small pots. Divide and replant roots of perennials in early spring.
Cultivation Water well in dry weather; remove faded flower-spikes to avoid self-sown seedlings, which can become a nuisance. Pull up and discard biennials after flowering. Perennials are short lived and can be replaced by young plants from seed.
Pruning Cut dead stems of perennials to ground level in autumn.
Pests and Diseases Root rots may be a problem on heavy, waterlogged soil.

Above *Omphalodes verna*

150mm (6in) wide, in June. Needs shelter from severe frost. Has a musk-like odour.
O. × scilloniensis (hybrid; Isles of Scilly). Height 1.2m (4ft); spread 600mm (2ft). Serrated grey-green leaves, white-felted beneath. White flowers, 30mm (1¼in) wide, cover bush in May–June. Not very hardy.

Site Sunny, sheltered from cold wind.
Soil Preferably well-drained.
Propagation Put semi-hardwood cuttings in sandy compost under cover in August; provide heat if summer is cool.
Cultivation Plant in April–May. Water well if dry weather follows. Protect during first winter.
Pruning If plants become leggy with age, cut back hard in spring just as growth is starting.

Omphalodes

BORAGINACEAE   Navelwort
Hardy annuals and perennials, mainly from south-eastern Europe, western Asia and Mexico, useful in the rock garden. The species listed are perennials suitable for the rock garden or front of boarder.
O. cappadocica (Turkey, Caucasus). Clump-forming species, 150–225mm (6–9in) high and 450mm (18in) wide. Heart-shaped, bright-green foliage. Dense sprays of sky-blue flowers in May–June.
O. luciliae (Turkey, Greece). Somewhat smaller plant notable for the greyish green colour of its foliage. Delicate, pale-blue flowers from May to early autumn.
O. verna (European Alps), blue-eyed mary. Height 150mm (6in); spread 250mm (10in). Early-flowering species, forms tufts of long-stalked mid-green leaves and open sprays of bright-blue flowers in February–May. There is also a white form, 'Alba'.

Site For *O. cappadocica*, a cool position is best; for *O. luciliae*, a sunny spot (or alpine house); for *O. verna*, light shade.
Soil Leafy loam, not particularly rich, with additional limestone grit for *O. luciliae*.
Propagation Divide *O. cappadocica* and *O. verna* in March or September; plant out directly, or pot up. Divide *O. luciliae* carefully in June–July and pot up in gritty soil.
Unrooted branches, if potted firmly, root quickly if placed in a closed frame.
Cultivation Alpine-house treatment for *O. luciliae* is preferable, as it is prone to slug attack outside. *O. cappadocica* and *O. verna* do well in moist, shady woodland conditions. *O. verna* spreads by means of runners.
Pests and Diseases Slugs are a nuisance.

Above *Olearia macrodonta*

Olearia

COMPOSITAE   Daisy bush
Evergreen trees and shrubs from Australasia, whose chief garden attraction is the clusters of white, daisy-like flowers in summer. Not fully hardy, olearias grow best in coastal gardens in south and south-west Britain, though *O. × haastii* may succeed elsewhere.
O. × haastii (natural hybrid; New Zealand). Height 1.2–1.8m (4–6ft); spread slightly more. Deep green leaves with white underfelt. Flattish flower-clusters, 75mm (3in) wide, in July. Hardy except in very severe winters.
O. macrodonta (New Zealand), New Zealand holly. Height 3m (10ft); spread 2.1m (7ft). Dark grey-green, shiny, holly-like leaves, white-felted beneath. White flowers in clusters,

Above *Ornithogalum nutans*

Ornithogalum

LILIACEAE

Bulbous perennials from the temperate zones of Europe, Asia, and Africa, with narrow leaves and racemes of starry, six-petalled, mostly white flowers. Most species are tender and only those listed thrive in Britain, where they make attractive border plants.

O. balansae (N.E. Turkey). Height about 100mm (4in); spread 75mm (3in). Smaller version of *O. umbellatum* (q.v.), but with broader leaves lacking silvery stripe. Green-striped white flowers in March–April.

O. nutans (W. Europe to W. Turkey), drooping star of Bethlehem. Height 250–350mm (10–14in), occasionally more; spread about 125mm (5in). Leaves very narrow, channelled. Flowers in racemes, each one nodding, 20–30mm ($\frac{3}{4}$–$1\frac{1}{4}$) long, with silvery white and green, waved petals in April–May.

O. umbellatum (Europe, North Africa), star of Bethlehem. Height 150–300mm (6–12in); spread 100–125mm (4–5in). Leaves very narrow, with silvery-white mid-rib. Flowers in umbel-like clusters, each about 40mm ($1\frac{1}{4}$in) wide, glistening white, green-striped in bud. Blooms open in sunshine only, just as the leaves die away, in early summer.

Site Best in full sun (but *O. nutans* likes part shade).
Soil Well-drained, but *O. nutans* is best where the soil stays moist.
Propagation Separate offsets or bulblets, or divide clumps when dormant. Sow seeds when ripe or in spring.
Cultivation Plant in autumn.
Pests and Diseases Slugs may eat leaves and flowers.

Osmanthus

OLEACEAE

A small genus of slow-growing evergreen shrubs or small trees of attractive shape, mainly from Asia, with strongly fragrant white flowers. The species listed are reasonably hardy and widely available.

O. × burkwoodii (syn. × *Osmarea burkwoodii*). Upright habit. Height and spread 1.8m (6ft) or more. Leaves glossy, dark green. Small white, tubular flowers in clusters in April–May. Can be grown as a formal hedge.

O. delavayi (China). Rounded shrub about 1.5m (5ft) tall, slightly less wide. Small, dark green, toothed leaves. Tubular, jasmine-scented flower clusters in April, followed by black berries.

O. heterophyllus (syn. *O. aquifolium*; Japan). Height and spread 1.8–2.4m (6–8ft). Mid-green leaves with holly-like prickles. White tubular flower clusters in September–October.

Site Sun or dappled shade.
Soil Any except waterlogged or shallow chalk.
Propagation Layer in autumn. Insert semi-hardwood cuttings in sandy compost under cover in July–August.

Cultivation Plant in late spring or early autumn; mix plenty of peat into soil when planting.
Pruning Remove dead growth in late spring.

Below *Osmanthus delavayi*

Osmunda

OSMUNDACEAE

Handsome hardy and tender ferns of worldwide distribution, cultivated for their handsome foliage and useful for shady parts of the garden.

O. cinnamomea (North and South America, West Indies, E. Asia), cinnamon fern. Perennial. Height 600–900mm (2–3ft); spread 600mm (2ft). Bold divided, bright green foliage covered in dense rusty scales when young. Fertile fronds yield upright spikes of dark brown spores.

O. claytoniana (syn. *O. interrupta*: E. North America, Himalayas, China), interrupted fern. Perennial. Height 300–600mm (1–2ft); spread 600mm (2ft). Handsomely divided sterile fronds surround striking upright fertile ones with dense gathering of spores in their midst.

O. regalis (cosmopolitan, including Britain), royal fern. Perennial. Height up to 2m (6$\frac{1}{2}$ft); spread 1.2m (4ft). Large leathery fronds that change colour with age from lime

Above *Osmunda regalis*

green, through pink, to deep rusty red; last tints are short-lived as first sharp frost shrivels delicate leaflets. Cultivars include 'Cristata' (crested fronds); 'Purpurascens' (purplish foliage); 'Undulata' (crumpled fronds).

Site All tolerate full sun, but plants prefer at least dappled shade.
Soil Rich, peaty, acid preferred, but plants tolerate neutral or slightly alkaline soil if it has sufficient moisture.
Propagation While it is possible to increase all the osmundas from spores, it is not very reliable, for the spores of all species contain a little chlorophyl which disappears within a day or two of harvesting and renders them useless. Perpetuate good forms of cultivars by careful division in spring.
Cultivation All like a damp situation; *O. regalis* will grow in the margins of a pool. Protect emerging shoots with dry bracken or straw in early spring.

Oxalis

OXALIDACEAE

A large and attractive genus of mainly small annuals, perennials, shrubs and bulbous plants of worldwide distribution. The small hardy perennials are useful in the rock garden. Those listed are bulbs or perennials; some are invasive.

O. adenophylla (Chile). Height 75mm (3in); spread 200mm (8in). Forms a fibre-coated bulb from which arise wrinkled glaucous leaves that die down in winter. Pink, cup-shaped flowers, 25mm (1in) across, borne on long stems in May–July.

O. enneaphylla (Patagonia, Falkland Islands). Height 75mm (3in); spread 150mm (6in). Spreads by means of scaly tubers producing crinkled, grey foliage. White, 25mm (1in) wide, funnel-shaped flowers in June–July. Interesting cultivars include the miniature 'Minutaefolia' (miniature, 50mm (2in) tall); 'Rosea' (pale pink flowers).

O. inops (South Africa). Height 100mm (4in); spread 200mm (8in). Invasive bulb whose light-green leaves appear in spring. Rose-pink, funnel-shaped flowers in June–August.

O. laciniata (Patagonia). Height up to 100mm (4in); spread up to 375mm (15in). Similar to *O. enneaphylla*, but glaucous leaves more divided, with wavy, purple margins. Smoky blue to dark-veined, light purple flowers, 25mm (1in) across, in May–August. A hybrid between this species and *O. enneaphylla*, *O.* × 'Ione Hecker' has 65mm (2½in) wide funnel-shaped flowers of lavender blue veined with purple.

O. magellanica (South America). Forms prostrate carpet of bronze-green leaves. White cup-shaped flowers produced in May–June. May be invasive in moist, peaty soils.

Site Sun or part shade.
Soil Preferably enriched with leaf-mould or peat, but must be free-draining.
Propagation Remove offsets of *O. adenophylla, O. enneaphylla, O. inops* and *O. laciniata* in March–April, and pot in a peaty mixture with grit. Divide *O. magellanica* at same time, and plant where it is to grow or pot up.
Cultivation Add peat as top-dressing on plant clumps when they are established.
Pests and Diseases Greenfly may attack leaves and flower stems.

Below *Oxalis adenophylla*

Pachysandra

BUXACEAE   Japanese spurge

Shrubs and sub-shrubs, native to Asia and North America, forming prostrate carpets with inconspicuous spikes of white or pinkish flowers. The species listed is valuable as evergreen ground-cover for shady places in the garden.

P. terminalis (Japan). Height up to 300mm (1ft); spread 600mm (2ft) or more depending on situation. Diamond-shaped, partly toothed, leathery, pale-green leaves clustered at ends of short stems. Spikes of small white flowers on ends of stems in February–March. 'Variegata', with leaves variegated with white, is attractive but spreads more slowly than its parent.

Site Prefers shade, however dense; will not thive appy in open situation.
Soil Must be moist and fertile; dislikes dry, chalky soils.
Propagation Divide and replant rooted pieces in March–April.
Cultivation Mulch in early spring with leaf-mould or compost to help plants spread.

Below *Pachysandra terminalis* 'Variegata'

Above *Paeonia mlokosewitschii*

Paeonia

PAEONIACEAE   Peony

Tuberous-rooted, clump-forming, hardy herbaceous perennials and shrubs, native to Europe, Asia, and western North America, with handsome lobed or dissected foliage and saucer- or bowl-shaped flowers, often large and colourful. Favourites for herbaceous and mixed borders.

P. delavayi (S.W. China). Deciduous shrub. Height and spread about 1.5m (5ft) or more. Dissected leaves 200–300mm (8–12in) long. Flowers 70–90mm ($2\frac{3}{4}$–$3\frac{1}{2}$in) wide, maroon-red, opening widely in June.

P. lactiflora (syn. *P. albiflora*; Siberia, Tibet, China), Chinese peony. Herbaceous perennial. Height 600–900mm (2–3ft); spread to 600mm (2ft). Dissected leaves, usually red-tinted when young. Flowers fragrant, bowl-shaped, to 100mm (4in) wide, usually white, sometimes pink or red. Represented in gardens mainly by its many cultivars, some of hybrid origin. Following are recommended: 'Bowl of Beauty' (mallow-purple, filled with pale yellow staminodes); 'Felix Crousse' (rose-red, double); 'Karl Rosenfeld' (deep crimson, double); 'La Cygne' (creamy-white, double); 'M. Jules Elie' (lilac-pink, double); 'Sarah Bernhardt' (apple-blossom-pink, double); 'The Moor' (maroon-crimson, single); 'Victoire de la Marne' (carmine-red, double); 'Whitleyi Major' (sometimes listed as *P. whitleyi*: pure white, single).

P. lutea (S.W. China). Height and spread 1.5–2m (5–$6\frac{1}{2}$ft).

peony. Deciduous shrub. Height and spread 1–2m (3¼–6½ft). Leaves dissected (in some forms almost ferny), often grey-green and pinkish when young. Bowl-shaped, pink to white flowers, 150–200mm (6–8in) wide, open in early summer. Many good cultivars of hybrid origin, including 'Chromatella' (double, sulphur-yellow, very large); 'Comtesse de Tudor' (double, salmon-red); 'Godaishu' (syn. 'Large Globe', semi-double, white with yellow centre); 'Reine Elizabeth' (syn. 'Queen Elizabeth', double, deep salmon-pink); 'Rock's Variety' (single, white, each petal with large, basal crimson-magenta blotch).

P. tenuifolia (S.E. Europe to Caucasus). Herbaceous perennial. Height and spread 300mm (1ft) or more. Leaves bright green, elaborately cut into slender, grassy segments creating a lacy effect. Flowers crimson, cup-shaped, about 60mm (2½in) wide, in late spring or early summer. One of the smallest and most attractive species.

Site Preferably sunny, but some shade tolerated.
Soil Well-drained but moisture-retentive, with plenty of humus.
Propagation Divide perennials in autumn or early spring. Take cuttings of shrubs in autumn in a cold frame (rooting is unreliable); or layer in spring. Sow seeds of shrubs and perennials when ripe, or as soon afterwards as possible; germination may take 1½ years, and seedlings take several years to reach flowering size; cultivars do not come true to type but can be interesting and sometimes good.
Pests and Diseases Peony blight (or wilt) often serious; peony blotch (or leaf-spot) can mar foliage.

Below *Paeonia lactiflora* 'Whitleyi Major'

Shrub, much like *P. delavayi*, but with brighter green leaves and yellow flowers. Natural variety *P. l. ludlowii* (Tibet) can reach 3m (10ft) tall and bears flowers 90–125mm (3½–5in) wide.

P. mlokosewitschii (Caucasus). Herbaceous perennial. Height 600–750mm (2–2½ft); spread 450–600mm (1½–2ft). leaves cut into large, oval, grey-green leaflets. Flowers bowl-shaped, 75–115mm (3–4½in) wide, lemon-yellow in April–May. Pale pink hybrids sometimes masquerade under this name.

P. obovata (China, Japan, Sakhalin). Herbaceous perennial. Height and spread 450mm (1½ft) or more. Dissected, grey-green leaves, copper-tinted when young. Rose-purple, bowl-shaped flowers, about 70mm (2¾in) wide open in May–June.

P. officinalis (France to Balkans), common peony. Herbaceous perennial. Height and spread to 600mm (2ft). Leaves extensively dissected. Flowers red, 80–125mm (3–5in) wide, bowl-shaped in May–June. Cultivars include 'Alba Plena' (double white); 'Anemoniflora' (deep pink with crimson and yellow petaloids); 'J.C. Weguelin' (crimson); 'Lize van Veen' (double white, flushed pink); 'Rosea Superba' (double bright pink); 'Rubra Plena' (double deep red, an old cottage-garden favourite).

P. peregrina (syn. *P. decora*, *P. lobata*; Romania, Italy, Balkans). Herbaceous perennial. Height and spread about 600mm (2ft). Similar to *P. officinalis*, but flowers more cup-shaped, and intense satiny red. Cultivar 'Sunshine' has salmon-red flowers with an orange patina.

P. suffruticosa (syn. *P. moutan*; Bhutan, Tibet, China), tree

green, ivy-shaped leaves. Pink or lilac flowers in summer. Cultivars include 'L'Élégante' (purple-veined white flowers, cream-edged leaves that turn purple in strong light).

Site Open, full sun.
Soil Moderately fertile; over-rich soil encourages leafy growth at expense of flowers.
Propagation Sow seeds in January–February in greenhouse or propagator at 16–18°C (60–65°F); pot on seedlings individually into 90mm (3½in) pots; plant out after risk of frosts has passed. Take softwood cuttings from over-wintered plants in March–April, inserting in sandy compost in greenhouse or frost-free frame.
Cultivation Give plants occasional high-potash feed.

Remove dead flower-heads. Lift best plants and over-winter them in pots of almost dry compost in frost-free place to provide cuttings in the following spring.
Pruning Cut back lifted plants by one third before potting them up for over-wintering.
Pests and Diseases Caterpillars sometimes eat leaves and flower buds. Black leg (bacterial disease) can affect the bases of unrooted cuttings; rust may infest leaves.

Above *Pelargonium × domesticum* 'Grand Slam'

Pelargonium

GERANIACEAE

Tender perennials and shrubs of Africa grown for their showy flowers. They are particularly useful in summer bedding schemes and in tubs and hanging baskets. Although commonly known as geraniums they are easily distinguished from the (mostly winter-hardy) species of the crane's-bill genus *Geranium* (q.v.).

P. × domesticum, regal pelargonium. Height 300–600mm (1–2ft); spread 200–600mm (8in–2ft). Branching plants with sturdy stems and toothed, usually mid-green leaves. Round heads of brightly coloured, often double flowers carried above foliage on slender stalks in June–August. Many cutivars in white, pinks, salmon, rose, violet, orange, scarlet; also bicolours. Examples: 'Grand Slam' (rose red) and 'Lavender Grand Slam' (both with abundance of large blooms); 'Black Butterfly' (very dark blooms with pink butterfly markings); 'Princess of Wales' (frilled, strawberry-pink flowers).

P. × hortorum, zonal pelargonium. Height 150mm–1m (6in–3¼ft); spread 150–600mm (6in–2ft). Rounded, soft, palmate leaves with dark band or zone. Some cultivars grown for variegated or coloured leaves as well as their flowers (which are chiefly in shades of pink or red), notably 'Mrs Henry Cox' and 'Golden Harry Hieover'. Good summer-flowering cultivars include 'Paul Crampel' (scarlet); 'Snowstorm' (prolific, white); 'King of Denmark' (double-flowered, salmon-pink). Some cultivars can be raised from seed, including 'Sprinter' (early flowering, bright scarlet); 'Picasso' (glowing carmine with orange eye); 'Startel' (ragged petals, jagged-edged leaves, various colours). 'Orange Cascade' and 'Red Fountain' have cascading habit.

P. peltatum, ivy-leaved geranium. Height 150mm (6in); spread up to 1.2m (4ft). Trailing stems carry fleshy, mid-

Below *Pelargonium peltatum* 'L'Élégante'

Penstemon

SCROPHULARIACEAE

Shrubs and perennials, native mainly to North and Central America. All have striking tubular blossoms that add colour to rock gardens and borders.

P. barbatus (syn. *Chelone barbata*; North America). Half-hardy. Height 900mm (3ft); spread 450mm (1½ft). Bushy, much-branched plant with glossy, lance-shaped leaves. Striking red or carmine tubular flowers, about 25mm (1in) long, borne in erect spires in June–August. Cultivar 'Coccineus' is clear scarlet.

P. campanulatus (Mexico, Guatemala). Height 450–600mm (1½–2ft). Hardy shrubby plant with dull green, lance-shaped leaves. Erect spires of bell-shaped flowers of pink, purple, or violet abundant in June. Varieties include 'Evelyn' (pink); 'Garnet' (wine-red).

P. hartwegii (Mexico). Half-hardy, often treated as an annual or biennial. Height 600mm (2ft); spread 300mm (1ft). Vigorous leafy, bushy plant with dark green foliage. Scarlet funnel-shaped blossoms in compact spikes in June–July. Parent of race of garden hybrids, of which selected strains for raising from seed are available for use in bedding schemes.

P. newberryi (W. North America). Hardy alpine. Height and spread 300mm (1ft). Shrubby mounds of dark green leathery leaves. Innumerable little rose-red tubular flowers in July.

P. pinifolius (California). Hardy alpine. Height 150mm (6in); spread 225mm (9in). Dense clusters of bright green, needle-like foliage. Tiny, vivid scarlet tubular flowers in July–August.

Site Open, sunny.
Soil Free-draining.
Propagation Most are raised from seed sown in trays in greenhouse; those used for bedding should be sown in gentle heat in February. Species can be sown at any period in the summer. Short cuttings of non-flowering stems can be taken in July–August and rooted in a mixture of equal parts peat and sharp sand in a propagator; transfer these to pots when they have rooted; over-winter in cold frame or cool greenhouse. Named varieties can be propagated only in this manner; also best for rock-garden kinds.

Cultivation Plant in spring (alpines can be planted autumn-spring). Take a few cuttings (as previously described) and over-winter them in a cold frame in case severe weather kills main plants. Leave old foliage on plants for winter protection.

Pests and Diseases Slugs attack young shoots.

Below Penstemon campanulatus 'Evelyn'

Pernettya mucronata

Pernettya

ERICACEAE

Hardy, evergreen, low-growing shrubs, native to Mexico, South America, New Zealand and Tasmania. The only garden species is grown for its colourful berries.

P. mucronata (S. America). Height 1.2–1.5m (4–5ft); spread 600–900mm (2–3ft). Dense habit. Small, pointed, glossy leaves cover stems. White, bell-heather-like flowers, 3mm ($\frac{1}{8}$in) long, carried in leaf axils in May–June. Male and female flowers usually carried on separate plants. Clusters of round berries, varying from white through pink to red and purple in September and lasting throughout winter. Good forms include 'Alba' (white fruits); 'Atrococcinea' (red-purple); 'Lilacina' (lilac). 'Bell's Seedling' (dark red) is hermaphroditic, setting fruits on its own.

Site Full sun preferred, but tolerates, shade.
Soil Lime-free; preferably moist, peaty loam.
Propagation By cuttings of cultivars (these will not come true from seed). Take 50mm (2in) stem cuttings in September–October and root in mixture of peat and sand. Can also be raised from seed. Sow in October in lime-free compost; grow on in pots for two years before planting outside.

Cultivation Plant outdoors any time between September and May. Set out in blocks of three or more cultivars to aid pollination.

Pruning In winter prune old, leggy plants to improve shape and encourage new growth lower down.

Petunia

SOLANACEAE

Perennials, usually treated as half-hardy annuals, from North and South America, with colourful, funnel-shaped flowers. The hybrid cultivars listed are widely used for bedding and as container plants.

P. × hybrida. Source of many popular cultivars. Height 225–300mm (9–12in); spread up to 300mm (12in). Flowers in a range of colours and bicolours produced in profusion all through summer and into autumn. Two most important groups of cultivars: Multiflora (large numbers of blooms about 50mm (2in) across); Grandiflora (larger flowers, 75–100mm (3–4in) across, but fewer of them per plant). Good Multifloras include 'Sugar Plum' (lavender with deeper-coloured veins); 'Resisto Mixed' (weather-resistant blooms in blue, red, pink, yellow and white); 'Multiflora Double Mixed' (large, frilled, fully double flowers). Good Grandifloras include 'Cascade Mixed' (mixed colours, suitable for baskets and bedding);; 'Cherry Frost' and 'Blue Frost' (both with white, waved edges); 'Razzle Dazzle' (blue, red, and purple flowers with broad white stripes) 'Super Fanfare Mixed' (large, very double flowers). Dwarf varieties and trailing petunias are also available.

Site Open, sunny, and warm.
Soil Reasonably fertile, free-draining.
Propagation Sow in greenhouse or propagator in a temperature of 15°C (60°F) in March; prick off into boxes; harden off; plant out in May.
Cultivation Give an occasional high-potash feed. Deadhead plants regularly. Discard after flowering.
Pests and Diseases Aphids may attack young shoots. Virus diseases may stunt and distort growth.

Above *Phacelia campanularia*

Phacelia

HYDROPHYLLACEAE

A genus of annuals and perennials native to North and South America, suitable for borders or rockeries.

P. campanularia (California). Height 225mm (9in); spread 150mm (6in). Fragrant dark green, rounded leaves. Pure gentian-blue, bell-shaped flowers, 25mm (1in) across, in June–September; popular with bees.

P. tanacetifolia (California). Height 600mm (2ft); spread 300mm (1ft). Hairy, dark green leaves, divided into leaflets. Fragrant, lavender-coloured flowers in July.

Below *Petunia × hybrida* 'Resisto Mixed'

Site Full sun.
Soil Well-drained, moderately fertile.
Propagation Sow seeds where they are to flower in May–June; thin out to 150mm (6in) for *P. campanularia*, and 300mm (1ft) for *P. tanacetifolia*. Seed can also be sown in September in sheltered areas but needs winter cloche protection.
Cultivation *P. tanacetifolia* will probably need staking in windy situations.
Pests and Diseases Slugs sometimes a problem.

Above *Philadelphus* 'Manteau d'Hermine'

Philadelphus

PHILADELPHACEAE   Mock-orange
Deciduous, bushy shrubs, native to North America, Europe, and eastern Asia, with showy, freely produced flowers, most of them giving off the scent of orange blossom. The plants are sometimes confusingly called syringa; they are in fact unrelated to the genus *Syringa* (q.v.), lilac.
P. 'Beauclerk'. Open structure with arching branches. Height up to 2m (6½ft); spread 2.5m (8¼ft). Flowers fragrant, creamy white flushed with pink in centre, to 75mm (3in) across, in June–July.
P. 'Belle Étoile'. Compact bush. Height up to 1.5m (5ft); spread 2m (6½ft). Flowers abundant, very fragrant, white flushed with red in centre, 50mm (2in) across, in June–July.
P. coronarius (S.E. Europe, W. Asia), mock-orange. Vigorous, erect-branched. Height up to 3.5m (12ft); spread 2.5m (8¼ft). Flowers creamy white, strongly fragrant, 25mm (1in) across, in early June. Variety 'Aureus' has bright yellow young foliage, greenish yellow later.
P. 'Manteau d'Hermine'. Compact, dwarf bush. Height up to 1m (3¼ft); spread 1.2m (4ft). Flowers double, creamy white, fragrant, in June–July.

P. 'Virginal'. Vigorous, erect bush. Height up to 2.5m (8¼ft); spread 1.8m (6ft). Flowers double, white, fragrant, 50mm (2in) across, in June–July.

Site Preferably in full sun (but *P. coronarius* 'Aureus' retains foliage colour longer if grown in semi-shade). Excellent for shrubberies and borders, the larger ones as specimens.
Soil Fertile; preferably a good loam.
Propagation Take soft-wood cuttings, 100mm (4in) long, from side shoots; root in a frame in late June–July. Can also be grown from hard-wood cuttings in sandy soil in October.
Cultivation Plant container-grown shrubs throughout the year. Water frequently if planted in late spring or summer.
Pruning Cut back flower-bearing shoots after flowering to a developing young shoot low down; this will flower the following year. Hard prune any weak growths.

Phlomis

LABIATAE
Herbaceous perennials and shrubs native to the Mediterranean region and eastward to China. Only a few are worthy of garden cultivation. There is, however, one excellent and widely available species.
P. fruticosa (Mediterranean), Jerusalem sage. Hardy evergreen shrub. Height 900mm (3ft); spread 600mm (2ft). Grey-green, woolly, wedge-shaped leaves. Yellow, hooded flowers, each 25–30mm (1–1¼in) long, carried in clusters in leaf axils in June–July.

Site Sunny position, preferably sheltered from cold winds.
Soil Well-drained.
Propagation Sow seeds under glass in spring. Alternatively, take cuttings in August–September, and root them in cold frame.
Cultivation Plant in October–April. Feed with general fertiliser once a year. Replace worn-out old plants regularly with young ones.
Pruning Remove unwanted and frost-damaged branches in spring.

Below *Phlomis fruticosa*

Phlox

POLEMONIACEAE

Annuals and perennials, native to North America, with attractive, sometimes scented, flowers; widely grown as alpines and border plants.

P. douglasii (W. United States). Perennial. Height 150mm (6in); spread 450mm (18in). Alpine species forming a spreading mat of sharply pointed mid- to deep green leaves. Pinkish lavender flowers, about 13mm (½in) across, carried in profusion in early summer. Varieties include 'Daniel's Cushion' (very free flowering, with large rose-pink blooms); 'Kelly's Eye' (red centres to clear-pink flowers).

P. drummondii (Texas). Half-hardy annual. Height 150–300mm (6–12in); spread 225mm (9in). Pale green, lanceolate leaves. Clustered flower-heads in shades of pink and white from mid- to late summer. Varieties include 'Dwarf Beauty Mixed' (various flower shades on compact, bushy plants); 'Twinkle Mixed' (clusters of flowers with star-like cut petals).

P. maculata (United States). Perennial. Height 600mm–1m (2–3¼ft); spread 450mm (1½ft). Herbaceous plant with lanceolate, mid-green leaves. Tall panicles of lilac flowers in mid-summer. Varieties include 'Alpha' (spikes of soft rose-pink); 'Omega' (very pale, almost white flowers, tinged with purple).

P. paniculata (United States). Perennial. Height 1–1.2m (3¼–4ft); spread 450–600mm (1½–2ft). Mid-green, lance-shaped leaves. Dense panicles of purple-pink, usually fragrant flowers. Many garden varieties include 'Balmoral' (clear pink); 'Brigadier' (glowing salmon-scarlet); 'Eventide' (deep mauve); 'Harlequin' (variegated foliage and violet-purple blooms).

P. subulata (E. United States), moss phlox. Perennial. Height 100mm (4in); spread 300–450mm (12–18in). Alpine forming mossy mats of deep-green, needle-like leaves. Small, purplish pink flowers in spring or early summer. Varieties include 'Oakington Blue Eyes' (attractive pale blue); 'Temis-caming' (glowing rose, early free-flowering).

Site Light shade or full sun.
Soil Rich and moisture-retentive for *P. maculata* and *P. paniculata*; ordinary well-drained for others.
Propagation Sow *P. drummondii* in greenhouse or propagator in March or early April at 15°C (60°F); prick off into boxes; harden off before planting out in May. Take cuttings of alpine species in early summer, using strong, non-flowering shoots 40–50mm (1½–2in) long. Pot up individually when rooted; over-winter in cold frame; plant out in following spring.
Cultivation Water in dry spells. Deadhead to prolong flowering. Stake taller varieties with twiggy sticks or canes and string. Discard annuals after flowering. Divide border plants regularly to maintain vigour.
Pruning Cut down dead stems of perennials in autumn.
Pests and Diseases Stem and bulb eelworm may infect shoots, stunting growth.

Right *Phlox paniculata*

Phormium

AGAVACEAE (LILIACEAE)

Two-species genus of evergreen perennials, native to New Zealand, distinguished mainly for their striking foliage, although flowers are also produced. They are not fully hardy but will survive most winters.

P. tenax, New Zealand flax, flax lily. Height 1–3m (3¼–10ft); spread about 1.2m (4ft). Specimen or border plant with leathery, sword-like mid- to dark green leaves up to 2.7m (9ft) long and 100–125mm (4–5in) wide. Dark red flowers

carried on spikes up to 900mm (3ft) long in July–September. Hardy, but may suffer damage in very cold winters. Established varieties include 'Purpureum' (bronze-purple leaves); 'Variegatum' (cream- and green-striped leaves). There is also a wide range of attractive modern hybrids with colourfully striped leaves.

Site Sunny aspect preferred
Soil Reasonably fertile.
Propagation Sow seeds in spring under glass; prick off into boxes; transplant to frame or nursery bed to harden off; plant out in spring of following year. Alternatively, divide and replant old specimens in spring.
Cultivation Plant in late spring. In cold areas protect plants in winter by covering with straw or plastic sheeting.
Pruning Cut out dead flower stems as soon as they fade.

Right *Phormium tenax*

Photinia

ROSACEAE

Evergreen and deciduous trees and shrubs, native mainly to south, south-east, and east Asia, which bear small white flowers in corymbs or panicles in spring, followed by small red fruits. The hybrid cultivar listed is grown mainly for its attractive foliage.

P. × fraseri 'Red Robin'. Makes a dense bush. Height 2m (6½ft); spread 2.4m (8ft). Young leaves remain bright red over a long period, later turn dark, glossy green.

Site Best in full sun; shelter from strong winds in colder areas.
Soil Reasonably fertile. Plant is particularly good on chalk soils, producing a *Pieris*-like effect from red young leaves (*Pieris* cannot be grown on chalk).
Propagation Put semi-ripe stem cuttings with heel in warm frame in late summer; grow in containers until planting.
Cultivation Plant from containers at any time. Water frequently if planted late spring or summer.

Below *Photinia × fraseri* 'Red Robin'

Above Phuopsis stylosa

Phuopsis

RUBIACEAE

A genus of only one species, valuable as a decorative, late-flowering plant for large rock gardens or for ground-cover on banks.

P. stylosa (Caucasus). Height 300mm (12in). Whorls of slender, pointed leaves clothe stems, which bear heads of small pink flowers in late summer. Plant has a pungent scent, most noticeable after rain. May spread rapidly.

Site Preferably in direct sun, but tolerates part shade.
Soil Good drainage essential; add chippings to heavier soils.
Propagation Divide in spring; pot them up or plant them out where they are to grow.
Cultivation Add top dressing of fresh soil after plant has been in for a while.
Pruning Remove dead growths in late autumn.

Phygelius

SCROPHULARIACEAE

Almost hardy evergreen shrubs, native to South Africa, usually treated as herbaceous perennials for sheltered borders. All have orange or red flower panicles and an erect, bushy habit.

P. aequalis (South Africa). Height 600–750mm (2–2½ft); spread 450–600mm (1½–2ft). Mid-green, toothed leaves. Orange flowers on stalks in July–October. Cultivar 'Yellow Trumpets' has yellow flowers.

P. capensis (South Africa), Cape figwort. Height 750–900mm (2½–3ft); spread 450–600mm (1½–2ft). Leaves mid- to dark green, held on open framework of thick branches. Brick-red flowers on stalks appear in July–October. Hardy except in severest winters. Best form is 'Coccineus', with vivid scarlet flowers throughout summer and autumn.

Site Sunny, sheltered, preferably against a south- or west-facing wall.
Soil Light, well-drained.
Propagation Sow seeds under glass in spring; pot-up singly; overwinter in frame; plant out following April. Divide and replant old specimens in spring. Take cuttings in late summer.

Cultivation No staking necessary, but tie in *P. capensis* to supports if grown as wall shrub. Water in dry spells. Mulch in spring.
Pruning In spring cut back to ground level those grown as herbaceous plants; trim shrubs to shape, remove dead wood.

Below *Phygelius capensis*

Phyllitis

POLYPODIACEAE

Hardy and tender perennial ferns from Europe, Asia, and South America. All have solid glossy rather unfern-like fronds. One species is suitable for British gardens.

P. scolopendrium (syn. *Asplenium scolopendrium*, *Scolopendrium vulgare*; Europe, including Britain), hart's-tongue fern. Evergreen. Height 150–450mm (6–18in); spread 300mm (12in). Bright green, entire fronds arranged in shuttlecock-fashion around crown of plant. Varieties include 'Capitatum' (frilled edges); 'Crispum' (heavily crested); 'Digitatum' (finger-like crests); 'Laceratum' (irregularly margined).

Site Shade preferred, but full sun tolerated if there is sufficient moisture.

Soil Alkaline preferred, but will also grow in neutral and acid soils. Plenty of organic matter, preferably well rotted, is beneficial

Propagation Best by division or removal of adventitious plantlets from main root-stock in early spring. Cultivars can be propagated in this way or by frond bases (hairy pieces of stem at base of frond); remove lower part in spring and place in very sandy compost in trays in greenhouse; plant out following year.

Cultivation Plant from pots at any season. Moist conditions preferred, but some cultivars grow effectively in rock garden. Remove old, dying, and decaying fronds each spring.

Pests and Diseases Vine weevil sometimes attacks those growing on a rock garden in warm summers, making indentations in leaf edges.

Below *Phyllitis scolopendrium*

Physalis

SOLANACEAE

Annuals and perennials native to Asia and America, grown mainly for the decorative inflated calyx surrounding the fruit. Good for cutting and drying.

P. franchetii (Japan), bladder cherry. Height and spread 450–600mm (1½–2ft). Upright plant with loosely erect stems and green triangular leaves. White, open, bell-shaped flowers, 13mm (½in) across, form in upper leaf axils in July-August, followed in September by bright orange-red, papery 'lanterns' (calyces), 50–60mm (2–2½in) long. *P. alkekengi* is similar.

P. peruviana (South America), Cape gooseberry. Similar in habit to *P. franchetii*; sometimes grown as an annual for its edible cherry-like fruits.

Site Preferably sunny and open: 'lanterns' are slow to colour in shade.

Soil Must be well-drained, especially in winter.

Propagation Divide roots in early spring. Sow seed of *P. peruviana* under glass in March–April.

Cultivation *P. franchetii* may be invasive; dig out surplus roots in October–March.

Above *Physalis franchetii*

Physostegia

LABIATAE Obedient plant

Hardy perennials, native to North America, grown for their showy spikes of tubular, lipped flowers. The species listed is good for cutting.

P. virginiana (United States). Herbaceous. Height 600–900mm (2–3ft); spread 600mm (2ft). Sturdy erect plant with stout stems and light green pointed, toothed leaves. Terminal spikes of tubular pink flowers, pinched and lipped at ends, 40mm (1½in) long, ranked in distinct rows around stem in August–September. Flowers stay in position if moved from side to side – whence the plant's common name. Cultivars include 'Rose Bouquet'; 'Summer Snow'; 'Vivid' (fuchsia-pink, compact, 300mm (1ft) high).

Site Preferably sunny and open: some shade tolerated.

Soil Reasonably moist and fertile; plant will grow on chalky soil.

Propagation Divide roots in autumn or early spring; plant only vigorous ones.

Cultivation Stake taller varieties when plants are 150mm (6in) high. If some (especially 'Vivid') become too invasive, dig out surplus roots in autumn or spring.

Below *Physostegia virginiana*

Picea

PINACEAE   Spruce

Evergreen, coniferous, usually large trees widely distributed in cooler regions of the northern hemisphere. All species have needle-like leaves borne on short 'pegs', which remain when the leaves fall; the cones are pendulous and fall intact after the winged seeds are released. Numerous dwarf forms have been raised, bringing these trees within the scope of the smallest garden; the following are typical.

P. abies (Europe) 'Nidiformis', a form of Norway spruce, the familiar Christmas tree. Flat-topped, spreading habit, height 1m (3¼ft); spread 3m (10ft). Sharp-pointed, green leaves, densely arranged. Attractive, bright green young growths.

P. glauca (North America) 'Albertiana Conica'. Popular dwarf form of Canadian or white spruce of dense, conical habit. Height 2m (6½ft) or more; spread 1m (3¼ft) or more. Leaves bright green, slender, and soft to touch.

P. mariana (North America) 'Nana', a form of black spruce. Slow-growing, dense, bun-shaped, height 450mm (1½ft); spread 750mm (2½ft). Foliage blue-grey, leaves sharp-pointed, prominently banded with white.

P. pungens (W. United States) 'Globosa', a form of the blue or Colorado spruce. Dense, rounded, with conspicuously blue foliage. Height 1.2m (4ft); spread 1.5m (5ft). 'Hoopsii' is a new, slow-growing blue spruce of conical habit. Height up to 3m (10ft) or more; spread 1.2m (4ft) or more. Vibrant blue-grey foliage. 'Procumbens' (syn. 'Glauca Procumbens') has prostrate branches that spread across ground surface and rise very little. Height 900mm (3ft); spread 4–5m (13–16½ft). Foliage grey-tinged blue. Upright shoots occasionally produced. A striking plant.

Site Full sun preferred, but most situations will do. Best effects obtained by planting in groups with other dwarf conifers and shrubs in a bed or rock garden.

Soil Must not be too dry; avoid shallow chalk.

Propagation Take semi-ripe cuttings, 50–75mm (2–3in) long, in August and insert in shaded frame.

Cultivation Plant container-grown specimens at any time. Water frequently if planted in late spring or summer. Keep area around plant free of weeds and grass.

Pruning Remove reverting shoots. Cut out ascending shoots on *P. pungens* 'Procumbens'.

Pests and Diseases Red-spider mites can be a problem.

Below *Picea pungens* foliage

Above *Pieris formosa forrestii*

Pieris

ERICACEAE   Lily-of-the-valley bush

Hardy evergreen shrubs native to Japan, Himalaya, China, and North America. All are shrubs of compact habit and have waxy flowers somewhat resembling those of lily-of-the-valley (*Convallaria*, q.v.).

P. 'Forest Flame'. Height and spread 1.8m (6ft). Brilliant red young shoots appear in spring; they age through pink and creamy-white to green. Flowers in large, drooping clusters in April–May.

P. formosa (Himalaya, W. China). Height 1.8–3.5m (6–12ft) or more; spread 3–4.5m (10–15ft) or more. Young spring growths are copper-red. White lily-of-the-valley flowers appear in April–May. Variety *P. f. forrestii* (China) retains bright-red spring colour longer; at its best in selection 'Wakehurst'.

P. japonica (Japan). Height and spread 1.8–3m (6–10ft). Leaves glossy and coppery when young. Flowers broader than those of other pieris, and carried earlier in the year, in March–April. Cultivars include 'Red Mill' (deep brown-red leaves – a good new form); 'Variegata' (leaves variegated with creamy white, flushed pink when young – associates well with rhododendrons and azaleas).

Site Sheltered position in part shade preferred.

Soil Lime-free loam, with good moisture-retention.

Propagation Take semi-ripe cuttings, 75–100mm (3–4in) long, in August and root in sandy soil in cold frame; pot them up the following spring. Or sow seeds in November–March in mixture of sand and peat. *P. formosa* can be increased by layering in September.

Cultivation Plant out in October or April. Mulch around plants with leaf-mould each spring. Do not let the soil dry out between watering in warm, dry spells.

Pruning Dead-head. Lightly reduce any straggly shoots.

Platycodon

CAMPANULACEAE   Balloon flower

A hardy perennial, native to China and Japan, with curiously shaped flower buds and bell-shaped, open blooms. It is useful in borders and rock gardens.

P. grandiflorum (China). Height 600mm (2ft); spread 450mm (1½ft). Mid-green, ovate leaves. Flower buds have inflated, balloon-like appearance, and open to pale-blue bells. Varieties include 'Album' (white flowers); 'Mariesii' (compact habit, deep blue flowers).

Site Full sun. 'Mariesii' is best form for rock gardens.
Soil Well-drained.
Propagation Sow seeds in spring in unheated greenhouse or frame, or in sheltered position outdoors; transplant seedlings to permanent positions as soon as they can be handled. Plants three years old or more can be carefully divided in spring.
Cultivation Established plants resent disturbance. In exposed conditions support growth with twiggy sticks.

Below *Platycodon grandiflorum*

Above *Polemonium caeruleum*

Polygala

POLYGALACEAE

A large genus of annuals, perennials, and shrubs of world-wide distribution that includes the following dwarf plants suitable for the rock garden.

P. calcarea (W. Europe, including Britain), milkwort. Native to chalk downs, therefore a lime-loving plant. Forms loose mats of dark-green foliage 50–75mm (2–3in) high. Tiny bright-blue flowers in racemes in May–August. May be short-lived.

P. chamaebuxus (Europe), ground box. Dwarf, 150mm (6in) high, spreading evergreen highland shrub with dark green leaves. Cream and yellow flowers appear April–June. Most readily available as cultivar 'Grandiflora' (syn. 'Purpurea'), with carmine and yellow flowers.

Polemonium

POLEMONIACEAE

Annuals and perennials native to North and South America, Asia, and Europe. The species listed makes a good border plant.

P. caeruleum (Europe, including Britain, Asia), Jacob's ladder. Height 450–900mm (1½–3ft); spread 450mm (1½ft). Hummocks of attractive dark-green, fern-like foliage. Strong stems with blue or white flowers, 25mm (1in) across, in May–July. Similar, larger and better, but not so readily available, is *P. foliosissimum*.

Site Open; avoid frost-pockets.
Soil Good, free-draining.
Propagation Divide root-stocks in the dormant period.
Cultivation Clean up old foliage in autumn.

Site For *P. calcarea*, open, well-drained, ideally on limestone scree; for *P. chamaebuxus*, light shade preferable.
Soil For *P. calcarea*, open, gritty, alkaline; *P. chamaebuxus* prefers moist spot in peat garden.
Propagation Sow *P. calcarea* in January–February in seed compost, adding crushed chalk or limestone if necessary; plant out following spring. Take soft cuttings of *P. chamaebuxus* in June–August and put in shaded frame; plant out following spring.
Cultivation Good drainage essential for *P. calcarea*; moist peat or leaf-mould desirable for *P. chamaebuxus*.

Right *Polygala chamaebuxus*

Polygonatum

LILIACEAE   Solomon's seal

Herbaceous perennials native to Europe, Asia, and North America. The hybrid listed is the most readily available form and is good for cool, shady situations.

P. × *hybridum* (*P. multiflorum* of gardens; Europe, including Britain). Hardy. Height and spread 600–750mm (2–2½ft). Elegant plant with arching stems and oblong, veined, green leaves which turn attractive yellow in autumn. Greenish white, bell-shaped flowers, 13mm (½in) long, in clusters in May–June. Good for cutting. Cultivar 'Striatum' has white-striped leaves.

Site Shade preferred, but plant will grow in sun if its roots are kept cool.
Soil Well-drained but moisture-retentive in growing season.
Propagation Divide rhizomes in October–February.
Cultivation Plant in October–March. On dry soils incorporate peat or compost to conserve moisture; also apply this as surface mulch in spring.
Pests and Diseases Sawfly caterpillars may strip leaves in June.

Right *Polygonatum* × *hybridum*

Polygonum

POLYGONACEAE   Knotweed

Annuals, perennials, and deciduous climbers of cosmopolitan distribution in the northern hemisphere. Most of those listed have bold foliage and attractive spikes or panicles of small, bell-shaped flowers, and are suitable for borders.

P. affine (Himalaya). Herbaceous perennial. Height 200–300mm (8–12in); spread 600mm (2ft) or more. Mat-forming with lance-shaped leaves. Cylindrical spikes of red flowers carried well above foliage in late summer and autumn. Varieties include 'Darjeeling Red' (deep crimson); 'Dimity' (opens palest pink, ages red); 'Donald Lowndes' (rose-pink). All these have rust-brown leaves in winter.

P. amplexicaule (Himalaya). Herbaceous perennial. Height 1–1.2m (3¼–4ft); spread to 1m (3¼ft). Clump-forming, with broadly lance-shaped leaves up to 200mm (8in) long. Red flowers in dense, slender spikes, 150mm (6in) long, in summer-autumn. Varieties: 'Atrosanguineum' (crimson flowers); 'Firetail' (similar but brighter flowers in stronger spikes); *P. a. pendula* 'Arun Gem' (dwarf, with pendent bright pink spikes).

P. baldschuanicum (syn. *Bilderdykia baldschuanicum*; S. Tadzhikistan), Russian vine, mile-a-minute. Very fast-growing, woody, twining climber. Height 15m (50ft) or more; spread to 10m (30ft). Leaves deciduous, ovate to lanceolate. Flowers cream, slightly pink-tinted, in large, fluffy panicles in summer-autumn. *P. aubertii* (W. China, Tibet), silver lace vine, is virtually identical but has white or green-tinted flowers.

P. bistorta (Europe to C. Asia), bistort, Easter ledges, snakeweed. Herbaceous perennial. Height to 600mm (2ft); spread 1m (3¼ft) or more. Rhizomatous, spreading underground to form large, dense colonies. Leaves mostly basal, broadly oval, 125mm (5in) or more long, on long stalks. Dense, poker-like spikes of pink flowers open in summer–

autumn. Variety 'Superbum' is larger in all its parts. Good for ground-cover.

P. campanulatum (Himalaya), lesser knotweed. Herbaceous perennial. Height 1m (3¼ft) or more; spread 1.2m (4ft) or more. Rhizomatous, forming loose colonies. Stems erect, branched, leafy, each leaf handsomely and boldly veined. Small pink bells carried in large panicles in summer–autumn.

P. macrophyllum (syn. *P. sphaerostachyum*; Himalaya, W. China). Herbaceous perennial. Height and spread 450–600mm (1½–2ft). Neatly clump-forming; otherwise similar to *P. bistorta* with clear pink flowers above narrow leaves. (The plant generally listed as *P. sphaerostachyum* is more robust, with deeper pink flowers).

P. vacciniifolium (Himalaya). Perennial, botanically a shrub. Height 100mm (4in); spread 600mm (2ft), sometimes more. Mat-forming, with densely interlacing, wiry stems. Leaves deciduous, ovate, small. Pink flowers in slender spikes in autumn.

Site Sunny sites preferred; part shade tolerated by *P. baldschuanicum*, *P. bistorta*, *P. campanulatum*, and *P. vacciniifolium*.
Soil Well-drained, moisture-retentive, humus-rich.
Propagation Divide perennials at planting time.

Take cuttings from mat-forming perennials in spring, from climbers in late summer.
Cultivation Plant in autumn–spring in mild spells. Mulch with organic matter every other spring.

Below *Polygonum campanulatum*

Potentilla

ROSACEAE   Cinquefoil

Hardy annuals, perennials, and shrubs of cosmopolitan distribution, mainly in the northern hemisphere. The perennials are good summer-flowering rock or border plants, and the shrubs are ideal for borders or for ground-cover. Most kinds have single, saucer-shaped flowers.

P. atrosanguinea (Himalaya), Himalayan cinquefoil. Perennial. Height 300mm (12in), spread 450–600mm (1½–2ft).

Leaves grey-green, resembling those of strawberry plant. Flowers appear in June–September. Of little garden value, but following hybrids are worth growing: 'Gibson's Scarlet' (vigorous grower, masses of large, single, intense-red flowers); 'Glory of Nancy' (greyish foliage, semi-double flowers of rich orange-crimson); 'Wm Rollison' (bright orange-flame flowers); 'Yellow Queen' (pure yellow flowers, earlier than most).

P. fruticosa (N. hemisphere), shrubby cinquefoil. Shrub. Height and spread 1.2–1.5m (4–5ft). Compact, with pale to mid-green, small, multi-lobed leaves. Buttercup-yellow flowers, 25mm (1in) across, carried in groups of two or three in May–August. Cultivars include 'Katherine Dykes' (primrose yellow); 'Mandschurica' (white flowers, grey leaves); 'Princess' (pink); 'Red Ace' (vermilion-flame); 'Royal Flush' (rose pink); 'Tangerine' (copper red).

P. verna (syn. *P. tabernaemontani*; Europe), spring cinquefoil. Shrub. Height 50–75mm (2–3in); spread up to 600mm (2ft). Low-growing, evergreen, mound-forming. Bright yellow flowers, 13mm (½in) across, on slender stems in April–May. Cultivar 'Nana' is less vigorous.

Site Bright sun preferred.
Soil Well-drained.
Propagation Perennials by division in October or March; alternatively, sow seeds in spring. Seeds of shrubby species can be sown in March; or take 75mm (3in) cuttings of half-ripe shoots in autumn and root in cold frame.
Cultivation Plant in October– April. Perennials like mulch of well-rotted manure in spring.
Pruning Short-lived perennials should be cut back when last flowers fade in autumn; most others die back naturally. Shrubby species benefit from dead-heading of flowering shoots and removal of weak and old stems.

Below Potentilla atrosanguinea 'Gibson's Scarlet'

Above *Primula pulverulenta*

Primula

PRIMULACEAE

Hardy and half-hardy annuals, biennials and perennials, native to Europe, Asia, Africa, and North and South America, popular in rock gardens, borders, and containers for their showy flowers.

P. alpicola (Tibet, Bhutan), moonlight primula. Hardy perennial. Height 200–450mm (8in–1½ft); spread 300mm (1ft). Pendent, creamy white, fragrant flowers in May–June above oval green leaves; flowers and stems covered in white meal. Varieties include 'Alba' (white); 'Violacea' (deep purple).

P. aurantiaca (W. China). Hardy perennial. Height 300– 450mm (1–1½ft); spread 300mm (1ft). Candelabra-type primula with tiered whorls of orange-red flowers in June– July above coarse, rounded or ovate green leaves. Likes damp conditions.

P. auricula (Europe). Hardy perennial. Height 150mm (6in); spread 200mm (8in). Alpine species, producing bright yellow, fragrant flowers in April–May among smooth green leaves. Varieties include 'Blue Bonnet' (violet, edged white); 'Dusky Yellow'; 'Old Irish Blue' (blue with white centre).

P. beesiana (W. China). Hardy perennial. Height 600mm (2ft); spread 300mm (1ft). Candelabra-type with whorls of rose-carmine flowers in June.

P. bulleyana (W. China). Hardy perennial. Height 600mm (2ft); spread 300mm (1ft). Candelabra-type with whorls of orange flowers in June–early July.

P. capitata (Bhutan, Sikkim, Tibet). hardy but short-lived perennial. Height 150–250mm (6–10in); spread 150mm (6in). Crowded heads of bell-shaped, deep-violet blooms in

June–July. Small, oblong-lanceolate leaves, often coated beneath with meal (which often also covers flower stems).

P. cockburniana (W. China). Hardy perennial. Height 150–250mm (6–10in); spread 250mm (10in). whorls of delicate orange-red flowers on slender stems above soft green, ovate leaves in June.

P. denticulata (Himalaya), drumstick primula. Hardy perennial. Height and spread 300mm (1ft). Large globular heads of purple or lilac flowers in March–May, followed by large, obovate, green leaves. Varieties include 'Alba' (white); there are also seed strains in reds and violets.

P. florindae (Tibet), giant Himalayan cowslip. Hardy perennial. Height 900mm (3ft); spread 600mm (2ft). Large pendent, bell-shaped, yellow flowers in dense clusters in June–July. Large aromatic leaves, green with reddish stalks. One of few primulas to grow in shallow water. Good seed strain: 'Art Shades' (yellow, orange, pink, brown).

P. pulverulenta (W. China). Hardy perennial. Height 600–900mm (2–3ft); spread 600mm (2ft). Candelabra-type with whorls of red flowers (coated with white meal) in May–June above handsome, soft green leaves. Good variety: 'Bartley Strain' (soft pink to rose-pink).

P. rosea (Himalaya). Hardy alpine perennial. Height and spread 150mm (6in). Rose-pink flowers in March–April, long before smooth green leaves. Varieties include larger-flowered 'Grandiflora'.

P. sikkimensis (Himalaya, Burma, Yunnan). Hardy perennial. Height 600mm (2ft); spread 450mm (1½ft). Clusters of pendent, yellow, fragrant blooms on stout stems in May–June above elliptical, bright green leaves.

P. veris (Europe, W. Asia), cowslip. Hardy perennial. Height and spread 150–200mm (6–8in). Deep yellow, fragrant flowers in neat heads in April–May above soft green leaves.

P. vulgaris (syn. *P. acaulis*; W. and S. Europe, including Britain), primrose. hardy perennial. Height 150mm (6in); spread 150–200mm (6–8in). Clusters of ovate, green leaves studded with sulphur-yellow flowers in April–May. Varieties include 'Mother's Day' (mixed colours), which is better as a container-grown plant.

Polyanthus (hybrids bred from *P. veris* and *vulgaris*; sometimes listed as Polyantha primroses). Hardy perennials. Height and spread 150–200mm (6–8in). Many colour combinations; large blooms borne in whorls on stout stems in April–May. Good cultivars include 'Blue Cockade' (violet-blue); 'Colossea' (mixed); 'Cowichan' (mixed, without central eye); 'Crimson Giants' (mixed); 'Pink Foam'.

Site Alpine species prefer cool, partly shady site on rock garden. Primrose and cowslip types will grow in full sun or part shade. Candelabras prefer dappled shade.

Soil Gritty, free-draining for alpine types; heavy, moist, with plenty of organic matter for other types.

Propagation All except named cultivars come true from seed. Sow as soon as possible after ripening; prick out seedlings into pots and grow for one season in frame; plant out where they are to grow in autumn or early spring. Some Candelabras can be increased from root cuttings taken in autumn; all can be successfully divided.

Cultivation Alpine primulas like a layer of grit around their collars; they should be divided regularly. Candelabra primulas, primroses, and polyanthus are easygoing but need dividing every few years immediately after flowering.

Pests and Diseases Slugs troublesome in spring; vine weevil may attack young pot-grown plants. Soft rots, grey mould, and primula leaf spot may infect plants.

Below *Primula* Polyanthus mixed

Above *Prunella grandiflora*

Prunella

LABIATAE   Self-heal

Hardy, ground-covering perennials, native to Europe, with tubular flowers on short spikes. Useful rock-garden plants.
P. grandiflora (Europe). Height 150–300mm (6–12in); spread 450mm (1½ft) or more. Fast-growing plant; needs to be controlled as it is invasive. Leaves ovate, shiny, mid-green. Purple flowers in May–October. *P. g. webbiana* is very similar but with more densely packed flower-spikes. Less-invasive forms include 'Loveliness' (compact, lilac flowers); 'Little Red Riding Hood' (free-flowering, with reddish pink blooms).

Site Sunny or shady, where plants can be kept under control.
Soil Any ordinary garden soil.
Propagation Divide plants in early autumn or spring.

Cultivation Remove dead flower-heads regularly in summer. Divide plants every two or three years to keep them under control, replanting small portions.

Prunus

ROSACEAE

A large genus of deciduous and evergreen trees and shrubs, widely distributed mainly in northern temperate regions, providing spectacular flowering displays in spring. It includes plum, apricot, almond, peach, cherry, cherry laurel and Portugal laurel. Those listed are deciduous unless otherwise stated.
P. × amygdalo-persica. Hybrids between almond and peach species. Cultivar 'Pollardii' is a small, spreading tree. Height to 8m (26ft); spread 6m (20ft). Leaves lanceolate, long-pointed. Bright-pink flowers, deeper pink in centre, 50mm

(2in) across, before leaves in March. Fruit intermediate between that of parents.
P. avium (Europe, including Britain), gean, wild cherry. Vigorous tree, conical when young. Height up to 20m (66ft) or more; spread 10m (33ft). Leaves oval, long-pointed, sharp-toothed, yellow or red in autumn. Masses of white flowers, 20mm (¾in) wide, in April. Excellent in open woodland. Cultivar 'Plena' (syn. 'Multiplex') has larger, very double flowers.
P. × blireana (garden hybrid), ornamental plum. Round-headed tree. Height and spread up to 5m (16½ft). Leaves bronze-red when young, becoming almost green. Flowers bright pink, double, rosette-like, appear before leaves in March–April.
P. cerasifera (Balkans), cherry plum, myrobalan. Round-headed tree. Height up to 10m (33ft); spread 8m (26ft). Small white flowers, profusely borne in March–April, the first opening before leaves. Fruits red, plum-like, edible. Cultivars include 'Nigra' (deep-red, later purplish leaves, pink flowers); 'Pissardii' (similar to 'Nigra' but flowers pink in bud, opening white).
P. × cistena, purple-leaf sand cherry; hybrid of *P. cerasifera* 'Pissardii' (q.v.). Height and spread up to 1.8m (6ft). Leaves red when young, bronze later. Small, white flowers in April, followed by deep purple, cherry-like fruits. Can be used for hedging.
P. glandulosa (N. China, Korea), ornamental almond. Shrub. Height and spread up to 1.5m (5ft). Compact habit, with ovate, pointed, mid-green leaves. Usually represented by cultivars 'Alba Plena' (double white flowers) and 'Sinensis' (syn. 'Rosea Plena', similar but with double pink flowers), both of them good for autumn leaf colour.
P. × hillieri. Hybrid of *P. sargentii* (q.v.). Height and spread up to 10m (33ft). Young leaves bronze, colouring richly in autumn. Pale pink flowers freely borne in April. Cultivar 'Spire' is a narrow tree with upright branches and 2.5m (8¼ft) through head, excellent in confined spaces.
P. laurocerasus (S.E. Europe, W. Asia), cherry or common laurel. Vigorous, wide-spreading, evergreen shrub or small tree. Height up to 6m (20ft); spread up to 7m (23ft). Leaves leathery, glossy green, oblong, up to 200mm (8in) long. Flowers small, white in racemes in April, followed by purple-black fruits. Commonly planted as hedge, but also good as isolated specimen. Cultivars include 'Otto Luyken'

Below *Prunus avium*

(very compact to 1.2m (4ft) tall, 1.5m (5ft) across, narrow, dark green leaves); 'Rotundifolia' (best hedge form, shorter leaves, vigorous, upright habit); 'Zabeliana' (very narrow, willow-like leaves, horizontal or slightly ascending branches, to 1m (3¼ft) tall and 4m (13ft) across).

P. lusitanica (Spain, Portugal), Portugal laurel. Evergreen shrub. Height and spread up to 6m (20ft); sometimes a small tree up to 10m (33ft) or more. Leaves ovate, up to 125mm (5in) long, dark, glossy-green on red petioles. Flowers white, fragrant, in racemes in June; fruit red, then black. Hardier than *P. laurocerasus* and more lime-tolerant.

P. padus (N. Asia, N. Europe, including N. Britain), bird cherry. Vigorous tree, conical when young. Height up to 10m (33ft) or more; spread 8m (26ft). Small, fragrant, white flowers borne in dense racemes in May, followed by small, black fruits. Cultivars include 'Colorata' (smaller tree with bronze and pink flowers); 'Watereri' (more vigorous, with flowers in longer racemes).

P. sargentii (N. Japan, Sakhalin). Broad-headed ornamental cherry tree up to 8m (26ft) tall and more across. Leaves obovate, taper-pointed, red when young and colouring brilliant orange and red in early autumn. Flowers 40mm (1½in) across, rich pink, covering the tree in March–April. Cultivar 'Rancho' has ascending branches and larger, deeper-coloured flowers.

P. spinosa (Europe, including Britain, N. Asia), blackthorn, sloe. Dense, twiggy, spiny shrub up to 4m (13ft) tall and as much across. Small white flowers in March–early April, usually before leaves. Fruits bitter, blue-black. Good cultivar is 'Purpurea' (leaves purple-red).

P. subhirtella (Japan). Early-flowering ornamental cherry tree that has given rise to several outstanding forms: 'Autumnalis' (height and spread 8m (26ft), semi-double, very pale pink flowers in mild periods from November through winter, with final burst of pinker flowers in early spring); 'Autumnalis Rosea' (similar, but with deeper-pink flowers); 'Pendula Rosea' (mushroom-headed, weeping tree up to 3m (10ft) tall by 5m (16ft½) across, with pale pink flowers in March–early April); 'Pendula Rubra' (similar, but with deeper-pink flowers).

Left, below *Prunus tenella*   **Above** *P. triloba*

P. tenella (S.W. Russia, C. and S.E. Europe), dwarf Russian almond. Shrub up to 1.2m (4ft) tall and as much across. Glossy green leaves. Abundant small pink flowers in April. Fruits velvety, like small almonds, sometimes borne after hot summers. Cultivar 'Fire Hill' is the best form, with bright rose-red flowers.

P. triloba (China). Ornamental almond, usually represented in gardens by cultivar 'Multiplex', a choice shrub up to 3m (10ft) tall and as much across (but easily contained by pruning). Leaves usually three lobed at the tip. Flowers pale pink, very double, 40mm (1½in) across, profusely borne in late March–early April.

P. × yedoensis, Yoshino cherry. Small tree with arching branches up to 5m (16½ft) tall and 6m (20ft) across. Leaves long-pointed, with slender teeth. Flowers pink in bud, opening nearly white and wreathing the tree for several weeks in March–April.

Japanese Cherries. The hybrid forms listed below mostly originated in Japanese gardens, have long been grown there, and provide spectacular spring-flowering trees; but they are not long-lived in Britain.

P. 'Amanogawa' (syn. 'Erecta'). Narrow, erect-branched tree up to 6m (20ft) tall and 1.2m (4ft) wide. Flowers semi-double, pink, fragrant, in large clusters April–early May.

P. 'Cheal's Weeping' (syn. 'Kiku-shidare Sakura'). Weeping tree up to 2.5m (8¼ft) high and 3m (10ft) across. Flowers bright pink, very double in late April.

P. 'Kanzan'. Most widely planted Japanese cherry. Distinct vase-shaped head of ascending branches until quite old. Height and spread up to 10m (33ft). Flowers large, double, purplish pink, profusely borne amid bronze young leaves in late April–early May; autumn colour, yellow or orange.

P. × 'Pink Perfection'. A hybrid between 'Kanzan' and

'Shimidsu Sakura' raised in Britain. Height and spread 8m (26ft). Flowers like those of 'Kanzan' but paler pink and white, produced in April–May.

P. 'Shimidsu Sakura' (syn. 'Longipes'). Beautiful flat-topped, spreading tree up to 6m (20ft) high by 10m (33ft) across. Large, semi-double, pure white flowers with frilled petals in clusters along branches in mid-May.

P. 'Shirofugen'. Spreading tree up to 8m (26ft) tall and 10m (33ft) across. Flowers double, pink in bud opening to white, in May; fragrant, 50mm (2in) across, turning pink before falling. Flower colour contrasts beautifully with deep-red young foliage.

P. 'Shirotae', Mount Fuji cherry. Low, wide-spreading tree up to 5m (16½ft) high and 10m (33ft) across. Young leaves green with long, slender teeth; yellow in autumn. Flowers white, fragrant, 50mm (2in) across, semi-double or single, in hanging clusters in April.

P. 'Tai-Haku', great white cherry. Vigorous tree with large leaves, bronze-red when young, yellow or orange in autumn. Height 8m (26ft); spread 10m (33ft). Flowers, 65mm (2½in) across – largest of any cherry – pure white, single, in mid- to late-April.

P. 'Ukon'. Vigorous tree with widely ascending branches. Height 8m (26ft); spread 10m (33ft). Flowers semi-double, an unusual shade of pale greenish yellow in late April, contrasting with bronze young leaves. Flowers quickly fade to white in full sun, but retain colour if tree is given light shade by neighbouring trees.

Above *Prunus* 'Cheal's Weeping' **Below** *P.* 'Tai-Haku'

Site Best in full sun; only evergreen species tolerate dense shade. Early-flowering trees most effective if given dark, evergreen background to show up flowers.

Soil Any reasonable soil, but *P. laurocerasus* can become chlorotic on shallow chalk (*P. lusitanica* is a good substitute on such soil).

Propagation Species by seed (where available), sown in a cold frame or the open ground. Large-flowered trees by budding (July) or grafting (March). Small-flowered trees and shrubs by 75mm (3in) cuttings in cold frame in July. Evergreens by late-summer cuttings in gentle heat.

Cultivation Plant open-ground shrubs and trees in November–March. Plant container-grown shrubs at any time, watering well if planted in late spring or summer. Container-grown trees best planted in early autumn–late spring; water well. Hedging plants should be set about 450mm (18in) apart.

Pruning Cut back young shoots of *P. glandulosa* and *P. triloba* to two or three buds after flowering.

Pests and Diseases Aphids and caterpillars can cause problems; bullfinches eat flower buds. Bacterial canker, honey fungus, peach-leaf curl, and silver leaf occasionally occur.

Pulmonaria

BORAGINACEAE   Lungwort

Herbaceous perennials native to Europe. Most form low clumps of prettily marked leaves, with clusters of drooping bell flowers in early spring, and make good ground cover for shady parts of the garden.

P. angustifolia, blue cowslip. Height 225mm (9in); spread 450mm (1½ft). Low plant with rough, tongue-shaped, dark-green leaves. Short-stemmed clusters of drooping, cupped flowers, 8mm (⅓in) across, pink turning blue in March. Cultivars include 'Mawson's Variety' (rich blue).

P. officinalis, Jerusalem cowslip. Evergreen. Height and spread 225–300mm (9–12in). Light green leaves blotched and spotted with grey-white. Flowers pink in bud, opening blue in April–May.

P. rubra. Evergreen. Height 300mm (1ft); spread 600mm (2ft). Rich green, downy, pointed leaves. Rose-red flowers in January–March.

P. saccharata. Evergreen. Height 300mm (1ft); spread 450mm (1½ft) or more. Broad pointed leaves, handsomely blotched and spotted with creamy white. Bold clusters of flowers pink, turning blue, 15mm (½in) across, in April–May. Cultivars include 'Argentea' (leaves silvery white); 'White Wings' (white flowers).

Site All prefer shade, and make fine ground-cover.
Soil Reasonably moist and fertile.
Propagation Divide clumps, preferably in autumn, or immediately after flowering.
Cultivation Mulch in early summer to conserve moisture. Water in dry weather. Remove dead leaves in autumn.
Pests and Diseases Slugs may eat young shoots in spring. Mildew may occur on leaves.

Below Pulmonaria saccharata

Above Pulsatilla vulgaris 'Rubra'

Pulsatilla

RANUNCULACEAE

A genus of attractive hardy perennials (formerly listed under *Anemone*, q.v.), mainly from the European mountain regions, which look well on the rock garden.

P. alpina (Europe). Stems, up to 300mm (12in) high, bear single white flowers 50mm (2in) wide and flushed blue-grey on the outside, followed by fluffy silver seedheads. The finely cut leaves form bold tufts.

P. vernalis (Europe). Height 150mm (6in). One of the loveliest of all alpine plants, but difficult to grow outside alpine house. The plant, clothed in attractive silky hairs, bears 50mm (1in) wide flowers, pearly white inside and pale violet outside, appear in April–May.

P. vulgaris (Europe), pasque flower. Most easily grown of the genus; variation in flower colour gives rise to several named forms. Type species bears purple flowers on 300mm (12in) stems in April–May above fernlike, finely cut foliage. Some nurserymen offer seedlings on a 'pot luck' basis; others offer named selections, notably 'Barton's Pink' and 'Rubra', the latter in glowing red shades.

Site Open sunny situation.
Soil Alkaline, free-draining.
Propagation Sow fresh seed in June–July, potting up when true leaves appear; water until they become dormant – young plants will be ready following spring. To perpetuate named forms, take root cuttings: remove roots at least 6mm (¼in) thick from clumps lifted in July–August, taking only one third from each plant. Slice into 25mm (1in) lengths and insert in pots of compost, with top-dressing of fine sand. Cover with glass and place in a frame; turn glass daily.
Cultivation Plant in September. Choose site carefully as, once planted, pulsatillas resent disturbance.

Pyracantha

ROSACEAE Firethorn

Evergreen shrubs native to south-eastern Europe and Asia. All have spiny branches, bright, small summer flowers, and prolific autumn berries and make fine wall shrubs and hedging plants.

P. atalantioides (China). Height and spread 3–4.5m (10–15ft). Vigorous shrub with glossy, deep green leaves. White flowers in clusters in June. Crimson berries. Form 'Aurea' has bright yellow berries.

P. coccinea (S. Europe). Height and spread 3–4.5m (10–15ft). Pointed leaves of mid-green. White flowers in clusters in June. Bright red berries. Form 'Lalandei' has broader leaves and orange-red berries.

P. rogersiana (syn. *P. crenulata*; China). Height 2.5–3m (8¼–10ft); spread 3.5–4.5m (12–15ft). Narrow leaves of mid-green. White flowers in clusters in June–July. Orange-red berries. Form 'Flava' has bright yellow berries.

Site Best against a wall (any aspect).

Soil Well-drained, reasonably fertile.

Propagation Take cuttings of firm young growths, 75–100mm (3–4in) long; root in propagating frame in summer. Or sow seeds in cold frame or greenhouse in October; prick off into pans or boxes when manageable; pot up and plant out following autumn.

Cultivation Plant in spring or autumn. Wall plants need trellis or wires for support. Tie in vigorous growths in growing season. Can be grown as hedging; set plants 375–600mm (15–24in) apart.

Pruning Trim wall plants and hedges after flowering; free-standing shrubs can be left to develop naturally.

Pests and Diseases Aphids and scale insects may attack stems and leaves. Fireblight can cause die-back in branches.

Below *Pyracantha atalantioides* 'Aurea'

Above *Pyrus salicifolia* 'Pendula'

Pyrus

ROSACEAE Pear

A small group of deciduous trees, sometimes shrubs, native to temperate regions of Europe and Asia. The two species listed make good decorative trees.

P. calleryana (C. and S. China). Large shrub or small tree in the wild, usually represented in gardens by the form 'Chanticleer', a vigorous, conical tree, 12m (40ft) high and 5m (16½ft) across. Leaves dark glossy green, persistent, turning rich purple and claret in autumn. White flowers profusely borne in spring.

P. salicifolia (S.W. Russia, Turkey, N.W. Iran), willow-leaved pear. Best garden form is 'Pendula', a dense, bushy tree with pendulous branches, height 5m (16½ft), spread 4m (13ft), with striking, narrow, silvery grey leaves. Creamy white flowers borne in dense clusters as the young leaves emerge. Fruits small, brown, pear-shaped. One of the best trees for a small garden.

Site Full sun. *P. calleryana* 'Chanticleer' is useful as a street tree and in other restricted positions.

Soil Any except waterlogged.

Propagation Graft in March. Bud in July–August.

Cultivation Plant container-grown trees at any time; others in November–March.

Pests and Diseases Woolly aphids and scale insects are common pests. Susceptible to fire blight.

Ramonda

GESNERIACEAE

Hardy evergreen natives of southern and eastern Europe, of which one species makes a popular addition to the rock garden.

R. myconi (syn. *R. pyrenaica*; Pyrenees). Forms flat rosettes, about 225mm (9in) wide, of crinkly, hairy leaves with toothed edges. From centre arise 100–150mm (4–6in) tall flower-heads of lavender-blue in April–May. Cultivars include 'Alba' (white); 'Rosea' (pink).

Site North-facing or shady.
Soil Enrich with peat or leaf-mould; must be free-draining.
Propagation Leaf cuttings best: detach some leaves in June–July, making sure to obtain dormant buds. Insert each leaf one third of its length into sand and peat mixture in shaded frame; they should be ready for potting on at end of August. Young plants should be grown on ready for planting in autumn of year following.
Cultivation Plant in spring between peat blocks or rock crevices; place plants on their sides to prevent water collecting in centre of rosettes.
Pests and Diseases Slugs are a pest, eating holes in leaf centres.

Below Ramonda myconi

Ranunculus

RANUNCULACEAE   Buttercup

Large genus of annuals and perennials native to temperate regions of both hemispheres. Some are garden weeds, but those listed are suitable for borders or rock gardens.

R. aconitifolius (Europe), fair-maids-of-France. Perennial. Height 600mm (2ft); spread 450mm (1½ft). Mid-green toothed, lobed leaves. Small white flowers borne freely on slender stems in May–June. Species usually represented in gardens by 'Flore-pleno', fully double form.

R. acris (Europe), meadow buttercup. Perennial. Height 450–600mm (1½–2ft); spread 450mm (1½ft). Familiar wild-flower of field and verge, with glistening, golden, cup-shaped blooms. Cultivated form is 'Flore-pleno', a double-flowered mutant commonly known as bachelor's buttons.
R. asiaticus (Orient), peony-flowered ranunculus. Tuber-ous-rooted perennial. Height 300mm (1ft); spread 150mm (6in). Free-flowering, generally with semi-double flowers in wide colour range in June–July from spring planting.

Site Open, sunny or part shaded.
Soil Free-draining, reasonably fertile loam.
Propagation Sow seeds of *R. asiaticus* in March in greenhouse or propagator; prick out into boxes in a cold frame; plant out in flowering positions in September. This species forms clusters of tubers which can be separated in autumn and planted separately. Other species increased by division in autumn or spring.

Cultivation Plant claw-like tubers of *R. asiaticus* in March–April, with the claws pointing downwards. In mild areas and in light, free-draining soils they can be left in situ; in later years they will flower in spring. Better results obtained by lifting tubers in autumn and storing in a frost-free place over winter. Keep all species well supplied with moisture in dry spells.

Below Ranunculus acris 'Flore-pleno'

Reseda

RESEDACEAE

Annuals and biennials, from the Mediterranean eastward to central Asia, grown in borders for their sweetly scented flowers, very attractive to bees. The species listed is good for cut flowers.

R. odorata (North Africa, Egypt), mignonette. Hardy annual. Height 300–600mm (1–2ft); spread 200–300mm (8–12in). Upright plant with spoon-shaped or three-lobed leaves and erect, branching stems. Compact spikes of small reddish-yellow flowers, 6mm (¼in) across, very fragrant, in July–September.

Site Sunny but cool; shelter plants from wind which will otherwise disperse scent.
Soil Must be rich, moist, and well-drained; some lime addition necessary if soil is acid.
Propagation Sow outdoors in March–April where plants are to flower. Water drills before sowing: seed germinates slowly in dry soil. Sow seed in pots in September for flowering under glass.
Cultivation Thin seedlings in open when large enough to handle; water in dry weather to maintain growth.

Right *Reseda odorata*

Rheum

POLYGONACEAE   Ornamental rhubarb

Herbaceous perennials native to Siberia, Himalaya, and eastern Asia; grown for their large decorative leaves and towering flower spikes.

R. alexandrae (Szechwan, Tibet). Height and spread 1m (3¼ft). Large, oval, prominently veined leaves grow from base of plant. Flower spikes, 300mm (1ft) or more long, produced in June–July, protected by attractive creamy-white, papery bracts.

R. palmatum (China). Height up to 2m (6½ft); spread 1.2m (4ft). Lobed green leaves with strong rhubarb-like stalks. Huge spires of tiny red flowers in June–July. An imposing plant when grown for its foliage alone. Cultivars include 'Atrosanguineum' and 'Bowles Crimson' (both with red-flushed foliage, richer red flowers).

Site Best in the open; plants need ample room to develop.

Soil Heavy, moisture-retentive.

Propagation Sow seed in spring; grow young plants on in pots until large enough to plant out in permanent positions. Propagate named forms by division in autumn.

Cultivation Plant at any time in dormant season. If very fine foliage is required, seed heads should be removed in their formative period. Remove all dead and decaying foliage in autumn. Clumps should not be divided until they have several strong crowns. Water often in summer dry spells.

Pests and Diseases Rhubarb crown rot sometimes occurs.

Right *Rheum palmatum* 'Atrosanguineum'

Above *Rhododendron* 'Fastuosum Flore Pleno'

Rhododendron

ERICACEAE

A large genus of evergreen and deciduous shrubs and trees widely distributed in temperate regions of the northern hemisphere and in the Malaysian highlands. After 200 years of hybridization they have become available in a huge variety of sizes in almost every colour. The flowers have five to eight lobes, are funnel-shaped, bell-shaped, or tubular, and are capable of creating spectacular displays over many months. The genus includes azaleas. Rhododendrons can conveniently be divided into several groups.

Hardy Hybrids
Mainly late-flowering, very tough and hardy, often large evergreen shrubs with bold leaves and large, showy flowers; may take 10–25 years to attain sizes given.
R. 'Blue Peter'. Strong-growing, upright habit. Height 3m (10ft); spread 5m (16½ft). Flowers funnel-shaped, pale violet-blue (paler in centre), 75mm (3in) across, freely borne in conical trusses in late May.
R. 'Britannia'. Slow-growing, compact, rounded bush. Height 1.8m (6ft); spread 2.5m (8¼ft). Flowers broadly bell-shaped, 75mm (3in) across, deep, glowing red in compact trusses in late May–early June.
R. 'Cunningham's White'. Compact. Height 3m (10ft); spread 4m (13ft). Flowers funnel-shaped, 50mm (2in) across, pale mauve at first, later pure white, spotted with yellow and purple in May. An old favourite, very hardy.
R. 'Cynthia'. Very vigorous. Height up to 6m (20ft); spread 7m (23ft). Flowers broadly funnel-shaped, 75mm (3in) across, deep rose-pink, in large conical trusses in May.
R. 'Fastuosum Flore Pleno'. Tall, domed bush. Height 3m (10ft) or more; spread 5m (16½ft). Flowers funnel-shaped, double, mauve, 65mm (2½in) across, in late May–June.

Left *Rhododendron* 'Elizabeth'   **Above** *R.* 'Cynthia' (with *R.* 'Goldsworth Yellow')

R. 'Gomer Waterer'. Very tough, compact bush. Height 3m (10ft); spread 4.5m (15ft). Flowers broadly funnel-shaped, 75mm (3in) across, mauve in bud, opening white, flushed mauve-pink on the edges, in large, dense, rounded trusses in early June.

R. 'Mrs A. T. de la Mare'. Compact bush. Height 2m (6½ft); spread 3m (10ft). Flowers funnel-shaped, 100mm (4in) across, with frilly margins, pink in bud, opening white with a green flare, slightly fragrant, in compact trusses in June.

R. 'Mrs G. W. Leak'. Vigorous, compact bush. Height and spread 4.5m (15ft). Flowers pale pink, heavily blotched with reddish-purple, in compact conical trusses in May.

R. 'Pink Pearl'. Vigorous, large, compact bush. Height and spread 5m (16½ft). Flowers broadly funnel-shaped, 100mm (4in) across, pale pink fading to nearly white, in large, conical trusses, in May–June.

R. 'Purple Splendour'. Compact, vigorous, upright branched. Height 2.5m (8¼ft); spread 3.5m (12ft). Flowers broadly funnel-shaped, 75mm (3in) across, deep purple with black-ish markings, in dense trusses in late May–June.

R. 'Sappho'. Large, dome-shaped bush. Height 4.5m (15ft); spread 6m (20ft). Flowers broadly funnel-shaped, 75mm (3in) across, white, prominently blotched with blackish purple, in dense, rounded trusses in late May to June.

Evergreen Species & Compact Hybrids

R. 'Bluebird' (*R. augustinii* × *R. intricatum*). Dwarf, small-leaved shrub. Height and spread 900mm (3ft). Flowers almost saucer-shaped, rich violet-blue, 50mm (2in) across, in small clusters in April.

R. 'Elizabeth' (*R. forrestii repens* × *R. griersonianum*). Compact, spreading bush. Height 1m (3¼ft) or more; spread 3m (10ft). Flowers funnel-shaped, deep scarlet, 75mm (3in) across, in April.

R. 'Fabia' (*R. dichroanthum* × *R. griersonianum*). Spreading

Above *Rhododendron* 'Praecox' **Right** *R. williamsianum*

habit. Height 1.8m (6ft); spread 3m (10ft). Flowers orange-red, nodding in lax trusses, funnel-shaped 75mm (3in) across, in late May–June.

R. 'Humming Bird' (*R. haematodes* × *R. williamsianum*). Compact, rounded bush. Height and spread 1.8m (6ft). Leaves glossy green, rounded. Flowers widely bell-shaped, deep glossy scarlet, 50mm (2in) across, somewhat nodding in open trusses in April–early May.

R. impeditum (China). Dense, dwarf, spreading shrub. Height 300mm (1ft); spread 450mm (1½ft). Tiny, aromatic leaves. Pale purplish-blue flowers cover plant in April–early May.

R. pemakoense (Tibet). Dense, dwarf, sometimes suckering shrub. Height 450mm (1½ft); spread 600mm (2ft). Tiny, dark green leaves, scaly and greyish-blue on undersides. Flowers relatively large, 50mm (2in) across, widely funnel-shaped, purplish-pink, often completely hiding the foliage in late March–April.

R. ponticum (Spain, W. Asia, Caucasus). Species (and its hybrids) commonly naturalised on acid soils in Britain. Dense, vigorous shrub or small tree, height 6m (20ft); more across. Flowers funnel-shaped, 50mm (2in) across, mauve or purple in rounded trusses in June. Can be used to make effective shelter belts and hedges. Form 'Variegatum' has conspicuously margined creamy white leaves.

R. 'Praecox' (*R. ciliatum* × *R. dauricum*). Charming, often semi-evergreen shrub. Height and spread 1.5m (5ft). Flowers funnel-shaped, rose-purple 40mm (1½in) across, borne

in clusters in February–March; can be damaged by late frosts.

R. 'Scarlet Wonder' (*R.* 'Essex Scarlet' × *R. forrestii*). Compact bush making a low mound. Height 600mm (2ft); spread 1m (3¼ft). Leaves glossy green, deeply veined. Flowers bell-shaped, 50mm (2in) across, bright scarlet in May.

R. williamsianum (China). Distinctive, charming small bush. Height and spread 1.5m (5ft). Leaves rather small, rounded, glaucous beneath. Flowers nodding, pale pink, broadly bell-shaped, 50mm (2in) across, in loose clusters in April.

R. yakushimanum (Yakushima, S. Japan). Very dense, slow-growing, dome-shaped bush. Height up to 1.2m (4ft); spread 2m (6½ft). Leaves with margins curled under, strikingly white-felted when young. Flowers bell-shaped, pink in bud, opening to white, 50mm (2in) across, in dense, rounded trusses in late May. One of the most beautiful rhododendrons, particularly FCC form. Recently several promising hybrids have been raised and are now available. Flower colour varies, and many have leaves conspicuously orange-felted on undersides.

Deciduous Azaleas

Famed for their riotous colour in late spring and early summer. Many have fragrant flowers and attractive autumn foliage. Can be divided into several groups: Ghent azaleas (Gh), with rather small, scented, honeysuckle-like flowers with protruding stamens in late May; height 1.8–2.5m (6–8¼ft), spread 1.5–2.5m (5–8¼ft). Knap Hill azaleas (Kn), with large, trumpet-shaped, brilliantly coloured, usually unscented flowers in May; height 1.8–2.5m (6–8¼ft), spread 1.8–3m (6–10ft). Mollis azaleas (M), with large, unscented flowers before the leaves in early May; height 1.2–1.8m (4–6ft), spread 1.5–2.5m (5–8¼ft). Some examples:

R. 'Cécile' (Kn.). Large, pink flowers with yellow flare.

R. 'Christopher Wren' (M). Compact bush, leaves bronze in autumn. Flowers deep yellow with orange flare.

R. 'Coccinea Speciosa' (Gh). Spreading habit. Flowers bright scarlet-orange. An old favourite.

R. 'Daviesii' (Gh). Creamy white, flared yellow, fragrant, late.

R. 'Gibraltar' (Kn). Red in bud, opening brilliant orange-red with frilled margins.

R. 'Homebush' (Kn). Deep, glowing pink, semi-double in dense, rounded trusses.

R. 'Klondyke' (Kn). Young foliage bronze-red. Flowers deep golden-yellow, flushed red.

R. 'Koster's Brilliant Red' (M). Brilliant orange-red.

R. 'Strawberry Ice' (Kn). Pale pink with yellow flare.

Evergreen Azaleas

Generally lower-growing and more spreading than deciduous azaleas, making low mounds often completely covered with blooms at flowering time. Can be grouped as follows. Kaempferi azaleas (Kf), sometimes semi-evergreen, with flowers single, about 50mm (2in) across, in mid- to late May; height 1.2m (4ft), spread 1.5m (5ft). Kurume azaleas (K), with flowers single or double, about 25mm (1in) across, in April–May; height 1.2m (4ft), spread 1.8m (6ft). Vuyk azaleas (V), with generally large flowers, 50–75mm (2–3in) across in May; height about 1m (3¼ft), spread 1.2–1.5m (4–5ft). Following are especially notable:

R. 'Addy Wery' (K). Flowers deep orange-red, compact habit.

R. 'Blaauw's Pink' (K). Rich salmon-pink, partly hose-in-hose.

R. 'Blue Danube' (V). Deep violet-blue, 75mm (3in) across.

R. 'Hinodegiri' (K). Bright red, very freely borne.

R. 'Hinomayo' (K). Bright phlox-pink, vigorous, free-flowering, very hardy.

R. 'John Cairns' (Kf). Deep orange-scarlet, leaves bronze in winter.

R. 'Kuro-no-yuki' (K). White with slight green flare, hose-in-hose, dwarf habit.

R. 'Orange Beauty' (V). Flowers 40mm (1½in) across, salmon-pink, slightly frilled, early May, height 1m (3ft), spread 1.5m (5ft).

R. 'Palestrina' (V). White flushed with green, 50mm (2in) across, upright habit.

R. 'Rosebud' (V). Double, bright pink flowers 50mm (2in) across; spreading habit.

R. 'Vuyk's Rosy Red' (V). Large, deep rose-pink flowers with slightly frilled lobes.

Site Most prefer light shade, but hardy hybrids, small-leaved rhododendrons, and azaleas generally thrive in full sun except in driest positions. Those that flower early are best not planted where late frosts are a problem.

Soil Well-drained but moisture-retentive acid soil: almost all are lime-haters.

Propagation By seed: sow in warm frame or greenhouse in February–April with no heat; but cultivars do not come true from seed, and species will hybridise with any nearby rhododendrons. By cuttings: take 75mm (3in) cuttings of side shoots of evergreens (including azaleas) in September–October in closed frame, having removed terminal bud; take 75mm (3in) cuttings of young growth of deciduous azaleas in spring under mist. By grafting: graft 75mm (3in) shoots of previous year's growth onto *R. ponticum* stock in January–February under glass with bottom heat. By layering: wound bark on low branch and peg down into soil enriched with peat and sharp sand in autumn–spring.

Cultivation Best planted in early autumn, or in spring if watered frequently during dry periods. Incorporate peat into humus-poor soils and sand and peat into heavy ones. Water well and mulch after planting.

Pruning Not usually necessary except to restrict growth: cut back lightly to a whorl of leaves in spring. Remove suckers from grafted plants. Remove flower-heads after blooming. Old, straggly hardy hybrids benefit from heavy pruning or pollarding in late winter; this will induce more-compact new growth.

Pests and Diseases The most serious are aphids, rhododendron bug, azalea gall, bud blast, and honey fungus.

Below Rhododendron
'Addy Wery' (evergreen azalea)

Above *Rhus typhina*

Rhus

ANACARDIACEAE   Sumach

A large genus of trees, shrubs, and climbers, mainly from temperate regions of Asia and North America. All have compound leaves and bear small flowers, often in conspicuous panicles.

R. typhina (E. North America), stag's-horn sumach. Deciduous, spreading tree or large shrub with stout, densely hairy shoots. Height 6m (20ft) or more; spread 8m (26ft). Pinnate leaves turn brilliant orange and red in autumn. Greenish flowers in conical panicles in June–July, followed on female trees by clusters of crimson fruits in autumn. Cultivar 'Dissecta' ('Laciniata' of gardens) has finely cut leaves, also with striking autumn colour.

Site Open, in full sun.

Soil Fertile; plant likes chalk, but tolerates others.

Propagation Root cuttings in sandy soil in early spring.

Cultivation Plant container-grown subjects at any time. Water frequently late-spring and summer plantings.

Pruning Plants can be kept low and shrubby, with large leaves for foliage effect, by cutting back in April to within one or two buds of old wood.

Pests and Diseases Coral-spot fungus may be a problem.

'Albidum' (white-tinged pink); 'Brocklebankii' (gold foliage, pink flowers); 'King Edward VII' (crimson); 'Pulborough Scarlet' (crimson).
R. speciosum (North America). Height 1.8–3m (6–10ft); spread 1.2–1.5m (4–5ft). Tender deciduous shrub. Leaves deeply lobed, mid-green. Bright red fuchsia-like flowers, 25mm (1in) long, carried in clusters in April–June.

Site Sun or light shade. *R. speciosum* is not fully hardy so requires shelter of south- or west-facing wall.
Soil Well-drained.
Propagation Hard-wood cuttings, 250–300mm (10–12in) long, in autumn (75–100mm (3–4in) long in the case of *R. laurifolium*).
Cultivation Plant in October–March. Mulch in spring with well-rotted manure or compost.
Pruning Remove old or diseased wood in spring.
Pests and Diseases Aphids may infest leaves. Leaf spot may occur.

Robinia

LEGUMINOSAE

Elegant, mostly hardy, deciduous trees and shrubs from North America, with brittle, spiny shoots and pea-shaped flowers in pendulous racemes. The two listed make good specimens for larger gardens.
R. 'Hillieri' (hybrid). Round-headed tree. Height 8m (26ft); spread 6m (20ft). Freely-borne lilac-pink, slightly fragrant flowers in June.
R. pseudoacacia (E. North America), false acacia, locust tree. Height up to 25m (80ft); spread 15m (50ft). Deeply furrowed bark. Leaves yellow in autumn. Flowers white, fragrant, in racemes up to 150mm (6in) long, in June. Cultivars include 'Bessoniana' (vigorous, upright habit, almost spineless branches); 'Frisia' (height up to 15m (50ft), spread 6m (20ft), with vivid yellow foliage); 'Umbraculifera' (syn. 'Inermis', mop-head acacia, a dense-headed, spineless tree up to 5m (16½ft) high and wide).

Site Full sun; strong winds may damage brittle branches.
Soil Well-drained; plants tolerate dry soils. Very fertile soils increase danger of wind damage.
Propagation *R. pseudoacacia* by seed in spring. Cultivars by grafting on to roots or shoots of *R. pseudoacacia* in spring.
Cultivation Plant at any time in November–March.
Pruning Cut out any dead wood in July–August.

Above *Ribes sanguineum* 'Pulborough Scarlet'

Ribes

GROSSULARIACEAE Flowering currant

Tender and hardy shrubs native to northern temperate regions and South America. Six of the 150 species are especially popular for their decorative flowers; blackcurrants, red and white currants, and gooseberries also belong to this genus.
R. alpinum (Europe). Height 900mm–1.8m (3–6ft); spread 900mm–1.2m (3–4ft). Hardy, deciduous, bushy shrub, with mid-green, deeply toothed leaves. Insignificant yellow-green flowers, 25–40mm (1–1½in) long, in April. Red berries produced in autumn if both sexes are grown.
R. aureum (North America), buffalo or golden currant. Height 1.8–2.5m (6–8¼ft); spread 1.2–1.5m (4–5ft). Hardy, deciduous shrub with pale-green, toothed leaves which turn to orange in autumn. Bright-yellow flowers, 10mm (⅜in) long, smelling of cloves, produced in April. Black autumn berries. (*R. odoratum* is similar, larger-flowered, but is not so readily available.)
R. laurifolium (China). Height and spread 450mm (18in). Hardy evergreen shrub, ideal for a rock garden (or for pot-culture under glass). Leaves are pale green and leathery. Unisexual: male flowers are green-yellow, 8mm (⅓in) long, female flowers are shorter; both are produced in spring. Purple-black fruits are produced if both sexes are grown.
R. sanguineum (North America), flowering currant. Height 1.8–2.7m (6–9ft); spread 1.5–2.1m (5–7ft). Hardy deciduous shrub with mid- to dark-green leaves, pale on underside. Deep pink flowers, 10mm (⅜in) long, in March–May. Blue-black berries appear in autumn. Varieties include

Below *Robinia pseudoacacia* 'Frisia'

Above *Rodgersia tabularis*

Rodgersia

SAXIFRAGACEAE

Hardy herbaceous perennials, native to China and Japan, bearing attractive foliage and flower plumes.

R. aesculifolia (China). Height 600mm–1.2m (2–4ft); spread 1m (3¼ft). Handsome horse-chestnut-like leaves emerge from hard, woody rootstock. Plumes of frothy white flowers up to 600mm (2ft) long in June–July.

R. pinnata (China). Height 600mm–1.2m (2–4ft); spread 600–900mm (2–3ft). Coarse green leaves divided into large, finger-like segments. Much-branched heads of fluffy pink flowers in July. Variety 'Superba', with attractive purplish bronze foliage, is especially fine.

R. podophylla (Japan). Height 600mm–1.2m (2–4ft); spread 600–900mm (2–3ft). Handsome spreading, divided leaves. Creamy-white frothy flower heads up to 450mm (1½ft) long in June–July.

R. tabularis (China). Height and spread 1m (3¼ft). Large, pale green, plate-like leaves 300–600mm (1–2ft) across on stout stems. Feathery white plumes of blossom in July.

Site Sheltered, sunny preferred, but most plants tolerate dappled shade.
Soil Moist, peaty.
Propagation By seed sown in early spring in a cold frame. Alternatively, root-stocks can be divided in dormant period.
Cultivation Plant at any time in dormant season. Old foliage should be cleared away in autumn, when a top dressing of leaf-mould or coarse peat should be applied.

Romneya

PAPAVERACEAE   Tree poppy

A genus of two herbaceous perennials, native to North America, with poppy-like flowers and dissected leaves. They are reliably hardy only in sheltered locations in the south and south-west of Britain.

R. coulteri (California). Height 1.2–1.8m (4–6ft); spread 900mm–1.2m (3–4ft). Blue-green, deeply lobed leaves. Fragrant white flowers, 100–125mm (4–5in) across, with deep yellow stamens, in July–September. *R. c. trichocalyx* is almost identical, but a little more slender in habit and with hairy buds. The hybrid 'White Cloud' is better than its parents.

Site Sheltered, light.
Soil Light, must be well-drained. Plants thrive in chalky soil.
Propagation Sow seeds in early spring under glass. Take root cuttings in February, inserting in sandy soil.
Cultivation Plant out in April–May. Romneyas resent any kind of root disturbance, so avoid moving established plants. Over-winter plants in first two years with bracken or peat as protection against hard frost.
Pruning Cut all stems to a few inches above ground level in late October.

Below *Romneya coulteri*

Rosa

ROSACEAE   Rose

Hardy and some slightly tender deciduous and evergreen shrubs including bushy, trailing, and climbing forms; most have prickly stems and shoots. They are native mainly to temperate regions of the northern hemisphere. The flowers form singly or in clusters; some are small but most are medium-sized to large, single, semi-double or double.

Wild (Species) Roses

R. × dupontii (France; possibly a musk-rose hybrid). Upright and arching to 1.8–2.1m (6–7ft), fairly open growth, few thorns. Leaves light grey-green. Flowers in small clusters, 75mm (3in) across, single, scented, creamy white with some pink flushes and yellow stamens, in June–July.

R. fedtschenkoana (Turkestan). Upright and arching to 2.5m (8¼ft). One of few species roses to flower throughout summer, later blooms coming on new side shoots. Leaves soft grey-green. Flowers single, 50mm (2in), white with yellow stamens, in clusters; main flush in June–July. Orange hips. Suckers readily on own roots.

R. glauca (syn. *R. rubrifolia*; C. and E. Europe). Upright and arching to 2.25m (7ft), shoots plum red, practically thornless when young. Grown principally for foliage: leaves purplish red, with coppery sheen. Clusters of small, pink, single flowers carried fleetingly in June.

R. × harisonii (syn. 'Harison's Yellow'; United States, hybrid between *R. foetida* and *R. spinosissima*). Upright, irregular growth to 2m (6½ft). Bright green glossy leaves. Flowers in clusters, semi-double, petals wavy, bright yellow, in late May–June. Slight scent.

R. moyesii (N.W. China) 'Geranium'. Open, arching to 2.7m (9ft), almost thornless. Leaves dark green, more plentiful than in parent species. Flowers single, scentless, bright scarlet, singly and in small clusters all along shoots in June. Showy, bright red, flagon-shaped hips.

Left *Rosa* 'Henri Martin'   **Above** *R. moyesii*

R. × paulii (England, rugosa hybrid) 'Rosea'. Low-growing, wide-spreading, giving dense, healthy leaf coverage for ground cover. Height 1.2m (4ft); spread 3.5–4.5m (12–15ft) across. Very thorny. Flowers large, single, scented, pale pink with cream stamens, in clusters, in early June.

R. xanthina spontanea (N. China, Korea). Best-known garden form of this is 'Canary Bird'. Arching growth 2.1m (7ft) high and wide, less in standard form. Plentiful, small, fern-like leaves; chestnut-brown shoots. Flowers large, single, yellow, all along main shoots, in late April–May.

Old Garden Roses

R. × alba (origin uncertain), alba rose. Varieties include 'Maxima' (great double white or Jacobite rose), vigorous, upright, 2.1–2.5m (7–8¼ft) high, 1.8m (6ft) across; leaves plentiful, soft grey-green; flowers in clusters, medium size, creamy white, petals wavy, scented, in June–July. 'Königin von Danemarck', bushy, well branched, to 1.2m (4ft) high and wide; leaves soft grey-green; flowers medium-sized, very double, intense carmine-pink, quickly paling except in flower centre, in June–July.

R. × borboniana (China/damask hybrid), Bourbon rose. Varieties include 'Boule de Neige', upright and vigorous, less tall than most at 1.2m (4ft); leaves, large, dark green; flowers 75mm (3in), double, globular, creamy white, in clusters, in mid-June and recurrent. 'Mme Isaac Pereire', very robust to 1.8–2.1m (6–7ft); large, mid-green leaves; flowers in clusters, 100mm (4in), double, globular but reflexing, deep cerise-pink, outstanding fragrance, in mid-June and recurrent. 'Mme Pierre Oger', blush-pink sport of

similar but deeper pink 'La Reine Victoria'; slender grower to 1.8m (6ft), needing pillar support; flowers in clusters, medium size, globular with shell-like petals, colour deepens in hot sun, in mid-June and recurrent.

R. × centifolia (origin uncertain), cabbage rose. Varieties include 'De Meaux', dwarf centifolia at 1.1m (3½ft) for small gardens; lax, arching growth; flowers soft pink, globular, opening flat, some quartered, sweet scented, June–July. 'Fantin-Latour', very vigorous to 2.1m (7ft), less lax than most; large, matt, dark green leaves; flowers in clusters, medium to large, double, blush-pink, reflexing showing button eye, in June–July.

R. × centifolia 'Muscosa' (Holland or France; sport of *R. × centifolia*), moss rose. Varieties include 'Common Moss' (syns. 'Old Pink Moss', 'Communis'), the earliest known and still best; quite bushy but wide-spreading, up to 1.5m (5ft) tall; red-tinged moss; flowers in small clusters, fragrant, double and reflexing, pink, in June–July. 'Henri Martin', lax, reaching 1.5m (5ft) high by 1.2m (4ft); flowers medium size, double, light crimson, in clusters, in June–July.

R. chinensis (China), China rose. Varieties include 'Cécile Brunner' (syn. 'Mignon'), small, twiggy, airy bush to 1–1.2m (3–4ft) at most; leaves pointed, coppery green, very healthy; flowers in clusters, very small, double, shapely at first, blush-pink, scentless, in mid-June and recurrent. 'Mutabilis' (syn. 'Tipo Ideale'), to 1m (3¼ft) as free-standing bush, 2.5m (8¼ft) or more as climber against warm wall; deep green leaves; flowers single, loosely formed, changing from coppery flame to buff, to pink, to crimson, in mid-June and recurrent.

R. damascena (Near and Middle East), damask rose. Varieties include 'Ispahan', vigorous, upright, 1.5–1.8m (5–6ft); flowers large, semi-double, fragrant, soft pink, in clusters, in June–July. 'Mme Hardy', vigorous, bushy to 1.5–1.8m (5–6ft); leaves matt, light green; buds with long, feathery calyces; flowers double, some quartered, white with green

'eye', in small clusters, in June–July; not fully rain-proof.

R. gallica (C. and S.E. Europe, Near East), French rose. Varieties include 'Belle de Crécy', lax, bushy to 1.2m (4ft); flowers scented, double, blends of lilac, pink, grey, and purple, in June–July; leaves matt mid-green. 'Charles de Mills', compact, upright, twiggy, 1.2m (4ft); flowers 100mm (4in) across, moderate scent, opening flat, petals quartered, rich crimson-maroon, in June–July. 'Complicata', untypical semi-climber or vigorous scrambler; flowers 100mm (4in), single, pink with white eye, very profuse, in June–July. 'Empress Josephine' (syn. 'Francofurtana'), spreading and lax, 1.2m (4ft) high and wide; flowers double, loosely formed, bright pink, veined deeper, in June–July. 'Rosa Mundi' (syn. 'Versicolor'), compact, upright, twiggy, 1.2m (4ft); flowers semi-double, pale blush-pink, striped deep pink, petals wavy, in June–July.

Hybrid Perpetuals

Hybrids of *R. × borboniana* and China roses. Varieties include 'Baron Girod de l'Ain', 1.2m (4ft) high by 1m (3¼ft) wide, upright; flowers large, cupped, sweetly scented, deep crimson, petals irregularly scalloped and edged and flecked white, in mid-June and recurrent. 'Baronne Prévost', oldest (1842) HP still listed; sturdy and upright 1.2m (4ft); light green leaves; flowers in clusters, double, rose-pink, some quartered, in late-June and recurrent. 'Frau Karl Druschki' (syn. 'White American Beauty', 'Snow Queen'), tall and leggy to 1.8m (6ft); light green leaves; flowers large, high-centred, double, pure white, scentless, borne singly or in small clusters, recurrent. 'Général Jacqueminot', ancestor of most modern reds; upright to 1.2m (4ft) and compact; light green leaves; flowers large, fragrant, double and rather globular, bright crimson, in mid-June and recurrent. 'Mrs John Laing',

Below *Rosa gallica* 'Rosa Mundi'

Above *Rosa chinensis* 'Mutabilis'   **Right** *R.* 'Just Joey' (large-flowered)

height; flowers medium-sized, double, shapely, rose pink; scent moderate. 'Double Delight', freely branching to average height; semi-glossy leaves (may mildew); flowers double, shapely at first, creamy white, petal edges flushed cherry red. 'Dutch Gold', vigorous and upright; flowers bright yellow, shapely (some split centres). 'Ernest H. Morse', vigorous; flowers abundant, fragrant, crimson; a top selection. 'Fragrant Cloud', medium height and profuse bloom; large, dark green leaves; flowers large, in clusters, bright geranium-red; outstanding fragrance. 'Golden Times', dark green leaves; flowers pale gold, carried freely; good scent. 'Grandpa Dickson', outstanding for both garden and showing; very upright and compact; flowers shapely, weatherproof, pale yellow. 'John Waterer', flowers very shapely, deep crimson; scentless; above average disease resistance. 'Just Joey', deservedly a top seller; healthy; leaves dark green; flowers coppery orange and pink blend, profuse, very large with waved petals. 'Lakeland', average height; semi-glossy leaves; flowers soft pink, large and shapely; some of show standard but good for bedding. 'Mister Lincoln', tall, rather leggy, 1–1.2m (3–4ft); dark leaves; flowers double, scented, deep, dusky red, singly or in small clusters. 'Mullard Jubilee' (syn. 'Electron'), vigorous; very thorny; flowers profuse, large, double, deep pink; little scent. 'National Trust', bushy, below average height; flowers prolific, shapely, on small side, bright red; little scent. 'Pascali', tall and upright; healthy leaves; flowers double, rather small, shapely, white with creamy buff tints in centres; the best white in rain. 'Peace' (syn. 'Mme A. Meilland'), classic rose, strong-growing to 1.2m (4ft) or more; healthy leaves; flowers very large, pale yellow with pink flushes, petals waved; little scent; rather late into bloom; makes a good shrub rose. 'Piccadilly', vigorous to average height; bronze green, healthy leaves; flowers double, shapely, probably the best red and yellow bicolour.

about 1.5m (5ft) high and 1m (3¼ft) wide; light green leaves; flowers singly and in clusters, large, high-centred, fragrant, silvery pink, in mid-June and recurrent (quick to repeat). 'Reine des Violettes', untypical growth; bushy and spreading 1.5m (5ft) high, needing good soil; grey-green leaves; flowers medium-sized, double, in clusters, opening flat, cerise fading violet-purple, in mid-June and recurrent.

Large-Flowered Bush Roses (Hybrid Teas)
Originally these were hybrids of Hybrid Perpetuals and Tea roses. Upright, compact shrubs with stiff, straight shoots, usually branching. Average height 750mm (2½ft). All open in June and are recurrent to October. Varieties include 'Alec's Red', ideal bedding rose, average height, healthy, vigorous; flowers light crimson, large, double, rather globular, singly and in small clusters. 'Alexander', upright, reaching 1.2m (4ft); healthy; flowers large, fragrant, deep vermilion, double, opening loosely; a good hedging rose. 'Alpine Sunset', sturdy, a little below average height; flowers very fragrant, large, shapely, blends of creamy yellow and peach; healthy. 'Blessings', average height, healthy; flowers almost non-stop, each loosely double, light pink, little fragrance; ideal for bedding. 'Bobby Charlton', vigorous, upright; flowers double, high-centred, soft pink, reverse lighter, scented; ideal for showing; rather late into flower. 'Camphill Glory', vigorous and above average height; healthy mid-green leaves; flowers large, double, shapely, creamy pink flushed deeper pink; weather resistant; good for hedging or bedding. 'Cheshire Life', average height or a little less, dark green leaves; healthy; flowers double, medium-sized, bright orange-vermilion, carried freely. 'Congratulations', elegant and slender, almost thornless; healthy; above average

Above *Rosa* 'City of Belfast' (cluster-flowered)

'Pink Favourite', very strong growing and upright; exceptionally healthy; flowers large, in clusters, shapely, bright pink. 'Silver Jubilee', outstanding bedding rose; healthy; flowers prolific, shapely, coppery pink, fragrant. 'Troika', vigorous to average height or more; healthy; flowers large, shapely, coppery orange, veined scarlet. 'Wendy Cussons', vigorous and spreading, freely branched; flowers prolific, always shapely, strong cerise-pink; fragrant. 'Whisky Mac', vigorous; flowers double, cupped, amber-yellow; fragrant.

Cluster-Flowered Bush Roses (Floribundas)
Many of these descended from *R. polyantha* (syn. *R. multiflora*). Upright, compact shrubs with stiff, straight shoots, usually branched. Average height 750mm (2½ft). Flowers usually small, single, semi-double or double, carried in trusses in June or July and all are recurrent. Varieties include 'Amanda', very healthy and robust; flowers deep yellow, shapely, large for type. 'Anne Harkness', tall, upright, well branched; flowers double in very large trusses, buff-yellow, first flush later than most; makes a good hedge. 'Arthur Bell', tall grower; large, leathery leaves; very healthy; flowers quick-fading bright yellow, very fragrant, semi-double, in small clusters, large for the type. 'Bright Smile', dwarf up to 600mm (2ft); robust, bushy, and healthy; flowers semi-double in small clusters, bright yellow, paling a little. 'City of Belfast', just below average height; robust, healthy, and bushy; leaves red when young; flowers profuse, double, pure scarlet; die-back possible in cold areas, elsewhere a top choice. 'City of Leeds', average height and strong constitution; leaves dark green, glossy, small; flowers large, salmon-pink, in medium sized trusses. 'Dame of Sark', for large bed or hedge; healthy; tall and constantly in bloom; flowers, double, large, in medium trusses, orange-red with yellow reverse. 'Dearest', established favourite; bushy to

average height, leaves dark green, glossy; flowers camellia-like, double, soft salmon-pink, not rain-proof but fragrant; rose rust possible in eastern districts. 'Elizabeth of Glamis' (syn. 'Irish Beauty'), robust and upright on light soils, not so good on cold, heavy soils; flowers large, shapely, opening wide, soft salmon-orange, in medium clusters; fragrant. 'Escapade', bushy, upright, well-branched; glossy, healthy, light green leaves; flower colour unique, soft rosy lilac with white eye, in big trusses; fragrant. 'Evelyn Fison' (syn. 'Irish Wonder'), probably the best all-round red bedding rose; robust; dark green glossy leaves; flowers unfading scarlet, double, with waved petals, in trusses of medium size; rainproof; little scent. 'Eye Paint', sometimes classed as shrub rose; tall and bushy; dark green, semi-glossy leaves; flowers profuse in clusters at all levels, each single, bright scarlet with white eye and lighter reverse; a McGredy 'hand-painted' variety; black spot may occur. 'Fragrant Delight', bushy to average height or a little more; young leaves bronze tinted, then dark green; flowers shapely in good trusses, coppery salmon with yellow shadings; fragrant. 'Iceberg' (syn. 'Schneewittchen'), perhaps the best of all cluster-flowered roses; strong, tall, bushy, canes quite slender, will make a shrub rose if lightly pruned; flowers fragrant, white, camellia-like, in large and small clusters carried all over the bush. 'Korresia', probably the best modern yellow cluster-flowered variety; healthy, robust to average height; glossy leaves; flowers in medium clusters, double, shapely, profuse; fragrant. 'Lilli Marlene', slender grower; shoots plum-red, few thorns, leaves healthy, bronze-tinted; flowers widely spaced in trusses, double, dusky scarlet. 'Living Fire', upright and vigorous; leaves dark green, glossy, healthy; flowers double, rather globular, in medium trusses, bright orange-scarlet with yellow shadings. 'Margaret Merrill', bushy to average height; dark green, generally healthy leaves; flowers in medium trusses, large, shapely in bud, opening wide, white flushed pink, pink stamens; fine fragrance. 'Marlena', very short and bushy; dark leaves; flowers double, bright crimson; for container planting or small bed. 'Matangi', McGredy 'hand-painted' variety; healthy, glossy leaves; flowers large, orange-vermilion, feathering to white eye. 'Memento', very promising newcomer; bushy to below average height; flowers salmon-red, prolific. 'Mountbatten', outstanding, vigorous, bushy, healthy; flowers very large, small trusses, mimosa-yellow; some scent; voted Rose of the Year, 1982. 'Queen Elizabeth', a superb variety; very healthy, robust, and tall, 2.1–2.4m (7–8ft), but little spread; flowers pink, large, cupped on long, thornless stems; good for hedges or for cutting. 'Rob Roy', tall, slender; dark, glossy leaves; flowers double, shapely, bright crimson, well-spaced in truss. 'Southampton', robust, upright, above average height; health outstanding; flowers double, apricot-orange, flushed scarlet; some scent; for a big bed or hedge. 'Stargazer', very dwarf and bushy; flowers single in medium trusses, scarlet with yellow eye (scarlet fades to pink). 'Stephen Langdon', very robust; large, dark green, healthy leaves; flowers a little later than average, deep scarlet, large petals, small trusses; shapely at first, they open wide with waved petals. 'Sue Lawley', a McGredy 'hand-painted' variety; vigorous, well-branched; flowers large, opening wide, irregularly patterned soft carmine, pink and white, paling with age. 'Sunsilk', robust, well branched; leaves healthy; flowers very large, double, shapely, soft yellow; sometimes classed as large-flowered (hybrid-tea) type. 'Topsi', dwarf, bushy; some black spot and some die-back possible, but popular for bright orange-scarlet semi-double flowers in medium-sized trusses; a dazzler. 'Trumpeter', compact, low-growing; glossy, dark green, healthy leaves; flowers in large trusses, globular, double,

bright vermilion. 'Warrior', similar to 'Trumpeter', but leaves lighter, semi-glossy, and flower trusses smaller.

Modern Shrub Roses

Hybrids of mixed ancestry; no common characteristics. Varieties include 'Buff Beauty' (hybrid musk group), large and lax (needs support), reaching 1.5m (5ft); flowers fragrant, in clusters, buff-orange, in June–July and recurrent. 'Chinatown' (syn. 'Ville de Chine'), upright, cluster-flowered type; fine foliage; flowers very fragrant, large, double in small clusters, yellow, in June–July and recurrent. 'Cornelia' (hybrid musk), 1.5m (5ft), bushy; flowers strawberry-pink; double in clusters, in June–July and recurrent. 'Fred Loads', 1.5–1.8m (5–6ft), cluster-flowered type; flowers in huge trusses, semi-double orange-vermilion, in June–July and recurrent; scented. 'Frühlingsgold', tall, arching to 2.1m (7ft); flowers large, semi-double, primrose-yellow, in May–June (non-recurrent); fragrant. 'Golden Wings', a smaller, more bushy 'Frühlingsgold', 1.5m (5ft), but recurrent. 'Nevada', bushy, arching shrub 1.8m (6ft) high and 2.1m (7ft) wide; flowers profuse, large, semi-double, creamy white, in June and partly recurrent. 'Penelope' (hybrid musk), 1.8m (6ft) high and 2.1m (7ft) wide, bushy; dark green leaves; flowers double in clusters, profuse, peach-pink, in June–July and recurrent; fragrant. 'Pink Grooten-dorst' (rugosa), upright to 1.8m (6ft); flowers small in large clusters, pink, petals fringed like a carnation, in June; no scent. 'Roseraie de l'Hay' (rugosa), up to 1.8m (6ft); with fine, wrinkled, very healthy leaves; flowers double, wine-red, in clusters, in early June and recurrent; fragrant; good for hedges. 'Sarah Van Fleet' (rugosa), bushy to 1.8m (6ft); fine leaves; flowers early, pink, double, in clusters, in mid-June and recurrent; fragrant.

Above *Rosa* 'Roseraie de l'Hay' (rugosa)   **Below** *R.* 'Nevada' (modern shrub)

Climbing Roses

Hybrids of mixed ancestry. Varieties include 'Autumn Sunlight', 3–3.5m (10–12ft); flowers double in clusters, orange-vermillion, in mid-June and recurrent; fragrant. 'Compassion', also 3–3.5m (10–12ft), fine dark green, healthy leaves; good continuity; flowers double, shapely, pink and apricot blends, in June and recurrent; fragrant. 'Dublin Bay', short climber or shrub; flowers bright crimson, in June and recurrent; for pillar or low wall. 'Golden Showers', 2.5m (8¼ft), very upright; flowers loosely double, yellow, in clusters, in June and recurrent; also suitable as a shrub. 'Handel', 4.5m (15ft); dark, healthy leaves; flowers double, in clusters, creamy white, edged rosy pink, in June and recurrent; prone to mildew. 'Maigold', 3–3.5m (10–12ft); flowers double, opening flat, bronze-yellow, in May; fragrant. 'Mermaid', very vigorous, almost evergreen; big thorns; flowers large, single, sulphur-yellow, in small clusters all summer. 'Pink Perpétue', 3m (10ft); flowers double, in large clusters, rose-pink, carmine reverse, continuously from June. 'Swan Lake', vigorous to 3m (10ft); flowers large, shapely, double, white with pink flush, in June; little scent.

Ramblers

Non-recurrent hybrids of *R. wichuraiana* and some others. Small flowers in large clusters. Long, lax shoots develop from the base of the plant each year. Varieties include 'Albéric Barbier', 4.5m (15ft); almost evergreen; flowers in clusters, yellow buds, then creamy white, in mid-June; fragrant. 'Albertine', 4.5m (15ft); leaves dark green (may mildew); flowers in clusters, coppery pink, shapely in bud, opening loosely, in mid-June; fragrant. 'Félicité et Perpétue', 4.5m (15ft); bronze-green leaves, almost evergreen; flowers profuse, large clusters, many small petals, white, in mid-July. 'Sanders' White Rambler', 4.5m (15ft); bright green, glossy leaves; flowers in clusters, pure white, in mid-June–July.

Miniature Roses

R. chinensis minima. Suitable for troughs, tubs, lining paths, rockeries. Flowering in June–July; all recurrent. Varieties include 'Angela Rippon', 300mm (12in), bushy; flowers double, coral-pink, prolific. 'Baby Gold Star' (syn. 'Estrellita de Oro'), 450mm (18in), tall for the type; flowers double, bright yellow. 'Baby Masquerade' (syn. 'Baby Carnaval'), 450mm (18in), vigorous, bushy; flowers open yellow, changing to pink, then red (as in cluster-flowered parent). 'Bambino', bushy to 250mm (10in); flowers double, pink; slightly scented. 'Cinderella', 250mm (10in), flowers very double, shapely, blush-pink. 'Coralín' (syn. 'Carolyn'), upright to 375mm (15in); flowers double, coral-pink. 'Darling Flame', large, spreading; flowers very prolific, in clusters, double, bright orange-vermilion, yellow reverse. 'Easter Morning', 375mm (15in) or more; flowers double, ivory-white. 'Gypsy Jewel', 375mm (15in), spreading wide; flowers large, double, rose-pink. 'Judy Fischer', 225mm (9in), sturdy; flowers double, deep pink. 'Lavender Jewel', 250mm (10in), lax grower; flowers large, double, lavender-pink. 'Little Flirt', tall; flowers double, orange-red with yellow reverse, fading rather quickly. 'Magic Carrousel', 250mm (10in), popular exhibition rose; flowers double, white with pink petal edges. 'New Penny', 250mm (10in), bushy; flowers double, coral-pink. 'Perla de Alcanada' (syn. 'Baby Crimson'), old favourite, still very fine; 250mm (10in); bushy; flowers between semi-double and double, rosy red. 'Rise 'n' Shine', popular show variety (though black spot likely); 375mm (15in), bushy; flowers large, double, bright yellow. 'Sheri Anne', tall and upright show rose; flowers

Right *Rosa* 'Handel' (climbing)

orange-red; fragrant. 'Snow Carpet', good for ground cover, spreading to 600mm–1m (2–3ft) with dense coverage; dark green leaves; flowers with many small petals, white; slightly fragrant. 'Starina', outstanding variety in every way; 450mm (18in); flowers very large, bright orange-vermilion. 'Sweet Fairy', 200mm (8in) – a real miniature; flowers apple-blossom pink, each with up to 60 petals; fragrant.

Site Sunny, open.

Soil Well-drained, moisture-retentive loam. Some roses – rugosas and *R. pimpinellifolia* (syn. *R. spinosissima*) hybrids, for instance – thrive on light, sandy soils. Few do well on shallow chalky soils.

Propagation By cuttings of ripe, current-season's wood, taken in late August–November; plant outdoors in open spot shaded from mid-day sun; transplant following autumn. By budding on to root-stocks at mid-summer, and heading back stocks following February. For new varieties, by cross-pollination in summer, preferably under glass; stratify partly ripened seeds in November–February; sow in boxes under glass or in open.

Cultivation Prepare soil for planting in September, mixing in manure and/or compost. Plant late autumn or late spring, about 450–600mm (1½–2ft) apart for bedding. Support and train climbers and ramblers on pillars, arches, pergolas; climbers also on walls, along horizontal wires. Apply fertilisers in late February and mid-July. Mulch in April.

Pruning Large- and cluster-flowered roses (hybrid teas and floribundas) in March in south, April in north: remove dead, diseased and weak shoots; prune remaining main shoots to 150–200mm (6–8in) (large flowered), to 200–250mm (8–10in) (cluster flowered), cutting just above a bud. Species roses: remove dead or diseased wood when seen. Shrub roses and climbers: shorten laterals by two thirds in late autumn, main shoots by one third if overrunning space; remove dead wood. Ramblers: cut shoots that have flowered back to ground level; tie in shoots of current year in their place (if few, retain some old shoots, trimming laterals). Miniatures: remove dead wood, thin out if twiggy growth has become tangled; trim remainder to keep tidy.

Pests and Diseases Aphids (greenfly), caterpillars, in some districts leaf-rolling sawfly, are most common pests; also chafers, froghoppers, leafhoppers, red-spider mite (particularly on climbers against walls), rose-slug worm, scale insects, thrips, and tortrix moth. Black spot and powdery mildew are common diseases.

Below *Rosa* 'Starina' (miniature)

Rosmarinus

LABIATAE

A small genus of evergreen shrubs, native to Europe, grown mainly for the aromatic leaves, which are used as culinary herbs.

R. officinalis (S. Europe), rosemary. Erect or sprawling shrub with numerous spiky branches. Height 1.2–1.8m (4–6ft). Leaves mid- to dark green with silvery white undersides. Pale blue or violet flowers, 13–20mm ($\frac{1}{2}$–$\frac{3}{4}$in) long, carried in clusters on the branches in March–April (occasionally into autumn). Varieties include 'Albus' (white or very pale blue flowers); 'Miss Jessop's Upright' (light mauve); 'Prostratus' (syn. *R. lavandulaceus*; mat-forming, with paler leaves and violet-blue flowers).

Site Sunny or partly shaded.
Soil Well-drained, preferably not clay.
Propagation Take half-ripe cuttings, 100mm (4in) long, in summer and root in a cold frame. Alternatively, take hardwood cuttings, 150–230mm (6–9in) long, in September or March and plant directly in permanent positions.
Cultivation Plant in March–May.
Pruning Trim lightly with shears after flowering. In spring, cut out dead or damaged wood.

Right *Rosmarinus officinalis* 'Miss Jessop's Upright'

Rubus

ROSACEAE   Ornamental bramble

A genus of some 3,000 species, native to North America, Europe, China, and Japan, only a few of which are of garden value; raspberries, loganberries, and blackberries belong to this genus. The decorative species are grown mainly for the flowers, foliage, and colourful winter stems.

R. cockburnianus (syn. *R. giraldianus*; (China), white-washed bramble. Decorative deciduous shrub. Height 2.1–2.7m (7–9ft); spread 1.5–1.8m (5–6ft). Pointed mid-green leaves, pale underneath. Purple flowers, 13–20mm ($\frac{1}{2}$–$\frac{3}{4}$in) across, carried on erect canes in June. Stems covered in a pure white wax, popular for winter decoration.

R. deliciosus (N. America). Deciduous shrub with thornless stems. Height 1.8–3m (6–10ft); spread 1.8–2.4m (6–8ft). Pale green, deeply lobed leaves. White flowers carried individually on stems in May–June.

R. phoenicolasius (China, Japan), Japanese wineberry. Deciduous shrub with very bristly stems. Height 1.8–2.4m (6–8ft); spread 2.4–3m (8–10ft). Mid-green leaves, white on the undersides. Tiny pink flower-clusters in June–July. Edible scarlet berries, 20mm ($\frac{3}{4}$in) long, ripen in late summer; used mainly in desserts and jams.

R. × tridel 'Benenden'. A vigorous, deciduous hybrid between *R. deliciosus* and *R. trilobus*. Height 1.8–2.4m (6–8ft); spread 2.4–3m (8–10ft). Bristly branches bear pale to mid-green leaves. Masses of white saucer-like flowers, 40–50mm (1$\frac{1}{2}$–2in) across, with yellow stamens in the centre appear in May. Bears no fruit.

R. ulmifolius (Britain). Semi-evergreen shrub with arching, prickly branches. Height 900mm–1.2m (3–4ft); spread 2.4–

3m (8–10ft). Dark grey leaves, grey-green beneath. Pale lilac flowers, 20mm ($\frac{3}{4}$in) wide, produced in June–August. Represented in gardens by 'Bellidiflorus' (double pink flowers).

Site Sun or partial shade.
Soil Ordinary, but must be well-drained.
Propagation Take semi-ripe cuttings, 75–100mm (3–4in) long, in late summer, except for *R. ulmifolius*; propagate latter by layering in summer, severing new plants from old the following spring. Alternatively, increase all species by division in October–March.
Cultivation Plant in October–March. Mulch in spring with well-rotted farmyard manure or garden compost.
Pruning Decorative stem types should have all old branches cut out in early spring. All other types can have older wood removed in autumn.

Below *Rubus phoenicolasius*

Rudbeckia

COMPOSITAE

Annuals, biennials, and herbaceous perennials, native to North America, some of which make showy border plants and are used as cut flowers.

R. hirta (North America), black-eyed susan. Hardy annual or biennial. Height 300–600mm (1–2ft); spread 450mm (1$\frac{1}{2}$ft). Rough, bristly, green foliage on branched stems. Large, bright yellow or orange, daisy-like flowers up to 75mm (3in) across, with hard dark centres, in June–September. Many mixed strains are offered by seedsmen. Named Varieties include 'Marmalade' (orange shades); 'Rustic Dwarfs' (orange and brown shades).

R. laciniata (North America), coneflower. Perennial. Height up to 2m (6$\frac{1}{2}$ft); spread 900mm (3ft). Upright branched stems with dense, green, hairy leaves. Large yellow, somewhat drooping petals on flowers with raised, dark green cones in late July–September. Varieties include 'Golden Glow' (double yellow).

R. nitida (North America). Perennial. Height up to 1.2m

(4ft); spread 900mm (3ft). Bright green leaves on dense, bushy, upright growth. Soft yellow flowers up to 190mm (4in) across with green central disks. Varieties include 'Goldquelle' (double yellow); 'Herbstsonne' (single yellow).

Site Open, sunny preferred, but dappled shade tolerated.
Soil All revel in a medium to heavy, moisture-retentive loam, except for *R. hirta*, which needs dry, free-draining soil.
Propagation Annuals grown from seed in trays in cold frame or greenhouse. Perennials increased by division of the root-stocks in autumn.
Cultivation Plant at any time in dormant period. Stake taller plants, especially perennials. Clear away old foliage in autumn. Divide clumps only if they start to become congested.
Pests and Diseases Pests include leaf roller and peach-potato aphis. Powdery mildew, rust and stem rot sometimes troublesome.

Below Rudbeckia hirta 'Marmalade'

Ruscus

LILIACEAE

Evergreen shrubs, native to southern Europe and western Asia, in which the leaf-like structures are modified flattened stems, or cladodes. To attain berries – their chief attraction in the garden – plants of both sexes must be grown in close proximity.
R. aculeatus (W. Europe to Iran), butcher's broom. Height and spread 600–900mm (2–3ft). Small dark green cladodes, the shape of privet leaves, produced on erect green stems. Insignificant pale green flowers carried on upper surface of cladodes in spring, followed, on pollinated female plants, by cherry-red berries the size of marbles.
R. hypoglossum (Europe). Height 300–450mm (1–1½ft);

spread 600–900mm (2–3ft). Cladodes larger and lighter in colour than those of *R. aculeatus*. Yellow flowers appear in April–May, followed by red berries on females.

Site Sun or dense shade.
Soil Any, from heavy clay to shallow chalk.
Propagation Divide in spring; or sow seeds outdoors or in cold frame when fully ripe (usually September–October).
Cultivation Plant in groups of three or five (to aid pollination) in spring.
Pruning Remove dead or damaged growth in spring.

Above *Ruscus aculeatus*

Ruta

RUTACEAE   Rue

Hardy evergreen shrubs native to Europe. The species listed has decorative value as a foliage plant; its leaves can also be used as a culinary herb.
R. graveolens (S. Europe). Perennial. Height 600–900mm (2–3ft); spread 450mm (1½ft). Attractive shrub with deeply divided, grey-green leaves which are almost evergreen. Clusters of small yellow flowers, 13mm (½in) across, appear in June–August. Varieties include 'Jackman's Blue' (the best form: compact, 450–600mm (1½–2ft) high, with striking blue-grey leaves); 'Variegata' (greyish leaves marbled creamy white).

Site Sunny.
Soil Well-drained.
Propagation Take cuttings in August, using side-shoots 75–100mm (3–4in) long; root in boxes; pot up into small pots; put outside in a sheltered place or cold frame; plant out in spring. Seed can be sown in March–April; prick out seedlings into boxes, then into small pots; when well rooted, treat the same as cuttings.
Cultivation Plant container-grown plants at any suitable time; plant 300–450mm (1–1½ft) apart for growing as a hedge. Pinch out growing tips.
Pruning Cut out old wood in spring. Remove dead flowers.

Right *Ruta graveolens* 'Jackman's Blue' (foreground)

Salix

SALICACEAE Willow, osier

Deciduous trees and shrubs, native to temperate regions of Europe and Asia, ranging from dwarf alpines to tall specimens. Flowers appear as catkins, with male and female on separate plants.

S. alba (Europe, including Britain, W. Asia), white willow. Vigorous riverside tree with ascending branches. Height 25m (82ft); spread 15m (50ft). Leaves narrow, long-pointed, grey-blue, to 75mm (3in) long. Catkins in May. Varieties include 'Chermesina' (syn. 'Britzensis', young shoots bright red in winter); 'Sericea' (syn. 'Argentea', lower-growing with silvery foliage); 'Vitellina' (young shoots golden yellow in winter).

S. caprea (Europe, including Britain, N.W. Asia), goat willow. Large shrub or small tree. Best male form in cultivation is 'Kilmarnock' (syn. 'Pendula'), with stiffly pendulous branches, 3m (10ft) tall and 2.5m (8¼ft) across, and silky catkins dotted with yellow anthers in early spring. 'Weeping Sally' is a good female form.

S. × chrysocoma (syn. *S. alba* 'Tristis'), weeping willow. Vigorous, wide-spreading tree to 15m (50ft) tall and 20m (66ft) or more across. Slender, yellow shoots, pendulous to the ground; narrow, glossy green leaves up to 100mm (4in) long. Catkins in March–April. Not suitable for small gardens. Subject to canker.

S. daphnoides (Europe), violet willow. Open, spreading tree. height and spread 10m (33ft), with arching branches. Young shoots deep purple with glaucous bloom; leaves dark green, bluish beneath, 75mm (3in) long. Catkins in March.

S. elaeagnos (S. and C. Europe, W. Asia), hoary willow. Dense, bushy shrub. Height 3m (10ft); spread 4.5m (15ft). Distinctive, very narrow leaves, green above, white beneath, up to 125mm (5in) long. Catkins in April.

S. lanata (N. Europe, including Scotland, N. Asia), woolly willow. Dwarf shrub, 1m (3¼ft) tall and 1.5m (5ft) across. Leaves broad, nearly rounded, covered in dense silvery hair when young. Stout, silky catkins borne in May.

S. matsudana (N. China), Peking willow. Vigorous and elegant tree. Height 15m (50ft); spread 10m (33ft). Leaves narrow, slender-pointed, up to 100mm (4in) long. Green-yellow catkins in April. Best forms are 'Pendula' (graceful weeping tree); 'Tortuosa' (corkscrew or dragon's claw willow: ornamental form with contorted shoots and leaves).

S. purpurea (Europe, including Britain, North Africa, temperate Asia), purple osier. Graceful shrub or small tree with arching, often purplish shoots. Height up to 5m (16½ft); spread 6m (20ft). Leaves narrow, 75mm (3in) long, dark green above, glaucous beneath. Good varieties: 'Gracilis' (syn. 'Nana', dwarf, bushy form to 1.5m (5ft) high and wide); 'Pendula' (weeping tree good for small gardens).

S. repens (Europe, including Britain, N. Asia), creeping willow. Variable shrub, usually dwarf 450–600mm (1½–2ft) high, sometimes 1.8m (6ft) or more, spreading by underground stems. Leaves small, silky hair beneath. Silver-grey catkins in April–May. *S. r. argentea* is taller with leaves silky, hairy on both sides.

S. viminalis (Europe, including Britain, N. Asia), common osier. Vigorous shrub or small tree up to 6m (20ft) tall and wide. Leaves long and narrow, entire, dark green above, white hairy beneath.

Site Open positions in full sun, preferably near water; *S. lanata* good on large rock gardens.
Soil Moist preferred; most thrive in deep soil. *S. purpurea* is suitable for drier positions.
Propagation Take cuttings of leafless shoots, 300mm (1ft) long; root in open ground in November–March; dwarf species preferably by cuttings, 25–50mm (1–2in) long, in cold frame in June–July.

Cultivation Plant open-ground trees in November–March; container-grown plants throughout the year. Water frequently if planted in late spring or summer.
Pruning Those grown for coloured young shoots should be kept low and bushy by cutting back, just before bud-break in spring, to within one or two buds of old wood.
Pests and Diseases Canker can be caused by willow anthracnose.

Below Salix caprea 'Kilmarnock'

Salpiglossis

SOLANACEAE

Annuals, biennials, and perennials from South America. The species listed is grown for its splendidly showy flowers, which are also good for cutting.

S. sinuata (Chile), velvet trumpet flower. Half-hardy annual. Height 450–600mm (1½–2ft); spread 300mm (1ft). Branching plant with pale green, narrow leaves and tall graceful stems of pale green, narrow leaves and tall graceful stems of trumpet-shaped, velvety flowers all summer. Flowers may be red, pink, orange, gold, yellow or blue, heavily veined in a deeper shade, often with mottled gold throats. Varieties include 'Bolero' (extra large blooms); 'Splash' (compact, early flowering, with good colour range).

Site Open, sunny preferred.
Soil Any, reasonably fertile.
Propagation Sow in late April–early May where plants are to flower; thin seedlings to 250mm (10in) apart. They can also be sown in March in greenhouse or propagator; prick seedlings out into boxes; harden off; plant out in May.
Cultivation Support stems in exposed positions with twiggy sticks or split canes. Remove dead flower-heads.

Bright scarlet flowers in summer and well into autumn. (See note on cultivation, below.)

S. sclarea (Mediterranean), clary. Biennial, often grown as an annual; used as a culinary herb. Height 750mm (2½ft); spread 300–450mm (1–1½ft). Large, grey-green, ovate, aromatic leaves. Flowers are bluish, with conspicuous purple, pink or white bracts in August.

S. splendens (Brazil), bedding salvia. Half-hardy perennial grown as an annual. Height 150–350mm (6–14in); spread 250–300mm (10–12in). Bedding plant with ovate, toothed leaves. Dense spikes of scarlet flowers in June–September. Varieties include 'Blaze of Fire' (early and free-flowering); 'Dress Parade' (mixture containing pink, purple, scarlet and white flowers); 'Tom Thumb' (dwarf variety growing to 200mm (8in) high); 'Tetra Scarlet' (early flowering, with large spikes).

Site Warm, open and sunny.
Soil Moderately rich, free-draining.
Propagation Sow seeds of *S. argentea*, *S. farinacea*, *S. horminum*, *S. sclarea*, and *S. splendens* in greenhouse or propagator; prick out seedlings into boxes; harden them off before planting out in May. Take semi-ripe cuttings of *S. rutilans* and *S. officinalis* in September, using healthy side-shoots 50–75mm (2–3in) long; root in sandy compost in greenhouse or cold frame (keeping *S. rutilans* frost-free);

plant out in spring.
Cultivation *S. rutilans* may be grown as perennial in sheltered gardens in south-west Britain, but is variably hardy and best moved to a frost-free greenhouse over winter. Water all salvias in dry spells. Remove dead flower-heads.
Pruning Cut hard back over-wintered plants of *S. rutilans* and *S. officinalis* in early spring. Remove flower spikes and old leaves from *S. argentea* to encourage more woolly leaves.

Above *Salpiglossis sinuata*

Salvia

LABIATAE

A large genus of annuals, biennials, perennials, and shrubs of world-wide distribution, grown in mixed borders and as bedding plants for their leaves, bracts or flowers.

S. argentea (E. Mediterranean). Short-lived perennial, also treated as biennial. Height 1m (3¼ft); spread 600mm (2ft). Large, rounded, rumpled leaves covered in silky white wool make a handsome rosette. The wool fades when flower-spike pushes up in second year if plant grows as perennial.

S. farinacea (Texas). Slightly tender perennial. Height 450mm (1½ft); spread 300mm (1ft). Compact, branching plant with mid-green lanceolate leaves. Tall spikes of violet-blue flowers. 'Victoria' a vigorous variety with intensely blue, long-lasting flowers.

S. horminum (Europe). Half-hardy annual. Height 450mm (1½ft); spread 300mm (1ft). Grown for its brightly coloured, long-lasting bracts at tips of tall, branching stems. Varieties include 'Blue Beard' (bright purple bracts); 'Pink Lady' (purplish pink); 'Oxford Blue'; 'Bouquet Mixed' (blue, purple, pink, and white). Often incorrectly called clary (see *S. sclarea*, below).

S. officinalis (Europe), sage. Shrubby perennial; used as a culinary herb. Height and spread 450–600mm (1½–2ft). Lanceolate, grey, woolly, aromatic leaves. Spikes of purple flowers in June–July. Varieties include 'Icterina' (marbled mid-green and pale yellow leaves); 'Purpurascens' (deep bluish purple leaves); 'Tricolor' (leaves edged and mottled creamy gold; young leaves tinged pink and purple).

S. rutilans (syn. *S. elegans*; Mexico), pineapple sage. Tender perennial. Height and spread 450–600mm (1½–2ft). Mid-green leaves with strong pineapple scent when touched.

Below *Salvia splendens*

Sambucus

CAPRIFOLIACEAE   Elder

Hardy, mostly deciduous shrubs and small trees of cosmopolitan distribution mainly in the northern hemisphere. The species listed are grown chiefly for their clusters of flowers, fruits, and foliage.

S. nigra (Europe, including Britain, N. Africa, S.W. Asia), common elder. Shrub. Height up to 8m (26ft); spread 5m (16½ft). Leaves usually with five leaflets. Fragrant flowers creamy white, with flattened heads in early summer, becoming pendulous with black fruits in autumn. Varieties include 'Aurea' (lower-growing, with yellow foliage); 'Laciniata' (finely cut, lacy leaves); 'Purpurea' (young foliage flushed with red-purple).

S. racemosa (Europe, W. Asia), red-berried elder. Shrub. Height and spread 3.5m (12ft) or more. Leaves with five to seven leaflets. Flowers in ovoid panicles in April; bright red fruits in mid-summer. Variety 'Plumosa Aurea', with golden foliage and finely cut leaflets, makes a fine decorative shrub but is slower-growing.

Site Elders are very hardy and tolerate considerable exposure, but golden-leaved forms are better in more sheltered position, and may 'scorch' in full sun.
Soil Ordinary.
Propagation By 300mm (12in) long hard-wood cuttings in open ground in late autumn–early winter.
Cultivation Plant container-grown specimens at any time of year. Water frequently after late spring or summer planting.
Pruning Those grown for foliage can have two-year stems cut to ground and one-year stems reduced by half in winter. Old leggy specimens can be cut to ground in winter to induce more-compact habit.

Below *Sambucus racemosa* 'Plumosa Aurea'

Above *Sanguinaria canadensis* 'Multiplex'

Sanguinaria

PAPAVERACEAE   Bloodroot

A hardy woodland perennial from eastern North America, most commonly grown on rock gardens.

S. canadensis. Height 150–300mm (6–12in); spread to 450mm (1½ft). Leaves long-stalked, rounded, cut into overlapping lobes, glaucous, about 150mm (6in) wide. Flowers solitary, glistening white, 40mm (1½in) wide, with unfurling leaves in April–May. Variety 'Multiplex' (syn. 'Plena', 'Flore-Pleno') has fully double flowers.

Site Part shade; sheltered from strong winds.
Soil Moisture-retentive and humus-rich, neutral to acid.
Propagation Divide rhizomes immediately after flowering or when dormant. Sow seeds when ripe (the dry seeds may take as long as 18 months to germinate).
Cultivation Plant after flowering or in early autumn. Mulch with organic matter every other spring.

Santolina

COMPOSITAE   Lavender cotton

Hardy evergreen shrubs, native to Europe, suitable for shrub borders and rock gardens and also grown as dwarf hedges. Most have small button-shaped flowers and aromatic silvery foliage.

S. chamaecyparissus (syn. *S. incana*; S. France). Perennial. Height 450–600mm (1½–2ft); spread 450–600mm (1½–2ft). Silvery, finely divided leaves forming a low mound. Bright yellow flowers in June–August. *S. c. insularis* (syn. *S. neapolitana*; Mediterranean) is taller, more open, with larger, more feathery leaves; 'Nana' is a dwarf variety reaching 300mm (1ft); 'Sulphurea' has pale yellow flowers. *S. rosmarinifolia* (syn. *S. virens*; Spain, Portugal, S. France). Perennial. Height 600mm (2ft); spread 1–1.2m (3¼–4ft). Leaves emerald green and thread-like. Golden yellow flowers in June–August.

Site Full sun.
Soil Well-drained.
Propagation Take half-ripe cuttings, 50–75mm (2–3in) long, in July–September and put in cold frame or open ground; plant out the following spring. Can also be potted and planted out the following autumn.
Cultivation Plant container-grown plants at any time when weather is favourable. For growing as a hedge, plant 300–450mm (1–1½ft) apart; pinch out growing tips until plants are large enough for clipping.
Pruning Prune hard in spring to prevent plants becoming leggy. Clip hedges in summer before flowers expand and pull bushes open.

Saponaria

CARYOPHYLLACEAE   Soapwort

Annuals, biennials, and perennials native to Europe and Asia. They include mat-forming alpines or taller border plants, with bright pink, campion-like flowers.

S. ocymoides (European Alps). Hardy evergreen perennial for rock garden or dry wall. Height 75–100mm (3–4in); spread 300mm (1ft) or more. Vigorous, forming trailing mats of small green leaves. Profusion of bright pink, flat, rounded flowers, 13mm (½in) across, in May–August.

S. officinalis (Europe, S. Asia), soapwort, bouncing bet. Hardy perennial. Height 600–900mm (2–3ft); spread 600mm (2ft). Vigorous, erect plant with large, coarse, oblong leaves. Branching heads of flat, rounded, rich pink flowers, 20mm (¾in) across, in August–September. The double-flowered forms are better garden plants, but both types can be very invasive.

S. vaccaria (syn. *Vaccaria pyramidata*; Hungary), cow herb. Hardy annual. Height 600mm (2ft); spread 450mm (1½ft). Bushy, erect plant with pointed green leaves. Graceful sprays of pink or white star-shaped flowers, 13mm (½in) across, in July–September. Easy to grow, and the flowers are good for cutting.

Site Open and sunny.
Soil Well-drained, fertile.
Propagation Sow seed of annuals outdoors where they are to flower in April or September. Divide roots of perennials in October–March.
Cultivation Stake perennials when plants are 100–150mm (4–6in) high. Cut back after flowering to encourage further blooms.

Above *Santolina rosmarinifolia*   **Below** *Saponaria officinalis*

Sarcococca

BUXACEAE   Christmas box

Small evergreen shrubs native to Himalaya and China. All are slow-growing, have glossy foliage, and tiny, insignificant flowers, and in the garden are useful as shade-loving plants.
S. confusa (China). Height 1.8m (6ft); spread 1.2–1.5m (4–5ft). Elliptical leaves, dark green on upper surface and pale green beneath. Very fragrant, tiny white flowers with pink anthers in January–March, followed by shiny black berries.
S. hookerana (Himalayas). Height 1.8m (6ft); spread 900mm–1.2m (3–4ft). More erect than *S. confusa*, and not so hardy; usually represented in gardens by variety *S. h. digyna*. Narrow, pointed, mid-green leaves 50–90mm (2–3½in) long. Fragrant, tiny white flowers in November–February, followed by shiny black berries 6mm (¼in) across.

Site Wooded garden, or border in sun or shade.
Soil Fertile; chalk tolerated.
Propagation Sow seeds in nursery bed outdoors in March–April. Take semi-ripe cuttings in autumn and root in cold frame.

Cultivation Plants seem to thrive on neglect. Water well in dry weather.
Pruning Restrict to size; otherwise cut out old, damaged, or untidy stems.

Below *Sarcococca confusa*

Right *Saxifraga × apiculata*

Saxifraga

SAXIFRAGACEAE

A large genus of plants, native to Europe, Asia, and North and South America, varying greatly in foliage, flower, and size, and suitable for all corners of the rock garden and for troughs and other large containers.
S. aizoon (syn. *S. paniculata*; Europe). One of the silver saxifrages; a very variable species, but basically with grey, crinkly, white-edged leaves that form a spreading mat of

rosettes. Panicles, 300–400mm (12–16in) tall, bear masses of pure white flowers in June. Varieties include 'Rosea' (soft pink flowers); 'Lutea' (creamy yellow). Ideal for troughs and sinks.

S. × apiculata. Popular early flowering encrusted hybrid. Narrow leaves form tight, spreading cushions; stems 75mm (3in) tall bear abundant yellow flowers in March–April. There is a white form, 'Alba'.

S. 'Bob Hawkins'. Attractive mossy saxifrage, with variegated foliage and white flowers on 150mm (6in) stems.

S. burserana (E. European Alps). Kabschia species with many named forms; one of the best early flowering saxifrages, producing silvery rosettes of leaves and then pure white flowers on 50mm (2in) stems in February–March. Cultivars include 'Brookside' and 'Gloria' (large white flowers); 'Sulphurea' (pale lemon-yellow).

S. cochlearis (French Alps). Attractive silver saxifrage forming neat domes of silver-encrusted leaves. Elegant sprays of white flowers, on 150–225mm (6–9in) stems, appear in June. Cultivar 'Minor' is about half as tall; both especially suitable for sinks and troughs.

S. cotyledon (European Alps, Scandinavia). A silver saxifrage forming large rosettes of strap-like leaves, lime-encrusted on the edges. Flower stalks, 600mm (24in) tall, carry a mass of pure-white flowers in June–August. Several geographic variations and a few named forms; outstanding is 'Southside Seedling' with red-spotted white blooms.

S. 'Cranbourne'. One of the best Kabschia hybrids. Only 25mm (1in) tall, with almost stemless pink flowers in March.

S. fortunei (China, Japan, Korea). Large saxifrage, about 300mm (12in) tall, valuable for its late flowering. Needs a cool, shady situation. Bright green deciduous leaves, with red undersides, turn reddish bronze. Panicles of star-like white flowers appear in October–November.

S. grisebachii (Balkans). A Kabschia species better known in form of its cultivar 'Wisley', with silvery grey rosettes and flowering stems covered with bract-like crimson leaves. Plump red calyces conceal the pink flowers in late spring.

S. × jenkinsae. A Kabschia hybrid that forms tight mounds of grey rosettes from which arise short-stemmed rose-pink flowers, no taller than 25mm (1in), in March–April.

S. longifolia (Pyrenees). Rosettes of this silver species look well if planted in crevices, allowing the 300–450mm (12–18in) long panicles of white flowers (June) to tumble down over a rock. Hybrid 'Tumbling Waters' (also white) is outstanding, forming panicles up to 600mm (2ft) long.

S. moschata (Europe). A mossy species, flowering in April–May, usually represented in gardens by one of its cultivars or hybrids: 'Dubarry' (deep-red flowers, 100–150mm (4–6in) tall); 'Peter Pan' (clear pink flowers on crimson stems, 75mm (3in) tall); 'Pixie' (deep-red flowers, 50mm (2in) tall); 'Cloth of Gold' (bright-yellow foliage, white flowers, 75mm (3in) tall).

S. oppositifolia (N. hemisphere). Creeping saxifrage, variable in colour with some good forms. Prostrate mats of wiry shoots with slightly silvered leaves. Purple-red flowers at tips of shoots in March–April. 'Alba' (white) and 'Splendens' (crimson-purple) are good selected garden forms.

S. stolonifera (syn. *S. sarmentosa*; N. hemisphere), mother-of-thousands. Popular indoor plant that is more or less hardy outdoors in sheltered, shady sites in much of Britain. Spreads by stolons (runners). Rosettes of lightly marbled, rounded leaves. Stems 225–300mm (9–12in) tall, with red- and yellow-spotted white flowers in July–August.

S. umbrosa 'Elliott's Variety'. Compact cultivar with deep rose-pink flowers on 75–100mm (3–4in) stems. *S. u.* 'Variegata' has yellow-splashed leaves.

S. × urbium, London pride. Hybrid often listed as *S. umbro-*

sa, one of its parents. Well-known plant, possibly too vigorous for most rock gardens, but invaluable for a shady spot or awkward corner. Pale pink flowers on 300mm (12in) tall stems in late spring.

S. × 'Valerie Finnis'. *S. burserana* (q.v.) hybrid with best yellow flowers. Grey-green spiky leaves form a hummock about 100mm (4in) wide covered with large flowers on 50mm (2in) stems in March.

S. × 'Winifred'. Kabschia hybrid with deep crimson flowers in March.

Site Kabschia species flourish in scree or in a crevice, and do well in sinks and troughs; they need protection against strong sun in summer. Silver types are good crevice fillers and accept any situation except deep shade. Particular needs of other species are noted above.

Soil Most are lime-tolerant: well-drained alkaline soil is ideal, although some also like neutral soil.

Propagation Kabschia and silver saxifrages increased by detaching non-flowering rosettes in May–June and treating them as cuttings: insert in peat and sand frame; soak at first, but water sparingly through the winter; pot up in following autumn ready for spring planting. *S. oppositifolia* increased by taking soft tip cuttings in April–June, potting them up in the autumn. Other species can be increased by division.

Cultivation Most saxifrages planted out in spring or autumn (but *S. fortunei* should not be planted until April). Shade Kabschias from mid-day sun in summer.

Pests and Diseases Rust sometimes attacks saxifrages; affected plants should be destroyed.

Above Scabiosa atropurpurea

Below Saxifraga moschata 'Dubarry'

Scabiosa

DIPSACACEAE   Scabious

Annuals and perennials, native to Europe and Asia, bearing colourful, closely packed, domed heads of flowers that look attractive in borders and are also excellent for cutting.

S. atropurpurea (Spain, Portugal), sweet scabious. Hardy annual. Height 450–900mm (1½–3ft); spread 300mm (1ft). Bushy plant with rosette of lobed leaves and wiry branching stems. Compact domed heads of fragrant flowers, 50mm (2in) across, in all colours except yellow, in July–September. Makes long-lasting cut flowers, and oval seed-heads dry well for winter decoration.

S. caucasica (Caucasus). Hardy perennial. Height and spread 450–600mm (1½–2ft). Free-flowering plant with basal rosette of leaves and erect branched stems. Many round heads of lavender, blue or white flowers, up to 75mm (3in) across, in June–September. Good cultivars include 'Bressingham White'; 'Clive Greaves' (lavender); 'Moerheim Blue' (rich violet-blue).

Site Full sun, open.

Soil Well-drained, preferably alkaline.

Propagation Sow seed of annuals outdoors where they are to flower in April or September. Divide perennials every two or three years in early spring (*not* autumn); older plants soon lose vigour and flower less abundantly.

Cultivation Dead-head as blooms fade to encourage others to develop. Plant perennials in spring, especially on heavy soils. Stake taller forms.

Pests and Diseases Slugs and snails may attack plants. Root rots occur on heavy soils.

Schizanthus

SOLANACEAE   Butterfly flower, poor-man's orchid

Half-hardy annuals and perennials from Chile, with colourful flowers. Useful for summer bedding, for containers, and for cutting.

S. × *wisetonensis* (hybrid). Height 450–600mm (1½–2ft);

Above *Schizanthus* × *wisetonensis* (mixed varieties)

spread 200mm (8in). Erect plants with finely cut, feathery, light green foliage. Abundant orchid-like flowers in June–October in pink, salmon, red, yellow, or white; may also be veined or bicoloured. Varieties include 'Butterfly' (large blooms in shades of pink and white); 'Hit Parade', 'Star Parade' (more compact forms).

Site Warm, sunny and sheltered.
Soil Free-draining, preferably enriched.
Propagation Sow in greenhouse or propagator at 16–18°C (60–65°F) in February–April; prick out into boxes or individual pots; harden off before planting out in May. Or sow in flowering position in April; thin seedlings to 100–150mm (4–6in) apart.
Cultivation Pinch out tips of young plants to encourage branching. Grow in position of maximum light to keep plants sturdy and compact. Stake with split canes if necessary. Discard after flowering.
Pests and Diseases Aphids may attack growing tips.

Schizophragma

HYDRANGEACEAE

Hardy, deciduous, ornamental climbers, native to Japan and China, that use aerial roots to anchor themselves to walls, pergolas, tree-trunks, or trelliswork. All have masses of small creamy flowers surrounded by bracts.

S. hydrangeoides (Japan). Height and spread 6–9m (20–30ft). Deep green, broad, slightly hairy, coarsely-toothed leaves. Creamy white flower-heads, 250–300mm (10–12in) across, surrounded by pale yellow bracts, in July–August. A superb climber, but it is not commonly grown in Britain.

S. integrifolium (China). Height and spread 4.5–6m (15–20ft). Slender, pointed leaves with smooth or slightly serrated edges, bright green on upper surface, grey-green on underside. white flowerheads up to 300mm (12in) across, surrounded by 90mm (3½in) long white bracts, produced in July. Less vigorous but larger in all its parts than *S. hydrangeoides*.

Site Best on a sunny wall, but shade afforded by north-facing wall tolerated. Effective when climbing into large tree or over old stump.
Soil Water-retentive; rich loams preferred.
Propagation Layer mature growths in autumn; rooting takes a year. Seeds can be sown under glass in spring. Semi-ripe cuttings can be taken in July and August and rooted in a heated propagator.
Cultivation Plant out in October–April, avoiding coldest months. Mulch with well-rotted compost in spring. Train young growths until they support themselves.
Pruning Dead-head, and cut out unwanted growth in autumn.

Right *Schizophragma integrifolium*

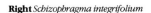

Schizostylis

IRIDACEAE   Kaffir lily

Perennials from South Africa with iris-like leaves and spikes of crocus-shaped flowers. The species listed is popular in herbaceous and mixed borders.

S. coccinea. Height to 600mm (2ft); spread 300mm (1ft) or more. Leaves narrowly sword-shaped, up to 400mm (16in) long, evergreen except in hard winters. Spikes of six-petalled, crimson flowers, 40–50mm (1½–2in) wide, appear in succession in early autumn to early winter. Varieties include 'Gigantea' (syn. 'Grandiflora', with larger flowers); 'Mrs Hegarty' (clear pink); 'Sunrise' (larger salmon-pink blooms).

Site Sheltered, preferably in full sun (but tolerates some shade).
Soil Rich, moisture-retentive.
Propagation Divide established plants in spring

every three years.
Cultivation Plant in spring. Mulch with organic matter every other spring.

Below *Schizostylis coccinea*

S. nutans (English bluebell): see *Endymion nonscriptus*.
S. sibirica (Turkey, Iran, Caucasus), Siberian squill. Height to 150mm (6in), but starts to bloom when shorter; spread 75–100mm (3–4in). Leaves broadly channelled, glossy. Flowers bell-shaped, nodding, bright deep blue in March. Varieties include 'Alba' (white); 'Spring Beauty' (deep electric blue, a little earlier).
S. tubergeniana (syn. *S. mischtschenkoana*; S. Caucasus, N. Iran). Much like *S. sibirica* but with paler blue flowers, each petal having a deeper blue mid-vein. Flowers start to open in late winter as soon as shoot breaks through soil.

Right *Scilla tubergeniana*

Scilla

LILIACEAE   Squill

Bulbous perennials from Europe, Asia and Africa. Those listed, with strap-shaped leaves and racemes of bell- or star-shaped flowers, look attractive in rock gardens or, naturalised, in lawns.

S. bifolia (Balkans, Asia Minor). Height to 100mm (4in) or more; spread 65–75mm (2½–3in). Leaves usually only two per bulb, narrow, and channelled. Flowers starry, rich mauve-blue, 13mm (½in) wide, in spring. Variety 'Rosea' has pink flowers.
S. campanulata (Spanish bluebell): see *Endymion hispanicus*.

popular evergreen, with rosettes of purple-green fleshy leaves that form a vigorous, spreading mat. Yellow flower-heads 50mm (2in) wide appear in May–June. 'Cape Blanco' is an outstanding form with white-powdered leaves; 'Purpureum' has larger purple foliage.

S. spurium (Caucasus). Mat-forming evergreen useful for ground cover. Starry pink flowers appear on 100mm (4in) tall stems in July–August. Variety 'Schorbusser Blut' has deep-red flowers in July–August.

Site Well-drained, sunny.
Soil Sedums thrive in any soil, the poorer the better.
Propagation Division is simple in all cases. Rosettes of *S. spathulifolium* can be detached

and inserted in the propagating frame, where they root readily.
Cultivation Plant out in October–April. Few problems except for curbing the most invasive species.
Pests and Diseases Aphids and slugs may attack plants.

Left *Sedum spurium*

Sempervivum

CRASSULACEAE   Houseleek

A genus of evergreen succulents from mountainous regions of Europe, western Asia, and North Africa. The plants form rosettes of varying size and colour that knit together to make attractive mats; the mostly star-like flowers are relatively unimportant. All do well on the rock garden.

S. arachnoideum (Alps), cobweb houseleek. Forms rosettes woven together with a white cobweb-like mat of hairs (whence its common name). Spreads to form a small hummock mostly no more than 25mm (1in) high. Bright rose-red flowers, 150mm (6in) tall, in June–July.

S. ciliosum (Bulgaria). Globose, grey-green rosettes with yellow flowers on 150mm (6in) stems appear in summer. The form 'Borisii' has more hairy rosettes, making them appear almost white.

S. giuseppii (Spain). Bright-green leaves with dark tips form the rosettes, the central leaves covered in hairs. Rose-red flowers on stems 75–100mm (3–4in) high in summer.

S. montanum (Europe). Variable plant with soft, matt, green rosettes, 25–50mm (1–2in) across. Pale red-purple flowers in June–August on 150mm (6in) tall stems.

S. tectorum (Europe), common houseleek. Most variable species; produces relatively large rosettes. All rosettes are 50–75mm (2–3in) high with 100–175mm (4–7in) spread; the rose-purple flowers are carried on 150–300mm (6–12in) stems in July. Many named forms include 'Commander Hay' (red leaves with green tips); 'Calcareum' (grey-green foliage and red tips).

Site Plants thrive in full sun.
Soil Poor soils promote better colours and firmer rosettes. Good drainage essential.
Propagation Remove non-flowering rosettes and insert them in sand frame in June. They root quickly and can be potted up during the summer for planting out the following spring.
Cultivation Sempervivums are best planted in spring. When established clumps begin to deteriorate, remove, propagate, and start again.
Pests and Diseases Rust sometimes attacks leaves.

Right *Sempervivum arachnoideum*

Site Sunny preferred, but part shade tolerated.
Soil Well-drained but moisture-retentive; moderately fertile.
Propagation Divide clumps or separate offsets when plants are dormant. Replant at once.

Flowering recurs in two years.
Cultivation Plant in autumn, the earlier the better.
Pests and Diseases Slugs occasionally eat bulbs or shoots in mild winters. Rust and smut may infect plants.

Sedum

CRASSULACEAE

A genus of mostly perennial evergreen and deciduous sun-loving plants of the northern hemisphere, suitable for the rock garden; larger species are available for the herbaceous border.

S. acre (Europe), biting stonecrop or wall-pepper. The type species, an invasive evergreen, is better ignored. Of its several forms, 'Aureum' is probably best for its yellow foliage; evergreen, 25–50mm (1–2in) tall, with flat yellow flower-heads appearing in June–July.

S. cauticolum (Japan). Height 100–150mm (4–6in); spread about 300mm (12in). First-rate deciduous plant with grey foliage and rose-purple flowers in August–September; its leaves turn reddish brown in mid-autumn.

S. hispanicum (S. E. Europe). A rather spready species, attractive for its light blue-green foliage, topped by 25mm (1in) tall pinky white flowers in summer.

S. kamtschaticum 'Variegatum' (E. Asia). Strikingly attractive form with variegated foliage. Orange-red flower heads appear late and turn deeper red in autumn.

S. spathulifolium (W. North America). Widely grown and

Senecio

COMPOSITAE

The largest genus of flowering plants, with about 3,000 species of annuals, biennials, perennials, succulents, shrubs, and trees from all over the world. Most of the popular garden forms have daisy-like flowers. Senecios are close allies of *Ligularia* (q.v.) and a number of formerly senecio species are now grouped in that genus of herbaceous perennials.

S. cineraria (syn. *S. bicolor*, *S. maritimus*, *Cineraria maritima*; Mediterranean region), sea ragwort. Half-hardy evergreen shrub. Height 600mm (2ft); spread 450–600mm (1½–2ft). Erect plant best grown as half-hardy annual. Oblong, deeply lobed leaves covered with white woolly hairs. Yellow flowers 25mm (1in) across in July–September. Varieties include 'Silver Dust' (most dwarf and compact form); 'White Diamond' (coarsely cut silver foliage).

S. compactus (New Zealand). Shrub, variably hardy. Height and spread 600mm–1.2m (2–4ft). Leaves oblong, wavy-edged, mid-green on upper surface, grey-white beneath. Bright yellow flowers in clusters 100–150mm (4–6in) wide in July. Requires protection in cold winters.

S. elegans (S. Africa). Half-hardy annual or biennial. Height 450mm (18in); spread 150–230mm (6–9in). Leaves dark green, 25–75mm (1–3in) long. Rose-purple flowers, 25mm (1in) across, carried in loose clusters in July–August.

S. 'Sunshine' (syn. *S. greyi* and *S. laxifolius* of gardens – not the true New Zealand species). Evergreen shrub. The best garden senecio. Height 900mm–1.2m (3–4ft); spread 1.2–1.8m (4–6ft). Leaves oval, mid-green, felted with grey-white hairs, up to 100mm (4in) long. Clusters of yellow flowers, 25mm (1in) across, in July–August. Not fully hardy in severe winters.

Site Annuals and biennials need bright sun; herbaceous perennials prefer part shade, although full sun is tolerated if roots are kept moist; shrubs prefer a sunny spot, and do well in coastal areas.
Soil Free-draining.
Propagation Sow annuals in pans or boxes in February–March. Seeds of *S. elegans* may be sown directly in flowering position in April. Lift, divide and replant perennials in spring. Take 75–100mm (3–4in) long semi-ripe cuttings of shrubs in late summer; root in cold frame; set out in nursery bed in following spring.
Cultivation Plant out annuals in May; *S. elegans* needs twiggy supports in exposed gardens. Plant shrubs and perennials in October–April. Stake perennials and other tall forms in exposed gardens.
Pruning Cut back perennials in November to ground level. Remove faded flower stems as soon as noticed, and dead or damaged wood on shrubs in spring.
Pests and Diseases Aphids may attack all species; thrips and chrysanthemum leaf miner may attack annuals and perennials; rust may occur on *S. elegans*.

Right Senecio 'Sunshine'

Sidalcea

MALVACEAE   Checkerbloom

Herbaceous perennials, native to western North America and Mexico, that make bold clumps of rounded leaves and elegant tapering spikes of flowers rather like small hollyhocks. The species listed is an easy-to-grow plant for sheltered, sunny borders.

S. malviflora (California). Height 750–900mm (2½–3ft) or more, depending on situation. Vigorous upright plant, making large clumps of rounded, slightly lobed and divided leaves. Flowers, up to 50mm (2in) across, on graceful erect spikes, round, shallowly funnelled, in pink or rose shades, in July–September. Cultivars include 'Croftway Red' (deep salmon); 'Rose Queen' (clear pink); 'William Smith' (large, salmon-red).

Site Preferably open and sunny.
Soil Fertile, reasonably moist; chalky soils tolerated.
Propagation Divide roots in early autumn or spring, retaining only healthy outer pieces and discarding remainder.
Cultivation Stake taller cultivars securely when plants are 100–150mm (4–6in) high. Remove central spike when flowers have faded to encourage side growths to develop.
Pests and Diseases Rust may appear on leaves.

Right *Sidalcea malviflora* 'Rose Queen'

Silene

CARYOPHYLLACEAE   Catchfly, campion

Annuals and perennials of the northern hemisphere, many of which are weeds. The cultivated species all have flowers with a tubular calyx and five notched petals, and most make good bedding, border or rock-garden plants.

S. acaulis (N. hemisphere), moss campion, cushion pink. Perennial. Height about 25mm (1in); spread to 300mm (1ft). Low-cushion-forming, with crowded shoots of tiny narrow leaves. Flowers, 13mm (½in) wide, deep pink, in summer. Often reluctant to flower.

S. armeria (Europe). Annual. Height 300–400mm (12–16in); spread 200–300mm (8–12in). Erect and well branched, with oval, stem-clasping, glaucous leaves. Flowers, pink or white, about 20mm (¾in) wide, in dense terminal clusters in May–September.

S. coeli-rosa (syn. *Lychnis coeli-rosa*, *Viscaria elegans*; S. Europe), rose of heaven. Hardy annual. Height to 450mm (1½ft); spread about 200mm (8in). Erect with slender but wiry stems bearing almost grassy leaves. Flowers about 25mm (1in) wide, rose-purple, in summer. Lavender, crimson, pink, and other shades, some with dark eyes, available in mixed strains.

S. schafta (Caucasus). Perennial. Height 150mm (6in); spread 200–300mm (8–12in). Tufted and spreading, with slender stems and small, ovate leaves. Pink flowers, 25mm (1in) wide, open in July–October. Good for rock gardens and dry walls.

Site Sunny; *S. schafta* tolerates some shade.
Soil Must be well-drained and moderately fertile, but *S. acaulis* thrives best in poor, gritty soil.
Propagation Divide perennials at planting time, or take cuttings in spring. Sow seeds of annuals in spring where they are to flower or, earlier, under glass.
Cultivation Plant perennials in autumn or spring.

Above *Silene coeli-rosa*

Silybum

COMPOSITAE

Biennial plants native to Europe, western Asia, and North Africa. The species listed makes an attractive border plant, especially in informal settings.

S. marianum (S. Europe, Asia, North Africa), Our Lady's milk thistle, holy thistle. Height up to 1m (3¼ft); spread 900mm (3ft). Handsome foliage plant with green, thistle-like leaves conspicuously veined and blotched with white. Fluffy rounded heads of rose-purple flowers produced in leathery, spine-tipped bracts in July–September.

Site Open and sunny preferred.
Soil Free-draining.
Propagation Sow seed where it is to flower in May–June; thin crowded seedlings.
Cultivation Easy plant to grow.
Remove flower-heads before seed blows about the garden.
Pests and Diseases Leaf miner sometimes attacks.

Below *Silybum marianum*

Sisyrinchium

IRIDACEAE

Herbaceous perennials from the Americas suitable for the border or rock garden. All have grassy or sword-shaped leaves and six-petalled, mainly starry flowers.

S. bermudianum (Bermuda), common blue-eyed grass. Height to 300mm (1ft); spread 150mm (6in). Tufted, with narrowly sword-shaped leaves. Flowers starry, violet-blue, 20–25mm (¾–1in) wide, in May–June. Several species from North America are very similar, notably *S. bellum* (but only 100mm (4in) or so tall) and *S. idahoense* (flowers with narrower, blue petals).

S. californicum (N.W. North America), golden-eyed grass. Height, spread, and overall appearance much the same as *S. bermudianum*, but flowers yellow. *S. brachypus* is a dwarf version, up to 150mm (6in) tall, with flowers in June–October.

S. striatum (Chile). Height 600mm (2ft); spread 300mm (1ft) or more. Robust, clump-forming, with greyish-green iris-like foliage. Flowers are pale yellow, 20mm (¾in) wide, in long spikes in summer–autumn.

Site Sunny preferred.
Soil Well-drained, moderately fertile.
Propagation Divide etablished clumps in September or March; sow seeds in spring.

Cultivation Plant in autumn or spring. Divide clumps every two years. Remove dead flower stems in autumn.

Below *Sisyrinchium striatum*

Skimmia

RUTACEAE

Hardy, evergreen bushy shrubs native to China and Japan. They are slow-growing and particularly useful in small gardens. Male and female flowers are borne on separate plants, so both sexes need to be grown in close proximity if the attractive berries are desired.

S. × 'Foremanii'. Height and spread 900mm–1.2m (3–4ft).

Evergreen female hybrid cultivar, with thick, oval, glossy, mid-green leaves, 75–100mm (3–4in) long. Creamy white, scented flowers appear in clusters, 50–75mm (2–3in) long, in March–April. Brilliant red berries appear in autumn and last through winter. Usually listed in nurserymen's catalogues as cultivar of *S. japonica* (q.v.).

S. japonica (Japan). Height 900mm–1.5m (3–5ft); spread 1.5–1.8m (5–6ft). Leaves mid-green and leathery. Creamy white, scented flowers appear in clusters, 50–75mm (2–3in) long, in spring. Bright red or orange berries produced in August–September. Varieties include 'Fragrans' (male, white, very free-flowering, strongly scented); 'Rubella' (male, with reddish-purple flower buds).

Site Sun or part shade.
Soil Well-drained.
Propagation Root 75mm (3in) long semi-ripe cuttings of lateral shoots in sandy soil in cold frame in summer. Sow seeds from ripe berries in cold frame in September. Prick out seedlings into pans or pots.
Cultivation Plant in October or April. Young leaves may be damaged by winter frost, so protect them against the worst weather.
Pruning Remove only dead or damaged wood.

Left *Skimmia japonica* fruits

Above *Smilacina racemosa*

Smilacina

LILIACEAE   False Solomon's seal

Hardy perennials native to Asia and North and Central America. The species listed needs a garden site resembling its woodland setting in the wild.

S. racemosa (North America), false spikenard. Height 600–900mm (2–3ft); spread 600mm (2ft). Arched stem clothed in lanceolate, glossy, light green leaves. Graceful panicles of tiny creamy white blossoms appear in May.

Site Must have shade or semi-shade.
Soil Damp loam preferred, but must not become waterlogged in winter.
Propagation Sow seed in cold frame in spring. Root-stocks can be divided in the spring and replanted immediately.
Cultivation Plant in spring and replanted immediately. Remove decaying foliage in autumn. Lift and divide only when growths become very crowded.

Above *Solanum jasminoides* 'Album'

Solanum

SOLANACEAE

Annuals, perennials, shrubs and climbers of cosmopolitan distribution. Included in this genus are familiar garden vegetables such as aubergines, tomatoes and potatoes, and weeds such as black nightshade. Most species have prominent flowers and berries.

S. crispum (Chile), Chilean potato tree. Scrambling, semi-evergreen shrub. Height and spread 4.5–6m (15–20ft). Glossy leaves, 75–100mm (3–4in) long, dark green on the upper surface, pale green beneath. Bluish purple star-shaped flowers, 25mm (1in) across, with prominent deep yellow anthers, appear in June–September. Variety 'Glasnevin' (syn. 'Autumnale') produces deeper-coloured flowers on into October.

S. jasminoides (Brazil), potato vine. Self-clinging evergreen climber. Height and spread 3–4.5m (10–15ft). Glossy leaves, 50mm (2in) long, mid-green. Pale blue, star-shaped flowers in July–November. 'Album' (white flowers) is a good form.

Site Best grown against south- or west-facing wall.
Soil Well-drained.
Propagation Take 75–100mm (3–4in) long cuttings of side-shoots in summer; root in propagator.
Cultivation Plant in April–May and secure to wall supports.

Pruning Cut out weak, damaged, or dead growths in spring. Restrict *S. crispum* where necessary by removing previous year's wood to 150mm (6in) from its base in spring.
Pests and Diseases Aphids may attack. Grey mould may occur in damp conditions.

Soldanella

PRIMULACEAE

A genus of small alpine plants with bell-shaped flowers from the European mountain regions, where they appear at the edges of melting snows; in cultivation they make good rock-garden plants.

S. alpina (Alps, Apennines, E. Pyrenees). Produces 200mm (8in) wide tufts of rounded kidney-shaped leaves about 75mm (3in) high. Fringed lavender-purple bells 15mm (⅝in) long borne on 75mm (3in) stems in spring.

S. montana. Similar to above, but generally larger and with flower-stalks about 150mm (6in) tall.

Site A small amount of shade in a cool place that does not dry out; a peat garden is ideal. Protect plants against excessive moisture in winter.
Soil Peat, leaf-mould, and sharp sand mixed into the soil are beneficial. Species listed will tolerate lime.
Propagation By division after

flowering; pot up or plant directly.
Cultivation Top-dress plants each spring with peat and leaf-mould mixture.
Pests and Diseases Slugs may eat young leaves, buds, and flowers.

Below *Soldanella alpina*

Right *Solidago* × *hybrida*

Solidago

COMPOSITAE   Golden rod

Herbaceous perennials, mostly native to North America. Easy border plants, they produce sprays of tiny yellow flowers from mid-summer and well into autumn, the best of them on bushy compact plants.

S. × *hybrida* (garden hybrid). Best forms for general garden use. Height 300–900mm (1–3ft); spread 300–450mm (1–1½ft). Bushy plants forming dense clumps of erect stems and narrow, pointed leaves. Graceful sprays or plumes, 150–300mm (6–12in) or more long, of tiny, bright yellow flowers in July–September. Numerous cultivars include 'Goldenmosa' (up to 750mm (2½ft) high, yellow foliage, August flowers); 'Golden Thumb' (syn. 'Queenie', 300mm

(12in) high bush, gold flowers in August–September); 'Lemore' (600mm (2ft) high, primose yellow flowers in September).

Site Full sun preferred; taller cultivars will grow well in light shade.
Soil Well-drained; acid or alkaline.
Propagation Divide clumps in autumn or spring, replanting only healthy outer pieces.
Cultivation Taller cultivars may need staking if grown on exposed sites.
Pests and Diseases Powdery mildew often appears on leaves in late summer.

Sophora

LEGUMINOSAE

Deciduous and evergreen trees and shrubs (and some herbaceous perennials) of cosmopolitan distribution. The species listed is hardy and deciduous but slow to flower.
S. japonica (China, Korea), Japanese pagoda tree. Handsome round-headed tree. Height 20m (66ft) or more; spread 15m (50ft). Leaves up to 250mm (10in) long, each with 9 to 15 leaflets. Flowers pea-shaped, creamy white, freely borne on older trees in large panicles in September, particularly after hot summers. 'Pendula' is a weeping form about 3m (10ft) tall and wide.

Site Open position in full sun preferred.
Soil Good, well-drained.
Propagation By seed. 'Pendula' by grafting on to *S. japonica* in March.

Cultivation Plant container-grown specimens in autumn to spring (or in summer if watered frequently).

Below *Sophora japonica* 'Pendula'

Above *Sorbus hupehensis*

Sorbus

ROSACEAE

Deciduous trees and shrubs, widely distributed in the northern hemisphere temperate zone, with simple, lobed or pinnate leaves and small, usually white flowers followed by often very showy fruits. There are two main groups of sorbus, as follows:

Mountain Ashes or Rowans
Leaves are pinnate, often colouring brilliantly in autumn. Fruits may be white, pink, yellow, orange, or red.
S. aucuparia (Europe, including Britain, Asia), mountain ash, rowan. Very hardy tree. Height up to 15m (50ft); spread 9m (30ft). Leaves with 11 to 15 leaflets, sometimes colouring well in autumn. Large, hanging clusters of orange-red fruits often taken early by birds. Varieties include 'Asplenifolia' (fern-like leaves with deeply toothed leaflets); 'Sheerwater Seedling' (narrow tree with erect branches); 'Xanthocarpa' (syn. 'Fructu Luteo', with orange-yellow fruits).
S. 'Embley' (*S. discolor* of gardens). Vigorous tree, upright-branched when young. Height up to 12m (40ft); spread 8m (26ft). Leaves up to 250mm (10in) long, with about 13 leaflets, scarlet in autumn. Bright red fruits in large clusters.
S. hupehensis (W. China). Compact tree. Height 12m (40ft); spread 8m (26ft). Leaves blue-green above; red in autumn. Fruits white, tinged pink, in August–September and persistent.
S. 'Joseph Rock'. Graceful, narrow tree. Height 12m (40ft); spread 5m (16½ft). Leaves with 15 to 21, rather small, glossy

green leaflets, turning orange, red and purple in autumn. Fruits small, yellow in August–September. One of the best for small gardens.
S. sargentiana (W. China). Open, sparsely branched tree. Height and spread up to 8m (26ft). Stout shoots and large, sticky buds. Leaves with 9 to 13 leaflets, each up to 125mm (5in) long, brilliant orange-red in autumn. Fruits orange-red in large clusters in September. One of the best for autumn colour.
S. vilmorinii (W. China). Dainty, spreading tree. Height and spread up to 6m (20ft). Fern-like leaves with 19 to 29 small leaflets, orange and red in autumn. Fruits red to white, flushed with pink in September.

Whitebeams
Leaves are toothed or lobed, often white-felted beneath. Fruits are usually red or brown.
S. aria (Europe, including S. England, Ireland), common whitebeam. Tree. Height 15m (50ft); spread 10m (33ft). Leaves elliptical, coarse-toothed, white-felted beneath. Scarlet fruits in September. Varieties include 'Decaisneana' (syn. 'Majestica', more upright, with large leaves and fruits); 'Lutescens' (young foliage silvery white).
S. intermedia (Scandinavia), Swedish whitebeam. Dense, round-headed tree. Height and spread 12m (40ft). Leaves ovate, with several lobes on each side. Fruits red in August–September. A common street tree.
S. 'Mitchellii'. Vigorous, round-headed tree. Height 15m (50ft) or more; spread 10m (33ft). Leaves large and rounded, up to 150mm (6in) long, white-felted beneath. Fruits brown, 13mm (½in) across, in August–September. (Now

regarded as broad-leaved form of *S. thibetica* and properly listed as cultivar 'John Mitchell' of that species.)

S. × *thuringiaca* (Europe). In gardens usually represented by variety 'Fastigiata', erect-branched, making a dense, broadly egg-shaped head. Height up to 10m (33ft); spread 5m (16½ft). Leaves up to 150mm (6in) long with two or four free leaflets at the base, orange and yellow in autumn. Fruits red, sparsely produced in August–September. Good for confined spaces.

Site Open, either sunny or partly shaded.
Soil Well-drained (rowans dislike, but whitebeams tolerate, shallow chalky soils).
Propagation By seed; but cultivars do not come true and species will frequently hybridise. Sow when ripe; over-winter in frame. Graft in early spring; bud in late summer.
Cultivation Plant open-ground trees in November–March; container-grown trees best planted in autumn–spring.
Pests and Diseases Birds frequently eat fruits. Plants are susceptible to fire blight.

Spartium

LEGUMINOSAE   Spanish broom

A genus of one hardy deciduous shrub, which grows into a gaunt bush when allowed to develop unrestricted.

S. junceum (Canary Is, S.W. Europe, Mediterranean). Height 2.5–3m (8¼–10ft); spread 1.8–2.5m (6–8¼ft). Bright green, smooth stems carrying very few narrow leaves, 13mm (½in) long, which fall soon after developing. Golden yellow, fragrant, pea-like flowers, 20mm (¾in) across, in June–August. Not fully hardy in severe winters.

Site Withstands gales well, so excellent for coastal gardens. Full sun preferred.
Soil Well-drained; dry conditions tolerated.
Propagation Sow seeds in pans or boxes in spring and keep in cold frame. Summer cuttings can be rooted in propagator.

Cultivation Plant in spring or autumn.
Pruning Prevent plants from becoming top-heavy by shortening previous year's growths to 25–50mm (1–2in) of old stems each spring. Dead-head to prevent seeding.

Below Spartium junceum

Spiraea

ROSACEAE

Hardy shrubs from the northern temperate zone, grown for their star-like flowers; some also have attractive foliage. They can be planted in shrub borders or used as decorative hedging.

S. × *arguta* (China), bridal wreath, foam of May. Deciduous. Height and spread 1.2–2m (4–6½ft). Graceful medium-sized shrub. Lanceolate leaves, small, toothed, and light green. Branches smothered in dense clusters of small, white flowers in April–May.

S. japonica (syn. *S. albiflora*, *S.* × *bumalda*; China, Japan, Korea). Deciduous. Height and spread 600mm–1m (2–3¼ft). Small shrub with rose-pink panicles of flowers throughout summer. Toothed, ovate leaves, pale green, sometimes cream and creamy pink when young. 'Anthony Waterer' is most commonly-grown cultivar, with brighter flowers and occasionally with strikingly variegated foliage; 'Goldflame' has coppery gold young leaves.

S. thunbergii (China). Deciduous. Height and spread 1.2–1.5m (4–5ft). A spreading shrub with arching stems and narrow, lanceolate leaves. White flowers carried in numerous clusters in March–April.

Site Open, sunny, sheltered from cold winds.
Soil Any; slightly chalky soils tolerated.
Propagation By soft or semi-ripe cuttings of healthy, non-flowering shoots in summer; insert soft-tip cuttings in peat and sand in a closed frame; semi-ripe cuttings need less-humid conditions. Hard-wood cuttings can be inserted outside in sheltered positions where they are to grow in October.

Left Spiraea japonica 'Anthony Waterer'

Cultivation Plant in November–March (container-grown specimens may be planted at any time if they are kept well-watered in dry weather). Young plants need support until established. Remove dead flower-heads.
Pruning Prune *S. japonica* to within a few inches of ground in early spring. Thin *S.* × *arguta* and *S. thunbergii* after flowering, removing old or weak branches.
Pests and Diseases Leaves sometimes eaten by sawfly.

Above *Stachys macrantha*

Stachys

LABIATAE

Annuals and perennials of wide distribution in the temperate zones. The garden species listed make useful ground-cover plants.

S. macrantha (syn. *Betonica grandiflora*; Caucasus). Perennial. Height 450–600mm (1½–2ft); spread 300–450mm (1–1½ft). Low-growing plant with broad, ovate, hairy and wrinkled leaves. Bold spikes of violet or magenta flowers freely carried in mid-summer. Variety 'Rosea' (syn. 'Superba') has attractive rose-pink blooms.

S. olympica (syn. *S. lanata*, *S. byzantina*; Caucasus), lamb's tongue, lamb's ear. Perennial. Height and spread 300–450mm (12–18in). Ovate leaves covered with silvery grey hairs give plant a soft, velvety texture. Spikes of purple flowers in July. 'Sheila MacQueen' has an improved form, with larger leaves and silver-tinged flowers. If plant is grown purely for foliage effect, non-flowering cultivar 'Silver Carpet' is better.

Site Sunny and open or part shade, at front of border. *S. olympica* looks bedraggled and is subject to mildew when wet: do not plant in drip-line of overhanging trees and shrubs. **Soil** Well-drained.

Propagation Divide plants in autumn or spring.
Cultivation Plant between October and April. Remove dead flower-heads. Divide plants every few years to keep them vigorous.

12m (40ft) or more; spread 8m (26ft). Attractive bark flakes in winter. Leaves yellow and red in autumn. Flowers cup-shaped, 50mm (2in) across, in July and August.

Site Sheltered, sunny, but with base of plants in shade.
Soil Well-drained, moisture-retaining, acid.

Left *Stewartia pseudocamellia* autumn foliage

Propagation By seed, layering, or 75mm (3in) cuttings in late summer in propagator or warm sand frame; over-winter young plants under glass.
Cultivation Plant from containers in spring.

Stipa

GRAMINEAE   Feather grass

Perennial grasses of elegant appearance from Europe and Asia. The species listed is useful as a specimen plant in lawns or borders; the plumes are decorative when cut and dried.
S. gigantea (Portugal, Spain, Morocco). Height to 2m (6½ft); spread about 1.2m (4ft). Clump-forming, with long, arching leaves, like a smaller pampas grass (*Cortaderia*, q.v.). Flowering panicles, up to 450mm (1½ft) long, of yellowish, glossy, oat-like spikelets with long awns, in June–July.

Site Best in full sun.
Soil Well-drained, preferably humus-rich.
Propagation Divide established clumps. Sow seeds under glass in spring.

Cultivation Plant in spring or early autumn. Flowers ready for cutting in July. Cut down plants in early winter.

Below *Stipa gigantea*

Sternbergia

AMARYLLIDACEAE

Hardy bulbous perennials from the eastern Mediterranean to the Caucasus and Iran. The species listed is the only widely available sternbegia.
S. lutea (E. Mediterranean). Height 100–150mm (4–6in); spread about 90mm (3½in). Leaves strap-shaped, glossy, rich green. Flowers 40–50mm (1½–2in) long, bright yellow, crocus-like, in September–October.

Site Full sun essential.
Soil Must be free-draining.

Left *Sternbergia lutea*

Propagation Separate offsets when dormant.
Cultivation Plant in late summer or early autumn.

Stewartia (syn. Stuartia)

THEACEAE

Evergreen and deciduous trees and shrubs, native to eastern Asia and eastern North America, whose garden appeal lies in their peeling bark and showy white summer flowers.
S. pseudocamellia (Japan, S. Korea). Deciduous tree. Height

S. rivularis (syn. *S. albus laevigatus*; North America), snowberry. Height 1.5–2m (5–6½ft); spread 2–2.4m (6½–8ft). Oval leaves, 40mm (1½in) long, pale green on upper surface, downy on underside. Small pink flowers appear in small clusters in July–September. Glistening white berries, up to 15mm (⅝in) in diameter, appear in October–February.

Site Sun or shade.
Soil Ordinary.
Propagation Take 200–250mm (8–10in) long hardwood cuttings in autumn. Remove unwanted suckers in autumn or winter.
Cultivation Plant in October–March. Mulch in spring with well-rotted manure or compost.
Pruning Thin out overgrown plants inb autumn–spring.
Pests and Diseases Leaf spot may occur.

Right *Symphoricarpos × doorenbosii* 'White Hedge' berries

Above *Stokesia laevis*

Stokesia

COMPOSITAE   Stokes' aster

Low, spreading, evergreen herbaceous perennial, native to North America, with distinctive blooms resembling large cornflowers with creamy centres. The flowers of the species listed are good for cutting.

S. laevis (syn. *S. cyanea*; S.E. United States). Height and spread 450mm (1½ft). Low, open plant with pale-green, lance-shaped leaves. Clusters of large, upward-facing flowers, 100mm (4in) across, powder blue, purple or creamy white, in July–September.

Site Full sun and shelter from cold winds preferred.
Soil Must be well drained (plant is short-lived on heavy, wet soils).
Propagation By root cuttings, 25–40mm (1–1½in) long, inserted in propagator in February. Careful division of plants in March is also possible. Sow seed under glass in February–March for planting out following spring.
Cultivation Stake with light, twiggy branches in May to prevent flowers being splashed in wet weather. In cold districts protect crowns in winter.

Symphoricarpos

CAPRIFOLIACEAE

Deciduous shrubs native to North America and China. All have small, bell-shaped flowers, but they are cultivated mainly for their autumn berries.

S. × doorenbosii. Height 1.5m (5ft); spread 1.2m (4ft). General appearance similar to *S. rivularis*, except fruits are smaller and white, tinged rose-pink. Varieties include 'Magic Berry' (rose-pink berries); 'Mother of Pearl' (white berries, flushed pink); 'White Hedge' (white berries in clusters).

Symphytum

BORAGINACEAE   Comfrey

Clump-forming, spreading perennials from the European Mediterranean to the Caucasus, with handsome large leaves and nodding, tubular flowers. Good for ground cover, especially at the edges of ponds or pools.

S. grandiflorum (Caucasus). Height to 300mm (1ft); spread to 900mm (3ft). Rhizomatous. Oval leaves 100mm (4in) long. Flowers, 13mm (½in) long, cream, in April–June. Hybrid *S.* × 'Hidcote' is taller, with blue flowers.

S. × *uplandicum* (*S. asperum* × *S. officinale*), Russian comfrey. Height to 1m (3¼ft); spread 600mm (2ft) or more. Oval leaves up to 250mm (10in) long. Flowers blue or purple in July–August. Cultivar 'Variegatum' (sometimes sold as *S. peregrinum* 'Variegatum') has leaves boldly cream-margined.

Site Part shade or full sun acceptable.
Soil Moisture-retentive, humus-rich preferred.
Propagation Divide established clumps in autumn or spring.
Cultivation Plant in autumn or spring. Cut down stems in autumn.

Above *Symphytum* × *uplandicum* 'Variegatum'

Syringa

OLEACEAE   Lilac

Hardy deciduous shrubs and trees, native to Europe and Asia, especially useful in the garden because their attractive, small, tubular flowers (often fragrant) open in late spring. The species listed are all deciduous.

S. × *hyacinthiflora* (hybrid between *S. oblata* and *S. vulgaris*). Large shrub similar to *S. vulgaris* (q.v.) but earlier-flowering. Variety 'Esther Staley' has flowers deep red in bud, opening pink in May.

S. × *josiflexa* (hybrid between *S. josikaea* and *S. reflexa*). Shrub up to 5m (16½ft) high and wide. Variety 'Bellicent' has fragrant, pale-pink flowers in large, graceful panicles in late May.

S. microphylla (N. and W. China). Compact shrub up to 2m (6½ft) high and wide, with rather small leaves. Variety 'Superba' has rose-pink and white, very fragrant flowers continuously in June–October.

S. × *prestoniae* (hybrid between *S. reflexa* and *S. villosa*; Canadian origin). Large hardy shrub up to 4m (13ft) tall and 3m (10ft) across. Variety 'Elinor' has large, upright panicles of lilac pink flowers in late May–June.

S. vulgaris (E. Europe), common lilac. Large shrub or small tree. Height 6m (20ft); spread 5m (16ft). Very fragrant flowers borne in conical panicles in May. Varieties include 'Charles Joly' (double, deep reddish purple); 'Firmament' (pink in bud, opening lilac-blue); 'Katherine Havemeyer' large double flower, lavender-purple fading to lilac-pink); 'Mme Lemoine' (large double, white); 'Primrose' (pale yellow in small panicles); 'Sensation' (flowers purplish red, edged white in large panicles); 'Souvenir de Louis Spaeth' (deep wine-red in long, slender panicles); 'Vestale' (white in dense panicles).

Site Best in full sun.
Soil Rich, well-drained; excellent on chalk.
Propagation Air-layer on old wood in spring or young wood in late summer; layering in early spring. Soft-wood cuttings, 75mm (3in) long with a heel, in June in warm sand frame; or semi-ripe cuttings in cold frame in August.
Cultivation Best planted in autumn. Remove flower buds in first year.

Pruning Dead-head after flowering, at least when young. Train larger shrubs to single stem by removing lower buds when established, then lower branches. Old, lanky specimens can be cut back hard in winter or early spring. Remove suckers from grafted plants and old trees.
Pests and Diseases Leaf miner and lilac blight occasionally a problem. Late frosts can damage the flowers.

Left *Syringa vulgaris* 'Souvenir de Louis Spaeth'

Tagetes

COMPOSITAE   Marigold

Annual and perennial plants, native to the southern United States, Central and South America. The species listed, the familiar garden marigolds, are annuals with bright yellow or orange daisy-like flowers; they are popular as border and bedding plants and also make good cut flowers.

T. erecta (Mexico), African marigold. Half-hardy. Height 600mm–1m (2–3¼ft); spread 300–600mm (1–2ft). Strong-growing, branching plant with deeply cut, dark green leaves. Large yellow flowers in July–October. Most of many garden varieties are double flowered. Examples include 'Jubilee' strain (very large orange, yellow and gold flowers, uniform growth); 'Inca Orange' and 'Inca Yellow' (dwarf forms, less than 300mm (1ft) high); 'Fantastic Mixture' (large flowerheads with curled petals, like chrysanthemums); 'Climax Mixed' (tall, with large blooms suitable for cutting).

T. patula (Mexico), French marigold. Half-hardy. Height and spread 150–450mm (6–18in). Bushy plant with deeply cut

leaves. Freely produced yellow-orange flowers in range of forms in June–October. Numerous varieties include 'Boy-O-Boy Mixture' (double, yellow, gold and brown); 'Honeycomb' (crested, golden-orange petals with bronze bases); 'Naughty Marietta' (single, yellow, blotched maroon); 'Scarlet Sophia' (double, russet-red laced with gold); 'Tiger Eyes' (central ruffled orange crest surrounded by bronze-maroon petals). Crossing French marigolds with *T. erecta* varieties has given rise to Afro-French hybrids – compact, vigorous, and early flowering. Good examples include 'Nell Gwynn' (very large, single, golden-yellow and bronze); 'Showboat' (double, deep yellow); 'Susie Wong' (single, clear, bright yellow).

T. tenuifolia (syn. *T. signata*; Mexico). Half-hardy. Height 450–600mm (1½–2ft); spread 300mm (1ft). Bushy, free-flowering plants with single blooms. Foliage light green and fern-like. Good varieties include 'Gem' strain (yellow, gold and orange, very compact); 'Paprika' (vivid crimson); 'Star Fire' (mixture of yellow, gold and bronze, including bicolours, on low-growing, branching plants).

Site Sunny and open.
Soil Any; well-cultivated poor soils tolerated.
Propagation Sow in March–April in greenhouse or propagator; prick seedlings out into boxes; harden off before planting out in May. Or sow where they are to flower in May.

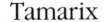

Left *Tagetes patula*

Cultivation Pinch out premature flowers buds from seedlings at planting time to encourage sturdy growth. Remove deadheads to prolong flowering and improve appearance. Discard after flowering.
Pests and Diseases Aphids can be troublesome on young shoots. Botrytis may infect flowers in wet weather.

Tamarix

TAMARICACEAE   Tamarisk

Hardy deciduous shrubs native to Europe, Asia, and Africa. Their feathery foliage looks delicate but can withstand heavy wind, making these plants ideal for coastal gardens.

T. pentandra (syn. *T. ramosissima*; E. Asia to E. Europe). Height and spread 3.5–4.5m (12–15ft). Pale to mid-green leaves are tiny, scale-like, and hug the stems. Small rose-pink flowers carried on 25–50mm (1–2in) spikes in late summer. The form 'Rubra' has red flowers.

T. tetrandra (Balkan peninsula). Height and spread 3–4.5m (10–15ft). General appearance similar to *T. pentandra*, but flowers appear in May on growth made the previous year.

Site Open, sunny.
Soil Well-drained; chalk tolerated.
Propagation Take 225–300mm (9–12in) hard-wood cuttings in autumn; root outdoors and leave for a year before transplanting to permanent position.
Cultivation Plant (from containers for best results) at any time, but preferably in autumn or spring.
Pruning In spring cut back most of previous year's growth on *T. pentandra*. With *T. tetrandra* cut back flowered shoots immediately blooms have faded.

Right *Tamarix pentandra*

Above *Tanacetum vulgare*

Tanacetum

COMPOSITAE

Hardy herbaceous perennials native to Europe, Africa, Asia, and North America.

T. haradjanii (syn. *T. densum amanum*, *Chrysanthemum haradjanii*; Turkey). Height 150–200mm (6–8in); spread 300mm (1ft). Forms dense carpet of finely divided, silver leaves. Clusters of tiny yellow flowers 3mm ($\frac{1}{8}$in) across in August. Good rock-garden plant.

T. vulgare (Europe, including Britain), tansy. Height 600–900mm (2–3ft); spread 600mm (2ft) or more. Erect plant with bright-green, finely cut leaves which smell of camphor. Clusters of bright-yellow, button-like flowers, 8mm ($\frac{1}{3}$in) across, in August–September. Common wayside plant; can become a nuisance and difficult to eradicate in gardens. 'Crispum' is an ornamental variety with curled leaves that can be used as a garnish.

Site Full sun; *T. haradjanii* grows best on rock gardens.
Soil Well-drained.
Propagation Divide plants in March. Take shoot-tip cuttings in April–September.

Cultivation Plant in spring or autumn. Cut off dead flower-heads.
Pests and Diseases Aphids may attack leaves. *T. haradjanii* may rot in wet winters.

Taxus

TAXACEAE   Yew

Evergreen conifers native to Europe, Africa, Asia, and North America. All the popular garden forms are very slow-growing, hardy, erect bushes or multi-stemmed trees.

T. baccata (Britain), common yew. Height 9m (30ft) or more; spread 4.5m (15ft) or more. Linear, needle-like, dark-green leaves 13–25mm ($\frac{1}{2}$–1in) long. Small, pale yellow male flowers cluster on undersides of previous year's stems; female flowers are green, solitary, usually unnoticed. Red cup-shaped berries with poisonous seeds follow the flowers. Best forms are 'Aurea' (golden-yellow leaves, more upright); 'Fastigiata' (Irish yew, green-black leaves, upright); 'Fastigiata Aureomarginata' (golden Irish yew); 'Standishii' (brilliant golden foliage, narrow-columnar, slow-growing). All except fastigiate (columnar) forms make good hedges.

Site Any, from full sun to deep shade. Do not plant near grazing land (all parts of the plants are poisonous). Tolerant of exposure to elements.
Soil Any, including chalk, clay, or acid peat.
Propagation Sow seeds in trays or boxes in autumn; allow to germinate in cold frame. Take sideshoot cuttings, 75–100mm (3–4in) long, of named varieties; root in cold frame in autumn.
Cultivation Plant in October–April; plant 600mm (2ft) apart for hedging. No staking required.
Pruning Remove stem or trunk suckers at any time. Clip hedges in spring. Old hedges can be cut back to old wood and will still sprout freely.
Pests and Diseases Scale insects and gall midges may attack.

Right *Taxus baccata*

Teucrium

LABIATAE   Germander

Perennials and shrubs mostly from the Mediterranean region. The garden species are suitable for rock gardens or as wall shrubs.

T. chamaedrys (Europe, S.W. Asia), wall germander. Evergreen. Height about 300mm (1ft); spread 600mm (2ft). Bushy shrublet with glossy, deep-green leaves. Rose-purple flowers, 10mm (⅜in) long, carried in spikes in mid- to late summer.

T. fruticans (Portugal, W. Mediterranean), tree germander. Height and spread 1.2m (4ft); or up to 2.4m (8ft) if trained on a wall. Bushy habit. Grey-green leaves, with under-sides and stems white-woolly. Flowers lavender-blue, 25mm (1in) long, in June–September.

Site Full sun preferred, but *T. chamaedrys* tolerates some shade. *T. fruticans* needs shelter.
Soil Must be well-drained; poor ground tolerated.
Propagation Take cuttings in late summer. Divide *T.*

chamaedrys in spring.
Cultivation Plant *T. chamaedrys* in autumn–spring, *T. fruticans* in spring only; latter needs protection in severe winters.

Right *Teucrium fruticans*

Above *Thalictrum speciosissimum*

Thalictrum

RANUNCULACEAE   Meadow rue

Perennials, native to Europe and Asia, mostly with handsome divided, fern-like leaves and branching heads of fluffy flowers. Garden species range from tiny alpines to plants for the back row of the herbaceous border.

T. aquilegifolium (Europe, N. Asia). Height 900mm (3ft); spread 300mm (1ft) or more. Bushy plant with much-divided, shining, grey-green leaves. Lilac or purple flowers in a dense head, 100–150mm (4–6in) across, without petals, fluffy, in May–July. 'Thundercloud' is a good cultivar.

T. delavayi (*T. dipterocarpum* of gardens; China). Height 1.2–1.5m (4–5ft); spread 450mm (1½ft). Erect, slender, elegant plant with wiry stems and small, round, blue-grey leaves. Delicate branching heads of dainty flowers, 13mm (½in) across, deep lilac with a tuft of cream stamens, in June–August. Cultivar 'Hewitt's Double' has deep mauve pompon flowers. Border plant of great beauty and distinction.

T. kiusianum (Japan). Height 100–150mm (4–6in); spread 75–100mm (3–4in). Miniature species with tufts of tiny fern-like leaves and small spikes of purple flowers in April–May. For the alpine house or for sinks and troughs.

T. speciosissimum (syn. *T. flavum glaucum*; Spain, North Africa). Height 1.2–1.5m (4–5ft); spread 600–900mm (2–3ft). Vigorous, erect plant with bold, divided, blue-grey leaves. Large pyramidal heads of yellow fluffy flowers in July–August. Leaves are good for cut-flower arrangements, but the flowers drop quickly.

Site All grow well in sun; *T. dipterocarpum* prefers cool, sheltered position in part shade.
Soil Fertile, reasonably moist.
Propagation Sow seed of species under glass in early spring. Divide roots of cultivars

in February–March, replanting only healthy outer portions of clumps.
Cultivation Tall species need firm support, staking when the plants are 150mm (6in) high in May. Water in dry weather to maintain growth.

Thuja

CUPRESSACEAE   Arbor-vitae

Evergreen conifers native to North America, China, and Japan. Most are slow growing and make fine specimen trees, according to size, for small or large gardens.

T. occidentalis (Canada), American arbor-vitae, northern white cedar. Height 15m (50ft); spread 4.5m (15ft). Mid-green, scale-leaves form flattened sprays, tansy-scented when bruised, and turning yellowish brown in winter. Cones yellowish and erect when young, turning brown and pendulous as they mature. Best forms include 'Alba' (white shoot tips); 'Aurea' (yellow leaves); 'Rheingold' (golden-

yellow, small tree about 3m (10ft) high and 1.8m (6ft) wide). *T. orientalis* (China), Chinese arbor-vitae. Height 4.5m (15ft); spread 3m (10ft). Mid-green foliage held almost vertically in flattened sprays. Cones pale brown. Many dwarf or near dwarf varieties, including 'Aurea Nana' (yellow green); 'Meldensis' (dark green); 'Rosedalis' (syn. 'Rosedalis Compacta', (yellow in spring, green in summer, purple in winter). Each of these varieties is about 600mm (2ft) high and 450mm (1½ft) wide.

T. plicata (North America), western red cedar. Height 21m (70ft); spread 7.5m (25ft) or more. Highly fragrant, glossy, green, scale-like leaves. Reddish brown trunk with spongy bark. Yellow-brown cones about 25mm (1in) long carried on mature trees. Best forms include 'Cuprea' (dwarf, cream foliage); 'Stoneham Gold' (golden yellow new foliage, dark green older foliage); 'Zebrina' (syn. 'Aureovariegata', gold and green sprays of foliage).

Site Sun or part shade.
Soil Ordinary.
Propagation Sow seeds in February; germinate in a cold frame. Take 50–100mm (1–4in) long cuttings of named varieties in autumn and root in frame.
Cultivation Plant in November–March. Water well in dry weather.

Thunbergia

ACANTHACEAE
Annuals and perennials native to Africa and Asia. The species listed is a tender, flowering, annual climber suitable for sheltered gardens.

T. alata (S. Africa), black-eyed susan. Height up to 3m (10ft); spread 450mm (1½ft). Twining plant with heart shaped, mid-green leaves. Showy, usually orange-yellow flowers with a long tube, generally dark brown, giving them characteristic 'black-eyed' appearance in June–September. Flowers occasionally may also be white or cream, with or without a dark tube.

Site Warm, sheltered sunny wall, fence, or post.
Soil Well-drained, fertile.
Propagation Sow in greenhouse or propagator in March in individual small pots; harden off before planting out in May. Or sow where they are to flower in late April–May.
Cultivation Provide strings, wires, or netting for stems to twine round. Water in dry spells during growing period. Discard after flowering.

Above *Thuja plicata* 'Zebrina'

Below *Thunbergia alata*

Thymus

LABIATAE Thyme

Hardy evergreen shrubs, native to Europe, that make attractive and useful rock-garden and edging plants. The aromatic leaves of two of the species listed are used as culinary herbs.

T. × citriodorus, lemon-scented thyme. Perennial. Height and spread 300mm (1ft). Hybrid with smooth, narrow, dark green leaves, lemon scented; culinary. Clusters of lilac flowers, 13mm (½in) long, in June. Varieties include 'Aureus' (yellow leaves); 'Silver Posie' (silver leaves).

T. richardii nitidus (syn. *T. nitidus*; Sicily). Perennial. Height 200mm (8in); spread 300mm (1ft). Small, ovate, grey-green leaves. Clusters of tubular, lilac flowers in May–June.

T. serpyllum (of gardens: now strictly *T. praecox arcticus*, but sometimes also listed as *T. drucei*; Europe, including Britain), wild thyme. Perennial. Height 75mm (3in); spread 600mm (2ft). Creeping plant with narrow, green, hairy leaves. Clusters of purple flowers, 13mm (½in) across, in June–August. Varieties include 'Album' (white); 'Bressingham Seedling' (pink); 'Coccineus' (red); 'Pink Chintz' (salmon pink).

T. vulgaris (S. Europe), common thyme, garden thyme. Perennial. Height 150–200mm (6–8in); spread 300mm (1ft). Long, narrow, dark-green leaves with strong scent when crushed; culinary. Clusters of lilac flowers 8mm (⅜in) long in June–August.

Site Bright sun.
Soil Well-drained.
Propagation Divide plants in March–April. Take 50–75mm (2–3in) long heel cuttings in May; pot up rooted cuttings and keep in peat and sand in cold frame until following September. Sow seed where it is to grow in April–May.
Cultivation Plant out rooted cuttings in September.

Above *Thymus vulgaris*

Tiarella

SAXIFRAGACEAE

Herbaceous perennials native to Asia and North America. Low-growing, with attractive leaves and short spikes of fluffy flowers, they make good weed-smothering ground-cover plants.

T. cordifolia (North America), foam-flower. Height 200mm (8in); spread 600mm (2ft) or more. Low carpeting plant, rooting out to form mats of soft green, pointed, lobed leaves, tinted or spotted with bronze. Erect spikes, 150mm (6in) high, of tiny cream flowers in May–June.

T. wherryi (North America). Height 150–130mm (6–9in); spread 300mm (1ft). Similar to *T. cordifolia* but spreads more slowly, making neat, tufted clumps of more-pointed leaves that colour well in autumn.

Site Cool, shady preferred; will grow in open if not too dry.
Soil Moist but well-drained, rich in humus; plants dislike dry, chalky soil.

Propagation Divide and replant rooted pieces in autumn or spring.
Cultivation Water in dry weather to maintain growth. Mulch in spring with leaf-mould or peat.

Left *Tiarella cordifolia*

Tigridia

IRIDACEAE   Shell-flower, tiger-flower, peacock-flower
Bulbous perennials from Central and South America. One half-hardy species with spectacular flowers is cultivated in Britain.

T. pavonia (Mexico, Guatemala). Height to 400mm (16in); spread 150mm (6in). Leaves narrowly lance-shaped, pleated, in fan-like tufts. Flowers somewhat iris-like, with three large petals, 75–125mm (3–5in) wide, in bright shades of yellow, red, purple, and white, and, within them, three smaller petals variously spotted and patterned, in July–September. Named cultivars hard to come by.

Site Full sun and shelter essential.
Soil Well-drained, fertile.
Propagation Separate offsets when dormant. Sow seeds under glass in spring.
Cultivation Plant in spring. Lift in autumn in cold winter areas and store just frost-free.
Pests and Diseases Slugs sometimes eat leaves and flowers.

Below *Tigridia pavonia*

Above *Trachycarpus fortunei*

Trachycarpus

PALMACEAE
A small genus of evergreen palms native to China and Himalaya. Only one species is in general cultivation, its decorative, fan-shaped leaves making it an ideal specimen tree for large lawns.

T. fortunei (syn. *Chamaerops excelsa*; China), Chusan palm. Height up to 10m (33ft); spread 2.5m (8¼ft). Slow-growing. Leaves 900mm (3ft) wide, divided into numerous narrow lobes. Large heads of tiny yellow flowers in late spring; sometimes followed by round, blue-black berries, 13mm (½in) across.

Site Bright light or part shade, with protection from north and east winds.
Soil Well-drained; rich loam preferred.
Propagation Pot up basal suckers in spring; root in frame or greenhouse. Or sow seeds in propagating frame in spring; pot on seedlings; plant out in fourth year.
Cultivation Plant out in late April–May. Occasional top-dressings of well-rotted manure or garden compost are beneficial.
Pruning Remove damaged leaves.

Above *Tradescantia* × *andersoniana*

Tradescantia

COMMELINACEAE

Hardy and tender perennials from North and South America. Several of the tender species are popular houseplants. The species listed is hardy and makes a good border plant; its attractive three-petalled flowers, carried on delicate umbels, last for just one day.

T. × *andersoniana* (syn. *T. virginiana*; N. America), spiderwort. Height 600mm (2ft); spread 450–600mm (1½–2ft). Long, mid-green, strap-like leaves. Violet-blue flowers in July–September. Hybrid cultivars include 'Carmine Glow' (pinkish red flowers, more-compact habit); 'Isis' (deep blue, long-flowering form); 'Osprey' (white flowers with fluffy blue central crest).

Site Sun or part shade.
Soil Any.
Propagation Lift and divide plants in spring. Or sow seed in greenhouse or propagator in March; prick out plants into individual pots; grow on in cold frame or sheltered bed; plant in flowering positions in autumn.
Cultivation Support with twiggy sticks or canes and string if necessary. Water in dry spells. Cut down dying foliage in late autumn.

Trillium

LILIACEAE

Hardy perennials, native to North America and Asia, that make useful plants for shady borders and rock gardens. All species have showy three-petalled flowers.

T. cernuum (E. North America). Height 450mm (1½ft); spread 300mm (1ft). Clusters of broad, green, rhomboidal leaves on stout stems. White (occasionally pink) flowers, 25mm (1in) long, in April–May.

T. erectum (E. North America), birth-root, lamb's quarters. Height 300mm (1ft); spread 250mm (10in). Clusters of broad rhomboidal, green leaves on stout stems. Flowers up to 50mm (2in) across, deep purple, and slightly malodorous, in April–May.

T. grandiflorum (E. North America), wake-robin. Height 300–450mm (1–1½ft); spread 300mm (1ft). Handsome oval green foliage in clusters on short, stout stems. Flowers white, ageing to pink (sometimes entirely pink), up to 50mm (2in) across, in April–June.

T. luteum (syn. *T. sessile luteum*; E. North America). Height 150–300mm (6–12in); spread 225mm (9in). short, rounded, green leaves heavily spotted with maroon, borne on short, stout stems. Yellow flowers, up to 25mm (1in) long, in May–June.

T. ovatum (W. North America). Height and spread 225mm (9in). Clusters of oval or rounded leaves. Striking white or soft-pink flowers, up to 40mm (1½in) long, in March–April.

G. recurvatum (North America). Height 300mm (1ft); spread 225mm (9in). Oval or rounded green leaves with brownish mottling, carried on strong, stout stems. Deep-purple to white flowers, up to 40mm (1½in) long, in April.

T. sessile (California). Height 150–300mm (6–12in); spread 150–225mm (6–9in). Rounded, mottled, green leaves in clusters on stout stems. Striking maroon flowers, 40mm (1½in) long, in March–April.

T. undulatum (E. North America), painted wood-lily. Height 300mm (1ft); spread 225mm (9in). Groups of rounded green leaves on strong stems. White flowers with distinctive purplish horseshoe-shaped markings in April–May.

Site Dappled shade preferred; open position tolerated if provided with sufficient moisture.
Soil Deep, rich, preferably acid (though plants will tolerate moderately alkaline conditions).
Propagation Divide rhizomes in late summer when foliage is dying down, or at any time in autumn–March.

Cultivation Plant as soon as possible after foliage dies down. Pot-grown plants planted during autumn or spring. Give top-dressing of peat or fine leaf-mould each spring. Divide clumps only when absolutely necessary.
Pests and Diseases Slugs often attack plants.

Below *Trillium sessile*

Trollius

RANUNCULACEAE   Globe-flower

Hardy herbaceous perennials, native to Europe, Asia, and North America, with showy globular or cup-shaped flowers and compact habit. They are moisture-loving plants that look attractive beside ponds or streams.

T. asiaticus (Siberia, Turkestan). Height 300–450mm (1–1½ft); spread 300mm (1ft). Compact mounds of finely toothed, bronze-green leaves. Deep yellow cup-shaped flowers, 40mm (1½in) across, in May–June.

T. chinensis (N. China). Height 300–450mm (1–1½ft); spread 300mm (1ft). Mounds of glabrous, round or kidney-shaped leaves on wiry stems. Handsome golden yellow, globular flowers, up to 50mm (2in) across, in May.

T. × cultorum (hybrid). Height 300–450mm (1–1½ft); spread 300mm (1ft). Garden hybrids derived from various species. Among the best are 'Earliest of All' (yellow); 'Fire-globe' (reddish-orange); 'Golden Queen' (yellow); 'Orange Globe' (orange).

T. europaeus (Europe, including Britain). Height 300–600mm (1–2ft); spread 450mm (1½ft). Bright green, lobed foliage in compact hummocks. Beautiful lemon-yellow globular blossoms, 50mm (2in) across, in April–July.

T. ledebourii (of gardens; Siberia). Height 600–900mm (2–3ft); spread 450mm (1½ft). Handsome lobed, green basal foliage on strong stems. Bright orange cup-shaped flowers, up to 75mm (3in) across, in May–June. (Plants sold under this name are strictly either *T. × cultorum* 'Golden Queen' or *T. chinensis*.)

T. yunnanensis (China). Height 600mm (2ft); spread 450mm (1½ft). Neat basal tufts of irregular or roughly oval green leaves. Bright yellow, flat flowers, 50mm (2in) across, carried on stout wiry flower stems in May.

Site Open preferred; but plants tolerate a little shade.
Soil Moisture-retentive, fertile.
Propagation Divide rootstocks in autumn. Sow seed of species in trays immediately it becomes available; it may take two seasons to germinate. Young plants are best grown individually in pots until they are ready for planting out.

Cultivation Plant at any time in dormant season, but early autumn or spring is preferable. Remove all old foliage in autumn. Divide roots only when they are overcrowded. Water often in dry spells.

Below *Trollius ledebourii*

Tropaeolum

TROPAEOLACEAE   Nasturtium

Hardy annuals and tuberous perennials, mostly climbing, from Central and South America. The popular garden species listed have showy, spurred flowers and attractive foliage.

T. majus (Peru), common nasturtium. Annual. Height (as climber) and spread (as ground cover) up to 3m (10ft). Leaves disc-shaped with stalk in middle. Red, orange, and yellow flowers, 50–65mm (2–2½in) wide, from June until first frost. Non-climbing forms include Tom Thumb dwarf strain, up to 250mm (10in) high, with single flowers. Semi-trailing forms include Gleam strains, up to 375mm (15in) high, with double and semi-double flowers.

T. peregrinum (syn. *T. canariense*; Ecuador, Peru), Canary creeper. Annual climber. Height 3m (10ft) or more; spread 1.5m (5ft) or more. Leaves pale green, deeply lobed. Bright yellow flowers about 20mm (¾in) wide, with two large, wing-like petals, in July–October.

T. speciosum (Chile), flame creeper. Rhizomatous climbing perennial. Height 3m (10ft) or more; spread about 1m (3¼ft). Stems very slender, set with small, leaves with radiating leaflets. Flowers 40mm (1½in) wide, vermilion-scarlet, in July–September. Seeds blue.

T. tuberosum (Bolivia, Peru) 'Ken Aslet'. Early-flowering form of a tuberous climbing perennial. Height 2–3m (6½–10ft); spread about 1m (3¼ft). Leaves rounded, broadly lobed, greyish-green. Orange-yellow-petalled, scarlet-spurred flowers, up to 40mm (1½in) long, in abundance in June–October. Tubers edible but of insipid taste.

Below *Tropaeolum majus*

Site Full sun or part shade for perennials; full sun preferable for annuals.

Soil Moisture-retentive for *T. speciosum*; well-drained and fertile for others.

Propagation Divide rhizomes of *T. speciosum* in spring. Separate tubers of *T. tuberosum* in autumn. Sow seeds of annuals in spring.

Cultivation Plant perennials in spring. Provide support for climbers (a shrub is ideal for *T. speciosum*). In cold areas, lift tubers of *T. tuberosum* and store frost-free.

Pests and Diseases Slugs and caterpillars may eat shoots and leaves.

Tulipa

LILIACEAE   Tulip

Bulbous perennials, native to Europe and Asia, with large, cup-shaped flowers, often very brightly coloured, and held well above the leaves.

T. fosteriana (C. Asia). Height 300mm (12in) or more; spread 200mm (8in). Leaves grey-green, narrowly ovate. Solitary flowers, 100mm (4in) long, brilliant scarlet with yellow-margined black blotch within, open in April. Cultivar 'Princeps' is 200mm (8in) tall and very sturdy.

T. greigii (Turkestan). Similar in size and appearance to *T. fosteriana*, but with leaves streaked and marbled dark purple-red.

T. kaufmanniana (Turkestan), water-lily tulip. Height about 200mm (8in); spread 150mm (6in). Leaves broadly oblong, somewhat grey-green. Flowers solitary, 75mm (3in) long, cream to pale yellow (its tapered buds flushed pink or red), in March–April.

T. tarda (syn. *T. dasystemon*; E. Turkestan). Height 100–125mm (4–5in); spread 75–100mm (3–4in). Leaves mostly

Above *Tulipa tarda*   **Right** *T.* 'Apeldoorn' (Div. 5)

basal, narrowly lance-shaped. Several flowers from each leaf-cluster, each about 40mm (1½in) long, opening widely, bright yellow with white petal tips, in March.

T. urumiensis (N.W. Iran). Almost identical to *T. tarda*, but with flowers entirely buttercup-yellow.

Hybrids

The first three species listed, and several others no longer widely grown, have been extensively hybridised to produce the wealth of tulip cultivars we grow today. Many of the hybrid varieties are better garden plants than the species. They are classified in groups according to flower shape, colour, height, and time of flower opening. The garden cultivars listed in each group below are good and typical.

Division 1: Single Early. Height 150–375mm (6–15in); April. 'Brilliant Star' (vermilion-scarlet); 'Pink Beauty' (carmine and white); 'White Hawk'.

Division 2: Double Early. Height 250–350mm (10–14in); April. 'Baby Doll' (buttercup-yellow); 'Carlton' (turkey-red); 'Peach Blossom' (silver-pink).

Division 3: Mendel. Height 400–500mm (16–20in); late April–May. 'Apricot Beauty' (salmon-rose); 'White Sail' (cream to white).

Division 4: Triumph. Height 450–500mm (18–20in); April. Like Darwin (Div. 6) but a little shorter and earlier. 'Bing Crosby' (scarlet); 'First Lady' (deep violet); 'Pax' (white).

Division 5: Darwin Hybrids (*T. fosteriana* × Darwin cultivars). Height 500–700mm (20–28in); April–May. Largest-flowered tulips. 'Apeldoorn' (orange-scarlet); 'Elizabeth Arden' (rose-pink); 'Golden Oxford' (rich yellow).

Division 6: Darwin. Height 550–750mm (22–30in); May–June. Tallest tulips, with almost flat-bottomed flowers. 'Alabaster' (white); 'Flying Dutchman' (cherry-red); 'Golden Age' (buttercup-yellow); 'Queen of the Night' (maroon).

Division 7: Lily-flowered. Height 450–600mm (18–24in), April. Flowers with pointed-tipped petals. 'China Pink' (satin pink); 'Dyanito' (red); 'Westpoint' (yellow).

Division 8: Cottage or Single Late. Height 350–650mm (14–26in); late April–May. Similar to Darwin but with ovoid blooms. 'Arctic Gold' (deep yellow); 'King's Blood' (cherry-red); 'Smiling Queen' (pink).

Division 9: Rembrandt. Height 550–750mm (22–30in); May. Darwin tulips with colour-breaking virus – flowers splashed and irregularly striped with contrasting colours or shades. 'May Blossom' (purple and cream); 'Zomerschoon' (pink and cream).

Division 10: Parrot. Height 400–600mm (16–24in); April–May. Mutants from other divisions, with fringed, waved and twisted petals. 'Black Parrot' (maroon); 'Texas Gold' (yellow, with red picotee).

Division 11: Double-late or peony-flowered. Height 400–600mm (16–24in); April–May. Flowers fully double. 'Gold Medal' (deep yellow); 'Mount Tacoma' (white); 'Symphonia' (cherry-red).

Division 12: Cultivars of *T. kaufmanniana* (q.v.); similar to parent but usually in two different shades of red and yellow.

Division 13: Cultivars of *T. fosteriana* (q.v.); similar to parent, but usually in shades of red, yellow, and white.

Division 14: Cultivars of *T. greigii* (q.v.); similar to parent, with leaves always maroon marbled or striped.

Site All require full sun.
Soil Well-drained, fertile.
Propagation Separate offsets or droppers when dormant.
Cultivation Plant in autumn, ideally not before October. On heavy soils lift the bulbs annually when the foliage yellows, storing them dry and warm until autumn.
Pests and Diseases In some areas and seasons fire disease, grey bulb rot, and slugs can be troublesome.

Left *Tulipa* 'Black Parrot' (Div. 10)   **Below** *T. greigii* 'Plaisir'

Valeriana

VALERIANACEAE

Hardy herbaceous plants, of cosmopolitan distribution, suitable for borders and rock gardens; good subjects for flower arrangements.

V. phu (Europe, Caucasus). Perennial. Height 750mm–1m (2½–3¼ft); spread 600mm (2ft). 'Aurea', the commonest garden form, has bright golden young foliage. Leaves at base of plant are ovate; those on erect stems are divided. Small, white, tubular flowers carried in densely packed panicles in July–August.

Site Open, full sun.
Soil Any.
Propagation Divide in spring.
Cultivation Stake with twiggy sticks or canes and string where necessary. If foliage only required remove flower buds as they form

Below *Valeriana phu* 'Aurea'

Verbascum

SCROPHULARIACEAE   Mullein

Hardy biennials and perennials, native mainly to southern Europe and western Asia. Tall-growing, with spires of yellow flowers, they make a good show at the back of borders or in island beds.

V. bombyciferum (syn. *V. broussa* of gardens; Asia Minor).

Biennial. Height 1.5–1.8m (5–6ft); spread 600mm (2ft). Large, pointed leaves, covered with silver hairs, form a spreading rosette. Flower spikes carrying dozens of bright yellow blooms in June–July.

V. chaixii (Europe). Perennial. Height 1.2–1.5m (4–5ft); spread 600mm (2ft). Woolly, pointed, silvery green leaves. Tall spikes of yellow flowers with maroon stamens in mid-summer.

V. × phoeniceum (hybrid). Perennial. Height 1–2m (3¼–6½ft); spread 450–600mm (1½–2ft). Garden hybrids with rough, pointed, mid-green leaves. Flowers in June–August. Cultivars include 'Gainsborough' (pale, clear yellow); 'Cotswold Queen' (tones of orange, yellow, and purple); 'Mont Blanc' (spikes of pure white flowers, silver-grey leaves); 'Pink Domino' (rosy pink flowers).

Site Full sun, reasonably sheltered.
Soil Well-drained, moisture-retentive, rich.
Propagation Sow biennials in greenhouse or cold frame in April; prick seedlings out into rows in sheltered bed; grow on until they are ready for planting in flowering positions in autumn. Perennials can also be raised from seed, but root cuttings must be taken to perpetuate named cultivars; take 75mm (3in) sections of healthy root in February and insert in pots of peat and sand in greenhouse; set out young plants in sheltered bed; transplant to flowering positions in autumn.
Cultivation Stake plants firmly. Cut down flower-spikes when flowers fade. Discard biennials after flowering.

Below *Verbascum × phoeniceum* 'Pink Domino'

Verbena

VERBENACEAE

Annual and perennial herbaceous plants, mostly from North and South America. Those listed are half-hardy perennials for the rock garden and border; they are also grown as annuals for summer bedding.

V. × hybrida (garden origin). Perennial treated as annual. Height and spread up to 600mm (2ft). Dark green, lanceolate leaves toothed and wrinkled. Rounded clusters of blue, red, pink, or white flowers, with and without eyes, freely carried in June–October. Varieties include 'Springtime' (early flowering, in a range of colours on compact plants); 'Tropic' (bright-scarlet blooms without eyes).

V. peruviana (S. America). Perennial. Height 75–100mm (3–4in); spread 300mm (12in). Low-growing, spreading rock-garden plant. Toothed, grey-green leaves. Brilliant scarlet, star-like flowers carried in great profusion in summer.

V. rigida (syn. *V. venosa*; Argentina, Brazil). Perennial treated as annual. Height 300–450mm (12–18in); spread 450mm (18in). Leaves oblong, deep green and toothed. Small violet flowers carried in dense clusters on erect stems in July–October. 'Alba' is a white-flowered form.

Site Sunny, open, but protected against wind.
Soil Light, free-draining, reasonably fertile.
Propagation Sow seeds in greenhouse or propagator in January–March at 20–25°C (68–77°F); prick off into boxes; harden off seedlings before planting out in May. Take cuttings of non-flowering side-shoots in August–September; root in sandy compost to over-winter in frost-free place.
Cultivation Pinch out growing tips when planting out to ensure sturdy, branching growth. Remove dead-heads.
Pests and Diseases Aphids may attack young shoots. Powdery mildew may be a problem in dry weather.

Below *Verbena peruviana*

Veronica

SCROPHULARIACEAE   Speedwell

Half-hardy and hardy annuals and perennials, native mainly to the northern hemisphere. Those listed are perennials suitable for rock gardens and borders.

V. exaltata (N. America). Height 1.5m (5ft); spread 600mm (2ft). Upright plant with narrow, lanceolate leaves. Spikes of lavender-blue flowers in mid-summer.

V. gentianoides (Caucasus). Height 300mm (1ft); spread 225mm (9in). Narrow, glossy leaves form rosettes. Tall stems carrying racemes of blue flowers in early summer. Varieties include 'Nana' (low-growing type suitable for rock garden); 'Variegata' (leaves marked with cream and white).

V. incana (syn. *V. spicata incana*; Caucasus). Height 300–450mm (12–18in); spread 225–300mm (9–12in). Foliage narrow, ash-grey. Flowers short, deep-blue spikes. Hybrid cultivars include 'Saraband' (violet-blue); 'Wendy' (deep lavender-blue).

V. longifolia (Europe, N. Asia). Height 1–1.2m (3¼–4ft); spread 450mm (1½ft). Slender lanceolate leaves carried in threes or opposite pairs. Racemes of small, deep-blue flowers in summer. 'Foersters Blue' is sturdy variety with rich blue flowers.

V. prostrata (Europe, N. Asia). Height 150mm (6in); spread up to 450mm (1½ft). Mat-forming species for the rock garden. Small, mid-green leaves. Freely carried, dense spikes of pale blue flowers in early summer. Very compact 'Lodden Blue' has more richly coloured blooms.

V. spicata (Europe). Height 300–450mm (1–1½ft); spread 300mm (1ft). Toothed, narrow, mid-green leaves. Spikes of small blue flowers. Varieties include 'Alba' (white); 'Bar-carolle' (rich rose-pink); 'Red Fox' (crimson).

V. teucrium (Europe, N. Asia). Height up to 375mm (15in); spread 600mm (2ft). Narrow, lanceolate, dark green leaves.

Slender racemes of light blue flowers. Varieties include 'Crater Lake Blue' (deep blue); 'Shirley Blue' (deep blue); 'Trehane (light blue, with yellow variegated leaves).

Site Full sun or part shade.
Soil Free-draining but moisture-retentive.
Propagation Lift and divide plants in early spring. Non-flowering shoots can be made into 50–75mm (2–3in) cuttings in August. Over-winter rooted cuttings in a sheltered place in 90mm (3½in) pots; plant in permanent positions in spring.
Cultivation Stake taller varieties with twiggy sticks or canes and string. Remove dead flower-spikes. Cut down dead stems in autumn.
Pests and Diseases Powdery mildew may be troublesome in dry summers.

Right *Veronica gentianoides*

Viburnum

CAPRIFOLIACEAE

Deciduous and evergreen shrubs, native mainly to eastern Asia, Europe, and North America, popular for their flattish rounded clusters of scented flowers (some bloom in winter), bright berries, and colourful autumn leaves.

V. betulifolium (China). Height and spread 2.5–3.5m (8¼–12ft). Bushy, deciduous shrub with dark green, coarse-toothed, oval leaves 50–100mm (2–4in) long. Tiny white flowers carried in flattened clusters, 50–100mm (2–4in) across, in May–June. Vivid red, currant-like berries produced (usually only on mature specimens) in autumn.

V. × bodnantense (hybrid). Height and spread 2.5–3.5m (8¼–12ft). Upright deciduous shrub with young bronze leaves ageing to rich green, oval, coarsely toothed, 50–100mm (2–4in) long. White-flushed pink flowers borne in rounded clusters, 25–50mm (1–2in) across, in December–February. One of the best winter-flowering shrubs, it is usually represented by 'Dawn', more heavily fragrant.

V. × burkwoodii (hybrid). Height 2.5m (8¼ft); spread 2.7–3.5m (9–12ft). Evergreen shrub with dark green, oval leaves, slightly toothed, 40–100mm (1½–4in) long. Waxy white flowers, pink in bud, carried in flat heads, 50–90mm (2–3½in) across, in March–May. Clone 'Park Farm Hybrid' is more spreading, with slightly larger flowers.

V. carlesii (Korea). Height and spread 1.5m (5ft). Deciduous shrub with oval downy leaves. Large, flattish heads of white flowers, pink in bud, in April–May; very sweetly scented. 'Aurora' is best form.

V. davidii (China). Height 600–900mm (2–3ft); spread 1.2–1.5m (4–5ft). Evergreen shrub with oval, prominently veined, dark green leaves 75–125mm (3–5in) long. White flowers carried in flat heads, 50–75mm (2–3in) across, in June. Followed by turquoise-blue berries, 6mm (¼in) across, if male and female clones grown in close proximity. Good as ground cover.

V. farreri (syn. *V. fragrans*; China). Height and spread 2.7–3.5m (9–12ft). Upright deciduous shrub with young bronze leaves ageing to mid-green, oval, pointed, coarsely toothed, 40–100mm (1½–4in) long. Fragrant white flowers, pink in bud, in November–March.

V. opulus (Britain), guelder rose. Height and spread 3.5–

4.5m (12–15ft). Bushy deciduous shrub with maple-like lobed, dark green leaves, 50–100mm (2–4in) across. Heavily scented white flowers carried in late spring in flat heads, 50–75mm (2–3in) across, surrounded by 20mm (¾in) wide white bracts. Translucent red berries in large clusters carried in autumn. Varieties include 'Fructuluteo' (yellow fruits); 'Sterile' (snowball tree with large, round, creamy white heads of sterile florets in early summer).

V. rhytidophyllum (China). Height 3–4.5m (10–15ft); spread 3–3.5m (10–12ft). Evergreen with elliptical, attractively corrugated leaves, 100–200mm (4–8in) long, glossy dark green on upper surface, grey with felt underneath. White flower-heads, 75–100mm (3–4in) across, in May–June, followed by oval fruits, red ageing to black.

V. tinus (Europe), laurustinus. Height 2–3m (6½–10ft); spread 2m (6½ft). Bushy evergreen shrub with oval, mid-green leaves, 40–100mm (1½–4in) long. white, pink-budded flower-heads, 50–100mm (2–4in) across, in November–May. Good varieties include 'Eve Price' (compact habit, pink flowers); 'French White' (white flowers); 'Variegatum' (creamy variegated leaves).

Site Full sun preferred; spring-flowering forms should be sheltered from north and east winds.
Soil Ordinary, not dry.
Propagation Sow seeds in cold frame when ripe (may take two years to germinate). Take semi-ripe cuttings, 75–100mm (3–4in) long, in summer. Take hard-wood cuttings in November; or layer long shoots in autumn and sever from parent plant a year later.

Cultivation Plant evergreens in September or April; deciduous forms in October–March. Those grown for their berries should be planted in groups to aid pollination.
Pruning Winter-flowering forms and evergreens pruned in April; summer-flowering types in February.
Pests and Diseases Aphids and whiteflies may attack.

Below *Viburnum davidii* fruits

Vinca

APOCYNACEAE   Periwinkle

Evergreen sub-shrubs, native to Europe, western Asia, and North Africa, that form trailing plants with long flexible stems and tubular flowers opening to a flat, round, five-petalled disc. They provide attractive ground cover in sunny or shady sites.

V. major (Europe), greater periwinkle. Height 300mm (1ft); spread 900mm (3ft) or more. Vigorous, low-growing plant with flexible, wiry stems, rooting out at the leaf joints and soon forming dense mats of foliage. Bright blue flowers, 25–40mm (1–1½in) across, in axils of leaves in March–June. Cultivar 'Variegata' (syn. 'Elegantissima') has leaves conspicuously splashed with creamy white; popular for cutting.

V. minor (Europe), lesser periwinkle. Height 225mm (9in); spread 450–600mm (1½–2ft). Of denser habit but spreading more slowly than *V. major*, with smaller, dark green, pointed leaves. Flowers bright blue, 25mm (1in) across, in March–August or later. Several cultivars with single or double, white, blue, or purple flowers; some with variegated leaves.

Site All grow well in shade; variegated forms best in sun.
Soil Well-drained, fertile; chalk tolerated.
Propagation Separate single rooted runners, ideally in early autumn or spring. Divide clumps of *V. minor* at same time.
Cultivation Water in dry weather; apply general fertiliser in early spring.

Below *Vinca major* 'Variegata'

Right *Viola* × *wittrockiana* mixture

Viola

VIOLACEAE   Violet, pansy

A large genus of annuals, biennials, and perennials of worldwide distribution, including species suitable for bedding, borders, woodland, and rock gardens. Most are easily cultivated and of high garden value.

V. 'Ardross Gem'. Perennial. Height 125mm (5in); spread 225mm (9in). Favourite rock-garden cultivar, with light blue flowers flushed with gold in May–September.

V. cornuta (Pyrenees), horned violet. Perennial. Height 225mm (9in); spread 450mm (18in) or more. Forms a dense mound of evergreen leaves. Violet-blue flowers from early summer to autumn. Varieties include white-flowered 'Alba'. A good front-of-the-border plant.

V. cucullata (E. North America). Perennial. Height 100–150mm (4–6in); spread 300mm (12in). Round, fresh-green leaves. Usually represented in gardens by its several cultivars and allied species such as *V. papilionacea* and *V. sororia*, all flowering in May–June. Typical are 'Freckles' (blue flecked with white); 'Striata' (white striped with violet-blue).

V. labradorica (North America). Short-lived perennial, but seeds freely. Height 100mm (4in); spread 300mm (12in). Usually represented by variety 'Purpurea', with purplish green leaves and dark violet flowers in spring and summer. A good spreader for the border front.

V. odorata (Asia, North Africa, Europe, including Britain), sweet violet. Perennial. Height 100mm (4in); spread 300mm (12in). Heart-shaped green leaves. Blue, violet, pink or white flowers in spring (and occasionally in autumn). Spreads by runners.

V. tricolor (Asia, Europe, including Britain), heart's-ease. Annual or short-lived perennial which seeds freely. Height

both single and mixed colours; good ones include 'Clear Crystals' (mixed); 'Roggli Swiss Giants' (single colours or mixed); 'Ullswater' (rich blue). Bloom in winter, spring, or summer, depending on variety.

Site Sunny or part shade.
Soil Moisture-retentive but well-drained; chalk tolerated. Add peat and leaf-mould.
Propagation Perennial types by cuttings rooted in frame in June–July or by division in early spring. Pansies and violas also from seed sown under glass or outdoors, as follows. Sow in July–August for winter and spring flowering; transplant to flowering sites in September–October. Sow under glass in February–March; for summer flowering; transplant to flowering sites in May. Outdoor sowings for summer flowers can be made in March–April. Consult seedsmen's catalogues for varieties best suited to blooming at particular times.
Cultivation Snip off faded flowers to ensure succession of blooms.
Pests and Diseases Aphids and slugs are likely pests. Mildew and rust may occur.

Vitis

VITIDACEAE   Ornamental vines
Evergreen or deciduous climbing shrubs native to the northern hemisphere. Most are vigorous and are grown for their attractive autumn foliage or for their fruits.
V. coignetiae (Japan), Japanese crimson-glory vine. Height and spread up to 25m (82ft) or more. Hardy deciduous climber with thick, lobed, pale green leaves up to 300mm (12in) across, turning gold, orange, and purplish red in autumn. Green flowers in May followed by barely edible purple-black fruits.
V. vinifera (Asia), wine grape. Height and spread up to 12m (40ft). Hardy deciduous climber with large lobed, mid-green leaves up to 150mm (6in) long. Oval fruits black with a blue bloom, or amber-green. Most cultivated grapes are grown from this species. Ornamental varieties include 'Apiifolia' (parsley vine, with deeply divided, dark green leaves); 'Brandt' (syn. 'Brant', attractive hybrid with red-purple autumn leaves and bunches of succulent sweet, aromatic grapes).

Site South- or west-facing site if fruits are to ripen properly. Vines are suitable for growing on pergola or trellis, or can be allowed to scramble through trees.
Soil Ordinary, moisture-retentive, neither very acid nor very chalky.
Propagation Take 'eye' cuttings under glass in December–January. Sow seeds in spring in pans or trays under glass. Layer one-year-old growths in April–August – a particularly successful method with *V. coignetiae.*
Cultivation Plant in November–March. Top-dress annually with well-rotted manure or compost.
Pruning Only to maintain spread in restricted area; in late summer.
Pests and Diseases Aphids and scale insects sometimes a nuisance.

Right *Vitis vinifera* 'Brandt'

about 100mm (4in); spread 300mm (12in). Fresh-green, indented leaves. Miniature pansy flowers in combinations of cream, yellow, blue, and violet in May–September. A parent of garden pansies.
V. × williamsii (*V. cornuta × V. × wittrockiana*) tufted pansy, bedding viola, violetta. Perennial. Height about 150mm (6in); spread 225mm (9in). Many cultivars, most of a single colour, including 'Irish Molly' (greenish yellow); 'Maggie Mott' (pale bluish mauve); 'White Swan' (white). Spring- and summer-flowering.
V. × wittrockiana (hybrid), pansy. Short-lived perennials. Height and spread up to 225mm (9in). Garden pansies with large flowers often blotched with blackish purple. Leaves fresh green and indented. Flowers red, yellow, blue, white, and violet in assorted combinations. Countless cultivars in

Weigela

CAPRIFOLIACEAE

Hardy deciduous shrubs, native to China and Japan, sometimes classified under *Diervilla*. The species listed has largely been superseded by hybrid garden forms. All thrive in urban, even industrial, atmospheres.

W. florida (China). Height 2m (6½ft); spread 1.8m (6ft). Spreading shoots carry light green, elliptical leaves, 50–100mm (2–4in) long and with prominent veins. Rose-pink, foxglove-like flowers, 25mm (1in) long, carried in clusters on previous season's wood in May–June. Varieties include 'Foliis Purpureis' (maroon-flushed leaves); 'Variegata' (beautiful compact shrub, with leaves edged pale yellow fading to white).

Modern Garden Forms. Many good cultivars exist of which parentage is uncertain, including 'Avalanche' (white); 'Bristol Ruby' (ruby red); 'Conquête' (deep pink); 'Looymansii Aurea' (pink, leaves yellow); 'Mont Blanc' (white). All flower in May–June.

Site Sun or part shade.
Soil Ordinary.
Propagation Take cuttings, 250mm (10in) long, of strong shoots in autumn; grow outdoors in nursery area; transplant to final positions a year later.

Cultivation Plant in October–March. Water well in dry weather.
Pruning Shorten or remove flowering stems immediately after flowering.

Below *Weigela florida* 'Variegata'

Wisteria

LEGUMINOSAE

Hardy, deciduous climbing shrubs native to the eastern United States, China and Japan. The popular garden species produce very fragrant mauve, blue, white, or pink pea-flowers in late spring.

W. floribunda (Japan), Japanese wisteria. Height and spread 9m (30ft). Vigorous grower with mid-green leaves composed of 13 to 19 leaflets. Fragrant, violet-blue flowers hang in clusters 250–300mm (10–12in) long – but usually only on mature specimens – in May–June. Varieties include 'Alba' (white); 'Macrobotrys' (lilac-blue, in long clusters); 'Rosea' (rose-pink, tipped purple).

W. sinensis (syn. *W. chinensis*; China), Chinese wisteria. Height and spread up to 25m (82ft). Very large species and probably the most popular. Dark green leaves composed of 9 to 11 leaflets. Fragrant, mauve flowers hang in clusters, 200–300mm (8–12in) long, in May–June. Commonest form is 'Alba' (white); 'Black Dragon' is deep purple, double.

Site South- or west-facing wall ideal. Wisterias are also good for growing against fences, arches, and pergolas, or through trees.
Soil Ordinary, not dry.
Propagation Plants from cuttings or layers flower more reliably than any others: buy these for preference. Sow seeds under glass in spring, or take hard-wood cuttings in autumn. Keep these under glass until well-rooted. Layer stems of *W. sinensis* in April–August; sever from parent plant a year later.
Cultivation Plant out in October–March; support plant against structure (wall, pergola, tree) until twisting stems and branches anchor firmly. Young plants will not flower until 5 to 10 years old.
Pruning Vigorous specimens on walls require hard pruning after flowering is over. Cut young stems back to three leaves when they are 450–600mm (1½–ft) long and continue this at intervals throughout the summer.
Pests and Diseases Aphids and thrips may infest and damage foliage.

Below *Wisteria sinensis*

Yucca

LILIACEAE

Long-lived evergreen perennials and shrubs native to North America, Mexico and West Indies. All have sword-like leaves and produce long panicles of bell-shaped flowers.

Y. filamentosa (S.E. United States), Adam's needle. Stemless species. Height 750mm (2½ft); spread 900mm (3ft). Erect, long, thin leaves of dull mid-green. Creamy white bell flowers, 50–75mm (2–3in) long, carried in clusters on stalks, 900mm–1.8m (3–6ft) high, in summer. Form 'Variegata' has leaves margined and striped yellow.

Y. flaccida (S.E. United States). Stemless species. Height 1.5m (5ft); spread 1.2m (4ft). Leaves 300–600mm (1–2ft) long, more grey and lax than those of *Y. filamentosa*. Clear white flowers, 50–65mm (2–2½in) long, in July–August.

Y. gloriosa (S.E. United States). Height and spread 1.2–1.8m (4–6ft). Leaves 450–600mm (1½–2ft) long, erect, deep green, carried at top of slow-growing woody stem or trunk. Cream flowers, tinged red, up to 75mm (3in) long, in September–November on stalks 900mm–1.8m (3–6ft) high. Only mature specimens flower.

Y. recurvifolia (S.E. United States). Height 1.2–1.8m (4–6ft); spread 1.8–2.1m (6–7ft). Leaves 450–600m (1½–2ft) long, arching, narrower than those of *Y. gloriosa*. Cream flowers, 50–75mm (2–3in) long, in July–October on stalks up to 1.8m (6ft) high. Only mature specimens flower.

Site Bright sun essential.
Soil Will grow well in poor sandy and chalky soils.
Propagation Sow seeds under glass in spring. Remove and replant rooted suckers in spring.
Cultivation Plant in April or September; or, if pot-grown, any time in summer.
Pruning Cut out dead leaves in spring. Remove faded flower-stalks in autumn.
Pests and Diseases Leaf spot may occur.

Right *Yucca gloriosa*

Zauschneria

ONAGRACEAE   California fuchsia

A genus of clump-forming perennials from western North America and Mexico, suitable for hot, sunny positions in the rock garden, where they will give a useful display of colour in late summer and autumn.

Z. californica. Herbaceous plant with woody-based stems that branch and grow to about 300mm (12in) high. Leaves grey and hairy. Tubular scarlet flowers produced at tips of stems in August–October. Of several cultivars, 'Glasnevin' can be recommended; it reaches 400mm (16in) and has green foliage.

Z. cana. Similar to above but with much narrower leaves.

Site Sunny, sheltered corner essential.
Soil Well-drained essential.
Propagation Division not easy. Take 50–75mm (2–3in) long cuttings of basal shoots in May and insert in sand in heated propagating frame; pot up rooted cuttings; over-winter under glass, ready for planting out following spring.
Cultivation In cold areas cover plants with bracken, leaves or a cloche in winter.
Pruning Cut plant down to ground in March.
Pests and Diseases Aphids can distort young growths.

Above *Zauschneria cana*

Zinnia

COMPOSITAE

Annual and perennial herbaceous plants, mainly from Central America. Those listed are showy annuals, with daisy-like flowers in a range of colours, for borders, bedding out, or cutting.

Z. angustifolia (syn. *Z. haageana*; Mexico). Half-hardy. Height 450–600mm (1½–2ft); spread 300mm (1ft). Light green, slightly hairy leaves and stems. Bright, daisy-like flowers in a range of colours in July–August. Good varieties include 'Chippendale' (bronze-red with gold tips to petals and gold stamens); 'Persian Carpet' (striking, richly toned, bi-coloured blooms).

Z. elegans (Mexico). Half-hardy. Height 600mm (2ft); spread 300mm (1ft). Pale green foliage. Bright purple flowers in July–September. A wide range of cultivars is available, including dahlia-flowered and cactus-flowered strains in many colours. 'Envy' has lime-green, double blooms popular with flower arrangers.

Site Sunny, sheltered.
Soil Free-draining, fertile.
Propagation Sow in greenhouse or propagator at 16–18°C (60–64°F); prick seedlings off individually into fibre or peat pots so they can be transplanted with minimum of root disturbance; harden off before planting out in May. Alternatively, sow where they are to flower in May, thinning seedlings to 300mm (1ft).
Cultivation Pinch out growing tips on young plants to encourage branching habit. Transplant with as little disturbance as possible to avoid a check to growth. Remove dead flower-heads and those spoiled by rain.
Pests and Diseases Viruses may stunt or distort growth. Grey mould occurs in cool, damp summers.

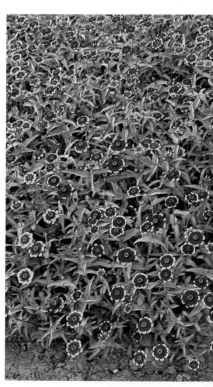

Right *Zinnia angustifolia* 'Chippendale'

Planning Your Garden

It's easy enough to grass over your entire plot and then to dig a border around the edge into which all plants are put. It has been done in countless gardens and it will be done in countless more. The only trouble is – it's boring.

True enough, the gardens which are most pleasant to be in are often the simplest, but they should also offer the spectator a few surprises. A garden where everything is predictable and can be taken in at a glance offers little temptation to explore.

Basic Considerations

It could be argued that it is unnecessary to plan a garden at all, but such an approach invariably leads to dissatisfaction with the result. Decide, once your land has been cleared and made ready for action, just what you require of your plot. A list of its potential attributes will make sure that all members of the family are catered for. Is there room for a swing, sand-pit, patio, greenhouse, vegetable garden, lawn, pool? Do you want one, some, or all of these?

This list is really the only thing that needs to be committed to paper so far as the general design is concerned. Planners will tell you that all good gardens start on a sheet of graph paper, which allows you to draw everything to scale. That's all very well for gardeners whose imagination can turn a paper plan into a garden in their mind's eye. But for those who would rather get out on the soil, the best advice is to do just that – the shape of the plot and its features can be marked on the earth rather than on paper.

Before you get to this stage, you will probably have a fairly good idea of what kind of a garden you want. There are two basic types – formal and informal. Formal gardens need not try to emulate Versailles in their complexity, but they will hopefully show a little more imagination than is evident in a lawn surrounded by a border. They may be basically angular in design – all squares and rectangles – or they may also incorporate circles, ellipses, and other shapes. Informal gardens use no geometrical designs: they are composed seemingly at random to produce a 'natural' effect.

With both these schemes the 'keep-it-simple' idea is important for two reasons: first, very fiddly shapes usually become irritating to look at over the years; second, they are usually difficult to maintain. Intricately shaped edges to lawns, for instance, are notoriously difficult to mow or to keep neat. Whatever the design, make sure that any powered equipment you own can be operated easily in the finished garden.

There is a trend that still persists in some quarters to design a garden that disguises the shape of the plot. If the garden is long and thin, the designer for some reason feels bound to make it appear short and fat; and vice versa. This is one approach to designing a garden, and there are occasions when it makes sense; but it should not be adopted as a matter of course. Some long, thin gardens are a delight *because* their length and narrowness are emphasised, creating (for example) a long vista into which plants encroach from the edges and make hidden nooks along the way. Such gardens can even be planted up with avenues of small trees down each side to make a slick formal effect. There is no reason why you should not choose an obvious design, provided it is pleasing to the eye – and straight lines often are.

Below In this well-designed country garden the architectural formality of the pool and fountain is balanced by cheerfully crowded borders and randomly curved edges to the lawn.

Filling in the Details

When you know what kind of garden you want, there comes a time when you have to start experimenting with shapes. The paper planner can simply doodle and decide which line looks best. The soil planner must get out on the earth and fiddle with shapes made with a length of hosepipe or trails of sand. These shapes can then be viewed from the windows of the house (both upstairs and down), and the location and size of beds and borders decided upon.

Large canes can mark the positions of trees; but always bear in mind (whether you plan on paper or soil) the size *at maturity* of the trees and shrubs you intend to include (the ultimate height and spread of the shrubs and trees are given in the A–Z section).

View the shapes you make from all sides so that they complement one another and the house. Remember that you are dealing not only with shape, size, texture and colour, but also with time. It alters the picture not merely with the changing seasons but also with the passing of the years as plants become larger and more handsome – or outgrow their welcome.

Focal points – trees, well-chosen ornaments, pots, tubs, even a lump of stone – are vital to give your eyes something to light on at the end of a bed or border, and to act as a 'full-stop'. Many garden ornaments available today seem incongruous when placed in small gardens. Don't feel that you have *got* to play host to a full-size Venus de Milo! Look instead for a handsome terracotta pot, a large rock – even the top of an old British Rail signal post (when painted white, these make superb pieces of wrought ironwork). Ornaments like this are unlikely to be found in a garden centre, where concrete statuettes are the order of the day. Junk shops, British Rail's Collector's Corner, and scrap-yards often yield rich pickings.

Above Even in a garden with well-stocked beds and borders, plants in handsome pots, tubs and troughs are useful for adding interest to paved areas such as patios and steps. **Left** An urn on this island bed makes a striking focal point; the effect is enhanced by the plainness of the surroundings.

Each garden feature will have to be positioned not only where it is convenient from your point of view, but also where it will flourish and be successful. A greenhouse, the vegetable plot, and a pond will all need full sun. The patio should be within easy reach of the kitchen if you plan to use it as an outdoor dining room in summer.

Bear in mind the aspect of the garden, too. Where does the sun rise and set? Will that patio be in the sun for more than a couple of hours? If a large tree is planted on the southern side, will the garden receive any sun at all?

Don't be ashamed of looking over the fence to see what your neighbour has done – not with a view to copying his design but to observe which plants are thriving and which look unhappy in this soil and locality. This will help you avoid making costly mistakes. If, for some reason, magnolias and rhododendrons always seem to fail in your locality, it is unlikely that you will do better with them than anyone else.

Know Your Soil

Much, of course, depends on the soil. It really does make sense to test the earth in your new garden to see what it is made of. There are three main factors influencing the nature of your soil: its organic matter and nutrient content; its drainage; its acidity or alkalinity.

The organic matter and nutrient content influence plant growth to a marked degree. Digging in compost and well-rotted manure is especially worthwhile; leaf-mould and peat are less nutritious but nevertheless are valuable soil conditioners. Plants feed greedily during the growing season, and helpings of fertiliser, natural or synthetic, at the correct rate will keep them growing healthily.

Good drainage is vital. Most plants hate waterlogged soil. It will seldom be necessary to lay a complete system of drains; but on heavy clay soil, digging in coarse grit and organic matter will help water to escape downwards more rapidly. Organic matter, on the other hand, will also hold on to more water in light, sandy soils where summer droughts are a problem.

Soil acidity is governed by the amount of free lime in the soil. A very chalky or limy soil is said to be alkaline; one which contains little lime is said to be acid. Soil acidity is expressed in the measure known as the pH scale. Small, inexpensive kits bought at garden centres can be used to test the soil in your plot. All you have to do is mix a soil sample with the indicator fluid and compare the colour of the liquid with the colours on the chart supplied. The kit will show the approximate pH value of your soil – whether it is acid or alkaline.

If your soil is very acid it may be 'sour', and helpings of lime will be beneficial. If the soil is alkaline there is little you can do to reduce its alkalinity in the long term, and you would be well advised to avoid planting acid-loving plants such as rhododendrons and camellias.

Even if you intend to do nothing about adjusting the pH of your soil, it is as well to know whether it is acid or alkaline so that you can garden *with* it rather than *against* it, putting in only those plants which will enjoy its degree of acidity or alkalinity.

Plants in Association

When you have made the overall plan for the garden, you can decide exactly which plants are to go where. Although all sorts of advice could be given here, in the end it all boils down to a question of taste. But a few general pointers may be welcome.

Never think of a plant in isolation: judge it as a companion for its neighbours. Plants should always be positioned to show one another off, not simply plonked into the soil.

Left A good colour sense enables the gardener to create vivid combinations. Here cool blue grape hyacinths (*Muscari*) and warm red azaleas complement one another to striking effect.

Above Blending of muted colours can achieve pleasingly subtle effects. Here blue and pink hybrids of forget-me-not (*Myosotis*) offer a pastel-shaded carpet to a scattering of yellow violas.

to overdo them. The same applies to evergreens and conifers. Both are vital to give a garden year-round form and texture, but if they are planted in quantity the plot may begin to look oppressive and unchanging.

Trees and shrubs are the backbone of any garden; border plants and bedding will flesh out the skeleton. Choose your plants not only with their shape and form in mind but also considering their seasons of interest. Make sure that there is at least a handful of flowers, fruits, and bright foliage to see you through the winter until the bright spring show begins once more.

Time and Space

Never imagine that your garden will one day be 'finished'. It is not a museum, and the picture it presents will always be changing. Some plants may outgrow their welcome or look better elsewhere in the garden. And even experienced gardeners frequently discover, or become interested in, plants they have hitherto ignored. Then, of course, new varieties of favourite species or hybrids are being introduced all the time. Finally, however attractive the overall scheme and the plants in it may be, many gardeners like to change things simply for the sake of change. All this makes gardening an exciting adventure.

The biggest decision you will have to make at planting time is how far apart to space the plants. They need room to grow, but while they are expanding the earth between them will look deadly dull. There are two ways around this. You can plant at the final spacing and fill in with annuals and bedding plants while the space is there, or you can plant rather more closely and thin out one or two plants later on. Most gardeners adopt a mixture of the two techniques, and there is no reason why the plants should not jostle one another for space if you like the feeling of a rather bountiful and overgrown garden. After all, it's more fun to snip back and thin out the plants you enjoy looking at than to spend all your time eradicating pernicious weeds. While considering the question of space, do make certain, before you plant trees, that your garden is large enough to cope with them when they are full-grown. If it is not, choose instead large, architectural shrubs: in 20 years' time they will present far less of a problem than a tree which is blocking your light, clogging your gutters, and threatening the foundations of your house. As in all garden-planning matters, a little thought at the beginning will save a lot of heartache later on.

Above A 'cottage-garden' border, in which the aim is to create an appealingly informal profusion of plants, calls for thoughtful balancing of colours, textures, shapes and sizes.

Rely on leaf shape, colour, and texture even more than on flowers. The leaves are in evidence for most of the year (all year if they are evergreen), whereas the flowers are fleeting. You will find that almost all flowers have more impact if they are shown off by a backdrop of handsome foliage than if they have to sit in mid-air.

Do not assume that all your leaves must be plain green. Well-placed variegated, grey- or purple-leaved plants make stunning features in their own right, although it is wise not

Plant Selection

One thing more than any other will determine how well a plant grows, and that is its environment. You can spend hours choosing the best specimen at the nursery; you can plant it well and pamper it; but if it does not like the spot you have chosen, nothing you do will enable it to thrive.

That is not to say that plants are temperamental. A few of them *are* notoriously difficult; but the vast majority simply have one or two dislikes when it comes to soil or atmospheric conditions. Each plant's whims and fancies are detailed in the A–Z section, but the lists on the following pages will help you to find a plant or group of plants for a particular spot or growing condition.

Do not regard the lists as exhaustive: they are limited in size by shortage of space. They offer an assortment of varied plants, but the fact that a certain plant has been omitted does not necessarily mean that it cannot grow under the particular conditions cited. Only if the A–Z section indicates that the plant dislikes such conditions would it be a waste of time to plant it.

Other categories deal with plants' ability to cover the ground and suppress weeds; their ability to grow against walls; the evergreen nature of their foliage; and their production of brilliant autumn tints or attractive fruits.

Use the lists as a source of inspiration; but if you want to fly in the face of the advice – by all means do so. Gardening is an adventure which will always offer a few surprises.

NOTE In most cases, the conditions defined by the heading apply to genera as a whole. If a genus is represented only by a particular species, the conditions defined may not be congenial to other members of that genus.

Plants for Chalky Soils

Gardeners who labour with chalky soils invariably bemoan the fact that they cannot grow rhododendrons and camellias, instead of rejoicing in the many hundreds of plants that will happily put up with alkaline earth. Certainly a chalky soil makes the planting of several genera inadvisable, for with their roots in alkaline soil they fail to extract all the nutrients they need, and their leaves turn yellow. But with all except the adamant lime-haters it is worth experimenting a little. Some plants hate very shallow soils over chalk, but will grow unperturbed if the earth is a little deeper even though markedly alkaline.

All have one thing in common: they will establish best where the ground has been well dug and enriched with organic matter before planting.

Acer (some)	*Cyclamen*	Lilium (some)
Agapanthus	*purpurascens*	Linaria
Ajuga	Daphne	*Magnolia kobus*
Allium	Deutzia	*Magnolia × loebneri*
Anaphalis	Dianthus	*Omphalodes luciliae*
Arbutus	Dierama	Papaver
Armeria	Eranthis	Parrotia
Aster	*Erica carnea*	Phyllitis
Aubrieta	*Erica × darleyensis*	Physostegia
Ballota	*Erica mediterranea*	*Polygala calcarea*
Betula	Euonymus	Polygonatum
Brunnera	Euphorbia	*Prunus lusitanica*
Buxus	Festuca	Pulmonaria
Campanula	*Ficus carica*	Pulsatilla
Caryopteris	Genista	Reseda
Cercis	Gentiana (some)	Rhus
Cheiranthus	Hebe	Sarcococca
Choisya	Helianthemum	Saxifraga
Cistus	Hepatica	Scabiosa
Clematis	Hypericum	Sidalcea
Coreopsis	Juniperus	Solidago
Corylus	Kolkwitzia	Syringa
Crataegus	Laburnum	Taxus
	Lamium	Vinca

Above Key to chalky-soil plants
1 *Agapanthus*
2 *Aster novi-belgii* 'Crimson Brocade'
3 *Lilium* hybrid
4 *Sidalcea* hybrid
5 *Papaver orientalis*
6 *Armeria maritima* 'Vindictive'
7 *Dianthus barbatus*
8 *Vinca major* 'Elegantissima'

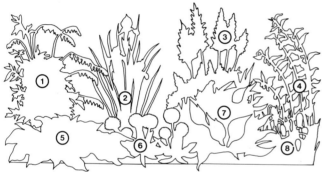

Left Key to plants for moisture-retentive or clay soils

1 *Dicentra spectabilis*   5 *Hosta crispula*
2 *Iris sibirica*   6 *Primula denticulata*
3 *Astilbe × arendsii*   7 *Lysichiton camtschatcense*
4 *Polygonatum × hybridum*   8 *Fritillaria meleagris*

Plants for Dry Soils

Light and sandy soils have many advantages: they are easy to cultivate, they warm up quickly in spring, and they drain well after wet weather. But in good summers the plants growing in them have to work hard to extract enough moisture to survive. You can always turn on a sprinkler, of course, but it makes more sense to use plants that are capable of tolerating, or even enjoying, some degree of dryness at the roots.

If sandy soil is all you have, and you want to grow plants that enjoy a modicum of moisture at the roots, there is only one thing for it: you must enrich your earth with plenty of organic matter – peat, compost, manure, leaf-mould and the like – to hold on to every last drop of water.

The plants in this list can usually tolerate dry conditions, but they will all need a helping hand in their youth. It is no good pushing their roots into dust and expecting them to survive. During the first year of establishment they will need to be soaked in dry spells so that the root system they develop is far-reaching and capable of searching for moisture. Organic matter is useful for these plants, too. And remember that when water is able to pass quickly through a soil, it often takes nutrients with it. Sandy soils are hungry soils: feed them regularly.

Plants for Moisture-Retentive or Clay Soil

There's no denying that clay soil is the most unpleasant kind to work, and the most back-breaking, too. But once plants are established within it they often do well, sinking their roots into a medium which seldom dries out at depth and so offers sustenance in dry summers, when plants on lighter soils are suffering.

Dig heavy soils in autumn so that the winter frosts can help shatter the clods and break them into more workable crumbs, and add as much organic matter and sharp grit as you can. Planting on soils like these is nearly always best carried out in spring, so that the plants do not have to sit through a cold winter in stagnant earth. When planting is completed, an organic mulch will prevent the surface from baking hard in the summer sun; it will be slowly incorporated by worms to make the soil easier for you to cultivate and more hospitable to your plants.

Ajuga	Iris (many)	*Ornithogalum*
Alchemilla	Lamium	*nutans*
Aruncus	*Leucojum aestivum*	Osmunda
Astilbe	*Leucojum vernum*	Polygonatum
Astrantia	Liriope	Polygonum
Brunnera	Ligularia	Primula (many)
Caltha	Lobelia (some)	Pulmonaria
Cimicifuga	Lysichiton	Rheum
Cornus	Lysimachia	Rodgersia
Dicentra	Lythrum	Ruscus
Dodecatheon	Matteuccia	Salix
Fritillaria meleagris	Mentha	Sidalcea
Gunnera	Mimulus	Smilacina
Hemerocallis	Monarda	Symphytum
Heuchera	Myosotis	Thalictrum
Hosta	*Narcissus cyclamineus*	Trollius

Acaena	Astrantia	Campanula	Crataegus
Acanthus	Aubrieta	Caryopteris	Crocosmia
Achillea	Ballota	Catananche	Cytisus
Agapanthus	Begonia (some)	Centaurea	Deutzia (some)
Ageratum	Berberis	Chamaecyparis	Dictamnus
Agrostemma	Bergenia	(some)	Dierama
Alchemilla	(some)	Cistus	Digitalis
Alstroemeria	Borago	Clarkia	Dimorphotheca
Alyssum	Buddleia	Convallaria	Echinops
Amaranthus	Buxus	Convolvulus	Echium
Anthemis	Calamintha	Corydalis	Elaeagnus
Arabis	Calendula	Corylus	Erigeron
Artemisia	Callistephus	Cosmos	Eryngium
Arundinaria	Calluna	Cotoneaster	Escallonia

Below Key to dry-soil plants
1 *Solidago*
2 *Kniphofia* hybrid
3 *Achillea filipendulina* 'Gold Plate'
4 *Pelargonium* 'Golden Harry Hieover'
5 *Hedera helix*
6 *Calendula officinalis*
7 *Gaillardia grandiflora*
8 *Paeonia*
9 *Lavandula spica*

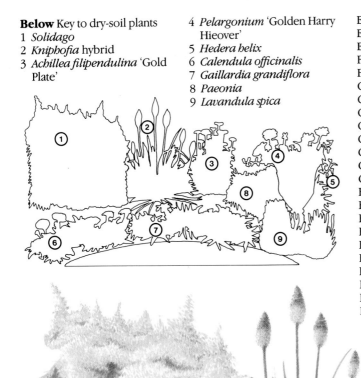

Eschscholzia	Ipomoea	Olearia	Sarcococca
Euonymus	Iris (some)	Osmanthus	Sedum
Euphorbia	Kniphofia	Paeonia	Sempervivum
Festuca	Lamium	Papaver	Skimmia
Ficus	Lathyrus	Pelargonium	Solidago
Gaillardia	Lavandula	Penstemon	Sophora
Galega	Lavatera	Phacelia	Spiraea
Gazania	Liatris	Philadelphus	Stachys
Genista	Limnanthes	Phlomis	Stipa
Geranium	Linaria	Phlox	Symphoricarpos
Gleditsia	Linum	Photinia	Tagetes
Godetia	Lychnis	Physalis	Tamarix
Gypsophila	Macleaya	Potentilla	Taxus
Hebe	Mahonia	Prunus	Thuja
Hedera	Malcomia	Pyrus	Thymus
Helianthemum	Matthiola	Rhus	Trachycarpus
Helichrysum	Mentzelia	Ribes	Verbascum
Helipterum	Milium	Robinia	Veronica
Hibiscus	Myrtus	Romneya	Viburnum
Hypericum	Nepeta	Rosmarinus	Vinca
Iberis	Nerine	Ruta	Yucca
Ilex	Nigella	Salvia	Zauschneria
Incarvillea	Oenothera	Santolina	Zinnia

Plants for Shade

All plants need light to survive, but not all of them need brilliant sunshine. Natives of woodland, in particular, are happiest when given some protection from the sun's rays. All the plants listed below will tolerate shade to a greater or lesser degree. Their entries in the A–Z section show whether or not they prefer part shade to heavy gloom, and whether or not they can put up with the dry earth that is often found under the canopy of large trees. In such spots try to be generous with soil enrichment: the plants you are putting in will have to share their food supply with established giants.

Acanthus	Berberis (some)	Digitalis
Aconitum	Bergenia	Endymion
Ajuga	Brunnera	Epimedium
Alchemilla (some)	Buxus	Erythronium
Allium cernuum	Caltha	Euonymus (some)
Allium moly	Camassia	Euphorbia
Anemone	Camellia	Gaultheria
Aruncus	Convallaria	Geranium (some)
Arundinaria	Corydalis	Hedera
Asperula odorata	Cyclamen	Helleborus
Astilbe	*Daphne laureola*	Hepatica
Astrantia	*Daphne mezereum*	Hosta
Aucuba	Dicentra	*Hypericum calycinum*

Ilex	Phyllitis	Skimmia
Lamium	Polygonatum	Smilacina
Lilium (some)	Polygonum (some)	Symphoricarpos
Liriope	Primula (some)	(some)
Lunaria	Prunella	Symphytum
Lysimachia (some)	Pulmonaria	Taxus
Mahonia	Ramonda	*Thalictrum*
Matteuccia	Rheum	*dipterocarpum*
Meconopsis	Rodgersia	Tiarella
Mentha	Ruscus	Trillium
Ornithogalum nutans	Sambucus (some)	Trollius
Osmunda	Sanguinaria	Viburnum (some)
Pachysandra	Sarcococca	Vinca
Pernettya	*Saxifraga fortunei*	Viola

Plants for Seaside Gardens

Coastal gardens have the great advantage of a fairly stable climate, thanks to the presence of the sea, whose temperature fluctuates very slowly. Such gardens, however, are apt to suffer at the hands of the wind, which lashes them with salt spray in autumn and winter.

Some plants can cope with this kind of treatment, and even though many of them look badly burned after a severe gale, they will soon produce new leaves when favourable weather returns.

Gardens right on the sea front are the most difficult to

plant, and it is essential that some form of windbreak is provided before planting gets underway. Wattle hurdles and other semi-permeable barriers should be erected before salt-tolerant hedges, such as tamarisk and juniper, are established to make a more durable shield.

That done, the gardener can experiment with a varied group of plants, even though his season may be shorter than that of gardens inland. The first gales of autumn are always awaited with dread!

Achillea	Dierama	Hypericum	*Primula vulgaris*
Agapanthus	Eccremocarpus	Ilex	and hybrids
Alstroemeria	Echinops	Iris	Pyracantha
Anemone	Elaeagnus	Jasminum	Ribes
Arbutus	Endymion	Juniperus	Romneya
Artemisia	Erigeron	Kniphofia	Rosmarinus
Arundinaria	Eryngium	Lathyrus	Salvia
Aucuba	Escallonia	Laurus	Sambucus
Berberis	Eucalyptus	Lavandula	Santolina
Bergenia	*Euonymus*	Lavatera	Scabiosa
Betula	*japonicus*	Leycesteria	Scilla
Buddleia	Euphorbia	Linaria	Sedum
Camellia	Fatsia	Lippia	Skimmia
Carpenteria	Festuca	Lychnis	Solanum
Caryopteris	Fremontia	Myrtus	Sorbus
Catananche	Fuchsia	Oenothera	Spartium
Ceanothus	Garrya	Olearia	Spiraea (some)
Centaurea	Gazania	Osmanthus	Symphoricarpos
Choisya	Genista	Passiflora	Tamarix
Chrysanthemum	Geranium	Penstemon	Trachycarpus
Cistus	Gypsophila	Phlomis	Tradescantia
Clematis	Hebe	Phormium	Tropaeolum
Cotoneaster	Hedera	Phygelius	Veronica
Crocosmia	Heuchera	Physostegia	*Viburnum tinus*
Cytisus	Hibiscus	Polygonum	Weigela
Dianthus	Hydrangea	Potentilla	Yucca

Plants for Ground Cover

Gardeners have been planting things closely together for hundreds of years, both for the mat-like effect of growth as well as to keep down weeds. Today the idea has caught on as a labour-saving device; but, unless care is taken in the early stages of establishment, ground-cover plants will save no labour at all.

The earth must be well cultivated, weeded and fertilised and the plants given every encouragement to grow well from the outset. This means that they will have to be thoroughly watered in dry spells, and that they will have to be weeded among until their leaves meet to form an impenetrable rug of growth. Only then can they be left to do the work of human weeders. If you make the mistake of planting ground-cover plants and leaving them alone, you will soon see them swamped by weeds.

When it comes to calculating how many plants you will need, bear in mind the ultimate spread of the species chosen. Plant so that the individuals will overlap slightly when they have been growing for a season or two.

Acaena	Gaultheria	*Pachysandra*
Ajuga	Geranium	*terminalis*
Alchemilla	Hebe	Pernettya
Arundinaria (dwarf	Hedera	Potentilla
species)	Helianthemum	Pulmonaria
Bergenia	Heuchera	Ruscus
Brunnera	Hosta	Santolina
Calamintha	Hypericum	Sarcococca
Calluna	Iberis	Skimmia
Cistus	Juniperus (some)	Stachys
Convallaria	Lamium	Symphytum
Cornus canadensis	Lavandula	Thymus
Epimedium	Liriope	Tiarella
Erica	*Lysimachia nummularia*	Vaccineum
Euonymus fortunei	*Mahonia aquifolium*	Vinca
Euphorbia (some)	Nepeta	Viola

Above Key to ground-cover plants
1 *Acanthus mollis*
2 *Brunnera macrophylla*
3 *Cistus* hybrid
4 *Pulmonaria saccharata* 'Pink Dawn'
5 *Calluna vulgaris*
6 *Epimedium* × *rubrum*
7 *Liriope muscari*
8 *Pachysandra terminalis*

Below Key to climbing plants
1 *Actinidia kolomikta*
2 *Clematis* × 'Jackmanii Superba'
3 *Parthenocissus henryana*
4 *Lonicera periclymenum*

Climbers and Wall Plants

Nowhere in the garden is a give-and-take relationship more apparent than on a wall up which plants have been trained: the building benefits from having its countenance brightened, and the plant enjoys the shelter and warmth the wall provides.

Not all the plants listed here are climbers, or grow so tall that their stems can be tied in as wall covering. Some of them simply enjoy the shelter. What all of them need in the early stages is generous watering; and whether they thrive or not may depend greatly on the particular aspect of the wall. The soil at the foot of a house wall with overhanging eaves or in the lea of rain-bearing winds is notoriously dry, owing to the fact that little rain reaches it. Soak it and keep it soaked until the plants are established.

Abutilon	× Fatshedera	Parthenocissus
Actinidia	Ficus	Passiflora
Camellia	Forsythia	Phygelius
Campsis	Fremontodendron	*Polygonum*
Carpenteria	Garrya	*baldschuanicum*
Ceanothus	*Hydrangea petiolaris*	Pyracantha
Chaenomeles	Ipomoea	Rosa (climbers and
Chimonanthus	Jasminum	ramblers)
Choisya	Lathyrus	Schizophragma
Clematis	Lippia	Solanum
Cobaea	Lonicera	Tropaeolum
Cytisus battandieri	*Magnolia grandiflora*	Vitis
Eccremocarpus	Myrtus	Wisteria

Plants for Hedges

If every garden was surrounded by fencing the prospect would be dull indeed. Hedges, even though they require additional labour, do have the advantage of greening up the scene; many bear attractive flowers.

As with any other plant, make sure you choose the right hedge for the job. Some hedges grow rapidly to great heights; others grow slowly. Some grow quickly in the early stages and then stop at a reasonable height. Some need twice-yearly trims with shears, others just a single pruning with secateurs. The A–Z section gives precise details of all the plants listed here. Whatever their stature, all hedges need well-prepared ground if they are to make an effective screen in the shortest possible time. Do not stint on the initial cultivation and soil enrichment.

Aucuba	Forsythia	Rhododendron
Berberis (some)	Fuchsia	Ribes
Buxus	Garrya	Rosa (some)
Carpinus	Ilex	Rosmarinus
Chamaecyparis (some)	Laurus	Sambucus
Chaenomeles	Lavandula	Santolina
Choisya	Ligustrum	Sarcococca
Cotoneaster (some)	Lonicera (some)	Skimmia
Crataegus	Myrtus	Symphoricarpos
× Cupressocyparis	Olearia	Tamarix
Elaeagnus	Pernettya	Taxus
Escallonia	Potentilla	Teucrium
Euonymus	Prunus (some)	Thuja
Fagus	Pyracantha	Viburnum (some)

Plants for Autumn Colour

Some gardeners seem to regard autumn as the closed season: the rains come down and the gardener comes in – never to venture out again until the spring. If this is to be the case, the end of the season should certainly be as colourful as possible, and the following plants can be relied on in most autumns to produce vivid tints before shedding their leaves. Most of the plants listed concentrate the colour in their foliage; but one or two have colourful stems.

Acer	Betula	Enkianthus
Ajuga	Calluna (some)	Erica (some)
Amelanchier	Cornus (stems)	Fothergilla
Berberis (some)	Cotinus	Hamamelis
Bergenia (some)	Cryptomeria	Hosta

Hydrangea (some)	Prunus (some)	Sorbus (some)
Malus tschonoskii	Robinia (some)	Stuartia (stems)
Parrotia	Rosa (some)	Viburnum (some)
Parthenocissus	Salix (stems)	Vitis

Attractive Fruits

With most garden plants it makes sense to snip off all flowers as they fade. Not only is a plant's strength conserved if it does not have to make seeds, but it may also be persuaded to produce another flush of flowers. However, there are some plants whose seed-heads – be they berries, pods, or orbs of fluff – are so attractive that a few extra summer blooms can be forgone for the sake of an autumn and winter show of fruits.

All the following plants have bright fruits. On some, however, the berries are carried only by female plants that have been fertilised by nearby males. Such plants are indicated in the list.

Acaena	Ficus	Physalis
Allium (some)	Gaultheria	Picea (some)
Anemone (some)	Ilex (some)	Pulsatilla
Arbutus	Lagurus	Pyracantha
Aucuba (females)	Leycesteria	Rosa (some)
Berberis (some)	Lunaria	Ruscus
Briza	Mahonia	Sambucus
Catalpa	Malus (most)	Skimmia (females)
Cercis	Moluccella	Sorbus (many)
Chaenomeles	Nicandra	Stipa
Clematis (some)	Nigella	Symphoricarpos
Cotoneaster	Passiflora	Taxus
Crataegus (most)	Pernettya (females)	Vitis (some)

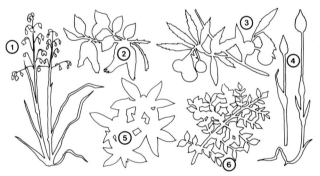

Evergreen Plants

Plant too many evergreens and your garden could take on the gloomy appearance of a cemetery, but plant just a few well-chosen forms and it will have a year-round framework that never looks totally bare.

Do not assume that all evergreens are dark and sombre. Many of them have light green or colourfully variegated foliage that may be cheered further by a crop of brilliant fruits. Planted in carefully selected sites so that they can come into their glory during the off season and yet be used as a backdrop to summer plants, evergreens will earn their keep as essential garden residents.

Acaena	Eucryphia (some)	Pachysandra
Arbutus	Euonymus (some)	Pernettya
Arundinaria	Euphorbia (some)	Phlomis
Aucuba	× Fatshedera	Phormium
Berberis (some)	Fatsia	Photinia
Bergenia (most)	Festuca	Picea
Buxus	Fremontodendron	Pieris
Calluna	Garrya	Pyracantha
Camellia	Gaultheria	Rhododendron
Ceanothus (some)	Hebe	(many)
Chamaecyparis	Hedera	Rosmarinus
Choisya	Hypericum (some)	Ruscus
Cistus	Iberis	Ruta
Convolvulus cneorum	Ilex	Santolina
Cordyline	Juniperus	Sarcococca
Cotoneaster (some)	Kalmia (some)	Senecio (most)
Cryptomeria	Laurus	Skimmia
× Cupressocyparis	Leptospermum	Taxus
Daboecia	Ligustrum (some)	Teucrium
Daphne (some)	Lonicera (some)	Thuja
Elaeagnus	*Magnolia grandiflora*	Thymus
Embothrium	Mahonia	Trachycarpus
Erica	Myrtus	Viburnum (some)
Escallonia	Olearia	Vinca
Eucalyptus	Osmanthus	Yucca

Left Key to plant fruits
1 *Briza media*
2 *Rosa moyesii*
3 *Arbutus unedo*
4 *Lagurus ovatus*
5 *Skimmia japonica*
6 *Cotoneaster horizontalis*

Plant Health

1: Identifying and Dealing with Common Plant Pests

PEST	PLANTS ATTACKED	DAMAGE CAUSED	CONTROL MEASURES	PROPRIETARY BRANDS
Aphids (greenfly, blackfly)	Many	Sap sucked; honeydew emitted; virus diseases spread	Spray with pirimicarb	Abol-G, ICI Rapid Greenfly Killer
Cabbage-root fly	Wallflower, cabbage and relatives	Leaves wilt; roots eaten away by white maggots	Dust soil with diazinon or chlorpyrifos	Fison Combat Soil Insecticide, Murphy Soil Pest Killer
Capsid bug	Many	Leaves tattered or with tiny holes; raised brown areas on fruits	Spray with systemic	Boots Systemic Greenfly Killer, Bio Systemic
Caterpillar	Many	Leaves, stems, flowers eaten	Spray with permethrin or trichlorphon	ICI Picket, May & Baker Caterpillar Killer
Chafer beetle	Roses, others	Foliage, flower buds eaten	Pick off by hand	
Earwig	Dahlia, others	Flowers, shoot-tips, young leaves eaten	Trap in straw-filled inverted flower pots on canes among plants; kill with malathion or HCH	Murphy Gamma-HCH; many proprietary malathions
Eelworm	Narcissus, phlox	Plants weakened, leaves and stems distorted	Destroy infected plants; do not grow these or related plants on site	
Flea beetle	Lunaria, stock, wallflower	Small holes in young leaves	Dust with derris	Many proprietary brands
Froghopper	Roses, others	Sap sucked under cuckoo-spit	Spray with fenitrothion	Murphy Fentro, PBI Fenitrothion
Leaf miner	Chrysanthemum, holly, others	Pale tunnels in leaves	Remove infested leaves; spray with pirimphos-methyl	ICI Sybol 2
Lily beetle (scarlet)	Lily and relatives	Leaves eaten	Spray with pirimphos-methyl	ICI Sybol 2
Mealy bug	Many	Sap sucked, virus diseases spread by small insect enclosed in white 'wool'	Spray with malathion	Many proprietary brands
Mice	Many	Seeds, young plants eaten	Set traps	
Narcissus fly	Narcissus	No flowers; weak, grassy leaves; maggots in bulbs	Destroy infested (soft) bulbs	
Rabbits	Many	Plants eaten; trees ring-barked	Fit rabbit-proof fence; also plastic guards around young trees	
Red-spider mite	Many	Sap sucked; foliage desiccated; fine webs spun	Spray with fenitrothion or malathion	Murphy Fentro, PBI Fenitrothion; many proprietary malathions
Rhododendron bug	Rhododendron	Leaves mottled, yellow above and brown below	Spray leaf undersides with pirimphos-methyl	ICI Sybol 2
Sawfly	Roses, polygonatum	Leaves eaten or rolled under	Spray in May, June with pirimphos-methyl	ICI Sybol 2
Scale	Many	Sap sucked, virus diseases spread by small, limpet-like insects	Spray with malathion	Many proprietary brands

PEST	PLANTS ATTACKED	DAMAGE CAUSED	CONTROL MEASURES	PROPRIETARY BRANDS
Slugs, snails	Many	Young plant leaves eaten	Scatter methiocarb thinly among plants	May & Baker Draza Slug Pellets, PBI Slug Gard
Slugworm	Roses	Leaves 'skeletonised' by yellow larvae	Spray with fenitrothion or derris	Murphy Fentro, PBI Fenitrothion; many proprietary derrises
Tarsonemid mite	Aster, begonia, impatiens, others	Stems, flowers distorted and scarred; leaves, stems spoon-like	Dig up and burn; grow unrelated plants in affected area	
Thrips	Gladiolus, roses, others	White speckles, then grey patches on leaves, flowers	Spray with fenitrothion	Murphy Fentro, PBI Fenitrothion
Tortrix moth	Roses	Leaves spun together; holes bored into flower-buds by maggots	Spray with fenitrothion	Murphy Fentro, PBI Fenitrothion
Vine weevil	Cyclamen, rhododendron, few others	Lower leaves holed and notched; grubs on roots; plants wilt	Dust lower leaves and soil with HCH	Murphy Gamma-HCH
Water-lily aphis	Water-lily, other aquatics; cherry and plum trees	Leaves distorted; flowers later discoloured	Hose aphids off water-lilies; spray trees with pirimicarb	Abol-G, ICI Rapid Greenfly Killer
Water-lily beetle	Water-lily	Leaves eaten; plants rot	Hose-off beetles; remove dead plant material	
Weevils	Many	Leaves eaten; larvae burrow into stems	Remove damaged stems; spray with fenitrothion	Murphy Fentro, PBI Fenitrothion
Whitefly	Many	Sap sucked; virus diseases spread	Spray with permethrin	Bio Sprayday, Bio Flydown, ICI Picket
Woodlice	Many	Leaves, stems, and rotting matter eaten	Trap in halved, scooped potatoes left by affected plants overnight	

2: Identifying and Treating Common Plant Diseases

DISEASE	PLANTS ATTACKED	DAMAGE CAUSED	CONTROL MEASURES	PROPRIETARY BRANDS
Anthracnose	Willow	Small brown canker on stems; die back of stem tips; brown-blotched leaves fall	Spray with thiophanate-methyl	May & Baker Fungus Fighter, Murphy Systemic Fungicide
Apple scab	Apple and relatives	Black spots on leaves; scabs on fruit	Rake up and burn infected leaves in autumn; spray with thiophanate-methyl	May & Baker Fungus Fighter, Murphy Systemic Fungicide
Azalea gall	Rhododendron	Hard green, reddish or whitish swellings on leaves and buds	Cut out and burn infected stems; spray with copper fungicide	Murphy Liquid Copper Fungicide
Bacterial canker	Cherry, plum trees	Leaves full of holes; stem cankers with oozing gum; general weakening	Cut out infected wood; spray with benomyl	PBI Benlate
Basal rot	Narcissus	Brown rot at base of bulb; white or pink fungus between scales	Destroy infected bulbs. Buy only from reliable sources	

DISEASE	PLANTS ATTACKED	DAMAGE CAUSED	CONTROL MEASURES	PROPRIETARY BRANDS
Blackleg	Pelargonium	Stem base turns black; grey fur and rot develop	Prevent by using sterile compost and good hygiene; ventilate plants well	
Blackspot	Roses	Leaves develop black spots, fall early	Rake up and burn all leaves at end of season; spray with bupirimate and triforine	ICI Nimrod-T
Botrytis (grey mould)	Many	Parts of plants rot, become covered in grey fur	Remove and burn infected parts; spray with benomyl	PBI Benlate
Bud blast	Rhododendron	Buds turn brown, develop black pin-head spore capsules, and fail to open	Cut off infected buds; spray with fenitrothion to control leafhoppers that spread the disease	Murphy Fentro, PBI Fenitrothion
Canker	Roses, other shrubs	Rough brown, often sunken areas on stems	Cut out and burn; spray with thiophanate-methyl	May & Baker Fungus Fighter
Chlorosis	Camellia, rhododendron, many others	Leaves yellowed; growth stunted on alkaline soils	Grow plants on acid soils. Water with iron sequestrene; feed well	Murphy Sequestrene
Clematis wilt	Clematis	Collapse of mature shoots, usually on young plants	Cut back to ground level; water with benomyl	PBI Benlate
Clubroot	Wallflower, cabbage and relatives	Roots swollen, smelly; plants stunted	Add lime to acid soil; improve drainage; dip young plant roots in thiophanate-methyl	Murphy Systemic Clubroot Dip
Coral spot	Many	Raised orange pustules on woody stems	Cut out infected wood and burn; paint wounds with sealant	May & Baker Seal and Heal Pruning Paint
Corm rot	Freesia, gladiolus	Corms rotting; leaves stunted, yellow	Destroy infected corms; water soil with benomyl	PBI Benlate
Crown rot	Rhubarb	Centre of plant brown, rotten	Destroy plants; improve drainage. Do not replant ground with rhubarb	
Die-back	Many	Woody stems die at tips	Cut out infected wood back to healthy tissue	
Fire	Tulip	Leaves, flowers streaked with strawy patches	Destroy infected bulbs; do not replant tulips on same ground. Prevent by spraying with mancozeb	PBI Dithane 945
Fireblight	Rose family: pear, hawthorn, cotoneaster, etc	Shoots, flowers looked burned, turn brown and wilt	Cut out infected stems back to healthy tissue; paint wounds with sealant	May & Baker Seal and Heal Pruning Paint
Fusarium wilt	Aster, sweet pea, others	Lower leaves, stem bases turn brown and rot	Destroy infected plants; do not grow again on same ground. Buy resistant varieties	
Heather wilt (Phytophthora root death)	Heath, heather	Leaves turn greyish, wilt and die	Destroy infected plants. If soil is alkaline, replace with peaty mixture	
Honey fungus	Many	Stems die back (or plants even die) for no visible reason. Fungal 'bootlaces' found in soil; honey-coloured toadstools on site	Dig up and burn infected plants; dig up all tree stumps. Water soil with recommended chemical	Bray's Emulsion

DISEASE	PLANTS ATTACKED	DAMAGE CAUSED	CONTROL MEASURES	PROPRIETARY BRANDS
Hyacinth yellows	Hyacinth	Yellow streaks on leaves; yellow slime in bulbs	Destroy bulbs; do not replant hyacinths in infected soil. Consult local horticultural adviser on further action	
Ink disease	Bulbous iris	Black patches on bulbs; also on flowers and leaves in wet weather	Burn infected bulbs. Prevent by spraying emergent leaves with mancozeb	PBI Dithane 945
Leaf spot	Hebe, daphne, other shrubs	Dark blotches on leaves	Spray with copper fungicide in spring. Prevent by growing in good soil	Murphy Liquid Copper Fungicide
Lilac blight	Lilac	Black spots on leaves; shoots wither	Cut out infected wood; spray with bordeaux mixture	Many proprietary brands
Mildew	Roses, many others	White powder or downy deposit on leaves and stems	Cut out badly infected growth; spray with benomyl	PBI Benlate
Peach-leaf curl	Peach and relatives	Leaves reddish, distorted; white fungal growth beneath	Destroy infected leaves; spray before leaves open with copper fungicide	Murphy Liquid Copper Fungicide
Peony wilt	Peony	On tree peonies, unopened buds rot; on herbaceous peonies, leaf bases turn brown and rot	Destroy infected buds or plants. Prevent by spraying with dichlofluanid	May & Baker Elvaron
Petal blight	Anemone, dahlia, chrysanthemum, others	Petals covered by translucent spots, especially in wet weather	Remove and destroy infected blooms	
Root rot	Many, especially perennials on badly drained soils	Roots turn brown and rot, killing plant	Destroy infected plants	
Rust	Antirrhinum, pelargonium, others	Yellow spots on upper leaf surfaces, orange pustules below	Destroy infected plants; spray others with mancozeb. Prevent by growing resistant strains	PBI Dithane 945
Scab	Crocosmia, freesia, gladiolus	Reddish brown spots on leaves; black spots on corms	Dip corms in calomel dust	Many proprietary dusts
Sclerotinia	Many, including dahlia, delphinium, sweet pea	White fungal growth rots stems, makes plant collapse. Black resting bodies overwinter in soil	Destroy infected plants. Do not grow dahlias on site	
Silver leaf	Cherry, peach, plum and relatives	Leaves look silvery; wood is brown when cut open	Cut out and burn infected growths; paint wounds	May & Baker Seal and Heal Pruning Paint
Smut	Anemone, others	Blisters, streaks, black spots on leaves	Dig up and burn infected plants	
Sooty mould	Many	Black deposit on honeydew excreted by aphids	Sponge off deposit; control aphids	Abol-G, ICI Rapid Greenfly Killer
Verticillium wilt	Aster, others	Stem bases go black; stems wilt	Grow resistant strains; rotate	
Virus	Many	Leaves distorted, marbled, yellowed; plant often stunted	Dig up and burn; control insect disease-carriers	
White rot	Mainly onion family	Base of bulb and roots rot, with white fungal growth	Destroy infected bulbs. Do not plant alliums on same site	

Index of Common Names

This index lists common names of genera and individual species described in the A–Z section. If you know a particular plant only by its common name, look that up in this index, which will direct you to the relevant genus in the A–Z section. In many instances where a genus has a common name, several of its species are known by variants or elaborations of that common name. Such variants are not listed in this index, but they will be found in the species descriptions under the appropriate generic heading in the A–Z section.

A

Acacia, false: *Robinia pseudoacacia*
Aconite, winter: *Eranthis*
Adam's needle: *Yucca filamentosa*
Alkanet: *Anchusa*
Almond, ornamental: *Prunus*
Alum root: *Heuchera*
Alyssum, sweet: *Lobularia maritima*
Angel's fishing-rod: *Dierama*
Angel's tears: *Narcissus triandrus*
Apple, crab: *Malus*
Apple of Peru: *Nicandra physalodes*
Arbor-vitae: *Thuja*
Archangel, yellow: *Lamium galeobdolon*
Aster, China: *Callistephus chinensis*
Aster, Stokes': *Stokesia*
Azalea: *Rhododendron*

B

Baby blue-eyes: *Nemophila menziesii*
Baby's breath: *Gypsophila*
Bachelor's buttons: *Kerria japonica* 'Pleniflora'; *Ranunculus acris* 'Flore-pleno'
Balloon flower: *Platycodon*
Bamboo: *Arundinaria*
Barberry: *Berberis*
Barrenwort: *Epimedium*
Bay, sweet: *Laurus nobilis*
Bear's breeches: *Acanthus*
Beauty bush: *Kolkwitzia amabilis*
Bee balm: *Monarda didyma*
Bellflower: *Campanula*
Bells of Ireland: *Moluccella laevis*
Bergamot: *Monarda*
Bindweed, field: *Convolvulus arvensis*
Birch: *Betula*
Birth-root: *Trillium erectum*
Bishop's hat: *Epimedium*
Bistort: *Polygonum bistorta*
Bitter root: *Lewisia rediviva*
Black cohosh: *Cimicifuga*
Black-eyed susan: *Rudbeckia hirta*; *Thunbergia alata*
Blackthorn: *Prunus spinosa*
Bladder cherry: *Physalis franchetii*
Blanket flower: *Gaillardia*
Bleeding heart: *Dicentra spectabilis*
Bloodroot: *Sanguinaria*
Bluebell: *Endymion*
Blue-eyed mary: *Omphalodes verna*
Borage: *Borago*
Bouncing bet: *Saponaria officinalis*
Box, Christmas: *Sarcococca*
Box, common: *Buxus sempervirens*
Box, ground: *Polygala chamaebuxus*

Bramble, ornamental: *Rubus*
Bridal wreath: *Spiraea* × *arguta*
Broadleaved kindling-bark: *Eucalyptus dalrympleana*
Broom, butcher's: *Ruscus aculeatus*
Broom, common: *Cytisus scoparius*
Broom, Moroccan: *Cytisus battandieri*
Broom, Mt Etna: *Genista aethnensis*
Broom, pineapple: *Cytisus battandieri*
Broom, Spanish: *Spartium junceum*
Broom, Warminster: *Cytisus* × *praecox*
Bugbane: *Cimicifuga*
Bugle: *Ajuga reptans*
Burning bush: *Dictamnus albus*; *Kochia scoparia* 'Tricophylla'
Burr, New Zealand: *Acaena*
Busy lizzie: *Impatiens*
Buttercup: *Ranunculus*
Butterfly bush: *Buddleia davidii*
Butterfly flower: *Schizanthus*
Button snake-root: *Liatris*

C

Cabbage palm: *Cordyline*
Calamint: *Calamintha*
Calico bush: *Kalmia latifolia*
Californian lilac: *Ceanothus*
Campernelle jonquil: *Narcissus* × *odorus*
Campion: *Silene*
Campion, rose: *Lychnis coronaria*
Canary creeper: *Tropaeolum peregrinum*
Candytuft: *Iberis*
Canterbury bell: *Campanula medium*
Cardinal flower: *Lobelia cardinalis*
Carnation: *Dianthus*
Castor-oil plant, false: *Fatsia japonica*
Catchfly: *Silene*
Cathedral bells: *Cobaea scandens*
Catmint: *Nepeta*
Cedar, Japanese: *Cryptomeria japonica*
Cedar, western red: *Thuja plicata*
Chalk plant: *Gypsophila*
Chamomile: *Anthemis*
Checkerbloom: *Sidalcea*
Cherry: *Prunus*
Cherry, bladder: *Physalis franchetii*
Cherry, cornelian: *Cornus mas*
Cherry laurel: *Prunus laurocerasus*
Cherry pie: *Heliotropium*
Cherry plum: *Prunus cerasifera*
Chilean fire-bush: *Embothrium coccineum*
Chilean glory-flower: *Eccremocarpus scaber*
Chilean potato tree: *Solanum crispum*
Christmas box: *Sarcococca*
Cider gum: *Eucalyptus gunnii*
Cinnamon fern: *Osmunda cinnamomea*
Cinquefoil: *Potentilla*
Clary: *Salvia sclarea*
Cobnut: *Corylus avellana*
Columbine: *Aquilegia*
Comfrey: *Symphytum*
Cone-flower: *Rudbeckia laciniata*
Cone-flower, purple: *Echinacea purpurea*
Coral bells: *Heuchera sanguinea*
Corn-cockle: *Agrostemma*
Cornel: *Cornus*
Cornelian cherry: *Cornus mas*
Cornflower: *Centaurea cyanus*

Cosmea: *Cosmos*
Cow herb: *Saponaria vaccaria*
Cowslip: *Primula veris*
Cowslip, American: *Dodecatheon*
Cowslip, blue: *Pulmonaria angustifolia*
Cowslip, Jerusalem: *Pulmonaria officinalis*
Crab-apple: *Malus*
Crane's-bill: *Geranium*
Creeping jenny: *Lysimachia nummularia*
Creeping wintergreen: *Gaultheria procumbens*
Crème-de-menthe plant: *Mentha requienii*
Crocus, autumn: *Colchicum*
Crown imperial: *Fritillaria imperialis*
Cup-and-saucer vine: *Cobaea scandens*
Cupid's dart: *Catananche*
Currant, flowering: *Ribes*
Curry plant: *Helichrysum angustifolium*
Cushion pink: *Silene acaulis*
Cypress, false: *Chamaecyparis*
Cypress, Leyland: × *Cupressocyparis leylandii*
Cypress, summer: *Kochia*

D

Daffodil: *Narcissus*
Daisy: *Bellis*
Daisy, African: *Dimorphotheca*
Daisy, Michaelmas: *Aster*
Daisy, moon: *Chrysanthemum uliginosum*
Daisy, Paris: *Chrysanthemum frutescens*
Daisy, Shasta: *Chrysanthemum maximum*
Daisy bush: *Olearia*
Dame's violet: *Hesperis matronalis*
Dead-nettle: *Lamium*
Dog's-tooth violet: *Erythronium dens-canis*
Dogwood: *Cornus*
Dusty miller: *Artemisia stelleriana*; *Centaurea cineraria*; *Lychnis coronaria*

E

Easter ledges: *Polygonum bistorta*
Edelweiss: *Leontopodium alpinum*
Elder: *Sambucus*
Elder, box: *Acer negundo*
Everlasting flower: *Helichrysum*

F

Fair-maids-of-France: *Ranunculus aconitifolius*
Fat-headed lizzie: × *Fatshedera*
Feather grass: *Stipa*
Fennel, finocchio: *Foeniculum*
Fern, cinnamon: *Osmunda cinnamomea*
Fern, hart's-tongue: *Phyllitis scolopendrium*
Fern, interrupted: *Osmunda claytoniana*
Fern, ostrich-feather: *Matteuccia struthiopteris*
Fern, royal: *Osmunda regalis*
Fescue grass: *Festuca*
Feverfew: *Chrysanthemum parthenium*
Fig: *Ficus*
Figwort, Cape: *Phygelius capensis*
Filbert: *Corylus maxima*
Firethorn: *Pyracantha*
Flame creeper: *Tropaeolum speciosum*
Flax: *Linum*
Flax, New Zealand: *Phormium tenax*
Fleabane: *Erigeron*

Foam flower: *Tiarella cordifolia*
Foam-of-May: *Spiraea × arguta*
Forget-me-not: *Myosotis*
Foxglove: *Digitalis*
Fuchsia, California: *Zauschneria*
Fumitory: *Corydalis*

G

Gean: *Prunus avium*
Gentian: *Gentiana*
Geranium, ivy-leaved: *Pelargonium peltatum*
Germander: *Teucrium*
Globe-flower: *Trollius*
Glory-of-the-snow: *Chionodoxa*
Gilliflower: *Dianthus caryophyllus*
Goat's-beard: *Aruncus*
Goat's rue: *Galega*
Gold dust: *Alyssum saxatile*
Golden bells: *Forsythia*
Golden rain: *Laburnum*
Golden rod: *Solidago*
Gooseberry, Cape: *Physalis peruviana*
Gooseberry, Chinese: *Actinidia chinensis*
Gorse, Spanish: *Genista hispanica*
Granadilla: *Passiflora edulis*
Grape hyacinth: *Muscari*
Grass, common blue-eyed: *Sisyrinchium bermudianum*
Grass, feather: *Stipa*
Grass, fescue: *Festuca*
Grass, golden-eyed: *Sisyrinchium californicum*
Grass, hare's-tail: *Lagurus ovatus*
Grass, pampas: *Cortaderia*
Grass, pearl: *Briza maxima*
Grass, quaking: *Briza media*
Guelder rose: *Viburnum opulus*
Gum: *Eucalyptus*
Gum cistus: *Cistus ladanifer*

H

Hare's-tail grass: *Lagurus ovatus*
Hart's-tongue fern: *Phyllitis scolopendrium*
Hawthorn: *Crataegus monogyna*
Hazel: *Corylus*
Heart's-ease: *Viola tricolor*
Heath: *Erica*
Heath, St Dabeoc's: *Daboecia*
Heather, ling: *Calluna*
Heather, bell: *Erica cinerea*
Heliotrope: *Heliotropium*
Hellebore: *Helleborus*
Heron's-bill: *Erodium*
Holly: *Ilex*
Holly, New Zealand: *Olearia macrodonta*
Holly, sea: *Eryngium*
Hollyhock: *Althaea*
Honesty: *Lunaria*
Honey locust: *Gleditsia triacanthos*
Honeysuckle: *Lonicera*
Honeysuckle, Himalayan: *Leycesteria formosa*
Hornbeam: *Carpinus*
Horsemint: *Monarda*
Houseleek: *Sempervivum*
Hyacinth: *Hyacinthus*
Hyacinth, grape: *Muscari*
Hyacinth, summer: *Galtonia*
Hyacinth, wild: *Endymion nonscriptus*

I

Indian bean-tree: *Catalpa*
Indian shot: *Canna*
Interrupted fern: *Osmunda claytoniana*
Ironwood, Persian: *Parrotia*
Ivy:*Hedera*
Ivy, Boston: *Parthenocissus tricuspidata* 'Veitchii'
Ivy, Kenilworth: *Linaria cymbalaria*

J

Jacob's ladder: *Polymonium caeruleum*
Japanese pagoda tree: *Sophora japonica*
Japonica: *Chaenomeles*
Jasmine: *Jasminum*
Jasmine, rock: *Androsace*
Jonquil: *Narcissus jonquilla*
Jonquil, campernelle: *Narcissus × odorus*
Joseph's coat: *Amaranthus tricolor*
Judas tree: *Cercis siliquastrum*
Juniper:*Juniperus*

K

Kaffir lily: *Schizostylis*
King-cup: *Caltha palustris*
Knotweed: *Polygonum*

L

Lad's love: *Artemisia abrotanum*
Lady's mantle: *Alchemilla*
Lamb's quarters: *Trillium erectum*
Lamb's tongue, lamb's ear: *Stachys olympica*
Larkspur: *Delphinium consolida*
Laurel, bay: *Laurus nobilis*
Laurel, common or cherry: *Prunus laurocerasus*
Laurel, mountain: *Kalmia latifolia*
Laurel, Portugal: *Prunis lusitanica*
Laurel, sheep: *Kalmia angustifolia*
Laurel, spotted: *Aucuba japonica*
Laurel, spurge: *Daphne laureola*
Laurustinus: *Viburnum tinus*
Lavender: *Lavandula*
Lavender, sea: *Limonium*
Lavender cotton: *Santolina*
Leopard's-bane: *Doronicum*
Lilac: *Syringa*
Lily: *Lilium*
Lily, day: *Hemerocallis*
Lily, foxtail: *Eremurus*
Lily, kaffir: *Schizostylis*
Lily, Lent: *Narcissus pseudonarcissus*
Lily, Peruvian: *Alstroemeria*
Lily, plantain: *Hosta*
Lily, torch: *Kniphofia*
Lily-of-the-valley: *Convallaria*
Lily-of-the-valley bush: *Pieris*
Lily turf: *Liriope*
Locust tree: *Robinia pseudacacia*
London pride: *Saxifraga × urbium*
Loosestrife, purple: *Lythrum salicaria*
Loosestrife, yellow: *Lysimachia vulgaris*
Love-in-a-mist: *Nigella damascena*
Love-lies-bleeding: *Amaranthus caudatus*
Lungwort: *Pulmonaria*
Lupin: *Lupinus*

M

Mallow, Indian: *Abutilon*
Mallow, jew's: *Kerria japonica*
Mallow, marsh: *Althaea officinalis*
Mallow, musk: *Malva moschata*
Mallow, tree: *Lavatera arborea*
Maltese cross: *Lychnis chalcedonica*
Maple: *Acer*
Marguerite: *Chrysanthemum frutescens*
Marigold: *Tagetes*
Marigold, Cape: *Dimorphotheca*
Marigold, marsh: *Caltha palustris*
Marigold, pot: *Calendula*
Masterwort: *Astrantia*
May: *Crataegus oxycantha*
Meadow rue: *Thalictrum*
Metake: *Arundinaria japonica*
Mexican orange-blossom: *Choisya ternata*
Mezereon: *Daphne mezereum*
Mignonette: *Reseda odorata*
Mile-a-minute: *Polygonum baldschuanicum*
Millet, wood: *Milium effusum*
Milkweed: *Euphorbia*
Milkwort: *Polygala calcarea*
Mint: *Mentha*
Miss Willmott's ghost: *Eryngium giganteum*
Mock-orange: *Philadelphus coronarius*
Moneywort: *Lysimachia nummularia*
Monkey-flower: *Mimulus*
Monkshood: *Aconitum*
Montbretia: *Crocosmia × crocosmiiflora*
Morning glory: *Ipomoea tricolor*
Mother-of-thousands: *Saxifraga stolonifera*
Mountain ash: *Sorbus*
Mugwort, white: *Artemisia lactiflora*
Mullein: *Verbascum*
Musk, lavender-water: *Mimulus ringens*
Musk, monkey: *Mimulus luteus*
Myrobalan: *Prunus cerasifera*
Myrtle: *Myrtus*

N

Naked ladies: *Colchicum*
Nasturtium: *Tropaeolum*
Navelwort: *Omphalodes*

O

Obedient plant: *Physostegia*
Old man: *Artemisia abrotanum*
Old man's beard: *Clematis vitalba*
Old woman: *Artemisia stelleriana*
Oleaster: *Elaeagnus angustifolia*
Onion: *Allium*
Orange-ball tree: *Buddleia globosa*
Orange-blossom, Mexican: *Choisya ternata*
Orchid, poor-man's: *Schizanthus*
Oregon grape: *Mahonia aquifolium*
Osier: *Salix*
Oswego tea: *Monarda didyma*

P

Pagoda tree, Japanese: *Sophora japonica*
Palm, Chusan: *Trachycarpus fortunei*
Pampas grass: *Cortaderia*

Pansy: *Viola*
Partridge berry: *Gaultheria procumbens*
Pasque flower: *Pulsatilla vulgaris*
Passion-flower: *Passiflora*
Pea, sweet or everlasting: *Lathyrus*
Peach: *Prunus*
Peacock-flower: *Tigridia*
Pear: *Pyrus*
Pearl everlasting: *Anaphalis*
Pearl grass: *Briza maxima*
Peppermint: *Mentha piperata*
Periwinkle: *Vinca*
Persian ironwood: *Parrotia*
Peruvian lily: *Alstroemeria*
Pheasant berry: *Leycesteria formosa*
Pheasant's eye: *Narcissus poeticus*
Pink: *Dianthus*
Plantain lily: *Hosta*
Plum, ornamental: *Prunus × blireana*
Poached-egg flower: *Limnanthes douglasii*
Polyanthus: *Primula*
Poppy: *Papaver*
Poppy, blue Tibetan: *Meconopsis betonicifolia*
Poppy, Californian: *Eschscholzia californica*
Poppy, plume: *Macleaya cordata*
Poppy, tree: *Romneya*
Poppy, Welsh: *Meconopsis cambrica*
Potato tree, Chilean: *Solanum crispum*
Potato vine: *Solanum jasminoides*
Primrose: *Primula*
Primrose, evening: *Oenothera biennis*
Prince's feather: *Amaranthus hypochondriacus*
Privet: *Ligustrum*
Pyrethrum: *Chrysanthemum coccineum*

Q

Quaking grass: *Briza media*
Quamash: *Camassia*
Quickthorn: *Crataegus monogyna*
Quince, flowering: *Chaenomeles*

R

Ragwort, sea: *Senecio cineraria*
Redbud: *Cercis canadensis*
Red-hot poker: *Kniphofia*
Rhubard, ornamental: *Rheum*
Rock rose: *Cistus*; *Helianthemum*
Rocket, sweet: *Hesperis matronalis*
Rose: *Rosa*
Rose, Christmas: *Helleborus niger*
Rose, Lenten: *Helleborus orientalis*
Rosemary: *Rosmarinus*
Rose-of-heaven: *Silene coeli-rosa*
Rose of Sharon: *Hypericum calycinum*
Rowan: *Sorbus aucuparia*
Royal fern: *Osmunda regalis*
Rue: *Ruta*
Rue, goat's: *Galega*
Rue, meadow: *Thalictrum*

S

Sage, common: *Salvia officinalis*
Sage, Jerusalem: *Phlomis fruticosa*
Sage, white: *Artemisia ludoviciana*
St John's wort: *Hypericum*

Salal: *Gaultheria shallon*
Scabious: *Scabiosa*
Sea pink: *Armeria maritima*
Sea ragwort: *Senecio cineraria*
Self-heal: *Prunella*
Setterwort: *Helleborus foetidus*
Shell: *Tigridia*
Shell-flower: *Moluccella laevis*
Shoo-fly plant: *Nicandra physalodes*
Shooting star: *Dodecatheon*
Silver-berry: *Elaeagnus commutata*
Silver-lace vine: *Polygonum aubertii*
Skunk cabbage: *Lysichiton americanum*
Slipper-flower: *Calceolaria*
Sloe: *Prunus spinosa*
Smoke tree: *Cotinus*
Snake's-head fritillary: *Fritillaria meleagris*
Snakeweed: *Polygonum bistorta*
Snapdragon: *Antirrhinum*
Sneezewort: *Helenium*
Snowberry: *Symphoricarpos rivularis*
Snowdrop: *Galanthus*
Snowflake: *Leucojum*
Snow-gum, alpine: *Eucalyptus niphophila*
Snow-in-summer: *Cerastium tomentosum*
Snowy mespilus: *Amelanchier*
Soapwort: *Saponaria*
Solomon's seal: *Polygonatum × hybridum*
Solomon's seal, false: *Smilacina*
Southernwood: *Artemisia abrotanum*
Sowbread: *Cyclamen*
Speedwell: *Veronica*
Spider-flower: *Cleome*
Spiderwort: *Tradescantia × andersoniana*
Spikenard, false: *Smilacina racemosa*
Spindleberry, spindle tree: *Euonymus europaeus*
Spiraea, blue: *Caryopteris*
Spruce: *Picea*
Spurge: *Euphorbia*
Spurge, Japanese: *Pachysandra*
Squill: *Scilla*
Star of Bethlehem: *Campanula isophylla*; *Ornithogallum umbellatum*
Starwort, summer: *Erinus alpinus*
Statice: *Limonium sinuatum*
Stock, night-scented: *Matthiola*
Stock, Virginian: *Malcolmia*
Stokes' aster: *Stokesia*
Stonecrop, biting: *Sedum acre*
Stork's-bill: *Erodium*
Strawberry tree: *Arbutus*
Strawflower: *Helichrysum bracteatum*
Sumach: *Rhus*
Sunflower: *Helianthus annuus*
Sun rose: *Cistus*
Sweet pea: *Lathyrus*
Sweet rocket: *Hesperis matronalis*
Sweet sultan: *Centaurea moschata*
Sweet william: *Dianthus barbatus*
Sycamore: *Acer pseudoplatanus*

T

Tamarisk: *Tamarix*
Tansy: *Tanacetum vulgare*
Tarragon, French: *Artemisia dracunculus*
Tea-tree: *Leptospermum scoparium* 'Nanum'
Thistle, globe: *Echinops*

Thistle, Our Lady's milk, or holy: *Silybum marianum*
Thorn: *Crataegus*
Thrift: *Armeria*
Thyme: *Thymus*
Tidy-tips: *Layia*
Tickseed: *Coreopsis*
Tiger-flower: *Tigridia*
Toadflax: *Linaria*
Tobacco plant: *Nicotiana*
Toetoe: *Cortaderia richardii*
Traveller's joy: *Clematis vitalba*
Trout-lily, American: *Erythronium revolutum*
Trumpet-flower, velvet: *Salpiglossis sinuata*
Trumpet vine: *Campsis*

V

Verbena, lemon-scented: *Lippia citriodora*
Veronica, shrubby: *Hebe*
Vine, ornamental: *Vitis*
Vine, Russian: *Polygonum baldschuanicum*
Vine, silver-lace: *Polygonum aubertii*
Vine, trumpet: *Campsis*
Violet: *Viola*
Violet, dame's: *Hesperis matronalis*
Violet, dog's tooth: *Erythronium dens-canis*
Violetta: *Viola × williamsii*

Viper's bugloss: *Echium*
Virginia creeper: *Parthenocissus*

W

Wake robin: *Trillium grandiflorum*
Wallflower: *Cheiranthus*
Wall-pepper: *Sedum acre*
Wand-flower: *Dierama*
Water-lily: *Nymphaea*
Whitebeam: *Sorbus*
Willow: *Salix*
Windflower: *Anemone*
Wineberry, Japanese: *Rubus phoenicolasius*
Winter sweet: *Chimonanthus praecox*
Witch-hazel: *Hamamelis*
Wolfsbane: *Aconitum vulparia*
Woodbine: *Lonicera periclymenum*
Wood-lily, painted: *Trillium undulatum*
Woodruff: *Asperula odorata*
Wormwood, common: *Artemisia absinthium*

Y

Yarrow: *Achillea*
Yellow archangel: *Lamium galeobdolon*
Yew: *Taxus*

Acknowledgements

The following photographs were taken specially for Octopus Books:
Michael Boys 9 above, 11 above, 14 below, 15 above right, 16 above, 17 below, 19 above, 23 below, 32 below, 33, 34 above, 39 below, 40, 46 below, 50 above, 54 left, 58 right, 60, 62–3, 64–5, 65 right, 70, 72–3, 76 left, 88 above and below, 90 left, 94 right, 95 below left and right, 100 below, 102 right, 104–5, 106 left, 106–7, 110, 112 above, 116, 118 right, 124 above, 127 above, 139 below, 145 below, 152 middle, 155 right, 158–9, 159, 160 right, 161 left, 177 above, 179 right, 184–5, 186 above, 187 right, 188 below, 191 above, 193 below, 194–5, 198, 200 below, 206–7, 212 left, 223 right, 224 left, 228, 229 above, 234, 241 right; Jerry Harpur 2–3, 4–5, 6–7, 8, 10–11, 14 left, 15 below right, 18 above, 24–5, 25 right, 28 above, 29 above, 32 above, 34 below, 35 above, 38 below, 39 above, 41 below, 42 left, 45 above, 46 above, 48–9, 49 below, 50–1, 52 left, 53 above, 55 above and middle, 58 left, 59 below, 62, 68, 68–9, 69, 71 middle and above, 72 left, 77, 79 below right, 80, 81, 82–3, 83 right, 87, 89 left, 93 below, 96 right, 97, 98 left, 99 right, 103, 104 below, 107 above, 108 left, 109, 110–11, 112 below, 115 right, 117 below, 119 above right, 120 middle, 124 middle, 125, 126, 127 below, 128 left, 129, 132 left, 134–5, 135 left, 136 above right, 137, 138, 140 right, 141, 142–3, 144 below, 145 above, 146, 148 below, 151 above right, 153, 154, 156, 160 left, 163 left, 165, 166–7, 168, 170, 171 above right, 173 right, 174, 175 left, 176, 177 below, 178, 179 left, 180 right, 181 above, 182–3, 183, 184 left, 186 below, 195, 199 below, 204 below, 207, 209 below, 210 left, 213 below, 214 left, 216 left, 218 left, 218–9, 219 above, 221 below, 224 above, 226, 227, 230 above, 231, 235, 236 left, 239, 240–1; Neil Holmes 17 above, 36 below, 37 below, 55 below, 90 right, 95 above, 122–3, 135 right, 196 left, 201 below, 205 above; George Wright 1, 10 left, 11 below, 12, 13 below, 16 below, 20 below, 21 above, 22–3, 27, 28 below, 47 above, 49 above, 53 below, 54 right, 56–7, 57 right, 60–1, 66–7, 73, 75 above, 79 above right, 84–5, 86 below, 92, 93 above, 99 left, 101 left, 102 left, 113, 114–5, 115 below, 120–1, 123 above, 128 right, 130 above, 136 above left, 136–7, 147 below, 150, 151 left and below right, 161 right, 163 right, 167 above, 169 above right, 172, 173 left, 187 left, 189, 190, 191 below, 192, 196 right, 197 left and below right, 201 above, 206 left, 210–11, 215, 220 left, 232, 233, 236 right, 237 left, 240 left.

The publishers thank the following individuals and organisations for permission to use these photographs:
A–Z Botanical Collection 84 left, 105, 142; Bernard Alfieri 123 below, 143, 208–9, 216 below; K. & G. Beckett 91 below, 98 right, 141 right, 171 below right, 175 right, 202–3, 217, 222–3; Pat Brindley 30–1, 35 below, 42 below right, 45 below, 57 left, 66 left, 149 above and below, 162 left and right, 204 above, 211 right, 237 above; Derek Gould 13 above, 18 below, 20 above, 23 above, 29 below, 31, 37 above, 38 above, 43 above and below, 47 below, 59 above, 64 right, 71 below, 74 left, 75 below, 79 left, 94 left, 96 left, 100 above, 101 right, 104 left, 108 right, 118 left, 119 below, 122 above, 130 below left and right, 131, 144 above, 147 above, 148 above, 155 left, 158 left, 167 below, 169 below right, 171 left, 202, 205 below, 220 right, 222 left, 223 left, 224–5, 225, 229 below, 237 below; Jerry Harpur Photo Library 238 (designers J and R Last), endpapers (Yeomans, Oxon); Tania Midgely 13 middle, 15 left, 24 left, 26, 74 right, 76–7, 86 above, 114 left, 121, 133, 138–9, 140 left, 157, 180 left, 181 below, 188 above, 199 above, 200 above, 206 below, 213 above, 214–5, 221 above; Photos Horticultural/Michael Warren 9 below, 64 left, 78, 82 left, 114 below, 117 right, 124 below, 208 above, 218 right, 234–5; Harry Smith Horticultural Photographic Collection 19 left, 21 below, 22, 26–7, 30, 36 above, 41 above, 42 above right, 44–5, 48 above, 52 right, 56 left, 61 below, 63, 89 right, 91 above, 107 below, 108 above, 119 above left, 120 below, 132 above, 132–3, 134, 140 above left, 152 above and below, 164 above and below, 169 left, 189, below, 193 above, 197 above right, 209 above, 212 right, 216–7, 230 below.